The Role of Play in Human Development

The Role of Play in Human Development

ANTHONY D. PELLEGRINI

2009

OXFORD
UNIVERSITY PRESS

Oxford University Press, Inc., publishes works that further
Oxford University's objective of excellence
in research, scholarship, and education.

Oxford   New York
Auckland   Cape Town   Dar es Salaam   Hong Kong   Karachi
Kuala Lumpur   Madrid   Melbourne   Mexico City   Nairobi
New Delhi   Shanghai   Taipei   Toronto

With offices in
Argentina   Austria   Brazil   Chile   Czech Republic   France   Greece
Guatemala   Hungary   Italy   Japan   Poland   Portugal   Singapore
South Korea   Switzerland   Thailand   Turkey   Ukraine   Vietnam

Copyright © 2009 by Oxford University Press, Inc.

Published by Oxford University Press, Inc.
198 Madison Avenue, New York, New York 10016

www.oup.com

Oxford is a registered trademark of Oxford University Press

Library of Congress Cataloging-in-Publication Data
Pellegrini, Anthony D.
   The role of play in human development / Anthony D. Pellegrini.
      p.   cm.
   Includes bibliographical references and index.
   ISBN 978-0-19-536732-4
   1. Play—Psychological aspects.   2. Play—Social aspects.   3. Symbolic play.
   4. Child psychology.   I. Title.
   BF717.P45 2009
   155.4'18—dc22

                                                            2008051545

1   3   5   7   9   8   6   4   2

Printed in the United States of America
on acid-free paper

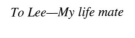

To Lee—My life mate

Acknowledgments

As a capstone to a career dedicated, in part, to the study of play, I must acknowledge a number of people. Most importantly, my work in this area has been guided by the writings of and discussions with Pat Bateson, Marc Bekoff, Gordon Burghardt, Bob Fagen, Greta Fein, Lee Galda, David Lancy, Serge Pellis, Peter Smith, and Brian Sutton-Smith. I must admit it was more than a little intimidating to reread the work of these scholars in preparation for writing this book. Having my work compared to this formidable body of work has been humbling.

I also acknowledge the following scholars for sending me copies of their work: Pat Bateson, Marc Bekoff, Rob Coplan, Sara Harkness, Jim Johnson, Angeline Lillard, and Serge Pellis. I also thank Erin and Bruce Tate for allowing me to play with and photograph Finn and Wyatt; Gini and Drew Woelflin for allowing me to photograph Henry; and Gumi Gossi, Kerri Lewis, and Serge Pellis for providing photographs.

Contents

The Role of Play in Human Development

1

Getting Here from There: An Introduction to My Study of Play

A PERSONAL INTRODUCTION

The decision to write an academic book is usually the result of an insight gained from deep and varied study of a topic, often across a number of years. My motivations are no different. I began studying play as a graduate student. At that time, I took classes addressing the educational, psychological, and anthropological dimensions of play and wrote one of my Ph.D. comprehensive, or in Ohio State University–talk, general exams, on the role of play in development. From the beginning of this process, I was exposed to an incredibly diverse literature on play and development, ranging from ethological descriptions of play and other forms of social behavior compiled by Blurton Jones (1972) and Bekoff (1978), to the obligatory Piaget (1962), the not-so-obligatory (at that time anyway) Vygotsky (1967), and psychoanalytical studies (e.g., Erickson, 1950, 1977). With this said, play was not the center of my intellectual universe while in graduate school. My dissertation addressed the role of preschoolers' private speech, testing the rival hypotheses posed by Piaget and Vygotsky. As part of my dissertation, I did, however, observe children in "free play" and videotaped their corresponding behavior and language.

Countless hours of viewing the videotapes of children's social behavior and language for my dissertation sparked a real interest in the language children used while engaged in pretend play. I was fascinated with the ways in which children used language to create and negotiate intricate pretend, social worlds. One of my first published papers on children's play came from these observations

(Pellegrini, 1982). It became clear to me that the language children used in pretending was not unlike the language of children's literacy events, as described initially by Basil Bernstein (1960, 1971, 1972) and M. A. K. Halliday (1969–1970) and later by David Olson (1977), Shirley Brice Health (1983) and Catherine Snow (1983). In both pretend play and early school-based literacy events, children used explicit language, not context, gestures, or shared knowledge, to convey information.

A few years later, I received a draft copy of a chapter on play written by Ken Rubin, Greta Fein, and Brian Vandenberg (1983). This chapter, the first and only chapter on play ever included in a *Handbook of Child Psychology,* is a comprehensive review of definitions, theories, and functions of play. On one very snowy day in our home in Georgia, my wife, Lee Galda, and I spent the day reading that chapter, drinking coffee, and enjoying the snow. Lee, whose interests were and continue to be in children's literature and early literacy, read the Rubin et al. paper and proclaimed after finishing the chapter that pretend play had very similar design features to those of narratives (Galda, 1984). That rather novel insight lead to an edited book on the relationship among play, narrative, and language (Galda & Pellegrini, 1985) and an empirical research program explicating the role of play in literacy generally, and narrative specifically (summarized in Pellegrini & Galda, 1998). It was apparent to us that specific ecologies, such as different peer configurations and different types of props, had important effects on both the generation of play and associated forms of oral language, and these forms of language were the precursors to school-based literacy.

Also about that same time, Peter K Smith and Kevin Connolly (1980) had just published their influential monograph, *The Ecology of Preschool Behaviour.* This work was very stimulating in terms of the evolutionary-oriented theory, which brought to mind my earlier affinity with Blurton Jones' (1972) work and that of zoologists studying play. The methodology in that book—very detailed behavioral observations of children in the natural ecologies—was also stimulating. It provided a way to chart the development of behavior in different ecologies across time. In 1983 I was awarded a Sara Moss Fellowship by the University of Georgia to go to Sheffield, England, to collaborate with Smith and Connolly on what I thought would be research on ecological effects on play. When I arrived and met Peter Smith for the first time, he told me that he was not working on ecology any more. Instead, he was now working on "rough-and-tumble" play (R&T). That was the beginning of my long collaboration with Peter Smith, my work in R&T (Pellegrini & Smith, 1998), and my interest in evolutionary theory and its role in play (Pellegrini, Dupuis, & Smith, 2007).

Since then, the evolutionary and animal play literatures have guided my research. This orientation has also impacted my thinking in this book. Indeed, play research seems to occupy a more important place in the study of nonhuman animal behavior than it does in the human case. As noted above, the topic has only been covered in one chapter in one of the six editions of the *Handbook of Child Psychology* (Carmichael, 1946, 1954; Eisenberg, 1998, 2006; Mussen, 1970, 1983). By contrast, biologists, such as K. Lorenz (1965) and E. O. Wilson (1975), have proclaimed play as a crucial area of study. Biological study of the role of play in ontogenetic and phylogenetic development has been especially impressive and relevant to our understanding of the role of play in human development (Bateson, 2005; Burghardt, 2005; Fagen, 1981). Consequently, an exchange between students of human and nonhuman play should be especially fruitful. With this said, the task ahead is a daunting one: Some ethologists have described the study of play as incredibly complex—akin to encountering a hornet's nest (Bekoff & Byers, 1981).

GETTING THERE FROM HERE

The organization of this book is pretty straightforward. In Chapter 2, I wrestle with the definitional problems associated with studying play. Rather than taking the position that play behaviors can placed on a continuum from "more" to "less playful" (Rubin, Fein, & Vandenberg, 1983), I advocated a more categorical stance, because two interrelated criteria, a means over ends and nonfunctional orientation, seem to be necessary, and perhaps sufficient, conditions for a behavior to be playful. These criteria, too, are important for the putative functions of play.

Chapters 3 and 4, respectively, address theories of play and the role of play in the development of behavioral plasticity. The epigenetic theories reviewed here have posited that play occurs during the juvenile period as a way in which to prepare the young organism to live in its specific niche. Play, in this view, has individuals experimenting with a variety of behavioral routines. In certain circumstances, the most effective of these novel routines could be used to change the course of adult practices. In Chapter 5, I discuss how different cultural practices shape behaviors and beliefs about play.

Cultural practices, in turn, are related to the function of play, which is addressed in Chapter 6. In that chapter, I discuss how the function of play is linked inextricably with gender. I demonstrate the ways that biological and social systems affect each other, and this is illustrated in the ways that boys' and girls' play have different functions in many societies.

In Chapters 7, 8, 9, and 10, I discuss social, object, locomotor, and pretend play, and games, respectively. In each chapter, I present the developmental course of each construct for boys and girls. While I discuss a variety of possible functions for each, I posit that the most important function for each form of play relates to behavioral flexibility.

In Chapter 11, I discuss the place of all forms of play in educational settings. This discussion is important in light of the continuing struggle between those wanting to minimize play experiences in school and increasing "basic skills instruction," and those advocating a more "whole child" approach to education, where play is central. In the final chapter, I address the issue of overblown claims, both against and for play, in education and human development more generally.

2

Play: What Is It?

THE APPEAL OF COMPLEXITY

The study of play is interesting for a number of reasons, not least of which is the sheer variety of scholarship on the topic. Scholars from anthropology (e.g., Bock, 2005; Lancy, 1996), through education (e.g., Fromberg & Bergin, 2006; Johnson, Christie, & Yawkey, 1999), history (e.g., Cross & Walton, 2005) and psychology (Burghardt, 2005; Smith, 1982), and zoology (e.g., P. Bateson, 2005; Fagen, 1981) have studied it. Consequently, the study of play has been subjected to an enormously rich variety of theory and methods. Despite this diversity, what all of these scholars agree on is that play is incredibly difficult to define. In this chapter, I will review a wide array of opinion on how behavior should be categorized as play ranging from structural, behavioral, to functional, consequential, and causal, motivational definitions.

What is a Category?

When social scientists observe any behavior, they typically parse discrete bits of the behavior into categories that are meaningful from a particular theoretical perspective. The ways these categories are formed also depend on the observers' either implicit or explicit definitions. In the more formal case, make no mistake about it: the way an individual parses behaviors is a theoretical act. That is, the way and degree to which definitions reflect one's concern with a specific behavior, function, hormone, or gene reflects one's theoretical orientation. Specific dimensions may be relevant to defining a category from one specific orientation, but not another. Indeed, one reason for the longstanding confusion in trying to define *play* is the lack of an explicit theory of play (Fagen, 1981).

Take the hypothetical example of observing mother–child interaction and trying to determine if the interaction is playful or didactic. If our theoretical orientation was to view play in terms of arousal (Berlyne, 1960; 1966), the observer might first want to distinguish between "specific" and "diverse" exploration by the dyad of their social and material environments. For example, when the mother presents the child with a novel object, their interactions could be described in terms of specific behaviors denoting exploration of the object: for example, increased heart rate, flat or negative affect (measured by facial expression or cortisol assays, for example), and distractibility. By contrast, a Piagetian (1962; 1970) theorist views the child as an egocentric being, and "assimilative" behaviors might be considered playful. For example, a child is presented with the same novel object by his mother, and the child drops it and picks it up repeatedly, while displaying a smile. Unlike the arousal case, the observer is not concerned with cortisol or heart rate, but is instead concerned with whether the child is using the object according to some extant action scheme.

Given the immense complexity and sheer volume of behavioral information presented to the observer, it strikes me as naïve to posit that behavioral categories "emerge" without theoretical bias, either implicit or explicit. While this position is associated with some forms of ethnography (e.g., F. Erickson, 1986), other ethnographers, most notably Bill Corsaro (1981; 1985), clearly delineated the "rules" followed in deriving behavioral categories, such as play. These rules are similar to those used by ethologists (Fagen, 1981; Hinde, 1974; Martin & Bateson, 1993) and psychologists to define categories used in human and nonhuman animal behavioral studies (e.g., Martin & Caro, 1985; Pellegrini, 2004). Generally, behavioral categories are defined in terms of structural, or physical, descriptions; function; causation; and motivation.

With this said, it is also very important to keep each of these dimensions distinct when defining play, or any other category for that matter. Specifically, definitions of play in terms of function typically involve comparisons with adult behavior and the degree to which it does or does not serve the same purpose. For example, playfighting is defined in terms of sets of physical behaviors, such as soft-hit, and is considered playfighting rather than "real" fighting, because it is *not* functional, in the sense that the blow does not hurt the other individual. Conflating the functional and structural aspects of definitions is problematic because "functions" of play, as will be discussed later in this book, are notoriously elusive (Bekoff & Byers, 1981; Martin & Caro, 1985). Relatedly, and perhaps more basically, play is often defined functionally in terms of *what it is not*. Taking the above example, playfighting is defined in terms of not being aggressive. Typically, the "not" categories, such as aggression, are also notoriously difficult, and some say impossible, to define (Hinde, 1974; Wilson, 1975).

From my point of view, it is necessary to include functional dimensions of play in its definition because specifying that play behaviors are not functional and do not serve an immediate purpose frees the organism from instrumental constraints that may limit other structural and motivational dimensions of play. For example, as will be discussed in the next section, by not being concerned that a behavior gets something done, the player is free to experiment with modifying that behavior and also varying the sequence in which it is expressed. Individual behaviors may be exaggerated or abbreviated and ordered in varied, novel sequences. Specific structural aspects of behavior, such as repetition, sequential variation, and exaggeration, are also crucial complements this definition of play.

DEFINING PLAY

Virtually all students of play acknowledge the difficulty (Burghardt, 2005; Fagen, 1981; Marin & Caro, 1985), or impossibility (Wilson, 1975), of trying to define it. Despite this state of affairs, it is also common to note that even though play is difficult to define, most people have no trouble recognizing it when they see it (e.g., Bekoff & Byers, 1981; Martin & Caro, 1985). Despite the frequency of this proclamation, it is not always the case that play can be reliably identified. As I will demonstrate, children, adolescents, and adults have sometimes have difficulty differentiating some forms of play from nonplay (Pellegrini, 1989; 2003; Smith, Smees, & Pellegrini, 2005).

Much of the confusion surrounding the definition of play is related to the fact that in the child development literature the term *play* is often used to label most forms of children's social and nonsocial behavior, regardless of whether it is play or not. So, two children sitting at a table talking with each other about the snacks they are eating could be labeled as play. From this viewpoint, virtually anything that children do has been labeled as play. For example, categories of children's social participation developed by Mildred Parten (1932) have been labeled as solitary *play*, parallel *play*, and cooperative *play* (all my emphasis) in author-itative reviews of children's play (e.g., Rubin et al., 1983) and peer relations (Rubin, Bukowski, & Parker, 1998), when the observed behaviors are not play, at least according to most formal definitions. More recently, children's social interactions in sex-segregated groups are also labeled play (Fabes, Martin, Hanish, Anders, & Madden-Derdich, 2003).

Equally problematic, as noted above, is that play is often defined in terms of what it is *not*. For example, when play is defined in terms of function, it is frequently noted that play behaviors resemble serious, or functional, behaviors, but they do not serve the same function if the behavior is playful.

Claims for the function, or utility, of play range across a very wide spectrum. At one end, play has been almost sanctified by some educators as they make claims about its being necessary for children's healthy development (National Association for the Education of Young Children, 1988; 1992; Singer, Golinkoff, & Hirsch-Pasek, 2006). For example, Robert Hinde (1974), a noted primatologist, claimed that "play consumes so much time and energy that it must be of crucial adaptive importance in development" (1974, p. 227; cited in Martin & Caro, 1985). In fact, we know very little about the amount of time and energy human (Bock, 2005; Pellegrini, Horvat, & Huberty, 1998; Pellegrini & Gustafson, 2005) and nonhuman animals (Martin & Caro, 1985) spend playing. Peter Smith (1988), a developmental psychologist and longtime student of play, has referred to this tendency to overestimate the importance of play in education and development as "the play ethos." When we do have empirical descriptions of nonhuman (Fagen, 1981) and human (Pellegrini et al., 1998; Pellegrini & Gustafson, 2005) play time and activity budgets, we find they are rather limited, accounting for between 2% and 10% of their time or energy—much less than typically claimed.

Espousing a more tempered position, midway along this continuum, the biologists Paul Martin and Tim Caro (1985) suggest that we know very little about play. Consequently, judgment about its role in development certainly should be withheld until we have a clearer picture of what it is we mean by "play" and how frequently it is observed. They, like most students of play, are certainly concerned about the ways in which play is defined. Definitions of play, like purported functions of play, can go on for pages in some books. To illustrate this problem, Robert Fagen (1981), in his seminal volume *Animal Play Behavior*, has a five-page appendix listing definitions of play. In terms of function, two primatologists, Baldwin and Baldwin (1977), have listed 30 possible functions of play.

Finally, some scholars suggest that play is a trivial or irrelevant construct (Schlosberg, 1947), or that any benefits associated with play may in fact be methodological artifacts (Smith, 1988). For example, Tony Simon and Peter K Smith (1983; 1985) found that when double-blind procedures were used, the putative benefits of play with objects for young children's problem-solving (e.g., Sylva, Bruner, & Genoa, 1976) disappeared. Similarly, when double-blind procedures were used by Smith and Whitney (1987) to test the widely reported role of play in children's creativity (Dansky & Silverman, 1973; 1975), these results were not replicated.

This state of affairs where play is simultaneously considered crucial and trivial, as well as clearly defined and poorly defined, has led some to consider studying it as akin to encountering a "hornet's nest" (Bekoff & Byers, 1981). One solution to this problem, proffered by one of the preeminent scholars in the field, Brian Sutton-Smith (1996), is to treat this seemingly chaotic or "ambiguous" state of affairs as representing different "rhetorics" of play. For Sutton-Smith (1996), "rhetoric is used in its modern sense, as being a persuasive discourse, or an implicit narrative, wittingly or unwittingly adopted by members of a particular affiliation to persuade others of the veracity and worthwhileness of their beliefs" (p. 8)." It is certainly the case, and Sutton-Smith also points this out, that different scientific and scholarly groups subscribe to different "rhetorics," and this reflected in their hypotheses and methods.

Contrast, for example, ethnographic and ethological perspectives for studying human development in general, and play in particular. Ethnographers typically want to understand the phenomena under study from the participants' points of view (Hymes, 1980a; 1980b). Thus, an important, and some would say necessary, condition for an ethnography (Hymes, 1980a) is for researchers to take on a participant-observer role. From this view, culture or behavior cannot be understood from the outside. Categories such as play are defined in terms of participants' perceptions. Ethologists, on the other hand, typically aspire to be a "fly on the wall," unobtrusively and objectively describing behaviors of their subjects (Pellegrini, 2004). They define a category in terms of its structural, functional, and contextual dimensions.

It is important to recognize, at least from my point of view, that these positions are complementary, not opposed. Take the case of trying to define the category "rough-and-tumble play (R&T)" or playfighting. Ethologists (e.g., Blurton Jones, 1972; Smith & Connolly, 1972) and comparative psychologists (e.g., Harlow & Harlow, 1965; Suomi & Harlow, 1972), for example, described R&T structurally, in terms of a variety of behaviors, such as soft hit, positive affect, and alternating roles. Factor analytic studies of children's R&T, generally, support the claims of Blurton Jones (1972) and Smith and Connolly (1972).

The factor structure of certain dimensions of play, however, can and does vary systematically. For example, the factor structures for the R&T of sociometrically defined "popular" and "rejected" children vary (Pellegrini, 1989). In this research, primary school children were categorized as either popular or rejected, defined by asking each child to nominate three individuals they "liked the most" and three children they "liked least." Popular children were defined in terms of "like most" / "like least," and were .66 of a standard deviation above the group mean for being liked and disliked, respectively. By contrast, rejected children were those whose "like least" / "like most" nominations were at or above .66 of a standard deviation.

For rejected children, the factor structure of R&T included both aggressive and seemingly playful behaviors. For popular children, on the other hand, R&T and aggression were separate factors. These separate factor structures are displayed in Table 2.1. For popular children, physically vigorous and playful behaviors seem to load on two factors—an R&T factor (1) and a playful provocation factor (2), the latter of which may be indicative of overtures to initiate R&T. The one aggressive behavior, "hit at," did not load on either factor for popular children.

By contrast, for rejected children, the aggressive and playful behaviors co-occurred, suggesting that the playful and aggressive categories were one and the same; their "playful" behaviors were not, in fact, very playful. Indeed, and by way of concurrent support, when we consider the behaviors in children's R&T, we find that for popular children R&T is followed by cooperative social games, not aggression; while for rejected children R&T is followed by aggression, and not games (Pellegrini, 1988).

Table 2.1   Factor structure of children's rough-and-tumble play and aggression

	Popular		Rejected	
Closed-hand hit			.86	
Tease		.94	.60	−.50
Kick at		.68		
Poke		.83		
Pounce			.83	
Playfight	.73		.89	
Chase	.69		.85	
Hold			.46	
Push	.74		.50	.50
Hit at			.95	

The factor structure of play also varies according the one's age. In a ground-breaking study, Sean Neill (1976) found that, for a sample of English adolescents,' unlike the case with younger children, R&T and aggression also co-occurred. This finding was replicated in a sample of American early adolescents (Pellegrini, 1994; 1995) and suggests that during adolescence, R&T may be used to serve a social-dominance function, and aggression is one of strategies used.

There is further evidence of the considerable variation in the ways in which individuals categorize R&T to be playful or not. For example, we find variation in how different individuals interpret exactly the same behaviors. In a study among young primary school children in Sheffield, England, Rebecca Smees, Peter Smith, and I (Smees, Smith, & Pellegrini, 2005) observed children's playground behaviors and videotaped children's R&T and aggression. As part of this study (Rebecca Smees' undergraduate dissertation at Sheffield), we showed these videotapes to three groups of subjects: the children who participated in the aggressive and R&T bouts (each participant was interviewed separately); children who were on the playground at the same time that the bouts were filmed but did not participate in the bouts, and the adult playground supervisors ("dinner ladies"). We asked the participants, among other things, if what they were viewing was playfighting or real fighting. Participants were interviewed on the day of the filming and again two weeks later.

If the structural definitions were sufficient to differentiate play from real fighting, we would expect no differences in interpretation among participants. Our original hunch was that there would be a difference, but one equivalent to a child culture versus adult culture difference—a view not unlike Sutton-Smith's differences in rhetorics of play. What we found, instead, was a participant versus nonparticipant difference. That is, children who played or fought with each other each agreed on what they saw, both on the same day and two weeks later. These views differed from both the playground supervisors' and those of the other children who were also on the playground with the participants! Regardless of my explanation for these particular differences, the important point is that different participants had different interpretations of what constituted play. To address this problem, I discuss various ways of differentiating play from nonplay behavior and suggest that behaviors should be coded categorically, as play or nonplay; and not continuously, as more or less playful.

Structural, Functional, and Causal Descriptions

At least initially, ethologists studying children's play were drawn to "objectively" observed and derived physical descriptions (i.e., motor patterns) of play as a way of combating what was viewed as introspective and subjective categorizations of behavior (Blurton Jones, 1972c). The paradigm of the miscategorization of children's behavior was, and continues to be, defining R&T as aggressive behavior (e.g., Ladd, 1983). A limitation of relying on purely structural descriptions for a definition of play is that they often include aspects of other, unplayful, behavior. For example, while running and jumping can be part of a constellation of playful

Table 2.2   Structural dimensions of play

Behavior	Example
Exaggerated movements	"Monster" steps
Variable sequence	Playing house where cook then buy a new stove
Incomplete sequence	Eat a pretend sandwich without making it

behaviors, they can also belong to the category of "games." In Table 2.2 I summarize some common structural characteristics used in defining play.

It should be noted that children's play is often characterized by behavior "play markers," the most basic marker of which is the "play face," observed in variety of species. The play face sends the message to other conspecifics that "this is play" (G. Bateson, 1972). The two photos below clearly show the similarities.

Definitions using structural, functional, and motivational criteria typically use a combination of these criteria because reliance on just one is not sufficient to differentiate play from other constructs (Burghardt, 2005; Martin & Caro, 1985). With that said, reliance on any list without specifying certain dimensions as necessary conditions is also problematic. I begin with describing the structural dimensions.

Structural, or physical, descriptions are based on muscle and body movements. These sorts of descriptions have been used by ethologists who have studied children's social behavior generally, and play more specifically. The volume edited by Blurton Jones (1972) and works by McGrew (1972) and Smith and Connolly (1972; 1980) are representative of this approach. Physical descriptions of play typically include: play face, soft-hit, alternating roles, run, jump, and incomplete or disrupted sequences of functional behavior. Examples of "play faces" are displayed in Figures 2.1 and 2.2.

Figure 2.1   Ape play face (Photo: Kerri Lewis)

Figure 2.2   Child (Henry) play face (Photo: Anthony Pellegrini)

From a functional perspective, a behavior would be considered playful if it resembled a functional behavior but did not serve that purpose. For example, playfighting resembles real fighting, but it is not used to defeat someone or to acquire a resource. Similarly, the behaviors used with toy pots and pans to cook an imaginary meal resemble the actions associated with actual cooking, but they are not in fact cooking.

Further, function can be classified along two dimensions (Hinde, 1975). First, *function*, in the biological, "ultimate," sense, refers to benefits associated with reproduction, or fecundity. So, frequency of and skill in playfighting during childhood might relate to boys' becoming bigger, stronger, and more competitive than their less-facile peers and, in turn, relate to their having access to "higher quality" mates and increased fecundity. These sorts of functions are "deferred." That is, play serves no function in childhood, but benefits associated with those juvenile play behaviors, such as fighting skills, are reaped in adulthood.

Function can also refer to the more proximal beneficial consequences of a behavior. For example, young girls' playing with objects, such as mortars and pestles, may relate to their ability to use similar objects to effectively and efficiently to process grain (Bock, 2005). Another immediate benefit relates to the effects of vigorous locomotor play on cardiovascular fitness (Pellegrini & Smith, 1998). One of the difficulties of solely functional definitions of play is that functions of play are very, very speculative. However, describing play in terms of function is crucial from my point of view. Specifically, if play is more concerned with means than ends, and not with the instrumentality of the behavior, then players are freed from constraints associated with using behavior efficiently to get things done. Instead, the player is concerned with the activity per se, and this enables players to recombine and modify individual behaviors and sequences of behaviors.

In Table 2.3 below, functional dimensions of play are summarized.

Table 2.3   Functional dimensions of play

Behavior	Example
Does not have a "real" consequence	Play fighting does not hurt others
Behaviors are similar to functional variants	Play fighting involves self-handicapping
More mean than ends oriented	Arranging blocks without a goal

Table 2.4   Causal dimensions of play

Behavior	Example
Interrupted by more serious concerns	Players are distractible
Relaxed motivation	Child chooses to do it, voluntarily
Characteristic of juveniles	Children play more than adults

Causal dimensions of play are antecedent conditions, such as the contexts in which the behavior is observed, or its motivational state. For example, it has often been observed that play occurs when organisms are in rather abundant and safe environments (e.g., Burghardt, 2005; Rubin et al., 1983), not when they are hungry or perceive danger. The characterization that play is observed primarily in juveniles is also a causal dimension: If a child is doing it, it is play. Above, in Table 2.4, I list some dimensions and examples of causal dimensions of play. In order to understand any behavior, play included, it is imperative to consider, not only structural dimensions, but also functional and antecedent conditions, and how these dimensions vary across the life span (Tinbergen, 1969).

PLAY DEFINED IN CHILD DEVELOPMENT

With all these criteria listed, most definitions of play are merely compilations of various lists, noting what is play and what it is not. Given these lists, we must then decide how to apply the criteria. Must a play behavior include a core of specific criteria to be considered "play," as in the case of Burghardt's (2005) definition? Or, alternatively, can a behavior be graded along a continuum from more to less playful, depending on the number of criteria met (Krasnor & Pepler, 1980)? Burghardt's (2005) criteria include many of the functional, structural, and causal criteria listed above:

Performance of the behavior is not functional in its form or context
Play is voluntary and done for its own sake
Play differs from serious behavior in terms of sequence, completeness, or exaggeration
Performed repeatedly
Performed when the individual is adequately provisioned, healthy, and safe

From Burghardt's point of view, *all* of these criteria must be met in order for a behavior to be considered play.

By contrast, Krasnor and Pepler (1980), and subsequently Rubin and colleagues (1983), defined playful behavior for children along a continuum from more to less playful, depending on the number of criteria met. Their criteria include structural, functional, and causal dimensions without explicitly labeling them as such. Their criteria include:

Flexibility, or the degree to which sequences of behavior vary from their functional variant

Positive affect, or the present of a play face, or its equivalent

Intrinsic motivation, or playing out of free choice and for its own sake

Non-literality, or pretending

Means/ends distinction, where players are more concerned with the process, or means, than the ends

Play from the points of view of Krasnor and Pepler (1980) and Rubin and colleagues (1983) is graded along a continuum where a behavior meeting three criteria is "more playful" than a behavior meeting two criteria. From this view, each of the dimensions of play is given equal weight; so, for example, a behavior characterized as having positive affect, pretense, and intrinsic motivation, such as a voluntary enactment of a dramatic script, would be considered more playful than one having two criteria, such as child's pretending to be a doctor, but not concerned with an accurate representation of that role. Unlike Burghardt's (2005) definition, then, no priority is given to any one or set of behaviors in characterizing an activity as play. As will be discussed below, some workers, as well lay observers, see it differently: while recognizing that play is a multi-dimensional construct, they also posit that some criteria are more important than others.

Play as Observable Behavior

Beginning with defining play in terms of observable behavior, and based on Piaget's (1962) theory of development, different forms of play correspond to different points, or stages, in ontogeny, though the categorization reflects the function rather than the structure of the behavior. The earliest form of play—functional, or practice play, which is similar to Groos's (1901) portrayal—corresponds to the sensorimotor period of development (approximately 0–2 years of age) and involves repetition of behaviors, routines, and subroutines that have been mastered. Such repetition is practice for mastering the adult variant of the behavior, a functional dimension. Esther Thelen's descriptions (1979; 1980) of infants' rhythmic stereotypies, or gross movements without any apparent function, such as body rocking and foot kicking, are a prime example of practice play.

Perhaps the most commonly studied form of human play is symbolic play. Symbolic play, also labeled pretend, fantasy, or make-believe play, is characteristic of the preoperational period in children's development. Symbolic play is a primarily assimilative behavior where a behavior is taken out of its functional context; for example, a using a banana to represent a pretend telephone. Further, and like practice play, symbolic play has the child recombining everyday behavioral sequences in novel orders.

Next, games-with-rules are the form of "play" engaged in by formal operational youngsters. As noted by Piaget (1962) and Rubin and colleagues (1983), games and play are different, primarily in terms of the means/ends criterion. Games are primarily accommodative and governed by *a priori* rules, such as the three-strike rule in baseball. Play, on the other hand, is primarily assimilative and rule-governed, but the rules are defined by the players, and they are in the constant state of renegotiation (Garvey, 1990; Sachs, Goldman, & Chaille, 1984). For example, when two preschoolers say they are going to "play Mommy and Daddy," they often begin by stating some role-related rule, such as "I'll be the daddy and you be the mommy" (Garvey, 1989; Pellegrini, 1982), or defining the context, such as "Let this be my sword." However, children typically change the rules in the course of the enactments; for example, "Daddies don't really do that." The difference between these rules and those of games is that play rules are flexible and negotiable where the rules of games are not, though (and as will be discussed in the chapter on games) there is also some negotiation in the rules of children's games.

Dispositional Criteria

The next dimension of play, according to Rubin and colleagues (1983), is dispositional, which roughly corresponds to the causal, motivational dimensions used in the nonhuman animal literature. The six dispositions include:

Intrinsic motivation
Attention to means over ends
Differentiation between play and exploration
Relation to instrumental behavior
Freedom from external rules
Active engagement

Beginning with intrinsic motivation, it is assumed that play is not a consummatory, instrumental behavior leading to a goal external to the behaviors themselves. For example, playful behaviors themselves are motivating, independent of any outcome of those behaviors. From this view, an adolescent's swimming laps for fun would be playful, but swimming to lose weight or to win a race would not be play.

"Means over ends," as discussed above, and briefly, sees the player more concerned with the behavior itself than with the functional outcome: It is the repeating of the movements of swimming or piling blocks up, rather than some outcome, that is important. Relatedly, play behaviors, in contrast with instrumental behaviors, do resemble the more serious versions, but they do not culminate in attaining the result. Furthermore, the behaviors of noninstrumental activity are typically more exaggerated, abbreviated, or sequentially disrupted.

"Exploration" is often confused with "play," yet there are very clear behavioral, structural, causal, and functional differences (Belsky & Most, 1981; Burghardt, 2005; Hutt, 1966; Pellegrini & Gustafson, 2005). Most basically, exploration is an information-gathering venture, whereas play is not concerned with an outcome such as gathering information. Over 40 years ago, Corrine Hutt (1966) differentiated play from exploration by noting their different motivations or causal antecedents. Exploration as it is concerned with gathering information is guide by the question, "What does *it* do?" By contrast, play is more person- than object- centered and guided by the question, "What can *I* do with it?" For example, when a child is presented with a novel object, she or he spends time exploring that object—touching, mouthing, rotating, and dropping it to find out what it does. Only after the object has been explored, and becomes familiar, can it be played with. Indeed, the child probably uses the attributes of the object discovered through exploration as a basis for play themes with it. For example, through exploration a child discovers that by pressing the top of a ballpoint pen, she can make the writing stylus come out of the bottom of the pen. This attribute can then be the basis of the child using that pen to give her baby doll a "shot" as she plays doctor.

Further, while the child at play is characterized as being relaxed, with positive affect and relatively low heart rate, and easily distracted, in exploration the child displays flat or negative affects, an increased heart rate, and is very difficult to distract.

Just as exploration precedes play in novel contexts, exploration also precedes play in ontogeny. Based on observations of infants in a laboratory setting, Belsky and Most (1981) found that exploratory behaviors were predominant relative to play during the first nine months of life. By 12 months of age, play and exploration were observed in close to equal amounts, and by 18 months of age, play was predominant. A similar pattern has been observed with nonhuman juveniles. For example, with domestic piglets, exploration is evidenced when they are presented with novel stimuli; as the objects become familiar, play increases (Wood-Gush & Vestergaard, 1991; Wood-Gush, Vestergaard, & Petersen, 1990). Similarly, among chimpanzees, exploration precedes play in ontogeny, and as exploration wanes, play increases (Loizos, 1967; 1969).

The rules dimension of play, as discussed above, relates to the absence of *a priori* rules and the presence of negotiated rules. In play the rules are flexible and negotiated by the players, not set in advance. Lastly, the criterion of "active engagement" is a vaguely defined construct and contrasted with states like daydreaming and boredom. The literature, however, does not usually specify what is meant by "active engagement." These distinctions between play and exploration are displayed in Table 2.5.

Table 2.5   Play and exploration

	Play	Exploration
Behavior	Low heart rate	High heart rate
	Positive affect	Flat/Negative affect
Function	Practice	Information gathering
Causal	Easily distracted	Deliberate
	Familiar context	Novel context
	What can I do with it?	What can it do?

Play as Context

Lastly, Rubin (1983) and colleagues defined play in terms of its contexts, a distinction close to the causal dimension used by ethologists. Contexts, from this view, are a limited set of antecedent conditions for play. The contexts described by Rubin and colleagues include:

Familiarity
Free choice
Minimal adult intrusion
Stress–free

A context can be familiar in terms of the materials and people present. As noted in the discussion differentiating play from exploration, individuals can only play with objects after they have become familiar with them. Similarly, individuals, either peers or adults, must be familiar to the child, and this probably relates to the stress-free criterion, Strangers tend to elicit fear and anxiety, and these conditions also inhibit dispositions necessary for play. Correspondingly, some animal researchers note that laboratory animals' play is an indicator that the animals are healthy and that their environments are not stressful (Martin & Caro, 1985).

Free choice and minimal adult intervention also tend to go hand-in-hand. These conditions seem to be prerequisites for individuals' being intrinsically motivated. In short, these contexts may be necessary for children to express the dispositional criteria and thus probably should be collapsed into one category, as suggested by ethologists, labeled "causal, motivational."

In an empirical test to determine the psychological reality of these criteria and the degree to which some criteria are more important than others, Smith and Vollstedt (1985) showed educated adults, both experienced and inexperienced with children, a series of videotaped play bouts. The participants were asked to rate each bout in terms of occurrence of each of the five criteria noted above. Smith and Vollstedt (1985) found that these adults could indeed identify play reliably, but they used multiple criteria to do so, with non-literality being the most important, and the means/end distinction and active engagement being relatively unimportant. These findings reflect the importance of fantasy as a "paradigm case" of play (Mathews & Mathews, 1982). On the other hand, these findings also may reflect the difficulty of presenting videotaped bouts that capture other criteria, such as means over ends and intrinsic motivation; or poorly defined constructs, like active engagement. Indeed, it is very possible that fantasy bouts also contain means-over-ends criteria. This study also highlights an associated problem—defining play that is not fantasy.

The Smilansky-Parten Matrix of Play Behaviors

Piaget's theory of human development generally (Piaget, 1970), and his theory of play more specifically (Piaget, 1962), are perhaps the most influential in all of child development. As we have seen already, his categorizations of play have been used as definitional criteria by Rubin and colleague (1983). These categories

Table 2.6   Smilansky-Parten play matrix

	Solitary	Parallel	Interactive
Functional			
Constructive			
Fantasy			
Games			

were also used earlier by Sara Smilansky (1968) as the basis for a way to categorize the cognitive dimensions of children's play. More specifically, Smilansky used Piaget's play categories (functional, fantasy, and games-with-rules), along with constructive "play," which Piaget (1962) did not consider play because it was more accommodative than assimilative, to the extent that in it children were more concerned with the result than with the means. These cognitive categories, in combination with a revised conceptualization of Parten's social participation scheme (solitary, parallel, and interactive), were used by Rubin and colleagues (e.g., Rubin & Maioni, 1975; Rubin, Maioni, & Hornung, 1976;' Rubin, Watson, & Jambor, 1978) to form a matrix of "play" behaviors, as displayed in Table 2.6.

The primary contribution of this matrix, despite some weaknesses, such as including "construction" as a dimension of play (Smith, Takhvar, Gore, & Vollstedt, 1986), is that it alerted researchers to the importance of both social and cognitive dimensions of play. Correspondingly, it alerted observers to the multidimensionality, or heterogeneity, of play as well the sophistication of different forms of play. For example, children who engage in solitary fantasy play tend to be unpopular with their peers and rated by their teachers as hyperactive; this was not the case for children engaging in interactive fantasy play (Rubin & Clark, 1982).

The clarity of this matrix and its ease of use has resulted in its being used to gather a vast amount of information on children's play (summarized in Rubin et al., 1983). The popularity of the matrix also reflects some problems not inherent in the matrix per se. Most basically, the matrix typically has been used to categorize all forms of children's behavior, whether the behaviors are play or not, and labeled as a corresponding form of "play." For example, in one series of studies the matrix was used to categorize the behaviors of preschool and primary school children on their school playgrounds (Frost & Sanderlin, 1985). In these cases, all of the behavior exhibited by children was forced into the matrix, whether it was play or not. Furthermore, it was used with primary school children even though it was designed for preschoolers, thus different levels of games or interactive behaviors, which are not play, are not captured. For example, chase behavior is common on the playground, but chasing, a form of locomotor play, does not readily fit into the Smilansky-Parten matrix—unless it is part of an interactive fantasy, where two children are pretending to be superheroes involved in a struggle, or an interactive game, where children are playing tag. A lesson here is that one should take great care before deciding to use an extant category system (Bakeman & Gottman, 1986; Pellegrini, 2004).

Table 2.7   Structural, functional, and causal dimension of play in social, locomotor, object-directed, and pretend

Domains	Social	Locomotor	Object-directed	Pretend
Structure	Reciprocity	Exaggerated movements	Altered action	Role enactment
Function	Self-handicapping	Soft-hit	Abbreviated action	Nonfunctional
Causal	Familiar peers	Spacious area	Familiar objects	All criteria

CONCLUSION

After reviewing the vast human and nonhuman animal play literature, it seems clear that play is a multidimensional construct and should be considered from structural, functional, and causal criteria, simultaneously. With this said, probably the most basic and necessary aspects of play relate to the means over ends and nonfunctional dimensions. As noted above, these dimensions of play enable the player to vary ordinarily functional behavior into different forms, durations, and sequences. In further recognition of the heterogeneity of play there is often overlap across the social, locomotor, pretend, and object-directed domains of play. For example, R&T is both social and locomotor play, and two children pretending to be doctor and patient, where one pretends a shoestring is a stethoscope, could be both social and object play. In Table 2.7 above, I schematize the functional, causal, and structural dimensions of play across domains. It should be noted that the examples in each of the cells for the structural, functional, and causal dimensions of this matrix could probably fit in a number of the cells. For example, "exaggerated movements" could be observed across domains.

3

Theories of Play

Theories from a wide variety of disciplines have examined the play of both human and nonhuman animals. Scholars from anthropology (e.g., Geertz, 1972; Lancy, 1996) to zoology (e.g., Burghardt, 2005; Wilson, 1975) have proffered theories to explain the existence and impact of play on individuals and societies. Currently, theories of play expounding the benefits of play are seemingly on the increase, and these efforts range from the credible to the incredible: Witness the recent cover story in the *New York Times Magazine* (Henig, 2008) on the value of play, or the Institute for Play suggesting a link between play deprivation and mass murder (Institute for Play: http://www.nifplay.org/about_us.html). In this chapter I limit the discussion to those theories with currency in the scientific literature, as judged (for better or worse) by their appearance in peer-reviewed scientific journals and academic books. Specifically, I discuss Piaget's and Vygotsky's theories of play first, seeing as they are arguably the most influential in studies of human play. Next, I discuss epigenetic theories derived from behavioral and evolutionary biology.

PIAGET'S AND VYGOTSKY'S THEORIES

Jean Piaget and Lev Vygotsky were, arguably, two of the most influential theorists in child development, generally, and children's play, more specifically. Each of their theories will be reviewed, with particular stress on the role of play in children's development.

Piaget's Theory

Piaget's (1983) equilibration theory viewed human development in terms of the interaction among assimilation, accommodation, and equilibration. Intellectual adaptation and growth for Piaget was a balance, or equilibration, between assimilation and accommodation. Growth and development are the result of a series of disequilibrations, or imbalances, that individuals have to correct. From this theory, assimilation is the process by which individuals subordinate the world they encounter to their own points of view. Play, for Piaget, was the paradigm of assimilation dominating accommodation. Different forms of play (functional, symbolic, and games) correspond to different developmental periods, respectively: sensorimotor, preoperational, and concrete operational. Importantly, Piaget viewed play as nonadaptive, a form of autistic thought that, with development, would be replaced by the rational, logical thought of adulthood (Harris, 2006).

Practice play is observed during infancy and involves infants repeating motor routines they have already produced or mastered but executing them in a nonfunctional context. In this way skills are refined and consolidated. For example, an infant learns that by swatting a mobile in his crib, he can make it spin. He repeats this movement with the mobile and then with other props in the crib, thus mastering the swat movement.

Piaget is perhaps best known for his work in symbolic play, arguably the most frequently examined form of play in child and educational psychology. Symbolic play occurs after the preoperational child has developed the ability to have one thing represent another, or what Piaget called the "semiotic function." In symbolic play, children practice having one thing represent something else; for example, having an empty tea cup represent a "real," full tea cup, from which a child is "drinking." As noted by Harris (2006), Piaget stressed that symbolic play was a form of autistic thought, where children interpreted and reenacted life events from their own, egocentric, perspective.

Games-with-rules is a form of collective behavior where children subordinate their behavior to an abstract set of rules that have been socially defined *a priori*. From this viewpoint, games are not "play," because they are not primarily assimilative activities, like the two other forms of play.

Vygotsky's Theory

Vygotsky's theory was formulated in the immediate shadow of the Bolshevik revolution in Russia. Vygotsky's brief, and that of his student A. R. Luria (1976), from the newly formed Soviet government was to construct a Marxist psychology. Karl Marx's theory, as expounded in his major work, *Capital,* was predicated on the proposition that human behavior could be changed by social and institutional forces, especially those forces realized through the means of production (Marx, 1906/1867). From this position, the role of social forces is paramount in shaping individual development to conform to societal norms. Marx also suggested that individuals' consciousness was realized through their work and their production.

Vygotsky's theory of play is a strange mixture of Marxist orthodoxy and the psychological theory of his contemporaries, especially Piaget and Freud. Like Piaget, Vygotsky was concerned primarily with symbolic play, where *play* was defined in terms of creating imaginary situations, yet he was critical of Piaget's view of the young child as nonsocial and egocentric (Vygotsky, 1962). Like Freud, Vygotsky saw play as being motivated by wishes that were unattainable in society, such as reducing or eliminating an undesirable condition. From these elements, Vygotsky's theory of play attempted to reconcile the tension between wishes that could not be fulfilled in reality but could in fantasy, and societal norms limiting those choices. Tension between these two opposing motivations was reduced by creating an imaginary world that also conformed to societal reality at some level. For example, two children enact a symbolic play bout where they want to ride a horse and each knows, in reality, they do not have access to a horse. To reduce this tension, the children use a broom to represent a pretend horse and further follow the societal rules that they know about horseback riding, such as galloping and making neighing sounds.

For Vygotsky, this representational process was seen a normal part of children's intellectual development—not as maladaptive or some inferior variant of adult intelligence. Indeed, symbolic play marked the start of children's being able to use symbols, and later signs, such as written words, to mediate their subsequent activity. Through symbolic play, posited Vygotsky, children learn to separate the meaning of a symbolic from its referent, and as a consequence, come to recognize the arbitrary relationhips between signs, such as words, and their referents. This ability to represent alternative realities, thought Vygotsky (1971), is later realized in art and aesthetic expression as well as in imagination.

Similarities Between Piaget's and Vygotsky's Theories

While different at some levels, the theories do share some ground, although in many cases the similarities are superficial. Specifically, both theories are concerned with symbolic play as well as being dialectic in nature (Bidell, 1988; Rogoff, 1988; Tudge & Winterhoff, 1991). By "dialectic," I mean that both theories are concerned with the processes of opposites being in conflict, such as assimilation and accommodation, and the pull of societal norms versus wish fulfillment, and its role in development. For Piaget (1966; 1983), the constructs of assimilation (i.e., the subordination of the outside world to one's own view of the world) and accommodation (i.e., domination of the internal by the external), and equilibration (i.e., a temporary balance between conflicting assimilation and accommodation) are crucial in this regard. Like Hegel's well-known thesis and antithesis, assimilation and accommodation are present and conflicting (in varying degrees) in all processes; balance, like the Hegelian synthesis, is represented by equilibration. Piaget (1966) considered pretend play an excellent example of an activity dominated by assimilation, while he considered imitation to be representative of accommodation.

For Vygotsky (1967) too, dialectical conflict is important. Children's pretend play, for Vygotsky, is a result of the conflict between their wishes and desires and their inability to meet them because of societal constraints. To resolve the conflict, children engage in pretend play whereby they can realize the "unrealizable." This cathartic aspect of his theory of pretend play has children addressing conflicts between individual and societal desires (see Fein, 1979, for a full discussion of this issue).

Another similarity is that both Piaget and Vygotsky acknowledged the importance of the social dimensions of cognitive development (Bidell, 1988; Chapman, 1986; Pellegrini, 1984). As noted above, Vygotsky specifically addressed the role of society and social interaction, especially the role of a more experienced tutor, in his theory. He did not develop it fully in his research program, possibly because of his untimely death. Piaget (1970), too, acknowledged the role of social factors in terms of facilitating or inhibiting development. For Piaget (1965), however, peers were a more potent spur to development than were adults. More is said about these social processes below.

In short, while there are similarities, the two differ considerably in their conceptions of social processes and the role of these processes in development, as well as in other related issues. These differences are not surprising in that Vygotsky and Piaget were interested in very different phenomena: Vygotsky was primarily interested in the use of sociocultural tools of thought, like language, while Piaget was interested in the development of logical thought (Rogoff, 1988).

Differences Between Piaget and Vygotsky

Most basically, Vygotskiian theory leads to a context-specific approach to cognition, not the central-processing position that characterizes Piaget's structural theory (Laboratory of Comparative Human Cognition [LCHC], 1983; Piaget, 1970). Furthermore, Piaget and Vygotsky made very different assumptions about the role of pretend play and interaction with peers and adults, specifically, in children's development.

First, pretend play was considered by Vygotsky (1978) as a first-order symbol system, like drawing and some very early writing. First-order symbolization involves symbols "directly denoting objects or actions" (ibid., p. 115), such as written symbols, like the symbol in Figure 3.1 representing a cat itself rather than the word *cat*. Second-order symbolization involves "the creation of written signs for the spoken symbols of words" (ibid., p. 115); thus, "cat" comes to stand for the word *cat,* which in turn stands for the cat itself. Early writing, according to this theory, should not initially be related to second-order symbol systems like reading. As writing becomes a linguistic, second-order symbolization process, it relates to reading. In short, Vygotsky's context-specific approach to cognition does not predict within-stage homogeneity for reading and writing at an early age; that is, writing and reading are different processes for young children.

Equivalence among cognitive processes, such as the equivalence of reading and writing during the early childhood period, is more consistent with a Piagetian, central processing, model, such that all dimensions of cognition are consistent within each developmental stage. In this model, all thought during the preoperational or concrete operation period should be at a similar level, except in usual

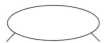

Figure 3.1 Written symbol for "cat"

cases of horizontal *decalage*. By contrast, studies following Vygotskiian theory, such as the research of Scribner and Cole (1978), treat literacy as a differentiated construct, whereas studies following Piagetian theory would treat reading and writing as a unified construct, usually called "literacy."

A second difference between Vygotsky and Piaget was in their conceptualizations of the functions of pretend play. Piaget (1932; 1966) considered pretend play primarily assimilative, or practice (see the Piaget [1966] & Sutton-Smith [1966] debate on this point). Because Piaget considered pretend play primarily assimilative, and not accommodative, he believed it should be minimally related to the creation of new knowledge. Indeed, Piaget (1970) considered activities dominated by assimilation as largely evolving in an egocentric or even autistic direction. "The most common form of this situation in the play of the child is the 'symbolic games' or fiction games, in which objects at his command are used only to represent what is imagined" (pp. 106–107). For Piaget, this form of thought was inferior to logical thought and destined to be replaced by more advanced forms of adult, logical thought.

Pretend and symbolic thought for Vygostsky were especially important in regards to children's literacy development (Pellegrini & Galda, 1993). As noted above, in pretend play children do things that they want to do in everyday life but cannot. The realization of this type of wish fulfillment is, however, limited by children's consideration of larger societal values. The rules in children's pretend play are based on societal rules; thus, a child enacting a mother in play would follow rules similar to those observed in society. In this way symbols become defined according to societal norms. In the process of trying to realize fantastic goals, children use make-believe. The symbolization inherent in make-believe is, for Vygotsky, a way in which children learn that one thing can represent another. This process is important in children's writing development. To quote Vygotsky (1978) on this matter: "Symbolic representation in play is essentially a particular form of speech at an earlier stage, one which leads directly to written language" (p. 111). So the extent to which play motivates or causes child development is very different for the two theories. For Vygotsky, but not Piaget, play is a causal force in the development of very specific areas and a force that can be later invoked through imagination later in life, in the ability to address hypothetical situations. As in pretending, addressing hypothetical situations in adulthood necessitates that individuals take a flexible stance towards a situations, seeing it from a variety of perspectives and simulating scenarios within each (Harris, 2006).

Importantly, the theories of Vygotsky and Piaget also make very different assumptions about the ways in which social interaction relates to children's development, and they diverge further regarding the influence of adults and peers in children's development. At the most general level of comparison, regarding the role of social interaction in children's development, Piaget was concerned with "intra-individual" development, assigning minimal effects to the role of social interaction in children's development. (See Bruner & Bornstein, 1989, and Tudge & Rogoff, 1989, for extended discussions of these issues.) Children's development, according to Piaget's equilibration theory, was a result of conceptual conflict encountered while they interacted with their physical and logical worlds (Piaget, 1983). As is well known, Piaget's (1967; 1974) young child was egocentric. Indeed, Piaget (1967) stated that children constructed symbols "in isolation" (p. 124); consequently he considered symbolic play to be the "purest form" (p. 126) of egocentric thought. For Piaget (Piaget & Inhelder, 1969), pretend play and egocentric thought characterized children from approximately three to six years of age.

Where Piaget (1965) did explicitly address the importance of social interaction for young children was in the realm of moral judgments, which he considered to be a branch of social knowledge (Kamii & DeVries, 1978). Indeed, this seems to be one of the few places where he explicitly outlined ways in which the social dimension of the environment affected development. In this realm, Piaget (1965) suggested that interaction with peers, not more-competent others, spurred development. Development was the result of conceptual conflict for Piaget; conflict is maximized in peer contexts and minimized in adult–child contexts. Piaget considered the unilateral roles that he thought typified adult–child interaction as inhibiting development.

On the other hand, Vygotsky (1962; 1978) and his student Luria (1961) stressed the role of more-competent others, often adults, in children's cognitive development. Through verbal interaction with a more-competent other about a specific task, children appropriate skills that become internalized. This is the well-known idea that higher cognitive functioning moves from the inter-psychological, or between-person, plane to the intra-psychological, or within-person, plane (Wertsch, 1978). Vygotsky's (1962) monograph on language and thought was, to a degree, a tract against Piaget's view of the socially insensitive child. Vygotsky considered children's cognitive development to vary as a function of social activity and of corresponding forms of language with a more-competent other (Pellegrini, 1984; Tudge & Rogoff, 1989; Vygotksy, 1962), usually an adult.

In short, Piaget and Vygotsky had very different views of the roles of pretend play and social interaction in children's development. Piaget saw the solitary child practicing, not learning, in pretend play. While a social component to development of the young child was acknowledged by Piaget, the peer context, not the adult–child context, was given primacy. By contrast, Vygotsky saw children's development as being spurred by pretend play with a more-competent other.

CURRENT EVOLUTIONARY-ORIENTED THEORIES OF PLAY

Parallel to the study of play in humans, biologists and comparative psychologists have also been studying play, but that of nonhuman animals. For the most part, this comparative and biological work has not invoked Piagetian and Vygotskiian theories, with the exception being where Piagetian theory was used to guide the study of nonhuman primates' play with objects (e.g., Parker, 1977). Instead, the study of nonhuman animal play has been guided by theories derived from Darwin's (1859/2006) theory of evolution by natural selection. In this section, I review selected evolution-oriented theories of play and relate them to the study of humans' play.

I was guided in this section by the heuristic advanced by the Nobel prize–winning ethologist Niko Tinbergen (1969), who noted that in order to understand any behavior, or class of behaviors, such as play, it is necessary to ask four questions that examine that behavior's antecedents, its function, and its ontogenetic and phylogenetic development. From that advice, in this section, I discuss those evolution-oriented theories of play that have been applied to the study of human play.

Sociobiology

Theory and related hypotheses associated with the general field of sociobiology were pioneered by two evolutionary biologists, Robert Trivers (1971, 1972) and W. D. Hamilton (1964), and more widely popularized by two eminent biologists, E. O. Wilson (1975) at Harvard, and Richard Dawkins at Oxford (1976). Indeed, Wilson nominated the study of play as one of the most important topics for sociobiological study.

Sociobiology arose, in part, as a counterpoint to group selection theory (Wynne-Edwards, 1962), a largely unexamined assumption that an individual's actions were naturally selected for in terms of their outcomes for the *group's* welfare. Group selection had been seen as the way to explain altruistic behavior (i.e., a behavior that benefits others, or the social group, but is costly to the actor). But group selection, as advanced by Wynne-Edwards, could not explain selfish behavior; it could not explain the complex patterns of selfish and altruistic behavior that are actually observed in all animal species.

Traditionally, sociobiology takes the gene, and the individual as a carrier of genes, as central in understanding the genetic evolution of behavior, including social behaviors such as selfishness or altruism. That is, the individual, or more exactly the gene, is considered the unit of natural selection, with selection at the group level seen as largely unimportant (though see Boyd & Richerson, 1985; Wilson & Wilson, 2007, for interesting discussions of this). From this viewpoint, individuals act to maximize their own reproduction, or fitness, and the subsequent survival and reproduction of their offspring. Any benefits to the group, such as low levels of intra-group conflict, are seen as byproducts of individual benefits; for example, low levels of conflict benefit individuals (e.g., of both high and low social dominance rankings) as well as the group, which comprises an aggregate of individuals.

Hamilton's (1964) kin selection theory was basic to changing this way of thinking with his notion of "inclusive fitness," defined as the sum of an individual's fitness plus the fitness of his or her kin. From this view, it is more likely to pay (in terms of fitness) to be altruistic to close kin (who are genetically more similar), than to more distant kin and especially non-kin. In other words, behavior that has costs for the individual performing it can still be selected for if it helps kin enough that there is a net benefit in terms of sharing genes and surviving.

Trivers (1971) extended the explanation to altruism and cooperative interactions with non-kin in his theory of "reciprocal altruism." He argued that individuals may cooperate with and be altruistic to non-related individuals, provided the other individuals reciprocate in kind; over time such reciprocity can be beneficial to each. Because of the possible problem of "free riders," however (individuals who take benefits but do not incur costs from reciprocating), reciprocal altruism is only likely among individuals who interact repeatedly and where there is a memory of reciprocity and sanctions against those who do not reciprocate. If reciprocal altruism has evolved, then individuals can benefit in the long term from taking risks or incurring costs for others, under the assumption that others will reciprocate by doing the same for them; this should minimize selfish behavior and cheating and maximize cooperation, group stability, and individual fitness.

The primacy of the gene, and individuals' phylogenetic history, was also espoused in sociobiologists' views of development. Development is seen as guided by genes, in turn, under the control of natural selection. As Wilson (1975, p. 145) put it: "The important point to keep in mind is that such phenomena as . . . the ontogenetic development of behavior, although sometimes treated in virtual isolation as the proper objects of entire disciplines . . . are really only sets of adaptations keyed to environmental changes of different durations. They are not fundamental properties of organisms around which a species must shape its biology." This argument suggests that an organism's development is the result of an evolved range of responses to a variety of possible environments. That is, although genes do not "determine" behavioral expression per se, they prescribe the capacity for behavioral expression across a range of possible environments, shaped by natural selection.

The role of the environment has typically been acknowledged in terms of what has been called a *range of reaction* (Gottlieb, 2003; Stamps, 2003). That is, genes prescribe a capacity to develop behaviors in environments that "trigger" (Wilson, 1975, p. 152) dimensions of that capacity. Different environments will facilitate or inhibit a phenotypic characteristic, but to similar extents for all genotypes. There continues to be a unidirectional effect of genes on behavior, though these theorists acknowledge that the environment moderates that effect. Such an approach was compatible with the traditional additive assumptions of behavior genetics analyses that apportioned variance to genetics, environment, and a gene-environment interaction conceived in additive terms (Gottlieb, 2003).

Two other aspects of sociobiology have had implications for the study of human behavioral development that I find less controversial. One is the priority accorded to cost–benefit analyses as a way to judge the adaptive value of a behavior (Barlow, 1989). A behavior is said to be functional and positively related to fitness, if benefits are greater than costs. Individuals for whom a behavior or strategy has benefits outweighing costs would be at an advantage relative to those for whom the ratio was zero or less. Stress on cost–benefit analysis is shared by the sister discipline of behavioral ecology (Krebs & Davies, 1993) as well as by game theorists (Maynard Smith, 1979), and this aspect continues to be important in ethology (e.g., Caro, 1995) and some areas of human development and the study of children's play (e.g., Pellegrini & Gustafson, 2005; Pellegrini, Horvat, & Huberty, 1998).

Another important aspect of sociobiology as applied to behavioral development is the idea that natural selection exerts pressure at all periods of development. An important corollary is that some adaptations may be age-stage specific. The importance of this position for developmental psychologists is that children's behavior, especially play, should be primarily evaluated in terms of the juvenile period per se, not necessarily for the benefit of that behavior for the mature adult. Consider three examples: (1) in infancy, sucking is functional and selected for during the period of infancy, while chewing food, not sucking, would be adaptive in the juvenile period; (2) in middle childhood, overestimation of one's cognitive abilities may help a child sustain interest in an activity that they might not otherwise engage in if their engagement was contingent upon approximating an adult ideal (Bjorklund & Green, 1992). Similarly, overestimation of one's strength may give a child more confidence in peer relationships (Omark & Edelman, 1976). What might be viewed as immature (such as overestimating one's own cognitive processes or one's strength) is in fact functional for children during this period; (3) in adolescence, increased risk-taking and distance from parental authority may be functional in raising status in the peer group and attracting the opposite sex, and more so than in earlier childhood, or adulthood (Arnett, 1992; Pellegrini, 2003).

By and large, sociobiologists have promoted a "general-purpose" view of adaptation. That is, they examined behaviors as being functional or adaptive in the species' natural environment, without paying so much attention to mechanisms and constraints that certain mechanism might impose on adaptation. Essentially, they focused only on the functional dimension of Tinbergen's "four why's." This was especially problematic in the human case, as the vast majority of us no longer live in environments resembling those in which we evolved. In addition, psychologists wished to say more about the cognitive mechanisms involved in behavior. Evolutionary psychology arose as a response to these needs.

Evolutionary Psychology

"Evolutionary psychology" is currently a label used to cover a variety of theories and propositions tying models of evolutionary biology to human behavior (Heyes, 2003; Symons, 1992). Because of this diversity and the resulting confusion among different positions, I will define it here more specifically, as following the theoretical tenets presented by Buss (1994), Cosmides and Tooby (1987), and Pinker (1997). This choice is based on the similarity of their positions as a group and their wide reach in the general human psychological literature.

Like sociobiology, evolutionary psychology shares a gene-centered view of human functioning, and it is seen by some as an offspring of sociobiology (e.g., Laland & Brown, 2002; Stamps, 2003); and the centrality of the theories of Hamilton and Trivers were especially important in Cosmides's and Tooby's original work (Cosmides & Tooby, 1987, 1992; Cosmides, 1989).

Cosmides and Tooby (1987) describe evolutionary psychology as the "missing link" between evolution and behavior. The goal of evolutionary psychology, from their viewpoint, is an adaptationist program aimed at recognizing specific functions (e.g., reproduction) associated with specific organs (e.g., the brain). From this position, the brain houses a variety of specific mechanisms (modules), and these mechanisms are adaptations that evolved to solve specific problems (Symons, 1989; Tooby & Cosmides, 1992). The stress on separate modules' being used to solve specific problems is based on the assumption that no general function could possibly maximize gene survival. Furthermore, a Blank Slate learning approach to solving such problems, labeled the Standard Social Science Model, is seen as inadequate by evolutionary psychologists (Cosmides & Tooby, 1987), as it was by cognitive psychologists (Bruner, Goodnow, & Austin 1956) and linguistics (Chomsky, 1957).

According to this variant of evolutionary psychology, mechanisms as adaptations are the proximal links between evolution by natural selection and behavior. This functional view generally leads to a search for mechanisms "designed" to solve the functional problems (Symons, 1989). It is also assumed that these proximal mechanisms are psychological, not behavioral, and that they reflect the outcomes of genetic evolution (Cosmides & Tooby, 1987; Symons, 1989).

Evolutionary psychologists posit that modules and other forms of brain-based mechanisms reflect the selection problems faced by ancestral humans in the Pleistocene era, the so-called Environment of Evolutionary Adaptedness (EEA), an environment implicitly assumed to be rather uniform across locations. Specifically, modules reflect the specific cognitive mechanisms used to solve problems faced in the Stone Age. Thus, modern humans are walking around with Stone Age psychological mechanisms and applying them to contemporary problems associated with fitness.

Modules are presented as "encapsulated units," each of which is independent of other modules. For example, a social exchange module should be independent of a language module (Cosmides, 1987; Tooby & Cosmides, 1992). A paradigm of a module cited by evolutionary psychologists is the language acquisition device (LAD) proposed by Chomsky (1965, 1975) to explain the acquisition of syntax (although Chomsky himself does not support the view of independent modules— Chomsky, 1994, cited in Maratsos, 1998, p. 424).

Evolutionary psychologists also assume that these mechanisms are "innate" (Cosmides & Tooby, 1987), or "instinctual" (Pinker, 1994), and designed to solve very specific tasks; this compartmentalized modular view has been called a "Swiss army knife" view of the brain. The specificity of the modules reflects the idea that no one solution would work to solve all of the problems encountered by humans; consequently, the modules are adaptations to the problems faced in the EEA.

Evolutionary psychology does not make central the role of experience during ontogeny, thus ignoring one of Tinbergen's four questions. Most important for my purposes is the lack of knowledge of how these modules develop within individuals from genes naturally selected to solve specific problems through childhood and adulthood (Karmiloff-Smith, 1998; Laland & Brown, 2002). Specific to the role of the environment in motivating and shaping development, Tooby and Cosmides do discuss the co-evolution of genes and the environment. They note that different aspects of the environment are "developmentally relevant" (Tooby & Cosmides, 1992, p. 84) at different periods in ontogeny. As a gene or set of genes are naturally selected over time, so too is the relevance of different aspects of the environment. While genes and environment interact, genes attend to only those aspects of the environment that are developmentally relevant, as determined by adaptations during the EEA. This environmental trigger view, as with sociobiology, is consistent with a *reaction range* of genes (Gottlieb, 2003, p. 339).

A similar debate regarding the primacy of environmental influences on behavior (i.e., learning) versus naturally selected, or "innate," adaptations was a crucial difference between Tinbergen's and Lorenz's views of instinct, leading Tinbergen to reconsider the importance of different experiences during ontogeny.

Behavioral Ecology

Behavioral ecological theory (Laland & Brown, 2002) has its roots in optimal foraging theory in biology (Krebs & Davies, 1997; Stephens & Krebs, 1986) and anthropology (Borgerhoff-Mulder, Richerson, Thornhill, & Volland, 1997; Cronk, 1991; Winterhalder & Smith, 2000). From optimal foraging theory (Stephens & Krebs, 1986), behavioral ecologists assume that individuals' behaviors reflect efforts to maximize their fitness, ultimately (Tinbergen's "functionality"). More proximally, optimality is assessed by documenting the degree to which benefits (i.e., resources, such as food or mates) are maximized in relation to associated costs (e.g., time and caloric expenditure and survivorship). Individuals' strategic choices are influenced by their ecologies (Tinbergen's "proximal causes") and their life histories (Tinbergen's "ontogeny"); thus, individuals choose from a variety of strategies to maximize access to resources while minimizing costs. The choice of specific strategies implemented may vary across the life span. So, rather than seeing strategies as reflecting some ideal, or generalized, environment, such as the "environment of evolutionary adaptedness" (Tooby & Cosmides, 1992), behavioral ecologists stress flexibility in response to varied ecologies, and individuals choosing from a variety of alternative strategies (e.g., Caro & Bateson, 1991) to maximize optimality.

Like their ethological predecessor Tinbergen (1969), behavioral ecologists often use field studies to determine how local ecologies influence behaviors and strategies (proximal forces) during ontogeny in the service of "ultimate function" (Krebs & Davies, 1993). Furthermore, and important from the point of view of developmental psychology, optimal strategies can vary according to one's life history. Life history theory is concerned with balancing the tradeoffs between different strategies for individuals' fecundity, survival, and physical conditioning during different points in ontogeny (Lessells, 1991). For example, Bock's (2005) work illustrates how one measure of cost (time taken away from work) associated with children's facility in an adult, economically productive role, outweighs the benefits of play (becoming more facile in those roles during play) among a pastoral group in Botswana at specific times in development. Playing at a simple activity, such as playfully pounding grain, resulted in girls' optimum cross-over from play to work (pounding grain as part of an adult activity) at a relatively young age. On the other hand, boys' optimum cross-over from playing with bows, arrows, and spears to the more skill-intensive activity of hunting occurred at a relatively late age. The tradeoff between the time spent in play refining hunting skills for boys was outweighed by the benefits associated with direct tutoring in adult hunting skills. As such, the choice of a specific strategy involves tradeoffs between costs and benefits in how individuals' solve fitness-related problems at different periods in development in different ecologies.

Epigenetic Theories of Play

Relatively recently, epigenetic theories have been applied to the study of human development and behavior. Lead by the theoretical and empirical work of the late Gilbert Gottlieb (1976; 1997; 1998; 2003), epigenetic theory specifies the ways genes and environment influence each other across ontogenetic development. Very briefly, as this will be discussed in much greater depth in the chapter on play and behavioral plasticity, during the early stages of the development of the organism through the juvenile period, the interaction between the individual and the environment determines the course of development. For example, the signals sent to a developing fetus that the maternal environment is stressed, as indicated by a lack of nutrients, results in the development of a smaller body size for the mature organism.

As we have seen, most theorists posit that play is observed only in situations that are safe and where the organisms are well fed. Indeed, one of the reasons for play being almost entirely limited to the juvenile period of development is most probably the fact that this period, especially for mammals, is characterized by parental protection and generally adequate provisioning (Burghardt, 2005), though providing contingently responsive stimuli in the environment, after a period of deprivation, may be especially supportive of innovative response (Fagen, 1981) At a more specific level, Gordon Burghardt (1984; 2005) has advanced his Surplus Resource Theory of Play.

Burghardt's Surplus Resource Theory

Surplus Resource Theory (SRT) is an evolutionary developmental model that specifies the resources necessary for play to develop in different species. These conditions include: Parental care and correspondingly long periods of immaturity; and the ability to metabolically thermoregulate and engage in and recover from vigorous activity. SRT should not be confused with the "surplus energy" theory, dating back to the German philosopher and polymath Friedrich Schiller (1795/ 1967). In Schiller's view, play was the result of a "surplus of energy" available after organisms' basic needs are met, a concept adopted in the nineteenth century by the British philosopher Herbert Spencer (1898). While the concept of "surplus energy" no longer is viewed as scientifically valid (e.g., Evans & Pellegrini, 1997; Rubin et al., 1983), the idea that play is supported only after organisms' basic needs are met is still current (Martin & Caro, 1985).

SRT posits that play can be observed only in those orders with surplus resources, and these orders include, not only mammals and birds, but also, and most controversially and originally, reptiles, fish, as well as some invertebrates. The extended juvenile period aspect of SRT, in addition to the safety associated with a protective parent during this period, is crucial to the role of play in developing the complex set of skills necessary for survival and reproduction. This is especially true for animals whose ecology is varied or unstable. From this position, individuals' behaviors are not triggered by an anticipated set of contingencies. Instead, juveniles use the resources afforded them (safety and provisioning) during this "sensitive period" to explore their environment and experiment with a variety of strategies that are effective in that niche. These environmental and behavioral factors, in turn, should affect subsequent gene expression and evolution. Play with juvenile age mates is especially relevant for humans in developing new strategies, because this context enables them to generate responses to novel environments.

By way of illustration, consider two children. Male 1 is a juvenile of around two years of age. This child's ontogenetic history from conception was a normal one, such that he and his mother were adequately nourished and he is securely attached. This "normal environment" prepares this child for being more physically active and competitive than females and after adolescence also being physically larger than females (Alexander, Hoogland, Howard, Noonan, & Sherman, 1979). His peer groups, too, should be sex-segregated so he, like similar boys, can be rough and active with each other and also learn their adult social roles. Girls' groups are more sedentary and nuturing where they learn their adult social roles.

By contrast, consider another two-year-old, Male 2, conceived and born to parents in a more severe ecological niche (where food is relatively scarce), such as the high Arctic. Children, but especially males, born to mothers in this sort of environment tend to be physically smaller, thus attenuating sexual dimorphism in size, as well as physical activity and aggression. Furthermore, the mating patterns in these sorts of ecologies (Alexander et al., 1979) tend to be monogamous rather than polygynous because both parents are needed to provision and protect offspring in such severe environments. Following sexual selection theory, the boys developing in this latter context should be less competitive, active, and aggressive because of lower levels of intra-sexual competition associated with monogamy. Correspondingly, children's peer groups should also be less segregated by sex. The roles they enact in these groups should also reflect the fact that both males and females take part in child-rearing.

Now consider a case where Male 1 at two years of age encounters a novel environment: He is placed in the severe context, similar to that described for Male 2. This scenario enables us to examine the ways that the environment affects genetic expression by demonstrating the degree to which this child uses play to explore different behavioral strategies that are adaptive to this new ecology and thus influence his evolution. Because his peer group will now comprise both males and females, his behaviors will become less competitive and active. In addition, the social roles that he enacts in pretend play will reflect those of the adults in the community and thus would be likely to include both nurturing and competitive roles.

These behaviors will, in turn, affect this child's morphology. Specifically, lower levels of exercise and vigorous behavior affect the immediate and future expression of the muscle and skeletal systems (Pellegrini & Smith, 1998). Additionally, the social roles learned and practiced in play during childhood should have an impact on his investment in his offspring—a phenotype that developed in response to this environment. The result would be an adult male who is more likely to be monogamous than polygynous and likely to investment in his offspring. Both of these behaviors should, in turn, impact his fitness, and consequently evolution.

In short, Burghardt's theory is important to the extent that it specifies the conditions under which play should be observed. Furthermore, with its focus on development, at both the ontogenetic and phylogenetic levels, it demonstrates how play—a quintessentially juvenile behavior—influences development both in ontogeny and in phylogeny.

Patrick Bateson's Theory

Patrick Bateson is a behavioral biologist at Cambridge University who, along with his students, has added considerably to our understanding of the role of early experiences and play, specifically in development (e.g., Bateson, 1964; 1976; Caro, 1989; 1995; Caro & Bateson, 1986; Martin, 1982; Martin & Caro, 1985). Also following the general epigenetic tack that experience and genes are inseparable parts of the same coordinated system, Bateson argues for a renewed stress on the role of ontogenetic development in explaining well-functioning, adaptive adult behavior and cognition. Correspondingly, he has, like his mentor Robert Hinde (1983), stressed the distinctions between concepts such as *instinct* and *innate* and the role of learning and experience in shaping subsequent adaptations.

Consistent with epigenetic theory, Bateson recognizes the role of behavior, especially play behavior, during the juvenile period, in shaping future development. For Bateson, play can be the leading edge of adaptive change, something he labels the "adaptability driver" (Bateson, 2006). Specifically, when organisms are faced with changes in their environment, their changes in these responses can be adaptive if they foster survival and reproduction, or not, if they do not. Responses to environmental change, especially if those changes are radical, require creativity in order to generate an array of responses that may work. Bateson suggest that play is an ideal candidate to be at the vanguard of this change.

The intrinsically motivating and noninstrumental dimensions of play during the juvenile period, for Bateson, are especially important for the creative responses to novel conditions. Recall that in play, individuals take extant behavioral routines and recombine, eliminate, and add elements. That such activity is intrinsically motivating means that the play will be sustained, thus increasing the likelihood of a solution's arising during play. Once a response is generated that solves the problem, it is likely to be used again by the originator and other conspecifics who have observed the effectiveness of the solution. Furthermore, those individuals using the response should enjoy selective advantage over those not using it. Correspondingly, solutions arising through play should be more likely to be selected, compared to other processes such as genetic assimilation and genetic inheritance. In both cases the probability of a complex solution (that is, one with a number of components) is much lower than in play. Novel behaviors in play are, first, responsive to novel conditions (unlike genetic assimilation) and, second, faster than most alternatives.

Bateson, in keeping with his developmental orientation, stresses the fact that natural selection works on all periods of the lifespan, not only on the mature adult. From this position, play can have immediate benefits, during childhood and also possibly deferred benefits at maturity. Clearly, children must survive childhood to reproduce later in development. Thus, the physically vigorous dimensions of rough-and-tumble play may be beneficial to immediate cardiovascular and muscular health. Play may also have benefits deferred until maturity, as in the case of children practicing social roles that they will hold as adults, such as girls playing at grinding corn and boys hunting with bows.

Evolutionary Developmental Psychology

The theories advanced by Gordon Burghardt and Pat Bateson are primarily concerned with the play of nonhuman animals, though they are certainly germane to the human case. Evolutionary developmental psychology, a theoretical orientation formulated primarily by Dave Bjorklund (Bjorklund & Pellegrini, 2000; 2002), is influenced by epigenetic theories, stressing important experiences during ontogenetic development, in human development. Correspondingly, evolutionary developmental psychology also considers humans' phylogenetic history, along with ontogeny, function, and causal dimensions of play behavior in order to fully understand it (Bjorklund & Pellegrini, 2002). There are four specific tenets of evolutionary developmental psychology that will be discussed in this chapter: Gene x environment interactions, individual differences, the role of behavior in ontogeny and evolution, and higher cognitive functions.

The notion of gene x environment interactions is at the heart of epigenetic theory, wherein one's genes and the environment in which they develop and are expressed cannot be separated (Gottlieb, 1998). In recognition of the importance of this interaction, behavior geneticists have also introduced models wherein one's genotype interacts with the environment (e.g., Caspi & Moffitt, 2006). An interesting example of gene x environment interaction was given by Robert Hinde (1983), when he noted the relationship between the mother's height and that of her offspring, arguably a relationship with one of the higher "heritability indices" in the human development literature. With this said, if the mother and her fetus experience a "severe" environment characterized by a shortage of food, then that relationship is substantially attenuated (Bateson & Martin, 1999), as discussed above in the example of the child conceived and reared in the high Arctic.

This example also points to the importance of ontogeny. Individuals experiencing a severe environment as fetuses are more likely to exhibit compromised morphological growth later in life. The importance of ontogeny is further recognized in evolutionary developmental psychology by stressing the effect of behavior during ontogeny as possibly affecting the course of evolution. Similar to Pat Bateson's notion of play acting as an "adaptability driver," outlined above, evolutionary developmental psychology recognizes the ways in which play can be at the vanguard of evolutionary change. As I will argue below, play during the juvenile period may enjoy especially important status in this regard as it affords opportunities to generate creative responses to perturbations in the environment. If these responses are adaptive, they should be imitated by other members of society and then selected.

Related to this general idea that play relates to behavioral flexibility, evolutionary developmental psychology posits that there should be individual differences, and correspondingly these difference should be realized in a variety of alternative responses to the environment (Belsky, Steinberg, & Draper, 1991; Caro & Bateson, 1986). Specifically, individuals' responses to their environment are not viewed as preprogrammed. Instead, the strategies used are in a close relation with their environment. Bateson and Martin (1999) use a jukebox metaphor to describe this process: the organism's behavioral developmental is chosen in response to the environment. Belsky (Belsky et al., 1991) and colleagues' hypothesized variation in alternative mating strategies in response to different environmental conditions is an example: in conditions of deprivation a strategy of frequent mating with minimal investment in offspring is pursued. By contrast, in abundant conditions a strategy of allowing more time between births and greater investment in each offspring is observed.

The next, and final, dimension of the theory concerns the role of higher cognitive processes in human development. In evolutionary developmental psychology, as in evolutionary biology, the "strategies" organisms enlist to solve problems are implicit- Organisms are not explicitly aware of their choices. As applied to the human condition, evolutionary psychologists suggest, these strategies are the remnants of our human history, used to solved problems in the Environment of Evolutionary Adaptedness (EEA). While evolutionary developmental psychology acknowledges the role of these implicit strategies, such as the use of specific signals to mark the playful tenor of an interaction, it is also concerned with higher cognitive functions that probably originated in social interaction between conspecifics (Hare, Brown, Williamson, & Tomasello, 2002; Humphrey, 1976; Jolly, 1966). In this model, consideration of social cognitive processes such as theory of mind and social pretend play are especially relevant. Specifically, and as will be discussed in the chapter on pretend play, when children engage in pretend play with peers, they gradually realize that they and their peers have different beliefs and desires.

In short, evolutionary developmental psychology is theory guided by the epigenetic view of development with its stress on the role of environmentally sensitive strategies during ontogeny to guide subsequent development and evolution. Play is an especially important behavioral strategy in this theory, as will be discussed in more detail in the next chapter.

CONCLUSION

To conclude this chapter, I have reviewed both traditional developmental psychological and evolutionary biological theories of play. The common ground between some of these theories was the stress placed on ontogenetic experiences in shaping development and possibly evolution.

4

Play and Behavioral Plasticity

As we have discussed in the preceding chapters, play is an interesting construct for a number of reasons, not the least of which is the fact that it is observed in most mammals and avian species (Fagen, 1981) and, possibly, even among some amphibians and reptiles (Burghardt, 2005). This has led many to consider the study of play an excellent context in which to make phylogenetic comparisons and, more generally, to study the role of play in evolution by natural selection.

Studying play within an evolutionary framework provides an opportunity to examine individual plasticity. As I will argue in this chapter, play during the juvenile period can be instrumental to behavioral and cognitive adaptations to novel environments. These changes, in turn, may also impact more distal evolutionary processes.

More generally, evolutionary theories used to explain the human condition have a long history in developmental psychology. Darwin himself (1871, 1877) applied his theory of evolution by natural selection to humans. Evolutionary theories were also taken up by others; for example by Spencer (1878, 1898), in his book *The Principles of Psychology*; additionally, in the early twentieth century by G. Stanley Hall. Hall (1904, 1916), the first president of the American Psychological Association, applied variants of this theory to humans' ontogenetic and phylogenetic development.

The years from the 1920s to the 1970s saw a largely dormant period in applications of evolutionary theory to human behavior, certainly in psychology and neighboring disciplines. This state of affairs has been ascribed to the reaction against an over-enthusiastic social Darwinism and to the influence of behaviorism on psychology (Plotkin, 2004). Yet evolutionary theory formed a paradigmatic bedrock for the sciences of botany and zoology, combining with genetics in the "modern synthesis," or neodarwinism (Huxley, 1942). Mostly relevant to psychology, it directly informed the study of animal behavior, within zoology. Ethologists such as Lorenz (1969, 1981) and Tinbergen (1951, 1969) continued a fruitful exploitation of evolutionary ideas in relation to animal behavior in natural habitats.

Lorenz (1966), in his controversial and popular book *On Aggression,* and Tinbergen (1969), in his Nobel Prize lecture, each specifically addressed the application of ethological ideas to human behavior. Soon after this, in the early 1970s, a group of ethologists with an interest in human development emerged, primarily in Germany and the United Kingdom. This group, which also included psychologists, used ethological theory and methods to examine human behavior and development, with much of the work being done with children (Blurton Jones, 1972a; Eibl-Eibeseldt, 1989; McGrew, 1972; Smith, 1974; Smith & Connolly, 1972). This body of work was never really mainstream in North American developmental psychology, perhaps because of its inductive orientation (Barlow, 1989), in contrast to the more deductive and experimental orientation of American psychology (Burghardt, 2005). Furthermore, much of the early human or child ethology work was rather atheoretical: evolutionary theory provided a backdrop to justify observations of humans (or children) in their natural habitat, but was only used scantily to make predictions regarding behavioral patterns or sequences of development.

This changed over the next decades with the advent of sociobiology. A landmark was the publication of Wilson's (1975) *Sociobiology* (which included a final chapter on the human species), detailing the application of theoretical perspectives from Hamilton (1964) and Trivers (1971; 1972). Since that time, we have witnessed a renaissance of evolutionary approaches to the study of human behavior, whether sociobiology (e.g., Dawkins, 1976; 1982), behavioral ecology (e.g., Krebs & Davies, 1993), or evolutionary psychology (e.g., Buss, 1989; Cosmides & Tooby, 1987; Daly & Wilson, 1983).

These primarily gene-centered views of behavior and evolution, epitomized in the "selfish" gene idea (Dawkins, 1976), especially as applied to humans, have resulted in sociobiology's being characterized by some as reductionistic and biological determinism (Laland & Brown, 2002). Relatedly, these approaches have paid little attention to the importance of development *per se,* as pointed out by recent exponents of evolutionary developmental psychology (Bjorklund & Pellegrini, 2000; 2002; Pellegrini, Dupuis, & Smith, 2007; Pellegrini & Smith, 1998), and by theorists emphasizing the importance of ontogenetic development in the evolutionary process via organic selection, epigenesis, or variants of these processes (Bateson & Martin, 1999; Gottlieb, 2003; Harper, 2005).

The relatively recent explosion of interest in the applications of evolutionary theory to human behavior has often resulted in a blurring of the assumptions and hypotheses associated with different models (see Burghardt, 2005; Heyes, 2003; Laland & Brown, 2002; Stamps, 2003). Correspondingly, there has been some tendency to label any theory of human behavior with an evolutionary orientation as "evolutionary psychology." This is problematic in that different theories take different stances, often rather subtle, on important issues relevant to evolution, such as the interrelated roles of the environment and ontogenetic development. Discussion of these issues is important not only theoretically but also for addressing the common misunderstanding, still often held in psychology, that invoking evolutionary theory smacks of biological determinism.

The importance of considering these specific issues was apparent in two recent personal experiences. In one case, I was reviewing a paper for an edited book written by a very well established and careful scholar. Yet, in reading the introduction to his chapter, the label "evolutionary psychology" was applied very loosely to virtually all theory that invoked propositions derived from Darwin's theory of evolution by natural selection. In the second case, I was at a symposium where Pat Bateson and the late Gilbert Gottlieb each made compelling arguments for an epigenetic view of development. They presented a long list of evidence from the history of evolutionary biology (dating from the nineteenth century) of ways that behavior affected evolution, rather than vice versa. In discussion, both suggested that dichotomies and misperceptions of biological determinism continued in psychology and that developmental psychologists have simply not read the different views of development in their journals.

In this chapter I hope I will remediate this problem. I will first remind readers of the principles of ethology and its concern with ontogeny, as voiced by Tinbergen (1951; 1969). I expand Tinbergen's concern with ontogeny by highlighting ideas advanced concerning epigenetic models of development (Gottlieb, 1998; 2003; Harper, 2005; Stamps, 2003) and organic selection (Bateson, 1988; 2003). This orientation also illustrates ways that environment and behavior interact with, and may subsequently shape, genotype.

Ethology and Tinbergen's Four Whys

Tinbergen and Lorenz were the founding fathers of ethology. *Ethology* is defined as the naturalistic study of behavior from an evolutionary perspective (Burghardt, 1973; 2005; Laland & Brown, 2002). Indeed, for this, they along with von Frisch (who studied bee behavior), shared a Nobel Prize for Physiology or Medicine in 1973. In a key statement of the principles of ethology, Tinbergen (1969) formulated four major issues (alternatively referred to as "four aims" or "four questions") in studying behavior: 1) proximal causes, 2) ontogenetic development, 3) adaptive value or function, and 4) phylogenetic history. This position clearly puts individual development (and indeed species development) on a par with studies of current mechanisms and adaptive function.

In traditional ethology, the first of Tinbergen's four whys was prominent, especially as applied to the study of instinct. Both Tinbergen and Lorenz studied instinctive behavior, or behavior reflecting a species' phylogenetic history rather than individual experience or reinforcement schedule (Burghardt, 1973). Instinct, in this early form, was considered to be "innate," and quite distinct from what was learned (Hinde, 1983; Laland & Brown, 2002). While it was thought that instinctive behaviors were triggered by environmental stimuli and that learning might affect the range of environmental triggers, the "instinctive responses" themselves were not considered to be affected. Lorenz's notion of *filial imprinting* is representative of this position: An organism is presented with a stimulus during a "critical period" in development, and the instinctual behavior is activated, although the stimulus features were largely acquired.

Tinbergen and Lorenz, however, came to have diverging positions on the constructs of learning and instinct. Tinbergen (1969) disagreed with the idea that the study of instinct should exclude factors external to the organism. Specifically, Tinbergen stressed the role of various forms of proximal antecedents to behavior, during ontogeny, in the study of behavior. Through the study of ontogenetic development, he argued, the relationship between an organism's phylogenetic history and its current behavioral repertoire could be properly understood. But the working out of such a program required further advances in evolutionary theory and our understanding of genetic processes. As will be discussed below, epigenetic theory (Gottlieb, 1998; Harper, 2005; Stamps, 2003) provided this impetus.

Consideration of the phylogenetic history of a behavior is also central to understanding that behavior, according to Tinbergen (1969). Indeed, it is common practice among both psychologists (Hall, 1904; 1916; Piaget, 1976) and evolutionary biologists (Bateson, 2005; Bekoff & Byers, 1981; Burghardt, 2005) to examine the extent to which specific behaviors, such as play, may have resulted from similar selection pressures, and to compare the development, function, and causes of these behaviors across different species.

G. Stanley Hall (1904; 1916), called by many (e.g., Cairns, 1983) "the father of child and developmental psychology" in the United States, was fond of comparing human behaviors to other species. Indeed, Hall used Darwin's theory of evolution by natural selection to formulate a theory of human development. Hall is remembered for his stress upon the stage-like progression of human development. For Hall, humans' ontogenetic stages were thought to be reenactments of their phylogenetic history. In this vein Hall is also remembered for the phrase "ontogeny recapitulates phylogeny," meaning that development within a species repeats the evolutionary history of the species. For example, the stages of child development were said to repeat the history of *Homo sapiens*. Some of Hall's famous examples include the following: Boys' tree climbing is a recapitulation of our primate past. Similarly, boys' play fighting (then it took the form of "cowboys and Indians") was a reenactment of our hunter-gatherer past.

Of course the accuracy of the notion that ontogeny repeats phylogeny is questionable. Specifically, and without going into detail right now (the role of play in evolution will be discussed later in this chapter), it is more likely that ontogenetic development influences phylogeny, as Hinde (1983) and Bateson (2005) suggest, rather than vice versa. The course of individual development, for example the age at which sexual maturity is attained, is affected by environmental factors (e.g., Ellis & Garber, 2000) and also influences the development of the species.

While psychologists and behavioral biologists continue to make cross-species comparisons, they have become more principled in their choices of species for comparison (Pellegrini & Smith, 2005). At one, and perhaps the least satisfactory, level we can choose species, *ad hoc*, as a basis for comparison: for example, comparing human behavior in one case with that of birds and in other cases with monkeys, and in yet other cases with that of apes. Such comparisons may, and correctly I think, raise the specter that we are merely constructing "Just so" stories. By contrast, comparing humans with the great apes is more satisfactory: the chimpanzees (*Pan troglodytes* and *Pan schweinfurthii*), bonobos (*Pan paniscus*), gorillas (*Gorilla gorilla*), and orangutans (*Pongo pygmaeus*) (Pellegrini & Smith, 2005). Though there are cases of convergent evolution where comparisons between very different species are warranted, such as humans and domestic dogs (Hare & Tomasello, 2005), chimpanzees and bonobos are often the best choice, given that they are our closest phylogenetic relatives (Wrangham, Chapman, Clark-Arcadi, & Isabirye-Basuta, 1996) as indicated by similarities in DNA evidence, and they have dispersal patterns similar to humans' (with males staying in a group and females often transferring to another group). For these reasons, they have been posited as especially informative comparator species (McGrew, 1981; Pellegrini & Smith, 2005; deWaal & Lanting, 1997).

Similarities between chimps and humans in terms of female dispersal, male residency, and polygyny are especially important when one examines social and locomotor play. For example, when males, not females, stay in the natal groups (females migrate), their social behavior is more gregarious, and their social groups become organized hierarchically, in terms of dominance. As a result, females and males segregate into same-sex groups to learn associated sex-specific roles. Specifically, the social skills learned in segregated groups should be related to males' and females' adult roles. This appears to be the case in chimpanzees; for example, males learn dominance and predation roles, such as patrolling (Mitani, Merriweather, & Zhang, 2000), and females learn to handle infants (Pusey, 1990). The case of male chimpanzees segregating is especially robust. The complexity of the skills associated with adult life may necessitate extended practice, and social play has been proffered as a context in which these skills have evolved (Alexander, 1989; Wrangham, 1999).

The juvenile and adolescent periods provide the social context to learn and practice adult roles. For males, skills related to dominance, such as detecting weaknesses in opponents and coordinating skilled movements, may need extensive practice, perhaps through play with peers, given the variety and complexity of skills to be learned (Alexander, 1989). That dominance skills are especially important to males' functioning (Wrangham, 1999) points to the development of these activities' taking place in a social context. Indeed, human cross-cultural studies show that male juveniles are socialized into more competitive and aggressive roles, especially in polygynous societies where roles are not stratified (Low, 1989; 2000). In female groups, too, roles are learned and practiced, and physically aggressive males are avoided. Females interact with other females in dyads and in these smaller groups use safer, indirect aggression to form these alliances and coalitions with other females (Campbell, 2002).

Meanwhile, a key methodological tool of the ethologists had more immediate application. Ethologists are naturalists, interested in organisms' behaviors in their natural context (Lorenz, 1981; Hinde, 1983). As a first-order exercise, ethologists typically construct "ethograms," or behavioral inventories of a species across the life span. Such observations should be made in the species' natural habitat, as this would be the context in which the behaviors evolved and in which their adaptive significance could be examined. Ethologists were not averse to subsequent experiments (with famous examples in Tinbergen, 1951), but observations in natural surroundings formed a bedrock for the meaningfulness of later, controlled study. This inductive approach in ethology was stressed by Lorenz and Tinbergen in direct contrast with the ethos in experimental and comparative psychology of the time of observing a few aspects of behavior in what was viewed by ethologists as rather impoverished experimental settings (Hinde, 1980).

It was this aspect of naturalistic observation that came to the fore in application of ethology to child development in the 1970s. Much of the work detailed in *Ethological Studies of Child Behavior* (Blurton Jones, ed., 1972) provides ethograms of children's behavior in various settings or situations. For example, Blurton Jones (1972b) described how *open-mouthed smile* (or *laugh*), *run, jump, open beat* (or *"soft hit"*) and *wrestle*, often co-occurred in a pattern he called *rough-and-tumble play* (as in Harlow's similar description in rhesus monkeys). Subsequent research has confirmed the coherence of the rough-and-tumble play pattern, as well as its relationship to affiliation, pro-social behavior, and (in adolescence) dominance and aggression (Pellegrini, 2006; Pellegrini & Smith, 1998). The rough-and-tumble pattern is different from actual aggressive behavior in all the ways Tinbergen described (causation, ontogeny, function, and species evolution). But this work was salutary for developmental psychologists who had often confused or confounded these two behavior patterns (Smith, 1974; Pellegrini, 2003).

Despite such valuable contributions, ethology remained at a largely descriptive level. Although some experimental work was carried out in this tradition (e.g., Pellegrini, Huberty, & Horvat, 1998; Smith & Connolly, 1980), significant theoretical inputs from evolutionary thinking were not readily available, and what there was was not widely used. This changed with the advent of sociobiology and evolutionary psychology, which were reviewed in the preceding chapter in this volume. In what follows I advance a more transactional view of the relationship between biology and the environment.

NOT A "MAIN EFFECT" VIEW OF EVOLUTIONARY HISTORY ON HUMAN BEHAVIOR: A TRANSACTIONAL VIEW OF THE ROLE OF PLAY IN HUMAN DEVELOPMENT

While I propose that evolutionary history has an impact on human development, I must further clarify the moderating role of context. This discussion is especially important given recent misunderstandings (e.g., Lickliter & Honeycutt, 2003) of some epigenetic theories, such as evolutionary developmental psychology (Bjorklund & Pellegrini, 2002). I stress that I do not take a deterministic view of phylogenetic history and genes on human behavior, or what John Archer (Archer & Lloyd, 2002) calls a "main effect model," even if continuity across common ancestry is found in dimensions of social behavior and organization (Bjorklund & Pellegrini, 2002; Pellegrini et al., 2007). This orientation leads to the position that genes, environments, and behavior dynamically influence each other (Bateson & Martin, 1999; Bjorklund & Pellegrini, 2002; Gottlieb, 1998; Pellegrini et al., 2007; Stamps, 2003).

By way of analogy, this orientation is akin to adding another, more distal, level to Bronfenbrenner's model of human development (1979; Bronfenbrenner & Ceci, 1994). For example, although Bronfenbrenner has a layer for SES, this does not translate into a main effect for SES. Instead, SES is influenced by and influences adjacent layers of context. This dynamic relationship is illustrated in work on "resilient" children (Masten & Coatsworth, 1998). Aspects of children's temperament and family moderate the effects of deleterious environments associated with low SES. By including an evolutionary layer, we are assuming that evolution by natural selection (rather than other explanations) influences, at a distal level, our current status as humans. This status is, however, dynamic and interacts with more proximal aspects of children's lives.

Specifically, the environment in which an individual develops, starting with conception, influences the ways that evolutionary history is expressed. Following Bateson and Martin's (1999) jukebox metaphor, individuals have a genetic endowment that can be realized through a wide variety of options: the specific developmental pathway taken by an individual is influenced by the perinatal environment (i.e., from conception through infancy) of the developing organism. Thus, many developmental pathways are possible, but which one is selected is determined by the transaction between the environment and the developing organism (Archer, 1992; Caro & Bateson, 1986).

A relevant aspect of the environment is nutrition as it affects sexual dimorphism in size, which, in turn, affects physically vigorous behavior, sex segregation, and play behavior. Specifically, the nutritional history of human mothers impacts the physical size of the offspring, and especially that of males (Bateson & Martin, 1999). Males' larger size, relative to females' (i.e., sexual dimorphism), may be one of the factors responsible for sex differences in social play, where males engage in R&T more than females (Pellegrini, 2004; 2006). These differences in size bias children to interact in sexually segregated peer groups where socialization practices further shape behavior (Pellegrini, Long, et al., 2007).

Consistent with this view, the availability of resources affects human mating systems and sexual dimorphism. The interactive nature of this system is illustrated by the fact that height is highly heritable, yet this relation is influenced by the fetus' perinatal environment; pregnant mothers experiencing nutritional stress will have relatively smaller offspring; this is especially the case for male offspring (Bateson & Martin, 1999).

Alexander, Hoogland, Howard, Noonan, and Sherman (1979) used the Human Relations Area File to examine ecologically abundant and stressed societies. They also partitioned human societies into ecologically imposed monogamy (e.g., Lapps of Norway, Cooper and Labrador Eskimos), polygynous (e.g., Bedouin Arabs and Khmer), and culturally monogamous (most Western societies). They found that the ecologically imposed monogamous groups lived in less abundant ecologies and were significantly less dimorphic than the other two, but there were no differences between the polygynous and culturally imposed monogamy groups. They argued that in ecologically imposed monogamous cultures, efforts of both parents are needed to protect and provision offspring. From this view, sexual dimorphism results from the confluence of ecological conditions and mating systems. Dimorphism is, in turn, hypothesized to be an antecedent condition for different energetic demands of males and females as well as an antecedent to both sex segregation and sex differences in play (Pellegrini, 2004).

Differences in body size are antecedents to differences in physical activity and associated with competitiveness, aggressiveness, and play such that males and females view themselves differently very early in development and then segregate (see Pellegrini, in press, for a fuller discussion). Later, these differences are translated into different social roles and differences in R&T and agonistic behaviors associated with different energetic demands. In short, the developmental option taken is related to the environment in which the individual develops. Given the vastly different environments into which individuals with the same genetic history are born, a single "genetic program" would not be equally effective across these different niches. This model is displayed in Figures 4.1 and 4.2 where abundant and thrifty ecologies, respectively, are modeled.

The Role of Ontogenetic Development and Play

Although evolutionary psychology stressed a consideration of psychological mechanisms, and thus focuses on the first as well as the third of Tinbergen's four whys, it typically does not focus on the second—ontogeny. This orientation has been brought into focus by recent critiques of the simple gene–environment interaction view found in both sociobiology and evolutionary psychology, and in

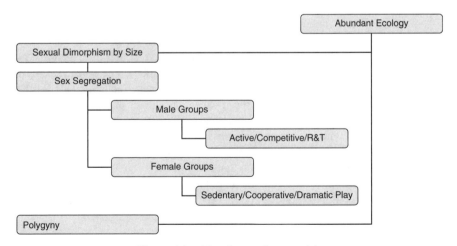

Figure 4.1   Abundant ecology models

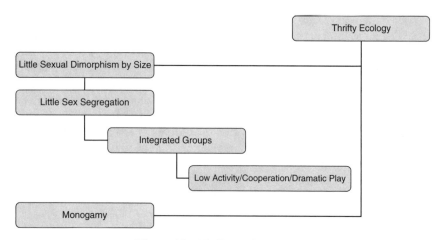

Figure 4.2   Thrifty ecology models

behavior genetics. Much of the argument centers on the limitations of the *range of reaction* view.

The reaction range is a high and low limit of responses to a "usual" environment and is set by the genotype, suggesting that behavioral responses at different times in ontogeny were naturally selected to be activated by a variety of environmental stimuli. So, given a variety of environments, but similar genotypes, the reaction range view would predict similar phenotypes. While genes and the environment do interact, the effects are linear.

By contrast, the *norm of reaction* view does not specify behaviors, or phenotypes more generally, given specific environments. Indeed, the developmental trajectories of individuals with the same genotype are not predictable. There is a true, non-additive, interaction between genotype and phenotype, so that the relative phenotypic position of different genotypes may vary substantially and nonlinearly, in different environments.

If gene x environment interactions are nonlinear, for which there are many examples (Gottlieb, 2003; Stamps, 2003), then by what ontogenetic process does this come about? The prime candidate explanation here is that of epigenesis, as argued, for example, by Stamps (2003) and Harper (2005). The epigenetic view points out that genes do not link directly to behavior; genes actually code for the production of proteins, initially in the micro-environment of the fertilized egg. There are many steps between genetic activity and behavior (see Gottlieb, 2003). Thus there is a complex system with possibilities of short-term and long-term feedback loops between phenotypic behavior and development in the next generations. It follows from this position that individuals' behaviors actively contribute, not only to their own development, but to subsequent evolution in a number of different ways (Bateson, 1998; 2003; 2005; Stamps, 2003; Waddington, 1959).

In short, the notion of the environment as a "trigger" in sociobiology and evolutionary psychology differs from epigenetic models of development, where the relationship between genes and environment is expressed in a norm of reaction, rather than a range of reaction (Gottlieb, 2003). Even though some evolutionary psychologists accept that individuals and their environments co-evolve (e.g., Cosmides & Tooby, 1987), my view is that this does not allow for behaviors to actually shape evolutionary processes, through such processes as epigenetic inheritance (Harper, 2005; Stamps, 2003) and organic selection (Bateson, 2005). The view presented below follows that developed by a group of ethologists (Bateson, 2003; 2005; Stamps, 2003) and psychologists (Burghardt, 2005; Gottlieb, 2003; Harper, 2005), and suggests that behavior and genes influence each other transactionally.

Transactions Between Genes and Environment

There is little dispute amongst those who accept evolutionary theory that the genotype influences the phenotype (including behavior), and that the details of this influence are affected by the environment—That genes and environment interact. But what about the influence of the environment and behavior on the evolutionary process *per se*?

Generally, evolutionary change is related to changes in gene frequencies in a species population; that is, to genetic evolution. But cumulative changes in behavior can also occur via cultural evolution, very obviously in humans (Boyd & Richerson, 1985; Tomasello, 1999; Tomasello & Call, 1997). While cultural evolution via social learning is rare in nonhuman species (Stamps, 2003), it can be viewed as just one mechanism for extra-genetic inheritance – passing on characteristics from one generation to the next without a change in gene frequencies.

The epigenetic view is that experiences during specific periods in development, such as sensitive periods, are used to gather information in the extant environment so as to forecast which behaviors will be adaptive to that environment. This then influences the development of offspring. The influence is not through the genotype, but at other points in the complex chain between genetic activity and phenotypic expression. For example, it might be via the nature of the egg cell provided by the mother, which will be the major part of the immediate environment for the new offspring. Essentially, epigenesis acts via changes in gene regulation, rather than changes in genes. Phenomena such as X chromosome inactivation, and genetic imprinting, are examples of this (Harper, 2005).

The main evidence for epigenetic processes comes from adaptations that may be adaptive over several generations, but may need to be reversed at some future point. A classic example is the effect of nutritional stress on the developing fetus (Harper, 2005; Susser & Stein, 1994; Tanner, 1970). Nutritional stress experienced by a developing fetus results in a "thrifty phenotype" (Alexander, Hoogland, Noonan, & Sherman, 1979; Bateson & Marin, 1999); e.g., a smaller body and less sexual dimorphism by size, and lower levels of physical activity.

Do such changes affect the genotype? While the genotypes of individuals are not changed via epigenesis, those of future generations might be changed if natural selection continues to favor the altered phenotypes. Harper sums up the intermediate position of epigenetic inheritance very neatly: "epigenetic inheritance, might be seen as something like an intermediate step between individual ontogeny and speciation in that it involves a (potentially) reversible, intergenerational transfer of an experience-dependent modification of the phenotype resulting from alterations in gene regulation" (Harper, 2005, p. 347).

In the longer term, there are processes that allow environmentally acquired behaviors to influence the genotype, without invoking discredited Lamarckian ideas. These ideas, or what has been broadly called organic selection, date back at least to Lloyd Morgan (1896) and Baldwin (1896). The basic idea is that in response to an environmental challenge, an organism may develop an adaptive response. But individuals with different genotypes may acquire or learn this new behavioral response with varying ease or efficiency. Although in each generation the new response is socially learnt, or at least environmentally acquired, nevertheless over a number of generations natural selection will favor those genotypes that more readily acquire this new behavior. Thus, genetic change will occur.

One version of this was described by Waddington (1957) as genetic assimilation. Waddington's experiments were with fruit flies, and involved developmental modifications to adult flies as a result of early stressors (such as heat shock), and subsequent artificial selection; but more naturalistic examples of this effect are available (see Bjorklund & Pellegrini, 2002). At least in Waddington's prototypic experiments, genetic assimilation involved delayed phenotypic response and rapid genetic change. Organic selection as described by Bateson (2005), however, is seen as distinct from genetic assimilation. It involves rapid, concurrent phenotypic change in response to a stressor and delayed genetic change via the occurrence of mutations. Mutational change can allow an adaptive, acquired characteristic to be expressed more easily. In either case, however, characteristics that are inherited extra-genetically (including social learning and epigenetic inheritance) may in the long term bring about genotypic change.

THE ROLE OF PLAY IN DEVELOPMENTAL ADAPTATION AND EVOLUTIONARY CHANGE

Play during the juvenile period is especially important in the processes of ontogenetic and phylogenetic development because in play, generally, new strategies and behaviors can be developed with minimal costs, and these strategies, in turn, can influence evolutionary processes (Bateson, 2005; Burghardt, 2005; Špinka, Newbury, & Bekoff, 2001). I suggest that play influences these processes by supporting the development of new strategies in novel environments during the juvenile period.

Play is an excellent choice to study this process because it is a paradigm of the application of evolutionary theory to the study of human development as it has been studied by ethologists (e.g., Burghardt, 2005; Caro, 1995), sociobiologists (e.g., Fagen, 1981, Wilson, 1975), and evolutionary psychologists (e.g., Symons, 1974). Indeed, E. O. Wilson (1975) suggested that play was one of the most important areas for sociobiological study. Play, of course, has also been studied extensively by developmental psychologists (e.g., Fein, 1981; Pellegrini, Dupuis,

& Smith, 2007; Pellegrini & Smith, 1998; Piaget, 1962; Rubin et al., 1983; Smith, 1982; Sutton-Smith, 1966; 1966).

As noted in the chapter defining play, across the varied disciplines there is general agreement on one of the defining attributes of play (Burghardt, 2005; Špinka et al., 2001) as being a seemingly "non-serious" variant of functional behavior. Playful behaviors resemble serious behaviors, but participants are typically more concerned with the behaviors themselves (i.e., "means") rather than the function (i.e., "ends") of the behavior. As a result, playful behaviors are also often more exaggerated than their functional counterparts, and the components of functional behavioral routines are often rearranged and abbreviated in play. For example, playfighting, though it resembles serious fighting in some ways, is just that—playful, not serious, and participants generally do not aim to hurt each other: There are hits, but they are exaggerated and soft, not hard, and participants typically reciprocate roles, alternating between the play aggressor and the play victim (Pellegrini & Smith, 1998). It follows then that play, relative to non-play, behaviors stress means over ends, as well as self-selection and intrinsic motivation, and variable behaviors.

Importantly, and as discussed in the definitional chapter, play occurs in safe and familiar environments during the extended and protected juvenile period and in the presence of adequate resources (Burghardt, 2005). Play also follows exploration of that environment. Exploration precedes play both ontogenetically—infants spend more time exploring than playing, and when they are toddlers their play increases (Belsky & Best, 1981)—and microgenetically (Hutt, 1966)—infants, toddlers, and children explore unfamiliar objects or environments before they play with them. Take, for example, a child entering a preschool classroom for the very first time. In the initial weeks of the experience, the child is apprehensive and spends time (often cautiously) exploring the physical and social environment of the school—exhibiting passive onlooker behavior (McGrew, 1972; Pellegrini & Goldsmith, 2003). Exploration is used to determine if the environment is dangerous, and if it is, how to avoid it (Špinka et al., 2001). Once it is determined that the environment is safe, then play occurs (McGrew, 1972; Pellegrini & Goldsmith, 2003).

When faced with a relatively novel, but safe, environment, play affords opportunity for behavioral and cognitive innovation and subsequent practice of newly developed behaviors and strategies (Bateson, 2005; Bruner, 1972; Špinka et al., 2001; Stamps, 1995; Sutton-Smith, 1966). For example, when horses are observed in novel, but safe, environments they exhibit locomotive play, possibly to learn and practice new behaviors appropriate for such an environment (Stamps, 1995). Play can also be induced in many animals by simply changing the environment. Many laboratory animals become playful when new bedding is introduced to their space, and pet owners may have observed how playful their dogs are with the appearance of new snowfall (Špinka et al., 2001). Less anecdotal, experimental evidence with mice suggests that locomotor motor play results in improved learning and plasticity, seemingly due to the increased synaptic plasticity and neurotransmission in mice engaging in play-like voluntary exercise, relative to controls (van Praag, Shubert, Zhao, & Gage, 2005).

The role of play in the development of innovation has been recently formalized by Špinka and colleagues (2001) in their "training for the unexpected hypothesis." They posit how locomotor and social play helps individual prepare for unexpected and novel environmental and social circumstances. The gist of the hypothesis is that, in the safe context of play, individuals appear to place themselves in unconventional and often disorienting positions. These novel behavioral situations afford an opportunity for them to experiment with a variety of routines in relatively safe circumstances and generate novel, and possibly adaptive, responses. With practice in play, individuals become facile at enlisting these processes and thus they become more accessible in times of need, such as during an emergency.

In a related vein, Povinelli and Cant (1995) provide an interesting example of the role of an uncertain environment in the evolution of behavioral flexibility. They compared the degree of behavioral flexibility in long-tailed macaques (*Macaca fascicilaris*) and orangutans (*Pongo pygmaeus*). Their hypothesis was that behavioral flexibility (i.e., having a variety of non-stereotyped locomotor behaviors in their repertoires) was a result of encountering uncertain environments in which to move (in these cases, arboreal clambering). Orangutans are physically larger than macaques, thus the niche of the orangutans is relatively unpredictable. For example, an animal the size of an orangutan (~ 40 kilograms) clambering from tree to tree will encounter tree limbs and vines that are relatively unpredictable because they bend extremely or could break. In order to move in these areas successfully, orangutans had to develop a very flexible behavioral repertoire to adjust to their unpredictable environment. Macaques, by contrast, are much smaller (~ 5.5 kilograms) and their locomotor repertoire through a similar environment is more predictable. Their weight does not perturb their travel as it does with the orangutan; consequently, their behavioral repertoire is much more stereotyped than that of the larger orangutan.

I now turn to an example of the role of play in affecting evolutionary processes. The nonhuman primate literature has long recognized the role of play in developing both normative behavior (Lewis, 2005) and psychopathology (Suomi, 1991; 2005; Suomi & Harlow, 1972). The experimental evidence from Suomi's laboratory is especially suggestive, which indicates that there are heritable individual differences in reactivity and aggression that are not optimal in terms of fitness and subsequent natural selection of those traits. Specifically, highly aggressive and highly reactive individuals are at a disadvantage compared to low aggressive and low reactive individuals, in competing for mates, reproducing, and protecting and provisioning offspring (Suomi, 1991; 2005).

Phenotypes associated with these genotypes can be changed by social rehabilitation regimens (i.e., younger conspecifics or nurturant adults) during the juvenile period. A hallmark of these social rehabilitation regimens is social play, first between juveniles and mothers, and then between juvenile peers (Suomi, 1991; 2005; Suomi & Harlow, 1972). For example, highly reactive monkeys (based on similar pedigrees) cross-fostered by a nurturant female are more playful, cooperative, and socially competent than are peer-reared monkeys. In playful bouts with adults and peers, juveniles learn appropriate social behaviors to function in their peer groups and to eventually mate. These behaviors are used to establish close relationships with both adults and peers during a juvenile's sensitive period of becoming socially competent. Additionally, these initial close relationships, such as an attachment relationship between the highly reactive monkey and a surrogate mother, enable the juveniles to establish close relationships with different adults in new social groupings, not unlike findings in the human attachment literature (Sroufe, Egelund, & Carlson, 1999). For example, in new social groups rehabilitated monkeys established relationships with nurturant foster grandparents who not only protected the reactive monkeys but also conferred their dominance status on the juveniles as well. The rehabilitated monkeys retained this dominance status, even when the older individuals left the group.

The behaviors of reactive individuals (whose reactivity was line-bred) can be changed during the juvenile period if they are reared by a nurturant mother. Following the notion of competitive exclusion (Bateson, 2005), these competent behaviors will be learned during this sensitive period, rather than less competent behaviors, such as stereotypic behaviors and social withdrawal, if the individuals are kept in a stable social environment, as was documented by Suomi and Harlow (1972).

In terms of moving from this behavioral level to the level of genes and behavior affecting evolutionary processes, recall that organic selection posits that organisms capable of change in their own lifetimes when exposed to environmental change, as was the case of a highly reactive individual being rear by a nurturant foster mother in a novel social environment, may pass this change on to their offspring by extra-genetic means. The social behaviors they learn in this relationship are generalized to other social groupings, even when that adult is no longer present. Indeed their dominance status is closely associated with the dominance of nurturant adults with whom they have a relationship. It is this elevated dominance status that should translate into the rehabilitated monkeys' mating with females with different genotypes. That is, dominant males, relative to subordinate males, are more likely to access females with "good genes," as evidenced by specific positive female morphological features, such as symmetry and physical attractiveness (Thornhill & Gangstead, 1993). Attractive females, in turn, choose to mate with dominant males (Pellegrini & Long, 2003; 2007). This sort of mating should result in selection's favoring the genes associated with social competence over high reactivity.

In summary, my position suggests play is an important mechanism in organic selection. While scholars from psychology (e.g., Bruner, 1972; Sutton-Smith, 1966; 1997), biology (e.g., Bateson, 1988; 2005; Bekoff, 1995), and philosophy (Carruthers, 2002) have posited links between play and creative responses to the environment for at least 40 years, I specify how play enables juveniles impact their own developmental trajectory as well as evolutionary processes. Play enables them to sample their environments and develop behavioral responses in a relatively low-cost fashion. In terms of impacting evolution, play behaviors and subsequent accommodations to behavioral routines and strategies represent a low-cost way to develop alternative strategies to a new and challenging environment. This is not to say that adults cannot also learn and develop alternative strategies, but it is probably less costly, and consequently more likely to spread through the population, if it is accomplished through play in childhood (Bateson, 2005). The ease with which play and play-related behavior spread through the population should relate to their being naturally selected.

When children are in a new but safe environment, they are able to experiment with a variety of behavior routines and subroutines. Like Sultan in Köhler's (1925) experiments, they construct through play varied responses to novel environments. Furthermore, the costs associated with constructing and practicing new behavioral routines are low because they are in a safe environment and the behaviors are non-serious. Costs are also minimized by the extended parental care characteristic of the human juvenile period. That play is characteristic of the juvenile period suggests that it is used during this sensitive period to gauge and construct behaviors that will be useful throughout the organism's development. From this view, play during the juvenile period is a low-cost strategy for developing phenotypes that will be adaptive to individuals' current and subsequent environments.

CONCLUSIONS

The case of children's play was presented as both a paradigm of a juvenile behavioral constellation as well as a behavioral construct that is important in ontogeny and as possibly affects evolutionary processes. Play in one's niche may enable individuals to forecast what their developmental niche will be in the future, a strategy that may be especially important in novel environments. Play enables individuals, after they have sampled their environments, to generate, in a rather low-cost manner, a repertoire of possible behaviors that is adaptive to their specific niche. This point was illustrated with gene x environment interaction derived from experimental studies of cross-fostered rhesus monkeys of differing genotypes. The initial phenotypical changes associated with play, such as increased exploration and cooperation, decreased aggression and stereotypic behavior, and dominance status were sustained across development. Selection should favor individuals exhibiting these new phenotypes more than those who do not.

5

Play in Culture

Why include a chapter on the role of culture in a book on the role of play in human development, especially one with an evolutionary orientation? After all, doesn't a biological orientation assume that social processes and, correspondingly, "culture" are reflections of some deeper-rooted phylogenetic past? Indeed, some biologically oriented psychologists assume that the standard social science model (Tooby & Cosmides, 1992), fails to acknowledge the importance of biological adaptations in studying culture.

By contrast, the epigenetic view of evolutionary biology (Gottlieb, 1992), and the one presented in this book, holds that behavior, or culture, more generally, is the result transaction between individuals' biology and their social and physical environments. Culture, from this position, can be viewed as socially transmitted practices and beliefs that influence any individual's ontogeny and any group's phylogeny. Indeed, the cumulative effects of cultural innovations across generations, or what Tomasello (1999) has labeled the "ratchet effect," is a primary way by which culture advances. That is, an innovative cultural practice, such as the invention of a specific tool, developed at point in time, will be transmitted to subsequent generations, thus each generation does not have to re-discover that innovation for itself. Clearly, this cumulative effect is characteristic of human societies.

Culture has not only been studied by "standard social scientists," such as anthropologists, psychologists, and sociologists. It has also been studied by primatologists (Hinde, 1999; Tomasello & Call, 1997; Tomasello, Kruger, & Ratner, 1993), sometimes as part of a larger debate on the degree to which monkeys and apes have culture. This debate is sometimes limited to specific types of socially transmitted knowledge, of the sort to be discussed in the chapter on pretend play, and the degree to which nonhuman primates demonstrate intentionality (Tomasello & Call, 1997). Most basically, studies of nonhuman primate culture outline the behavioral practices and traditions associated with learning life skills, such as potato washing, tool use, and mothering skills. Briefly, Tomasello (1999) doubts that nonhuman primates have "culture" in the sense that they purposefully teach conspecifics, based primarily on their lack of intentionality.

In this chapter, I examine the place of play within a variety of human cultures, including modern industrial, pastoral, and foraging cultures. This level of contrast is especially important to the extent that it relates to the costs and benefits associated with play in development. The assumption is that play is more likely to be observed in abundant cultures, such as most modern and pastoral societies, than it is in foraging societies. Consistent with the arguments advanced by Surplus Resource Theory (Burghardt, 2005), play is most likely to occur in groups where resources are abundant so that juveniles are afforded a prolonged and protected period to learn and develop skills. In more severe settings, more time is spent in economically productive activities, i.e., work, rather than play. Play, following the thesis advanced in this book, could be at the vanguard of shaping culture, as a way in which behavioral innovations invented in childhood are culturally transmitted. But first, I attempt to situate play in "culture" more generally.

THE IMPORTANCE OF "CULTURE"

Trying to define *culture* is a complex and controversial exercise, not unlike the one involved in trying to define play. By extension, definitions of culture applied to child development have been proffered by anthropologists from at least the first third of the twentieth century (e.g., Benedict, 1934; Mead, 1928; 1930; 1946) to the present (Lancy, 1996, in press; Harkness, 2002; Rogoff et al., 1993; Whiting, 1976). These definitions, generally, refer to culture as a set of customs, or routines, and beliefs that shape children's lives (Harkness, 2002). By extension, and from a more current view, customs are part of the everyday practices in which children are embedded and are not limited to ceremonial practices, such as rites of passage (Harkness, 2002). For example, Bock (2002) and Rogoff and colleagues (1993) have documented the ways children's play is embedded in everyday economic practices, such as weaving and food processing.

The study of play in different societies is interesting to anthropologists, psychologists, and evolutionary biologists for a number of different reasons. Perhaps most fundamentally, anthropologists, and especially ethnographers, are concerned, primarily, with the ways in which cultures operate. As noted above, anthropologists such as Margaret Mead (1928; 1946) and Ruth Benedict (1934) examined the specific conditions under which children were reared in a variety of societies. Indeed, Mead's work (1946; 1954) was foundational to the nascent field of research in child development for over one half of a century, since its inclusion in the first and second editions of *Carmichael's Manual of Child Psychology*.

Following on that tradition, Beatrice and John Whiting (1975) examined child rearing in a variety of societies, including the United States, in their famous "six cultures" study. Basic to this line of inquiry was the notion of a *setting*, or a place where children were assigned by adults (representing more general societal norms and ways that they sustained themselves) to participate in activities thought to be important for children's roles in those societies as adults. One of Whiting's students, Sara Harkness, along with Charles Super, formalized a model, the "developmental niche" (Super & Harkness, 1992), to represent more specifically the ways in which children are enculturated. In this chapter I will use the developmental niche as a heuristic to examine culture and play.

Psychologists are also concerned with culture. Perhaps most commonly, cultural differences are of interest to psychologists because they provide insight into psychological "universals," such as invariant stages of the development syntax (e.g., Slobin, 1970) or Theory of Mind (e.g., Lillard, 1997). Furthermore, Evolutionary Psychologists, especially those associated with the "Santa Barbara School" (e.g., Cosmides & Tooby, 1987, 1992), are interested in the culture of contemporary hunter-gatherers because they hypothesize that this environment is similar to the one from which contemporary humans evolved, a hypothetical environment labeled by Bowlby (1969) as the Environment of Evolutionary Adaptedness (EEA). From this position, examination of extant foraging societies (e.g., Gossi et al., 2005) should be important to understanding humans' current psychological status, reflecting those adaptations to the EEA.

Behavioral biologists, too, are interested in cultures, especially as they are associated with behavioral variations in different ecologies. More specifically, behavioral ecologists examine the cost: benefit ratios of different behaviors and strategies and suggest that individuals seek "optimal" solutions (Stephens & Krebs, 1986) to basic problems associated with growth, maintenance, and reproduction in their life histories. In a discussion of children's play with objects in a pastoral group in Botswana, John Bock (2005) demonstrated that boys' and girls' play with objects was related to their respective economic roles in adulthood: hunters and cooks/mothers. Time spent playing diminished as children's skills with objects increased; work with objects replaced play with objects so as to optimize time and energy expended in each activity.

In what follows, I examine play and culture, initially from an ethnographic perspective, using the developmental niche (Super & Harkness, 1986) as a heuristic. I will examine not only "traditional" societies, also differentiating pastoral from foraging societies, but also contemporary societies.

PLAY IN THE "DEVELOPMENTAL NICHE"

Ethnography is a branch of anthropology where researchers try to determine the ways meaning is made in each culture. This is often attained by determining the function of behaviors, rituals, etc., in their naturally occurring habitats (Hymes, 1980b). To this end, ethnographers rely on a variety of research techniques, but perhaps most importantly on participant observations—where the researchers participate in the culture in order to maximize their understanding of local meaning (Hymes, 1980b). This participatory, or "emic," stance is in contrast to the "outsider," or "etic," position, often used in ethology and psychology (Pellegrini, 2005), where observers maintain detached and "objective" orientations. A useful ethnographic model for examining the ways children are enculturated, the "developmental niche," was developed by Super and Harkness (1986).

Following the earlier "Whiting Model" (Harkness, 2002), the developmental niche's has three components: Social and physical settings; customs related to child care; and beliefs regarding childhood.

Social and Physical Settings

The first component of the developmental niche is concerned with social and physical settings in which children live, play, and work. For example, very common physical settings for young children in contemporary industrialized societies are the preschool or nursery school classrooms with their accompanying rich array of objects with which to interact, such as blocks, art materials, sand tables, and computers. The nuclear family is another common social setting children are embedded in, with an array of objects similar to what can be found in many schools (especially in middle-class homes). In terms of the peer dimension of such social settings, children are typically segregated into same-age groups with non-kin adult teachers/caregivers in schools, and with kin, typically a mother/grandmother and siblings, at home.

By contrast, consider the physical and social settings of some foraging groups, such as the Hazda, a nomadic group in Tanzania (Blurton Jones, Hawkes, & O'Connell, 1997). Mothers leave their young children (from about two and a half years old) behind in camp as they go out to forage for food. At this time, their social groupings consist of a wide age range of children (up to about five years old, at which point children also forage) as they are supervised by an older child. The objects they interact with are related to their adult roles: Girls have dolls and boys have bows and arrows.

More directly relevant to analyses of the developmental niche and the Whiting Model is Marianne Bloch's (1989) examination of play behaviors in physical and social settings for a American sample of middle-class children (infants to five years of age) and in a sample of Senegalese children (of roughly the same age as the American sample) living in polygynous groups in a rural fishing village. Bloch observed the play of children as well as the locations where they played and the social composition of their groups. For ease of exposition and comparison, I present these data for children's activities in different physical and social settings in tabular form, by country, in Tables 5.1–5.6.

Table 5.1   American: time spent in locations

Location	2–4 Years		5–6 Years	
	Males	Females	Males	Females
In house	.70	.68	.63	.65
In yard	.13	.14	.06	.10
In neighborhood	.09	.08	.12	.13
Outside neighborhood	.08	.09	.15	.09

Table 5.2   American: time spent in activities

Activities	2–4 Years		5–6 Years	
	Males	Females	Males	Females
Sleeping	.10	.10	.04	.02
Eating	.11	.12	.17	.15
Hygiene	.02	.02	.03	.03
Care By Others	.02	.02	.00	.00
Care Self	.05	.02	.05	.01
Work	.03	.03	.03	.13
Observe Others	.04	.01	.04	.02
TV/Objects	.11	.11	.12	.10
Social Interact	.08	.10	.05	.03
Play	.30	.29	.32	.30
School-related	.02	.03	.01	.08
At School	.02	.02	.01	.02

Table 5.3   American: time with different social participants in play

	All Play	Function	Construct	Pretend	Gross Motor
Solitary					
2–4					
Male	.17	.03	.01	.02	.06
Female	.17	.03	.00	.04	.07
5–6					
Male	.14	.03	.02	.01	.03
Female	.14	.02	.01	.02	.08
Different Partners					
2–4					
Male	.15	.03	.01	.03	.07
Female	.16	.03	.01	.02	.05
5–6					
Male	.18	.03	.03	.01	.08
Female	.16	.03	.01	.04	.03

Table 5.4   Senegalese: time spent in locations

Location	2–4 Years		5–6 Years	
	Males	Females	Males	Females
In house	.12	.13	.13	.12
In yard	.49	.64	.51	.50
In village	.13	.09	.07	.12
Out village	.04	.05	.08	.05
Elsewhere	.07	.02	.05	.00

Table 5.5   Senegalese time spent in activities

Activities	2–4 Years		5–6 Years	
	Males	Females	Males	Females
Sleeping	.04	.05	.02	.06
Eating	.12	.15	.08	.15
Hygiene	.02	.03	.02	.01
Care By Others	.00	.02	.00	.01
Care Self	.03	.01	.03	.01
Work	.03	.05	.13	.15
Observe Others	.11	.13	.08	.07
TV/Objects	.03	.02	.02	.01
Social Interact	.08	.10	.06	.03
Play	.21	.27	.22	.18
School-related	.00	.01	.03	.01

Table 5.6   Senegalese: time with different social participants in play

	All Play	Function	Construct	Pretend	Gross Motor
Solitary					
2–4					
Male	.19	.05	.02	.02	.11
Female	.13	.07	.00	.06	.04
5–6					
Male	.02	.00	.00	.00	.00
Female	.06	.00	.00	.03	.00
Different Partners					
2–4					
Male	.19	.01	.02	.02	.11
Female	.19	.02	.00	06	04
5–6					
Male	30	01	03	01	16
Female	22	00	00	07	06

Perhaps most interesting in Bloch's findings for the purposes of our discussion is the fact that "play" is the one activity accounting for highest proportion of time—around 20% for the Senegalese children and around 30% for the Americans. Furthermore, in both societies, social interaction with peers was more common than adult–child interaction. The primacy of interaction with peers, rather than adults, is probably due to the age of the children in both samples. As will be illustrated later in this chapter, interaction with peers typifies the juvenile period in many cultures, while interaction and play with adults, rather than peers, is more common in infancy.

Also very surprising was the relative equality in time spent in fantasy in both places, with the Senegalese actually spending a bit more time in pretend play than the Americans, though probably not statistically different. The reader must ask,

Why these similarities? Is it the case that these cultures are really more similar than different? These results might suggest that both Senegalese and middle-class American societies situate their children in similarly object-rich environments where the value of play, especially pretend play, is stressed.

Consistent with this explanation for the lack of differences in the observed pretend play of these two groups is that they are both relatively well off, in an economical sense. That is, both groups are probably well fed and safe, and both probably have the "surplus resources" necessary to support play. Furthermore and specific to the presence of pretend play, it may be that the skills necessary to flourishing in each society are sufficiently complex and symbolic that pretend play is important for learning associated skills, such as navigation for the Senegalese and school-related skills in both societies.

Besides research following the Whiting Model generally and the developmental niche more specifically, examination of the various social and physical settings of children's behavior and play are basic Vygotskian-oriented studies. This orientation, recall, posits that children become members of society by participating, in an apprentice-like fashion, in work-related activities, such as weaving, cooking and food preparation, and hunting (Morelli, Rogoff, & Angelillo, 1993; Rogoff et al., 1993). For example, Morelli and colleagues (1993) documented children's participation in work and play settings and adult and peer partners play in one foraging community (the Efe of Zaïre), a pastoral group (Mayans of Mexico), and two American communities (Salt Lake City, Utah, and Santa Cruz, California). In both the foraging and pastoral communities, children engaged in pretend play around work-related themes. Furthermore, and consistent with my interpretation of Bloch's data, more of their time was spent in work-related activities (~5%–7%) than in play (~3%–5%), perhaps reflecting the more severe environments of the foragers and pastoralists, relative to the Americans. In work settings, adults were the most likely social partners of children, while children played more frequently with peers, relative to adults. American children, by contrast, spent more time playing (~6%) than working (~3%), and when they played they frequently played with adults (~6%–7%), relative to the traditional societies (~1%–3%).

These findings are consistent with the Vygotskiian idea that enculturation into adult roles occurs in the context of participation in adult and work-related activities, or what Rogoff and colleagues (Rogoff, Mosier, Mistry, & Göncü, 1989) have labeled "guided participation." American children's play, on the other hand, tended to more frequently relate to school-lesson themes. While not work in the traditional sense, schooling and subsequent literate activities is the stuff of adult roles in contemporary industrialized societies. Indeed, and as will be discussed below, childhood activities that stress social and intellectual development, for example, are typical of offspring reproductive enhancing societies, rather than the economic productivity of production enhancing societies. In all cases, however, it seemed that adults were the important guides for children learning desired skills at work- and played-related activities. In many of these cases, however, adults do not teach children directly. Instead, their example is used to convey a skill, as in the case of Hazda fathers making bows and arrows while their sons observe (Blurton Jones, 1993). Thus, the physical and social settings overlap with customs of child care.

Customs of Child Care

The second component of the developmental niche relates to the societal customs surrounding child care. Again contrasting contemporary, industrialized societies with foraging societies, we find that the former typically stress close mother–child interaction. When care by children's kin is not possible, alternative child-care arrangements that approximate familial care, in terms of care being closely supervised by "qualified" and consistent adults, is sought out. The stress on state-level licensing of caregivers and facilities in modern society is a testament to this orientation. In many of these cases within modern societies, the definition of "high quality" child care are those conditions approximating the care provided by stay-at-home mothers in economically secure families.

A corresponding consequence of the primacy of the mother–child relationship in contemporary society is the importance of the mother–child attachment relationship (Bowlby, 1969) as an indicator of a high quality adult–child relationship. By extension, children's attachment relationships to their preschool teachers are part of the definition of a quality childcare program (Ritchie & Howes, 2003). The primacy of the mother–child bond cannot be overestimated in contemporary societies. The furor associated with daycare for infants, a time and place not consistent with the ideal of the EEA, is indicative of this bias (Belsky, 2001; 2003). Where modern parents cannot be the primary caregiver for their children, they aim to provide their offspring with a consistent and warm caregiver.

The importance of mother–child interaction, generally, and mother–child play, specifically, is only equivocally supported by the anthropological record (Lancy, 2007). For example, in many traditional societies, both pastoral, such as the Kpelle of West Africa (Lancy, 1996) and the Gusii of East Africa (LeVine & LeVine, 1966), and foraging societies, such as the !Kung, a one-time foraging group in northwestern Botswana and northeastern Namibia (Blurton Jones, 1993; Konner, 2005), children are left to play in a central area in camp in a mixed-age grouping, within sight and earshot of adults and typically cared for by older female children and adolescents—an area called by the "mother ground" by the Kpelle (Lancy, 1996). In the case of the Hazda, a foraging group living in northern Tanzania, for example, children are not directly supervised nor confined to camp explicitly (Blurton Jones, 1993).

The practice of adult, relative to peer, care varies with age and ecology in many societies. For example, with both the !Kung and the Hazda, (Blurton Jones, 1993) mothers carry their infants on their on gathering journeys, of approximately six and a half miles. The degree to which older children accompany adults on hunting or gathering outings depends on the cost–benefit tradeoffs between work and play. In the Hazda case, it is not uncommon for children as young as three years of age to gather, dig, and process baobab pods and roots or to run errands for adults, such as fetching water and firewood. The !Kung children, by contrast, stay in camp throughout their childhood and are more closely monitored by adults; and when they do forage, it is done in the camp, not outside of its boundaries.

The differences between the customs of child care for !Kung and Hazda reflect the cost: benefits associated with playing versus engaging in economically productive activities in each ecology. In the !Kung case, the ecology is more dangerous than the Hazda's, such that it is easier for children wondering outside of camp to get lost. Specifically, the topography of their living area is relatively hilly with rock outcroppings and deep valleys (Blurton Jones, 1993), and, when interviewed, parents do indeed express concerns with children getting lost. In the Hazda case, by contrast, distances are closer and food and water are typically more available. Because of the relative costs and benefits associated with economic and play activities, the Hazda children spend less time playing and move into economically productive activities at a younger age than do the !Kung's. Specifically, the costs (i.e., danger as well as caloric and time expenditure) associated with !Kung foraging in childhood means that they spend more time playing in childhood, and foraging is postponed until the mid- to late teenage years (Blurton Jones et al., 1997; Draper, 1976; Lee, 1979). The Hazda children, on the other hand, can move into economically productive activity with relatively low costs, and thus do so.

Beliefs and Expectations About Childhood

The third, and final, component of the developmental niche is concerned with beliefs and expectations regarding childhood. This component represents the cognitive processes that mediate children's experiences in different settings. Starting with modern industrialized societies, especially American and European societies, the dominant belief is that play is good for children and that children learn through play. A current volume on play, with the provocative title *Play = Learning* (Singer et al., 2006), is an exemplar of cultural bias. Consequently, children in this niche should have relatively large portions of their time and energy budgets dedicated to play. As we will discuss below, however, this orientation is not shared by all contemporary industrial societies.

A useful way of organizing beliefs and expectations about childhood can be derived from Nicholas Blurton Jones' (1993) behavioral ecological studies of childhood and play discussed in the preceding section. Recall that behavioral ecological theory is guided by the hypothesis that individuals' behaviors and strategies are biased toward optimal solutions to problems presented in their ecologies. In relatively severe and dangerous ecologies, such as some foraging societies, the stress is not on offspring reproduction, but on "enhancing survivorship." As with the !Kung discussed above, children are protected and indulged, and play is encouraged as the benefits associated with play are greater than the benefits, and associated dangers, of economic activity. Hazda society, not unlike fertile agricultural societies, has been characterized as a "production enhancer" because children are seen as providing economic benefit (Blurton Jones, 1993). In these cases, play is less valued than work because the latter is more beneficial, so children move from play into work at younger ages than they would in societies where young children have less economic benefits.

In most modern industrial societies where resources are generally abundant, juveniles have extended and protective childhoods. Beliefs and practices about childhood are characterized by having children spend time in activities that maximize their social and intellectual ability. Correspondingly, and consistent with Burghardt's (2005) Surplus Resource Theory, children in this sort of rich environment should spend a substantial portion of their time and energy budgets in play. From this view, play in childhood is thought to enhance children's social and intellectual skills necessary for success in adulthood. An important part of success, of course, is to maximize the reproduction of their offspring, thus this strategy has been labeled Offspring Reproductive Strategy. An implication of this strategy, not unlike the distinction between K and r reproductive strategies (Belsky et al., 1991), as will be outlined in my later discussion of social play and parent–child play, is that parents, in the K case, invest more of their resources in fewer offspring while in the r case, they maximize the number of offspring with minimal investment in each.

Mothers in middle-class families typically engage in the forms of play they think will maximize children's social and intellectual prowess. For example, while both recent Asian American immigrants to the northeastern United States and European American families frequently played with their preschool age children, the former group engaged in more constructive than pretend play, relative to the latter group (Parmar, Harkness, and Super, no date).

The Stress on Play in Contemporary Society: The Role of G, Stanley Hall for Play in America

The positive view of play in childhood has its roots in the Child Study Movement. The Child Study Movement in the United States began in the early twentieth century. Its origins can be traced to the influences of Darwinian theory applied to child psychology. This influence was due, perhaps most directly, to the theories and influence of G. Stanley Hall (1904; 1916). Hall was called by many (e.g., Cairns, 1983) the father of American psychology, generally, and a founder of child and developmental psychology in the United States, more specifically. Hall was the first American to receive a Ph.D. in psychology (from Harvard in 1878, under the supervision of William James) and the first American to be awarded a chair in psychology (at Johns Hopkins in 1884) (Cairns, 1983).

He was much more, however. He was a minister, an educational psychologist, a university professor and president, the first president of the American Psychological Association, and the founder and editor of a number of psychological journals. It may have been this great willingness and ability to cross intellectual boundaries and integrate a variety of disciplines that lead to his having such a great impact on our field. He took this knowledge of biology, psychology, and philosophy to guide the Child Study Movement across the United States.

As a child/developmental psychologist, Hall may be most remembered for his stress on the stage-like progression of human development. Hall thought these stages reenacted the history of the species (phylogeny). In this vein, Hall is perhaps best remembered for the phrase "ontogeny recapitulates phylogeny" (paraphrased from the German biologist Ernst Haeckel). For Hall, this meant that development within an individual (ontogeny) recapitulates, or repeats, the evolutionary history of the species (phylogeny). Some of Hall's famous examples include the following: Boys' tree climbing is a recapitulation of our primate past. Similarly, boys' play fighting was a reenactment of our hunter-gather past.

As previously noted the accuracy of the notion that ontogeny repeats phylogeny is not credible (see Bjorklund & Pellegrini, 2002; Hinde, 1983). Specifically and without going into detail (though see Bjorklund and Pellegrini, 2002, chap. 3, for an extended discussion) it is probably more likely the case, as argued in the preceding chapter, that ontogenetic development influences phylogeny. The course of individual development, for example the age of sexual maturity, influences the development of the species.

I also proffer a cautionary note. We should not be too hasty and laugh too visibly at the apparent foolishness of Hall's claim: Take pause. The history of science is too full of examples that seemed like certainties, only to later be discredited. That Newton's theory was displaced by Einstein's (Clark, 1971) should not discredit the historical importance of Newton for the physics of his day. In short, we should minimize the extent to which we view historical events from our contemporary eyes and try to view those events through the eyes of the actors of that day (Butterfield, 1965). From that view, Hall was very innovative.

Probably the most enduring aspect of Hall's theory was the stress on stages of human development and the corresponding importance he gave the role of play during childhood. Hall saw play as integral to childhood. Hall viewed childhood as a period during which children should be allowed unfettered time to explore and play. He warned against "unnatural" and "artificial" educational and pedagogical regimens because they interfered with the natural unfolding of children's developmental processes (Cairns, 1983, p. 52). Play, for Hall, ideally had children choosing activities and enacting them on their own terms. In this regard, play during childhood was stressed as a way in which children expressed their phylogenetic history. So children's play hunting or fishing expressed their foraging past!

Perhaps more interesting was Hall's view that play was not something that prepared individuals for adulthood. Unlike most of his contemporaries, such as Karl Groos (1898; 1901) and later Piaget (1932) and Vygotsky (1967), Hall considered play important to childhood *per se*—not as practice for adulthood. Indeed, this view is current among many developmental psychologists today who study play (Bjorklund & Pellegrini, 2002; Pellegrini, in press).

This work, along with that of other Darwinians, such as Groos (1898; 1901), stressed the notion of childhood as a distinct "stage" of human development. Correspondingly, play was seen as the way in which youngsters of this age came to know their world. Through play, children interacted with their physical and social world and "constructed" their mental worlds. If this view sounds reminiscent of Piaget, it is. After all, Piaget was trained as a biologist, and his general systems theory was a biological theory; his more specific notions of assimilation and accommodation are biological constructs.

The general Darwinian world view and Hall's theories, specifically, had an enormous impact on the new fields of developmental and child psychology as well as on nursery and primary school education in America in early twentieth century America (Cairns, 1983; Kessen, 1965). Specifically, Hall was the first president of Clark University, in Worcester, Massachusetts. Clark, traditionally, has been a bastion for the training of some of America's leading developmental psychologists. Clark's Child Study Institute was a laboratory where children were studied, and this knowledge was used to develop school curricula. John Dewey, another advocate of play, was among Hall's students (Cairns, 1983). When Piaget first visited the United States, he gave a series of lectures at Clark, as did Sigmund Freud.

At the same time, Hall was instrumental in founding the journal *Pedagogical Seminary* in 1891, renamed in 1927 the *Journal of Genetic Psychology* (Smith & Connolly, 1980). This scientific journal was the archival outlet for studies in child and developmental psychology in the first half of the twentieth century, providing an intellectual forum for the nascent science of child development. Indeed, the use of the term "genetic" in this context was synonymous with ontogeny—not with the influence of genes on behavior, as it is currently used.

The result was that American psychology was shaped by Darwinian and Hallian developmental theory. Childhood was seen as a unique stage, and children of this age should "play in order to develop properly." The intellectual ethos of the Child Study Movement was directly translated into educational programs and interventions for young children. The "nursery school" movement was being formulated at academic institutions in the United States (Teachers College/ Columbia under the influence of John Dewey) and at the child welfare stations at the universities of Iowa and Minnesota. Laboratory nursery schools were formed at both Iowa (see Thompson, 1944) and Minnesota (see Parten, 1932). Both being land-grant institutions, they were based on the agricultural extension model (Cairns, 1983). Apparently, an Iowa housewife and mother, Cora Bussey Hill, queried that if universities could help farmers grow bigger cattle and better corn—could they not help grow healthier children (Cairns, 1983)? Acting on this idea, researchers set up a "child welfare station" at Iowa (1917) and established a laboratory nursery school in 1921 (Cairns, 1983). Similar institutes and nurseries were established during the 1920s and 1930s at Minnesota, Toronto, Berkeley, Yale, and the Merrill-Palmer Institute in Detroit, not only as child advocates but also as centers where research knowledge and excellent pedagogy were designed and tested. The labs were used both to test developmental theories and to design curricula based on these theories. The Shirley G. Moore Laboratory Nursery at the University of Minnesota is still carrying out this work today. It is the center of a number of very active research programs and a place where preschool teachers are trained, and the importance of play is stressed in this curriculum.

With all of this said, antipathy towards play, however, does exist within parts of modern society. The reason proffered for the antipathy toward play by scholars is the influence of our Puritanical/Calvinist past. That is, the "work ethic" associated with Calvinism has permeated American (and indeed Anglo-Saxon) culture (see Tawney, 1926/1969). Consequently, this ethos tends to devalue all enterprises associated with pleasure and leisure. The result of this orientation has been that play has been devalued by most schools in the industrialized world.

As I will discuss below, this orientation is not limited to countries governed by Puritanical/Calvinistic leaders. For example, in much of medieval Europe, well before the Reformation, religious writers and moralists tried to govern children's play (Orme, 2001). In some cases they tried to discourage it, relating it to the frivolities of some adult practices. In other cases they lobbied to increase it, as in the case of encouraging boys' playing at war and play fighting as a way in which to prepare boys to defend their country (Orme, 2001).

Furthermore, play was discouraged by the explicitly anti-Christian, Marxist, ideology, following the line of valuing labor and being correspondingly disdainful of pursuits associated with frivolous leisure. This orientation reached a high point (or low point, depending on your values) during the Cultural Revolution in China when intellectuals (viewed as a non-laboring class) were "reeducated."

The Chinese Case

A team of American observers to Chinese schools in the mid-1970s found that schools discouraged intellectual elitism, a continuation of policies associated with Cultural Revolution (Kessen, 1975). Correspondingly, Chinese kindergarteners' love of labor is considered a virtue, and an objective of primary school education was the "participation and love for productive labor" (Kessen, 1975, p. 119). Similarly, with older children, the American team observed cases where primary schools were paired with a neighboring factory, and children were given jobs to complete in the factory. For example, children helped assemble badminton birds and shaped chess pieces.

Chinese nurseries and kindergartens made very limited provision for children's play. In the nurseries (that is, pre-kindergartens) the team of Americans observed, they found that indoor play was minimal, and where it was observed, was initiated by an adult with a child (Kessen, 1975). Furthermore, there was a paucity of play materials in the nurseries as well. Indeed, the observers noted a "uniform absence" of toys in many nurseries (p. 69). They concluded, however, the children did not seem the worse for it!

In kindergarten, however, there was a great variety of play materials, such as toy trucks and plastic animals and art materials available, and most kindergartens had an attached play yard with "substantial" play equipment (Kessen, 1975). Additionally, break periods were scheduled before classes and for ten minutes in between each class (about every hour). This, it seems, it similar to a periodic recess, or play break.

Children's behavior, both indoors and outdoors, was, however, adult-directed, not spontaneous or play-like in the way I have defined play in this book. For example, in outdoor play, children moved as a group from one activity to another—more like physical education than play. Similarly, the indoor play was also highly organized. The American observers concluded that children did not seem free to pursue their own interests. So, for example, children would be seated at a table with drawing materials and while they were not free to choose the activity, they could choose what to draw. Furthermore, and perhaps most telling, the Americans did not observe instances of kindergarten-age children engaging in dramatic play! Contrast this with the high frequency of dramatic play observed during the free play periods even in the most traditional American preschool classrooms.

When we move into Chinese primary school and examine the frequency of breaks during the school day, we find that a 30-minute break is given after the first and the third class periods (where each period is about 40 minutes). As with the breaks in kindergarten, they are structured and more like a physical education class than a recess period as we know it. Children were observed being guided through eye exercises (to prevent nearsightedness) and then doing calisthenics to recorded music.

The Soviet Russian Case

The extent to which play has been pursued as an area of scholarly activity or stressed in schools in the former Soviet Russia is both similar and different from the People's Republic of China. It is different to the extent that there was a history of Western-oriented developmental psychology at the very beginning of the Soviet experiment. Specifically, research on play in the Soviet Union in the 1920s was guided by Vygotsky, a developmentalist influenced by the American psychologist G. Stanley Hall's notion of stage theory and of "ontogeny recapitulating phylogeny" (Rahamani, 1973), and by his contemporary, Piaget (1932). This work, and the subsequent work of Zaporozhets and Elkonin (1971) and Repina (1971), stressed the role of play in children's development. Specifically, and following the contemporary *zeitgeist* of both Vygotsky and of Western psychology, play was conceptualized as practice for practical ends—learning and development. Play in childhood was practice at learning the skills necessary to become an adult. This view is consistent with that advanced by Piaget.

For Vygotsky, play, and as discussed earlier, was motivated by the tension within the child to fulfill desires and wants that are unattainable within socially acceptable norms. Take for instance the example where a child has a desire to own a horse. Because, in reality, he cannot attain that goal, he pretends a broom is a horse. In this view, children develop the ability both to control emotions and desires as well as gain practice at symbolic representation—or having one thing (a broom) represent something else (a horse).

These Western and non-Pavlovian principles, however, were suppressed with the succession of Stalin (Rahamani, 1973). At this time, psychology became much less developmental and much more oriented towards pedagogy, "shaping" the new Soviet man. Indeed, Western influences in psychology were suppressed and only Pavlovian theory was given currency (Rahmani, 1973). In terms of Soviet pedagogy, schools stressed the role of "work," in the form of class projects and learning specific skills, such as carpentry and dress-making (Bronfenbrenner, 1973, p. 52). Schools did, however, have recess periods, and the goal of recess, like education more generally, was to educate Soviet citizens (Bronfenbrenner, 1973). This entailed children's learning to cooperate with peers and internalizing socially minded and collectivist values. On the playground, this was accomplished by peer-guided games. So, not unlike Western views, play was seen by

Soviet psychologists and educators as training for adulthood. Consistent with Vygotsky's theory (1978), this was accomplished through social interaction. So, play has been treated in similar ways by the West and the East: An equal-opportunity target.

CONCLUSION

In this chapter I have explored the ways in which play varies in different cultures. Following a behavioral ecological orientation, the role of play in culture can be best understood by considering the relative values of play and work in the specific ecologies being observed. For example, in societies characterized as "production enhancers" (Blurton Jones, 1993), play would be replaced by work relatively early in ontogeny because of the relative ease and safety with which resources can be accessed. Bock's (2005) work with pastoral people in Botswana is illustrative of this case. By contrast, in survivorship-enhancing societies, such as the !Kung, children's lives are relatively dangerous, and their parents and communities shelter them from the dangers associated with economic activity. Adult-supervised play activities are a resulting practice.

Lastly, in relative abundant modern societies, children's lives are also sheltered, but with the purpose of enculturating children with the social and intellectual skills necessary to function in society. As we have seen, some societies, such as those in North America and Europe, stress play to meet those ends, while others are more skill-oriented. This level of variation across societies suggests that cross-cultural comparisons should include cost : benefit analyses of play versus work as part of their analysis.

6

Functions of Play

Hypotheses about functions of play truly do encompass the spectrum. Some behavioral psychologists, such as Scholsberg (1947), suggested that the construct was so unimportant that it should be relegated to the trash bin of science. At the other end of the continuum, some students of children's play (e.g., Singer et al., 2006) posit that children's play has benefits for a wide variety of social, emotional, and cognitive areas. Correspondingly, two primatologists, Baldwin and Baldwin (1977), have listed 30 possible functions of play. A more middling, and skeptical, position has been taken by the English psychologist and longtime student of play, Peter Smith (1982; 1988). Smith (1988) labels the unequivocal acceptance of the value of play as the "play ethos," roughly defined as the position that play is all good for all children.

Smith's skepticism is based, primarily, on the methodological limitations of the studies in educational and developmental psychology that have proposed such benefits. For example, benefits of pretend play in relation to preschool children's creativity and problem-solving cannot be replicated under double-blind conditions (Simon & Smith, 1983; 1985; Smith & Whitney, 1987). Similar levels of skepticism have also been voiced by the ethologists Paul Martin and Tim Caro (1985) and Lynda Sharpe (2006), though for different reasons. They are skeptical of a biological function of play due to its relatively low cost (in terms of time, energy, and survivorship). In their view, there should be correspondence between costs and benefits, with low costs relating to relatively limited benefits.

In this chapter I will first define what it is I mean by *function*, drawing from both the behavioral biology and the developmental psychology literatures. Before delving into the theoretical discussions of function, I will consider different ways that function is established. In further attempting to explicate the function of play, I follow Tinbergen's (1963) advice by simultaneously considering function along with the ontogeny and phylogeny of play, as well as proximal causes of play. As part of this discussion, I will consider the possible difference in functions of different forms of play for males and females. Guided by sexual selection theory (Darwin, 1871), I explore the hypothesis that males' and females' reproductive roles influence their play and its function.

WHAT IS MEANT BY *FUNCTION*?

How Is Function Determined?

In a formal, logical sense, *function* means that x causes y, or that y is "a function of" x. That is, a functional relation between two variables is also a causal one, where y is caused by x. Continuing with this philosophical level of analysis, British empiricists, such as John Stuart Mill (1843/1874) and Bertrand Russell (1959), specified the conditions necessary and sufficient for establishing that y is a function of x. In their view, three conditions are needed to establish a causal, or functional, relation between two variables. First, there must a significant co-variation between the two variables. For example, a first step in determining the causal role of social play (x) on boys' social affiliation (y) would be to demonstrate a significant correlation between the two variables.

Second, and with the first condition met, x and y should be in an antecedent/ consequence (temporal) relation. So x, social play, should precede y, social affiliation, in time. These two conditions can be met, and typically are, in many forms of naturalistic, longitudinal research where, for example, children are observed across time, and their behavior x, at time 1, predicts subsequent behavior y, at time 2.

In some cases, and in many of the social and behavioral sciences, predictive correlations are taken as evidence that one variable, x, is "beneficial" in terms of its predicting y, with the implication that the relation is causal. The obvious problem with using only the first two conditions to make functional, or causal, judgments is that there may be an unobserved, or mediator, variable between x and y. For example, we know that one form of children's social play, rough-and-tumble play (R&T), x, predicts peer affiliation, y, such that when R&T ends there is a statistically significant probability that they will next engage in cooperative games (Pellegrini, 1988).

There may be, however, a mediator between R&T and peer affiliation. Specifically, it may be the case that children who engage in R&T play may also have sociable temperaments, and it is this temperament that is responsible for both children's R&T and their peer affiliation. Schematically, the relationship can be represented as in Figure 6.1.

In this case, x and y are correlated, leading us to begin to make a causal inference. However, both x and y are also significantly correlated with m, as well as with each other. When the correlations between m and x and m and y are statistically controlled, the correlation between x and y becomes insignificant. This demonstrates that the relationship between x and y was not causal. Instead, it

Figure 6.1   The problem of a mediator variable

was due their each being inter-correlated with the mediator. Specifically, x was correlated with m which, in turn, was correlated with y and the relation between x and y was dependent upon each of them being correlated with m.

The third condition necessary for causality is to eliminate the possibility of mediators, as well as all other alternative explanations for the relations between x and y. The only way that we can be absolutely confident that all alternative explanations for the relations between x and y have been eliminated is to conduct a controlled experiment. In well-designed (i.e., internally valid) experiments, random selection of participants and random of assignment of participants to conditions assures us that all differences among participants in different conditions are equated and that the difference between participants in different conditions are only due to differences in the experimental treatments. So, in the case illustrated above, we can eliminate temperament as a mediator by randomly selecting a sample of children from the general population and then from that sample, randomly assigning children to different conditions: one where they are trained to engage in R&T and another where they are trained in peer interaction, without R&T. Randomization should guarantee that differences between groups will be randomly distributed across conditions, and any between-group differences in affiliation should be due to differences in the conditions.

I stress that the experiment must be internally valid in order to make valid causal inferences. More specifically, even though participants are randomly selected and randomly assigned, a confounding of variables will limit our understanding of the effect of x on y. In some cases, for example, experimental implementation of play regimens have confounded play with adults' coaching children in play (Smith, 1988); thus it is important to keep these effects separate in order to make inferences about the effect of play *per se*. For example, I conducted an internally valid experiment to determine the effects of dramatic play on children's story comprehension (Pellegrini, 1984), an example I'll discuss in more detail in the chapter on educational implications. In this experiment, children were randomly assigned to different experimental treatments, one of which was dramatic play with peers, to examine the relative effects on story comprehension. In addition to the peer-dramatic-play condition, there were peer interaction (without play) and adult-directed-interaction conditions (where conceptual disequilibration was facilitated). In this way we separated adult tuition from peer play.

Functional inferences for biologist, on the other hand, are often based on arguments by design as well as experimental and correlational studies (Hinde, 1980; Martin & Caro, 1985). Arguments by design typically involve finding structural similarities between an antecedent behavior, such as the quasi-aggressive behaviors associated with R&T, and a functional consequence, such as aggression.

Functional consequences for biologists also are typically related to survival and reproduction. For example, the punching and wrestling behaviors of R&T should relate to structurally similar behaviors in fighting and, ultimately, winning fights. Winning fighting, in turn, would predict access to mates and subsequent fitness. A correlation between these two features would provide empirical support for the argument by design. Of course there is always the possibility that the form of a behavior in play at time 1 is mediated by another factor, in its relation to the "serious" behavior at time 2. Another possibility is that the serious behaviors in adulthood are not related at all to the structurally similar juvenile behaviors!

Different Models of the Function of Play: Deferred, Immediate, and Accelerated Benefits

As noted above, psychologists typically equate function with beneficial conse-quences, and the array of beneficial consequences associated with play is staggering. For example in one recent book (ed. Singer et al., 2006), play is said to benefit children's: early literacy, self-regulation, mathematics, writing, uses of technology, and emotion learning. The theories enlisted to test these hypotheses in the child developmental and educational psychological literatures are typically derived from Piaget (1932) and Vygotsky (1967), both of whom stressed the role of pretend, or symbolic, play for subsequent, often deferred, symbolic func-tioning. For both Piaget and Vygotsky, like most developmental psychologists, the beneficial consequences associated with play during childhood are typically deferred, after childhood. As will be discussed below in much greater, the extent to which benefits associated with play during childhood are deferred or immediate is a matter of debate.

Biologists, too, have ascribed numerous benefits to play (e.g., Baldwin and Baldwin, 1978), but function, for biologists, as noted above, is related to adaptation in the context of fitness, or reproducing of viable offspring, in conjunction with ontogeny, phylogeny, and proximal causes (Tinbergen, 1969). A behavior or strategy will be favored by natural selection if the associated benefits outweigh the associated costs. Importantly, it is not the absolute costs that are important but the costs relative to benefits (Martin & Caro, 1985). Simply, benefits must exceed costs. Following Darwin's theory of evolution by natural selection, evolutionary biologists examine how behaviors and strategies at different periods during individuals' life histories are either favored or not favored by natural selection.

Also crucial to understanding function in the context of natural selection is that natural selection operates on all periods of development—not only adulthood. After all, infants and juveniles must survive into adulthood before they can reproduce! Life history theory suggests that we should examine the relative costs and benefits associated with play with regards to individuals' growth and maintenance, in addition to reproductive success at different periods in develop-ment (Stearns, 1992). Per this claim, play can have benefits during childhood or have them deferred until maturity, depending on the cost–benefit tradeoffs of different forms of play during childhood, and later in development.

So, for example, if we are concerned with the function of preschool boys' social play, we should not be immediately concerned with its role in the reproductive behavior, as they are many years from sexual maturity. Instead, we might look at the costs of the behaviors associated with social play in childhood, such as the caloric expenditure associated with physically vigorous behavior, and the benefits associated with the growth of muscular and skeletal systems during this period (Byers & Walker, 1995; Gunter, Baxter-Jones, Mirwald, Almstedt, Fuchs, Durski, & Snow, 2008). Take the case of one dimension of children's locomotor play, jumping: Periods of sustained jumping, though costly, during childhood have the benefit of increased bone mineral content during childhood (Gunter et al., 2008). Similar immediate effects are observed during adolescence: jumping increases youngsters' bone density (Young & Beck, 2008). This sort of development of the skeletal system during the juvenile period is relevant to later survival and later reproductive success, as bigger and stronger bones relate to physical stature, dominance status, physical attractiveness, and attractiveness to mates.

There are important theoretical implications for the function of play, depending on when the putative benefits of play are reaped. Are they deferred until maturity, as proposed by most theories of play, such as Groos (1898), Piaget (1932), and Vygotsky (1967)? Or are they more immediate to the period during which they are observed, following more current ethological theorizing (Bateson, 2005; Martin & Caro, 1985; Pellegrini, Dupuis, & Smith, 2007)?

Play Serving Deferred Benefits

The classical view of play is that it is practice for adulthood. For example, Piaget's (1932; 1983) view of development was that young children's behavior and thought were imperfect variants of adults', operational, thought. Play, from this view, is a way in which children can assimilate new information into extant cognitive structures, with the goal of progressing towards operational thought. This orientation of play as practice for adulthood goes back to at least Groos (1898; 1901) and has been restated in the contemporary developmental (Smith, 1982) and ethological (Fagen, 1981) literatures. This position assumes that play during the juvenile period has no immediate utility. Indeed, part of the definition of play is that it serves no purpose! It is an imperfect variant of adult behavior, but the play behavior affords individuals opportunities to master and practice these behaviors and skills.

Graphically, this "conventional" model of play (Martin & Caro, 1985) is represented in Figure 6.2.

The hypothetical data for this graph plot one trajectory for the development of a serious behavior where the subjects are playing and another trajectory where they are not playing. As can be seen, the hypothetical play and nonplay trajectories for the serious behavior co-occur during childhood, and then, for the play group, relative to the nonplay group, the behaviors and skills developed during childhood lead to improved serious behavior at maturity—a deferred benefit.

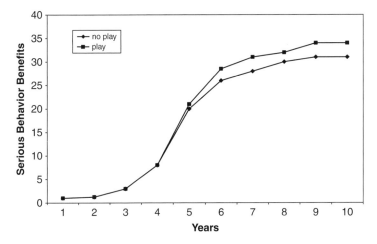

Figure 6.2   Play conventional practice model

An example of play as practice, common to both the human and nonhuman animal literatures, is the role of R&T during childhood and fighting skills in adulthood (e.g., Fagen, 1981; Groos, 1901; Smith, 1982). The premise is that the skills learned and developed in R&T during childhood, such as learning to land accurate blows, avoid attacks, and recognize dominant and subordinate peers, will be useful in adult, serious fighting (Fagen, 1981; Smith, 1982). Juveniles who engage in R&T should, as adults, be better fighters than those who did not engage in R&T as juveniles, though there is little support for this hypothesis (Sharpe, 2006). Pat Bateson (1981) has characterized this model as a "scaffolding" model of play: Play is used in the assembly of a skill, such as fighting, and when the skill is completed, the scaffolding is removed. In this case, a behavior, play, is being used in development (Bateson, 1976).

Play Serving Immediate Benefits

In contrast to the conventional deferred benefit model, in Figure 6.3, I graphically present an "immediate benefits of play" model (Martin & Caro, 1985).

The immediate benefits model of play is less commonly invoked that the deferred benefits model in the child developmental (though see Bjorklund & Pellegrini, 2000; Pellegrini & Smith, 1998) and nonhuman animal literatures (though see Bateson, 1981; Bekoff, 1978). In this model, the benefits of play are reaped at the period during which the costs are incurred. In further contrast with the conventional model, which views juvenile behavior and play as imperfect, the immediate benefits model posits that the play behaviors observed during the juvenile period are beneficial to the niche of childhood, specifically; they are not imperfect variants of adult behavior. For example, the form and behavior of a chrysalis are beneficial to that period, but not to behavior associated with being a butterfly; that is, a chrysalis makes an excellent chrysalis but a terrible butterfly

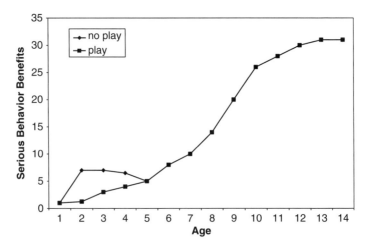

Figure 6.3   Play immediate benefits model

(Hinde, 1983). Juvenile behaviors and morphology are beneficial to that niche, a position that Bateson (1981) has labeled the "metamorphic" view of play. Play is beneficial to the juvenile period, but not beyond, except to the extent that it aids in the survival of childhood. Children are excellent at being children, but not excellent at being adults: Nor should they be.

This view explicitly addresses the notion that natural selection works on all periods of development. Affording infants and juveniles the time to engage in playful behavior for its own sake with little concern about adult-related economic productivity or reproductive roles should occur only in ecological niches with a relative surplus of resources (Burghardt, 2005).

A clear example of the immediate benefits of play is in the area of locomotor play (Byers & Walker, 1995; Pellegrini & Smith, 1998). Take for instance, one form of locomotor play, exercise play. It relates to immediate cardiovascular conditioning: When the exercise stops, so do the benefits, but they can be regained if exercise is resumed (Pellegrini & Smith, 1998). Additionally, a case can be made for the immediate benefits of pretend play, such that pretending in childhood is related to children's self-efficacy associated with their enactment of omnipotent social roles. For example, pretending to be a powerful adult or a superhero may afford opportunities for children to try out a number of different roles that, in reality, are not available to them. As with locomotor play, the benefits end when the play ends. Also in each case, the specific behaviors involved, whether they are repetitive movements or pretend role-playing, are unique to childhood and beneficial to that period.

Play as an Accelerated Developmental Benefit

The final possibility is that play accelerates normal development, as illustrated in Figure 6.4. In this case, the individual, under normal conditions, will develop

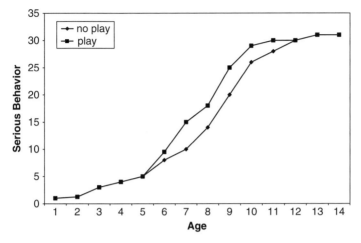

Figure 6.4   Play accelerated development model

a skill, with or without play. Play simply accelerates the development of that skill; thus, the benefits are also rather immediate, and short-term. This model also demonstrates a very important assumption, that there are multiple routes to competence, which is labeled by systems theorists (Bertalanffy, 1968) as "equifinality." From this view there is an individual skill to be learned (such as becoming literate) and there are a multitude of paths to this outcome.

In one case, a child may become literate through pretend play with one's peers. That is, in social pretend play, children learn to symbolically represent one thing for another and to reflect on the meaning and structure of language, skills that predict children's ability to use letters and words to represent meaning (Pellegrini & Galda, 1991). In another, equivalent case, a child can become literate without play and primarily through adult guidance. Examples of different pathways to literacy have been illustrated by Harold Stevenson and colleagues (Stevenson & Lee, 1990) in their comparisons among Taiwanese, Japanese, and American children. In the first two cases, children became literate with very little adult–child book reading; whereas in the United States, book reading is an important precursor to literacy (Bus, vanIJzendoorn, & Pellegrini, 1995).

As noted under each model, it is probably the case that different forms of play have different functions, and they depend on the ecological niche in which individuals develop. In order to understand function more fully, it should be clear from the above discussion that we need to also consider ontogeny, or the place of function during different periods of development. For example and as discussed above, play can serve different functions at different periods. It thus becomes very important in the discussion of function to determine the impact of different experiences at different periods of development. In the next section I will outline Niko Tinbergen's (1963) "Four Questions," one of which refers to function, which should be asked when trying to understand any behavior.

The "Four Whys"

As noted earlier, Niko Tinbergen, along with Konrad Lorenz and Otto von Frisch, shared the Nobel Prize in Physiology or Medicine in 1973 for their work in the biological study of behavior, or ethology. Tinbergen and Lorenz initially shared an interest in "instinctual" behavior. Instinct, or relatively uniform behavioral patterns, labeled "fixed action patterns," as defined by Tinbergen (1969), occurs in organisms at a very young age, trigged by a specific environmental cue, and with minimal learning. A classic example of "instinctual" behavior includes the imprinting demonstrated by Lorenz's (1969) goslings. In this case, goslings would follow the first animate beings they observed post-hatching. Imprinting, for Lorenz, was an instinctual behavior observed during a "critical period" in development and would work to support goslings' survival by ensuring that they stayed close to mother. Lorenz continued to hold to the idea that instinct was relatively fixed by nature with little room for plasticity of response and learning. He also held that these critical periods were relatively immutable: Opportunity to reap the function of the instinctual behavior would be taken during that point, or lost.

Tinbergen, with time, came to a different conclusion. He showed how seemingly instinctual behavior could be influenced by experiences during the ontogenetic development of an organism. For example, he showed how the timing and the function of a stickleback's attacking of red stimuli was modifiable. Subsequent work with filial imprinting in birds supported Tinbergen's views (e.g., Bateson, 1964). Furthermore, it has been shown how imprinting is influenced by experiential factors, such as hearing species-typical calls prenatally (Gottlieb, 1976; 1997). Further early imprinting experiences are not as permanent as Lorenz proposed (Cairns, 1979).

All of this is background for Tinbergen's proposal that, in order to fully understand function, researchers need to address four questions: How did the behavior develop ontogenetically? What are its immediate causes? How did it develop phylogenetically? What is its function? The answer to the final question is dependent on the other three.

In terms of the first, ontogenetic, question, it is important to chart the forms of play across ontogenetic development. What are its forms at different points in development? When does it start? Finish? Take locomotor play: It is probably the case that in infancy it takes the form of rhythmic stereotypies, and during childhood, it takes the form of exercise play (Pellegrini & Smith, 1998). Phylogenetically, we see that similar forms of behavior are observed in nonhuman animal species as well (Pellegrini & Smith, 1998; Stamps, 1995). The different forms of play at different periods of ontogeny probably also have different functions. As noted above, it is probably the case that some forms of play, such as exercise play, have immediate benefits, while others, such as R&T, have deferred benefits.

Immediate causes can be environmental, such as a spacious environment, and hormonal, such as the effects of androgens, generally, and testosterone, specifically. From this question, males and females have different environments in which to develop. Both hormonal and socialization events conspire to affect males' and females' play behavior and subsequent adult behavior. The different adult reproductive and social roles (i.e., adult function) for males and females should, in turn, relate to different immediate causes and ontogenetic and phylogenetic histories of play experiences for males and females.

More specifically, sex hormonal events during the perinatal period differentiate the amygdala and hypothalamus of males and females (Hines & Shipley, 1984), and both of these brain structures, in turn, affect social behavior, generally (Collaer and Hines, 1995) and play behavior, more specifically (Lewis & Barton, 2006). Indeed, the relative size of the amygdala and the hypothalamus are related to the frequency of social play in a variety of nonhuman primates (Lewis & Barton, 2006). It has been suggested that the development of the amygdala and the hypothalamus are especially important in sexually differentiated play behavior, such as R&T, and, relatedly, the ability to read facial expressions marking play.

SEX AND FUNCTION

Sex affects the expression of different types of play behavior, and correspondingly, the putative functions and ontogenetic and phylogenetic development of these behaviors. Sexual selection theory, as articulated by (Darwin, 1872), is certainly one powerful heuristic for examining and explaining sex differences in behavior generally (e.g., Archer & Lloyd, 2000) and in play specifically (e.g., Pellegrini, 2008).

Very generally, sexual selection theory predicts that adult reproductive roles shape the development of behaviors across the life span. In keeping with the position of this book, however, I also stress that the expression of any behavior is moderated by the individual's ecological niche. This is not to say that phylogenetic history is irrelevant. Certainly it is not. More specifically and importantly for the argument I will be making in this chapter, Wrangham (1987) has demonstrated that many features of human social organization share a common ancestry with African apes. Humans, like gorillas, chimpanzees, bonobos, and orangutans, have males having sexual relationships with multiple females and females migrating out of their natal groups. These differences in social organization, I will argue, have implications for sex differences in children's play.

In the next section I present a model for sex differences in the expression of play behaviors, their antecedents (primarily in the form of segregated juvenile peer groups) and subsequent functions. Guided by sexual selection and more recent theory, such as the theories of inclusive fitness (Hamilton, 1964), parental investment (Trivers, 1972), and social role theories (Eagly, 1997), I suggest that sex differences in play have antecedents in the mating systems of society (where males take multiple mates), male residency and female dispersion patterns, and the subsequent organizational effects of hormones on males and females. These initial differences are affected, in turn, by socialization in segregated sex peer groups during the preschool years.

Sexual Selection Theory

Sexual section theory, as proposed by Darwin (1871) and later refined by Trivers (1972), recognized explicit differences between males and females, especially in terms of morphology, with males generally being physically bigger, stronger, and having more visual "armature," such as prominent canines, antlers, and horns, than do females. For example, Darwin observed that males of many (but not all) species tend to be bigger, more physically active, and more physically aggressive than females. Darwin also pointed out that differences in size, aggression, and levels of vigorous behavior seemed to be related to differences in mating strategies. Specifically, in societies where males have multiple mates, such as polygynous (where males have many mates), relative to monogamous (where males and females form stable pair bonds) species, males are larger, more physically vigorous, and also more competitive.

Multiple males' competing with each other for access to single females is an important ecological antecedent to sex differences in morphology and behavior. Indeed, the need to be competitive results in males' being physically larger (i.e., sexual dimorphism in size) and more aggressive than females. Males' reproductive role in most polygynous contexts means that they invest more time and energy in competition with other males for mates and less time provisioning offspring than do females. Males, in this view, who hold substantial resources, as evidenced by their physical size and strength, should be able to defeat their competitors for access to mates. Furthermore, their resource-holding power should also lead them to be attractive to, and chosen by, females as mates. As I will discuss, this has implications for the sex differences in children's physical activity and aggression, such that juvenile males' play behavior is more physically vigorous and competitive (Pellegrini & Archer, 2005).

Females in polygynous relationships, by comparison, invest more in their offspring than males do. After all, they not only incur the cost of bearing the fetus to birth, but they must also protect and provision it until it is self-sufficient, or at least mobile. In the case of mammals generally, and primates specifically, this amounts to a substantial time and energy investment for females. Females, in this system, try to choose the fittest males to contribute "good genes" to their offspring and also to help with (especially) protection and possibly provisioning. This, too, has implications for females' play where juveniles play at mothering (Pusey, 1990).

Related to the importance of polygyny for males' and females' reproductive behavior is the role of male residency and female dispersal. For example, in the case of many human societies, as well as in chimpanzees and bonobos, females at maturity migrate out of their natal groups, while males remain in these groups (Wrangham, 1987; Wrangham, Chapman, Clark-Arcadi, & Isabirye-Basuta, 1996). The implication of these patterns is that males are more gregarious than females, and their social groups are organized hierarchically, in dominance hierarchies (Wrangham, 1987). As juveniles, both chimpanzees (Mitani, Merriweather, & Zhang, 2000) and humans alike (Pellegrini, 2004a; Pellegrini, Long, et al., 2007), segregate into same-sex groups to learn and practice the social skills associated with their adult reproductive roles. For example, in the case of chimps, male juveniles learn predation and dominance-relevant skills (Mitani et al., 2000) and females learn to handle infants (Pusey, 1990). A similar pattern holds, as we will discuss below, for human juveniles, where male groups are characterized by R&T (Pellegrini & Smith, 1998) and dominance-related interactions (Pellegrini, Roseth et al., 2007) and female groups are more sedentary, less aggressive (Pellegrini, Long, et al., 2007) and play has domestic themes (Garvey, 1990).

Consistent with theory, the converse also seems to be true, as in cases where reproductive roles are reversed (i.e., where males take on much care of offspring, relative to females). The best examples of these cases come from polyandrous (females take many mates) shore birds, such as the spotted sandpiper, *Actitis macularia* (Erckmann 1983) and the American Jacana, *Jacana spinosa* (Jenni, 1974). In these species, predictions hold: Females are larger than males, there is sexual segregation, and there is intra-sexual female competition where females are more aggressive than males.

There are also other cases of polyandry. Some bats and Australian marsupials have larger females and segregate by sex (e.g., Altringham & Senior, 2002; Altringham, personal communication, 18 April 2003; MacFarlane & Coulson, 2002). In Syrian golden hamsters, females are also larger and more aggressive than males (Pellis, personal communication, 21 April 2003; Siegel, 1985). These comparisons must be qualified, however, as these questions have not been thoroughly studied, to my knowledge (also see Ralls, 1976).

These examples illustrating the importance of mating systems and dispersal patterns for both adult role and juvenile behavior should serve as an important reminder to scholars choosing to compare human behavior to the behavior of other species. The choice of a comparison species is crucial. In the case of humans, closeness of a species both in terms of the DNA evidence as well as similarities of the mating and dispersal systems are important moderators of both social behavior and social organization. From this vantage point, comparing humans with the great apes is appropriate (McGrew, 1981; Pellegrini & Smith, 2005; de Waal & Lanting, 1997; Wrangham, 1987).

In the case of humans (as well as the great apes) (Pellegrini, 2004a), competition and direct aggression are especially evident when there is a shortage of females, and in polygynous mating systems. In the case of polygyny, there is greater variation in males' than females' reproductive success: One male copulates with a number of females, with the result that males compete with each other for the chance to mate with a limited number of females. This probably causes males to be more competitive and aggressive (direct) than females. Females, in turn, invest more in their offspring and are more nurturing than the males. The skills relevant to these adult reproductive roles should be learned in and developed in juvenile sex-segregated groups.

Darwin also suggested that females had an active role in securing mates; they were not passive pawns in the male reproductive game (see also Campbell, 2002; Smuts, 1987; 1995). Females' reproductive strategies relate to their actively choosing the best mates, and this often involves manipulating social relationships, such as alliances, to access mates and to protect themselves and their offspring.

Females' use of indirect and relational aggression is consistent with this view (Campbell, 1999).

Darwin could not, however, determine why males were competitive and females choosy, and not *vice versa.* Based on the earlier work of Bateman (1948), Trivers (1971) suggested that differences in parental investment are responsible for a number of sex differences, including levels of types of aggression, in different species. The basic consideration that sex is inexpensive for males (i.e., one-off mating efforts and no offspring care) and expensive for females (mating efforts, gestation, and provisioning and care of infants/juveniles) leads to the general rule that female investment leads to female choosiness and concerns with maximizing investment in offspring. Females are therefore likely to choose a male based on resource-holding power, such as physically attractive and physically large. Females also are less likely than males to risk harm or danger, in the form of direct competition, because it would compromise their ability to provision and protect their offspring. Females are therefore more concerned with "staying alive" (Campbell, 1999; 2002).

Behaviorally, this means that females in these species use more indirect and safer strategies to access and protect resources than males do. Males, on the other hand, are much less choosy in mating. This view is also supported by Buss's (1989) findings on human males' tendency toward promiscuity. The strategy of frequent mating and lack of paternal investment results in intra-sexual competition for mates, sexual dimorphism, and differences in R&T, social dominance, and aggression. The patterns related to mating strategies, competitiveness, and uses of different forms of aggression, however, are related to the environment in which individuals develop.

Sexually Segregated Groups as Proximal Cause for Differences in Play

Sexually segregated peer groups during the juvenile period provide the proximal context through which juveniles express their biological heritage, such as high or low levels of physical activity, and socialization biases to learn and practice in play those skills relevant to their specific niche and to subsequent adult reproductive roles. Given the different reproductive roles of males and females, especially in polygynous societies, sex differences are important and, correspondingly, are expressed in sexually segregated peer groups.

More specifically, males' early bias toward physically active behavior (Eaton & Inns, 1986) is an antecedent to rough and physically vigorous behaviors, such as exercise play, R&T, and aggression, which are learned and practiced in sexually segregated peer groups (Pellegrini, 2004a; Pellegrini, Long, et al., 2007). These behaviors are probably functional in terms of learning motor skills associated with males' competitive reproductive roles. In terms of more immediate function, they are also probably important for juveniles' social affiliation, cardiovascular fitness, and muscle/skeleton development (Byers & Walker, 1995; Pellegrini & Smith, 1998). Females avoid these active behaviors and interact with each other because they find vigorous behavior, especially in the presence of males, to be aversive and possibly dangerous. In these segregated groups, males and females learn and practice, possibly through observational learning and reinforcement (Boyd & Richerson, 1985), the social roles associated being an adult male or female.

More specific to the nature of sex segregation, it is important to note that in the animal literature it is labeled *social segregation* (Conradt, 1998; 2005) when it is used in the way I do here—to describe the sex composition of peer groups. Degree of segregation is often assayed in a variety of different ways. For example, it has been measured by the proportion of male or female preschool children in a group (e.g., Pellegrini & Long, 2003). It has also been measured in a study of early adolescents observed in a variety of unstructured venues (e.g., hallways, cafeteria, dances) the proportion of males: males + females in focal males' groups ranged from .92 to .77 across two years of observation (Pellegrini & Long, 2003).

Additionally, segregation can be measured more categorically. For example, in a study of primary school children's playground behavior, segregation was measured as presence in "mostly" segregated (where 60% or more were of the same sex) or "mixed" (where 40% or less were of the same sex) groups (Blatchford, Baines, & Pellegrini, 2003); both boys and girls were observed in the "mostly" segregated groups in 80% of the observations. Lastly, some scholars have defined and measured segregation more absolutely—whether the group was the same or mixed-sex and found that 39% and 40% of male and female groups, respectively, were segregated, or same-sex (Fabes, Martin, Hanish, Anders, & Madden-Derdich, 2003). Clearly, it is important to attend to the metric used in the research, given the variety used.

Difference in level of physical activity is an important condition that affects sexual segregation and the correspondingly different forms of play behavior in children's peer groups. Individual males and male groups are more physically more vigorous and competitive than females as individuals or in groups (Pellegrini, 2004a; Pellegrini, Kato, Blatchford, & Baines, 2002; Pellegrini, Long, et al., 2007). It is in these sexually segregated groups that different uses of rough and competitive social and locomotor play are learned and developed. This difference continues at both the individual and group levels throughout the juvenile period, despite sex differences in maturation (Eaton & Yu, 1989; Pellegrini, 2002).

That males are more active than females is probably due, following sexual selection theory, to their larger size (as adults) and corresponding need to develop skeletal, muscular, and neural systems associated with this difference (Pellegrini & Smith, 1998). These vigorous behaviors, in turn, relate to males' social roles as adults. Specifically, the vigorous activity characteristic of juvenile males' groups is related to the development of neural (cerebellar) and muscular systems used in behaviors associated with fighting and predation (Byers & Walker, 1995). Additionally, similarity in activity preference also relates, more immediately, to peer affiliation. Consequently, males use segregated groups, not only to affiliate with each other as they engage in vigorous physical exercise (Pellegrini, Horvat, & Huberty, 1998; Pellegrini, Long, et al., 2007) and competitive games (Pellegrini et al., 2002), but also to practice behaviors and roles related to physical aggression and dominance relationships during adolescence (Pellegrini & Long, 2003; Pellegrini & Long, 2007).

That most males are also highly active, relative to females, probably relates to more immediate functions being associated with physically vigorous play. Specifically, and as will be discussed below, the behavioral compatibility hypothesis for sex segregation states that same-sex juveniles interact and affiliate with each other because they have similar behavioral styles; they find similar levels of activity enjoyable, maximally motivating them for sustained engagement and corresponding skill development. In this view, behavioral compatibility probably motivates individuals to affiliate with peers having similar activity biases. As will be discussed below, the ways in which children are socialized moderates this activity bias.

There are numerous possible explanations for these differences in activity, but exposure to androgens prenatally has been proffered as one of the proximal mechanisms by which selection pressure is exerted and results in sex differences in physical activity (Archer & Lloyd, 2002). These hormonal differences, interacting dynamically with social reinforcement and modeling, may be responsible for males' preference for high-activity behaviors (Campbell et al., 2000; Pellegrini, Long, et al., 2007) and sex segregation (Martin & Fabes, 2001; Pellegrini, 2004a; Pellegrini, Long, et al., 2007).

More specifically, physical activity is an important influence on sex segregation (Campbell & Eaton, 1999; Eaton & Enns, 1986; Eaton & Yu, 1989; Martin & Fabes, 2001), but I also stress that culturally related sex role socialization practices probably moderate the role of physical activity in segregation (Huston, 1983). Early and persistent sex differences in physical activity, where males are more active than females, should bias physically active children to interact with each other, but socialization practices also interact with physical activity to affect segregation (Archer & Lloyd, 2000; Pellegrini, 2004a).

Consistent with social role theory (Archer & Lloyd, 2002; Eagly, 1997), male roles in contemporary society are higher–status than female roles, so males may be more reluctant to integrate than girls. Girls, on the other hand, should be more willing than boys to interact with opposite-sex peers because of boys' relatively higher status. Evidence supporting this argument comes from the finding that boys are more reluctant than girls to play with sex-role inappropriate toys (Serbin, Connor, Burchardt, & Citron, 1979) and have been socialized away from female roles and into male roles (Huston, 1983).

By extension, individual differences within each sex and differing socialization events impact sex segregation (Archer & Lloyd, 2002; Berenbaum & Snyder, 1995; Fabes, 1994; Maccoby & Jacklin, 1987; Martin & Fabes, 2001; Pellegrini, 2004a; Serbin, Moller, Gulko, Powlishta, & Colburne, 1994) such that some boys and some girls are more or less active than their same-sex peers, and these differences impact their degree of sex segregation. Highly active children of both sexes should be biased to interact with each other relatively early in the history of group formation because of behavioral compatibility (Ruckstuhl, 1998; Serbin et al., 1994) but this bias probably changes with time, due to socialization pressure.

Boys' and girls' different levels of sex segregation across the preschool period generally garners support from Legault and Strayer's (1990) observations that young (15–36 months of age) preschool girls, relative to boys, sexually segregated earlier in the school year. One hypothesis is that most girls, but especially low-activity girls, are repelled by high levels of activity, leading the high-activity girls to interact with boys, at least in the early phases of group formation, such as at the start of the school year; then to interacting with other girls as boys discourage integration. However, less-active females may also find the behavior of these high-activity-level girls noxious, leading the high-activity girls to keep to themselves, separate from both boys and low-activity girls. In this view, it is too general to document sex segregation solely in terms of boys interacting only with boys or girls only with girls. High-activity girls should interact with boys initially, but socialization pressures should lead them out of mixed-sex groups and into segregated groups with only other high-activity girls.

In our research we examined this sort of interaction between socialization and activity bias. Specifically, we studied preschool children in the University of Minnesota lab school throughout one academic year and showed that boys' and girls' peer groups were generally segregated, with segregation being defined as the ratio of same-sex / same + opposite-sex children in children's immediate peer group during each scan sample (Pellegrini, Long, et al., 2007). The segregation finding was apparent relatively early in the school year and remained so throughout the year. Segregation, however, was affected by the sex of the child and their levels of physical activity (observed and recorded simultaneously with the segregation information), as well as time of the year. Specifically, boys at all levels of physical activity, remained at relatively stable levels of segregation across the duration of the study. That high- and low-activity boys' level of segregation was stable is consistent with social role theory, among others, proposing that boys interacted with each other, rather than girls, because of their relatively high status.

High-activity girls started off the year interacting in integrated groups, possibly because their behavior was more compatible with boys' than with low-activity girls. As the year progressed, however, the high-activity girls became more segregated among themselves. This may have been due to their being expelled from boys' groups or leaving voluntarily (Lagault and Strayer, 1990). In short, highly active girls began the school year playing with boys possibly because of the compatibility of their behavioral styles and as the year progressed, socialization pressures may have moved these highly active girls into sex segregated groups.

Social role theory posits that boys (both high and low activity levels) may have been reluctant to interact with lower-status girls. This point is consistent with our finding that boys' segregation was more stable across the year than girls'. High-activity girls may have been, in turn, excluded from interacting with low-activity girls, possibly because of behavioral incompatibility, and interacted in segregated groups of high-activity girls. These trends, for both high- and low-activity boys and girls are displayed in the four panels in Figure 6.5.

Importantly, these results suggest a dynamic relationship between biology (physical activity) and socialization (differing role status of boys and girls).

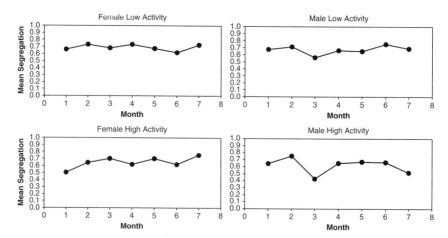

Figure 6.5   Mean segregation as a function of sex and median split of activity

From this view, physical activity alone does not lead to segregation. Consistent with the behavioral compatibility hypothesis, physical activity probably biased high-activity girls and boys to interact early in the school year. As the year progressed, however, socialization pressures may have resulted in either boys excluding lower-status girls from their groups or girls choosing to leave, even though they were active. For different reasons (i.e., behavioral incompatibility) these highly active girls may also have been excluded from or left groups of low-activity girls, thus forcing them to interact among themselves in segregated groups. This finding highlights the importance of specifying theoretically derived interactions between biological and socialization factors.

I must qualify this explanation, however, by stressing that the relationship between physical activity and sex segregation is a dynamic one and one where we are unable to specify directionality: Physical activity and sex segregation affect each other across time, and we do not make dichotomous judgments about the role of either biology (e.g., in the form of physical activity) or socialization (e.g., differential reinforcement) in this relationship. While the specific ways in which physical activity and social context interact are important to understand, it is not an easy task to untangle effects. For example, it is very difficult to determine the extent to which one factor is either an antecedent to or consequence of the other. Comparative, experimental research may be useful in untangling the directionality of effects. For example, and following Suomi's (2005) research described in Chapter 4, monkeys could be bred for high or low levels of physical activity and then observed in male and female peer groups.

Additionally, extant research suggests that there are other dimensions of behavior besides physical activity, such as R&T, which might be responsible for sex segregation (Fabes & Martin, 2003; Maccoby, 1998). From this view, the rough and quasi-aggressive behaviors associated with R&T may be noxious to girls and motivate them to interact in segregated groups. Alternatively, it may be the case that physical activity mediates the relationship between R&T and segregation because physical activity is significantly related to R&T ($r = .50$, $p < .005$, Martin & Fabes, 2001; $r = .48$, $p < .01$, Pellegrini, 1993) and segregation, as found in this study and in Martin & Fabes (2001). In our work in the university lab school, we could not test this hypothesis as we observed only very low levels of R&T. Perhaps this reflected school policy discouraging this sort of vigorous and quasi-agonistic behavior. It may be necessary to observe children in settings where R&T is more readily tolerated, and thus adequately sampled, as was the case in Martin and Fabes (2001).

CONCLUSION

The function of play is elusive. In some quarters play is a panacea for the early education and development of children. In others it is dismissed as pointless. Part of the reason for such wildly different claims is due to the fact that *function* is defined differently in a variety of fields. Perhaps most important, from my point of view, is that function should be considered along three possible different dimensions: immediate, deferred, and accelerated benefits. The extent to which any of these benefits is realized depends, not only on the form of play, but also on the ecology in which the individual is developing. Immediate and accelerated benefits are more likely to be associated with severe ecologies, given survivorship risks. By contrast, deferred benefits are more likely in abundance ecologies.

With this said, certain forms of play may have both immediate and deferred benefits during childhood. Specifically and as discussed above, take the case of social and pretend play. The immediate benefits probably relate to peer affiliation and bonding. That boys and girls have early and different activity levels biases them to play in sex-segregated groups, where this affiliation occurs. Deferred benefits are probably related to their adult reproductive roles, which are differentially socialized for boys and girls.

Specifically, for boys, rough and vigorous social play probably relates to their social dominance. Social dominance also serves a distal function because it relates to mate access and fitness in a variety of species, including humans (e.g., Buss, 1989; Noorwick & Van Schaik, 2004; Pusey, Williams, & Goodall, 1997). While fitness is obviously not an immediate, primary concern for preschool children, social dominance is relevant when we consider social dominance in terms of "competitiveness," or competing for resources, as well as physical conditioning. Specifically, and consistent with life history theory, an optimal strategy for preschoolers living in a stable and abundant ecology involves relatively high levels of competitiveness, which, in turn, should lead to increased physical activity, physical size, and fitness (Alexander et al., 1979; Lessells, 1991; Pellegrini, 2004).

As will be discussed in the chapter on social play, preschoolers' physical size has been linked theoretically and empirically, in some studies, to social dominance, or the ability to access and maintain resources (Pellegrini et al., 2007; Tremblay et al., 1993; for support, Hawley & Little, 1999). Thus, both locomotor and social play and related social dominance encounters in preschool may have immediate beneficial consequences, such as physical fitness and self efficacy, and these, in turn, should relate to ultimate function.

For girls too, play probably serves both immediate and deferred benefits, depending on the ecology. Like boys, girls play in sex-segregated groups based on both physical activity bias and socialization practices. Also like boys', social and pretend play has an immediate affiliative benefit of peer affiliation embedded in sex-segregated groups. The themes enacted in these groups follow adult reproductive roles, such that girls' typically enact domestic themes. Furthermore, girls' physically vigorous play, in the form of jumping, has both immediate and long-term benefits in terms of increasing bone mineral content in childhood (Gunter et al., 2008) and adolescence (Weeks et al., 2008).

Following from a sexual selection position, same-sex peers, in their segregated groups, compete with each other for status and control of resources, where the dominant members have preferred resource control, relative to less dominant individuals. More specifically, both females and males compete intra-sexually but using different strategies. Males' competition should be more direct and involve physical and aggressive strategies (Campbell, 1999; Pellegrini & Long, 2003; Savin-Williams, 1987), while females' should be less direct and involve using physical attractiveness, social ostracism, and ridicule (Campbell, 1999; Savin-Williams, 1987). From these competitions, theory predicts, females choose dominant males (Darwin, 1871).

Empirically, there is only equivocal support for the proposition that there are sex differences in play behaviors used in social dominance encounters. While males are more competitive and physically aggressive (Pellegrini & Archer, 2005), and female use less direct forms of aggression, especially in late childhood and adolescence (e.g., Savin-Williams, 1987), sex differences in the context of using these strategies to access resources has not generally been observed during early childhood, but becomes more apparent in adolescence (e.g., Savin-Williams, 1987). This may be due to the fact that many of the preschool samples are university-affiliated and therefore relatively low on rates of physical aggression.

The case is different during adolescence. Savin-Williams' (1987) study of adolescent males and females at summer camp showed that girls' antagonism was less direct than boys'. He also noted that dominant girls' tended to be tolerant and complimentary of their peers, perhaps as a way to build a strong peer network. Consistent with this idea, he found that females' dominance was ordered in a less hierarchical fashion than males'. Girls shared places in a dominance order, often with their friends. These findings are consistent with the idea of the use of alliances in social dominance (e.g., Roseth, 2006; de Waal, 1982).

So, to answer the question "What is the function of play?" It depends! It depends on how you define function, when, and for whom.

7

Social Play

In this chapter I examine the development and possible functions of social play in humans. Social play takes the form of interaction between children and adults and between children themselves, with the earliest forms of play occurring between children and adults, typically parents (Power, 2000), as part of their more general social interaction. For example, mothers playing peek-a-boo with their infants is one of the earliest, and pan-cultural, forms of social play (Bruner & Sherwood, 1976; Fernald & O'Neil, 1993). In peek-a-boo play, mothers and babies engage in routinized interactions typified by unpredictability (for the baby at least) in vocalizations, expectations, and facial expressions (Fernald & O'Neill, 1993), and high positive affect, some of the basic hallmarks of play, as I and others (e.g., Lillard, 2007), have defined it. Similar structural dimensions typify the social play between peers, whether that play revolves around themes of playfighting or domestic roles. Indeed, many major theorists (e.g., Bandura, 1986; Bowlby, 1969; Harlow, 1962; Trivers, 1972) suggest continuity between parent–child interaction and children's subsequent peer interactions, relationships, and group participation. That is, social interactions between infants and their parents are important for subsequent, competent social interaction, due to social learning, the nature of attachment relationships between the two, or some combination of both. For this reason, I will begin this chapter on social play with a discussion of parent–child play.

ADULT–CHILD PLAY

Adults generally, and mothers specifically, are often considered to be young children's very first "playmates." Mothers' role in children's social emotional development is assigned very high status indeed from theorists of a variety of stripes. At least since Freud (1940) described the mother–child relationship as unique, theorists have ascribed importance (e.g., Isaacs, 1972), though some would say undue importance and burden (Patterson, 1980), to their role in children's subsequent development. A problem associated with the study of social play involving both adults and children and peers is that many writers do not differentiate interactions which are "play," as defined in this book, from those more general forms of social interaction, which are not. Recall from our earlier discussion of definitions of play that all social interactions involving juveniles and between juveniles and adults are sometimes considered play by the simple fact that juveniles are involved. To avoid this problem, in this chapter I will attempt to address only the aspects of social behavior that clearly, for me at least, appear to be play, as displayed in Figure 7.1.

Regarding the play between juveniles and adults in most mammals, it typically involves kin, most often mothers and their offspring. Mother–offspring play among human and nonhuman primates provides some of the best examples. The examples of play between rhesus monkey mothers and offspring provided by Harlow (1962) and Suomi (Biben & Suomi, 1993; Suomi, 2002) and those between human mothers and their children provided by MacDonald and Parke (1984; 1986) show the relative similarity in the structure of the behavior across these primate species. Most commonly, in the human and nonhuman cases we observe exaggerated movements and the irregular patterning of those behaviors. Perhaps most importantly, in adult–child play the adults also engage in self-handicapping behavior. For example, they tend to make themselves weaker or slower so that the child too can get a chance to enact a variety of roles. Witness examples of fathers standing on their knees when wrestling with their sons and the ease with which they are toppled by their smaller and younger playmates. Adults

Figure 7.1   Mother and Juvenile chimp Play (Photo: Kerrie Lewis)

probably self-handicap as a way to keep children engaged in the play activity. Continued participation in a variety of social play themes probably helps children become socially competent, in a way similar to Vygotsky's (1978) idea of the zone of proximal development. Correspondingly, adults' behavior is guided by their aim to maximize children's participation in activities. The more competent children become, the less adults have to self-handicap to maintain children's participation. If adults did not self-handicap, children would very soon become uninterested because they would always be on the losing end. This lack of opportunity to play, in turn, would adversely affect social skills learning.

Why would parents waste their time and energy doing this sort of thing, you might ask? From an inclusive fitness perspective (Hamilton, 1964), it make sense that parents invest resources in their offspring to maximize the likelihood of their survival and eventual reproduction. That mothers' and fathers' genes (50% from the mother and 50% from the father) constitute their offspring's genetic endowment means that they will spend time and energy provisioning, protecting, teaching, and playing with their progeny to support their development and eventual reproduction. On the other hand, the offspring has genetic material unrelated to its mother (the other 50%). This, as will be discussed later in this chapter, leads to a conflict of interest between mothers and offspring, as they each try to maximize their own fitness (Trivers, 1972). So, eventually children will continue to try to "exploit" mothers' resources for their own ends and the mother will pull away from their children, to safeguard her resources for other offspring.

The quantity and quality of children's play with their parents also depends on their ecological niche. In many human societies adults do not play with children directly, nor direct the play of children's play with their peers (Lancy, 1996; Rogoff, Göncü, Mistry, & Mosier, 1993). In many traditional societies, as soon as children are mobile they interact with their peers in mixed aged groups and are attended to by older children, typically older girls. Parents usually spend their time protecting and provisioning their offspring, rather than playing with them.

That social play often occurs along with other forms of social interaction and other forms of play makes decisions about what counts as social play, as distinct from other forms of interaction such as comfort hugging or didactic interaction, less than clear-cut. Regarding different forms of play, in an earlier paper Peter Smith and I (Pellegrini & Smith, 1998) treated rough-and-tumble play (R&T) as a form of locomotor play. R&T is a form of play that is both social and locomotive, as it occurs with peers and adults, and it is also physically vigorous, as it has physical training benefits (Bekoff, 1988). Similarly R&T co-occurs with pretend play (Pellegrini & Perlmutter, 1987). Indeed, in their chapter on play Rubin and colleagues (1983, p. 723) use enacting *Star Wars* roles as an example of social pretending, not R&T. Correspondingly, Saltz and colleagues (Saltz et al., 1977), in their classic study of children's pretend play, parsed children's make-believe play into two categories: thematic fantasy play and social dramatic play. In the former case, children, mostly boys, enacted pretend roles associated with super-heroes, typified by playfighting, jumping, and running. Social dramatic play, by contrast, is more sedentary and involves enactments of social domestic roles, such as mothers and fathers (Garvey, 1990).

In this book, however, R&T will be treated primarily as social play because R&T must be social, by definition, while its levels of physical vigor are less important (Pellegrini, 2002). Indeed, in some treatments of "social play" only R&T is covered (e.g., Fry, 2005) because of the difficulty of disambiguating it from other forms of play and from other forms of social interaction. In this argument, social play will be defined in terms of R&T between children and between children and adults. Correspondingly, in separate chapters I will discuss the social and nonsocial aspects of pretend play and object play. I begin with a discussion of adult–child social play, generally, followed by discussions peer R&T.

Theoretical Bases

As noted above, many theories of social development assume that mother–child interaction is the base on which subsequent social relationships arc built. More specifically to mother–child play, rather than more general social interaction, Marc Bornstein and Catherine Tamis-LaMonda (1993) in their important review of parent–child symbolic play, present three theories that explain mothers' roles in facilitating children's subsequent play: attachment, ethology, and scaffolding. Scaffolding, as applied to mother–child interaction (Wood, Bruner, & Ross, 1976), is rooted in Vygotsky's theory (1962; 1976) that children's development is spurred by adults providing just enough support to maximize children's participation in social tasks. I will first cover attachment and ethological, evolutionary-oriented, theory, and then scaffolding.

Attachment and Evolutionary-oriented Theory

Attachment theory is based on Bowlby's (1969) melding of the ethological and psychoanalytical literatures. As noted above, Freud afforded the mother *the* primary role in children's social-emotional development. Correspondingly, Bowlby was impressed with both Lorenz's (e.g., 1965; 1981) and Harlow's (e.g., 1962) descriptions of early, "critical," periods in the development of nonhuman infants and especially the role of the mother in juveniles' subsequent development. *Attachment* refers to the close relationship between a parent, typically the mother, and child in terms of their affectional ties. Attachment between a child and mother is motivated to maximize the child's survival by having the child maintain proximity to the mother and using the mother as a "secure base" from which to explore the world (Bowlby, 1969).

Patterns of attachment between the child and mother have been characterized as secure, insecure-avoidant, and insecure-resistant/ambivalent (Thompson, 1998). Secure infants use their mothers as secure bases from which to explore the material and social world. These children also respond positively (e.g., smile, proximity-seeking) after mothers return from absence. By contrast, insecure-avoidant infants avoid mothers during reunions while insecure-resistant infants show signs of avoidance during reunion. Additionally, both groups are preoccupied with their mothers before they leave. These classifications will be useful later in our discussions of evolutionary-oriented explanations of differing styles of mother–child play and subsequent peer social play.

I base the discussion of ethological views of parent–child play on the "gene-centered" views of W. D. Hamilton (1964) and Robert Trivers (1972; 1974), which became important bases for other evolutionary-oriented theories of human development, such as sociobiology (e.g., Wilson, 1975) and evolutionary psychology (e.g., Cosmides & Tooby, 1992). Two propositions are crucial here. First, the notion of inclusive fitness proposed that individuals' social interactions are influenced by their degree of kin relatedness so that they can maximize the likelihood that their genes will survive and be passed on to subsequent generations. From this position, that mother and their offspring share 50% of the same genes suggests that they will be more cooperative with each other than in their interactions with other individuals who are less closely related, such as the mother and her nephew, with whom she shares only 25% of the same genes.

An important implication of the theory of inclusive fitness, however, is that mothers and their offspring will also, at some points in development, conflict with each other because they each want to maximize their own fitness, not that of their kin (Trivers, 1972). At some developmental point the fitness of the mother and her offspring actually come into conflict. From this view, mothers, at crucial points in development, will discourage children's interactions because they are "costly" to her in terms of caloric and time demands. For example, a three-year-old child demanding to nurse will be depleting mother's time and energy—resources that might go to a younger offspring. At such points in development, mothers will discourage the older child so that they can provision and protect the younger. Children, on the other hand, will try to exploit as much as their mothers' time and energy as possible so as to maximize their own fitness.

Some behavioral biologists (e.g., Zahavi, 1977), anthropologists (Chisholm, 1996; Chisholm, Burbank, Coall, & Gemmiti, 2005), and psychologists (e.g., Belsky, 2005; Belsky, Steinberg, & Draper, 1991) have proposed that the patterns of mother–child interactions, such as attachment and play behaviors, are the result of general environmental conditions and related mating strategies. In the first case, Zahavi (1977) suggested that mothers' willingness to play with their offspring could be used by their offspring as an indicator, of sorts, of mothers' willingness to contribute to their greater well-being.

Not dissimilarly, both Jim Chisholm and Jay Belsky and their colleagues suggest that the nature of the mother–child attachment relationship reflects the broader ecological niche of the mother–child relationship. Both of these positions are based explicitly on Trivers's (1974) proposal that the conflict of interest between mothers' and offspring's fitness affects mothers' willingness to invest in their offspring, and these decisions are based on mating strategies. Belsky and colleagues have taken the idea of K-selected (such as primates) and r-selected species (such as insects) (Wilson, 1975) to characterize the strategies that some parents use in response to environmental stability and stress. Belsky and colleagues (1991) suggest that mothers' highly invested in their offspring utilize strategies typical of K-selected species. K-selected species typically inhabit rather stable and enriched niches. Reflecting this stability and abundance, mothers have relatively few offspring and invest highly in each—assuming that their investment will "pay off" in terms of their offspring's surviving and reproducing.

In less stable and more impoverished niches, on the other hand, Belsky and colleagues suggest that mothers enlist strategies typical of *r*-selected species, where they invest minimally in offspring and instead invest in maximizing the number of births. Quantity of offspring is stressed rather than providing for the quality of each. In this pattern, insecurely attached children would typify the latter condition and secure attachment the former. Behavioral ecologically–oriented field work with different foraging populations (e.g., Blurton Jones, 1993), as discussed in the chapter on culture, provides empirical support to these claims.

Similarly, Jim Chisholm (1996) advances a life-history theory of attachment that reflects mothers' and children's ecological niche. In this view, organisms try to solve problems during different periods of ontogeny with different strategies. The chosen strategy reflects the optimal solution to the problem at hand. As noted early in this book, an optimal solution is one where benefits outweigh cost. Not unlike Zahavi's (1977) formulation, Chisholm suggests that children can gauge the supportiveness of their environment from their interactions with their mothers. From this, Chisholm predicted that insecure-resistant patterns of attachment resulted from mothers' inability to provision the infant, such as maternal depression or scarce food, while insecure-avoidant attachment resulted from mothers' unwillingness to provision the infant, such as concern with her own survival or another offspring. In this latter case, it might be more adaptive for children to avoid their mother and seek support from others.

For Chisholm, too, secure attachment relationships reflect stable and responsive care-giving. Secure children, in turn, are more willing than their insecure counterparts to explore their environments and take risks, perhaps because their secure attachment relationships buffer them from stressors (Chisholm et al., 2005). Especially interesting from the point of view of a main thesis presented in this book, Chisholm notes that secure attachment relationships moderate children's reaction to stressful and novel situations. As I have argued throughout this book, individuals try to maximize unexpected and unpredictable behaviors and outcomes through play in order to motivate sustained interaction. It may be that securely attached children are the players who *initiate* unpredictable behavioral routines in social play to maximize unpredictability.

Vygotskiian Theory

The role of mothers, adults, or more competent others, generally, in interacting and children's development is afforded a primary place in fostering children's cognitive development in Vygotsky's theory. Vygotsky's sociocultural theory was developed in the context of the newly formed Soviet state and had an explicit aim to formulate an explicitly Marxist psychology and account of human development (Luria, 1976). From this historical position, the role of social position and labor, or activity, were central to that brief (Fromm, 1968). Vygotsky's (1976) construct of the "zone of proximal development" is perhaps the clearest articulation of the ways these forces come together to scaffold children's development.

As is well known, the zone of proximal development is a construct developed by Vygotsky to represent children's competence, where *competence* is defined as the distance between children's levels of independent functioning in a specific task and their level of functioning with the assistance of an adult or a more competent other in that same task.

The role of adults in this model is to maximize children's participation in the cultural practices important to that culture; thus the metaphor of the child as "apprentice" has been used in reference to Vygotskiian theory (e.g., Reeder, Shapiro, Watson, & Goelman, 1996). Correspondingly, the appropriate metric for judging children's competence in the zone of proximal development is not how well they perform a task but the amount of adult support it takes children to participate in the task at hand. More competent children participate in a task with minimal adult support, whereas less competent children require more support, even though both sets of children may complete a task to equal levels of facility (e.g., Pellegrini, Brody, & Sigel, 1985a, b). So, for example, when we observed handicapped and non-handicapped children and their parents engaged in the construction of origami figures from models (Pellegrini et al., 1985b), there was no difference between the two groups of children in terms of the scored quality of their completed origami figures. The groups differed in how these figures were constructed, however. Parents of the handicapped children provided more support than did those of the non-handicapped children. They held their children on their laps, guided their hands while folding, and were less cognitively demanding (e.g., told children what to do, asked low-level questions). Thus, it took more parent support to enable the handicapped children to participate in and complete the task, relative to the non-handicapped children. If we were to only look at differences in the quality of the constructed origami figures, we would have missed this important point.

Consistent with this logic, parents' playful interaction with children should maximize participation and competence so that children's play with a parent should be more sophisticated, relative to their play alone or with peers. Bornstein's (2006) recent review of the parent–child play literature supports this position. Parents not only enjoy playing with their infants and children but they also "scaffold" children's pretending to higher levels than solitary play, consistent with Vygotsky's theory of the zone of proximal development. Also consistent with Vygotsky's theory, and as noted above, mothers seem to adjust their levels of interaction with their children to maximize their participation (Damast, Tamis-LaMonda, & Bornstein, 1996). As in some of my own work (Pellegrini, Perlmutter, Galda, & Brody, 1990), mothers' sensitivity to children's levels of participation was judged using sequential analyses. When children are struggling, mothers increase their support and lower their demands. By contrast, when children meet maternal demands, mothers tend to lower the support and increase the demands of their interactions.

So, parent–child play seems to be rather synchronized, with children and parents each sensitive to the other's behavior in the interest of maintaining the playful interactions and maximizing participation. Yet with all of this said, the extent to which adults, generally, and mothers, specifically, influence the quantity and quality of children's play is still debatable. While some of the literature presents evidence for the importance of mothers' roles in children's play, such as the relationship between attachment status and levels of symbolic play (e.g., Slade, 1987a, b) and the relations between the frequency of father–son R&T and sons' R&T with peers (Carson et al., 1993), a host of other findings do not support this link (see Fein & Fryer, 1995a, b, for reviews).

One of the reasons for this confusion may be the differential importance of adults for children of different ages. For example, in two naturalistic studies of young children in their preschool classrooms, I found that number of adults present correlated positively with the frequency of very young children's (~two-years-of age) pretend play but *negatively* with older children's pretend (Pellegrini, 1984; Pellegrini & Perlmutter, 1989). Younger children need adult support to play, but older ones do not. Indeed, adults may actually inhibit children's play, as implied in some definitions of play (Rubin et al., 1983).

These equivocal findings may also be due, according to Marc Bornstein (2006), to the fact that much of this research only examined the frequency and quality of mothers' play with their children without consideration of children's levels of sophistication. As noted above, different maternal strategies are effective with different children. The microanalytical work of Angeline Lillard and her colleagues has gone a long way towards addressing this concern. That is, the specific behavioral cues used to maintain mother–child interaction have been studied systematically by Lillard (summarized in Lillard, 2006) and her colleagues. Not unlike evidence from the nonhuman play literature, Lillard's findings are that mothers' behaviors signal their young children that "this is play," and children respond accordingly. Like using the "play face" as a signal, mothers smile more when they are pretending with their child than they do in realistic interactions. Furthermore, when pretending, mothers use onomatopoeia, slurping sounds, and exaggerated movements, such as holding a pitcher too high when pretending to pour a drink, to mark play. And, perhaps most obviously, mothers' use of the word "pretend," as in "let's pretend to cook," is a signal to play. Similarly to the notion of the zone of proximal development, Lillard (Lillard & Witherspoon, 2004) has shown that mothers guide children's participation in joint play. Lillard's close observations show that this is accomplished by mothers' paying very close attention to what it is their children are doing. With less experienced players, mothers' pretend actions were slower. Following the idea of the zone of proximal development, the goal of mothers' interactions is to maximize children's participation in play.

In short, mothers and their children seem to be very well attuned to each other during play. This synchrony is probably responsible for children's participation in play with peers.

SOCIAL PLAY WITH PEERS

There is evidence that both the quality of parent–child play and its quantity seem to predict the quality and frequency of children's play with peers. With that said, it also seems to be the case that some forms of peer social play can remediate deficits in early parent–child play. Two oft-cited cases come to mind: The first involves nonhuman primates and the second, children deprived of their parents during World War II.

The nonhuman primate example involves maternally deprived rhesus monkeys in Harry Harlow's lab at the University of Wisconsin. As is well known, Harlow conducted studies into the effects of various sorts of maternal deprivation on offspring behavior. Generally, maternally deprived infants, as juveniles, had a very difficult time with peer relations, often being very aggressive. The females were unwilling to mate, and when they did, they were often unwilling and unable to care for offspring adequately. In a landmark study, Steve Suomi, a student of Harlow's, and Harry Harlow (1972) paired these maladjusted monkeys with younger peers, or "normal" monkeys. They hypothesized that play between the maternally deprived monkeys, who were older, stronger, and less competent and the younger and smaller juveniles, would remediate the older monkeys' social problems. The idea was that by interacting with a nonthreatening conspecific (nonthreatening because they are younger and smaller) who were also socially unskilled, the maladjusted and the younger monkeys could learn socially competent social skills, such as turn-taking and inhibiting aggressive responses, especially during rough-and-tumble play by interacting with each other. This is what happened.

The second example of the importance of peer experiences involves a case presented by Anna Freud and Sophie Dann (1951). In this situation six children were orphaned when their parents were arrested by and executed under the Nazi regime. The children were moved from various orphanages, as well as having survived the concentration camp at Tereszin. After the camp was liberated by the Russians, these six children remained together, as a group, and along with many other, older children who also had survived concentration camps, were taken to England. The six children were taken to Bulldogs Banks in Sussex, England and were cared for by four adults. In the end, Freud and Dann argued that these children invested their "libido" in each other, instead of a parent, and as a result were not aggressive, cognitively delayed, or psychotic.

All of this, of course, is not to say that parent–child play is less important than peer social play, only that social play between peers is very important for social bonding and learning social skills. One of the foundational studies of preschoolers' social interaction and play, and one of the most frequently cited, was conducted by Mildred Parten (1932) as part of her doctoral studies at the University of Minnesota's Institute of Child Welfare. In fact, and perhaps ironically, Parten's study was of children's "social participation," not of play *per se* as we have defined it here. Specifically, Parten proposed a continuum of social participation so as to document differences between a child "actively playing in a group and one who is merely an accidental member" (p. 248). Her famous categories include: unoccupied behavior, onlooker behavior, solitary play, parallel activity, associative play, and cooperative play. Interesting from a definitional point of view, Parten explicitly refers to these categories as reflecting children's *social participation* while sometimes also using the word *play* to describe some of these activities. For example, in defining parallel *activity* (emphasis mine) Parten notes: "The child *plays* (emphasis mine) independently, but the activity he chooses naturally brings him among other children (p. 250). Corresponding in defining cooperative *play* (emphasis mine), criteria for play, *per se*, are not mentioned, but those for cooperative interaction are: "The child *plays* (emphasis mine) in a group that is organized for the purpose of making some material product, or striving to attain some competitive goal, or of dramatic situations of adult or group life, or of playing formal games" (ibid., p. 251). In the case of cooperative *play* (emphasis mine), some of the adjectives used to describe behavior, competitive and formal games, for example, are clearly not part of play. It seems from these examples that *play* is being used colloquially, as the behaviors children exhibit, not in a more exact sense, and as distinct from other forms of peer interaction that are not play. As discussed earlier, this habit of not differentiating social play from social interaction has continued, with the result that peer interaction and peer play are not differentiated in the literature.

Take the example of Ken Rubin's (Rubin, Maoini, & Hornung, 1976) influential melding of Parten's "social *play*" (emphasis mine, p. 414) categories with those of Smilansky (1968) where the "Definitions for the social play categories were taken directly from Parten" (p. 415). From this viewpoint and our discussions of Parten's definitions, all of children's behavior would be categorized as some form of play. Correspondingly, some schemes for differentiating social from nonsocial "play" among peers seemingly categorized all behavior into Rubin's adaptation of the Smilansky-Parten categories (e.g., Coplan, Gavinski-Molina, Lagace-Seguin, & Wichmann, 2001). Given this position, how would the following example be coded: Two preschool girls walking on the playground smiling, with their arms around each other? It is not play by most definitions, but it certainly is cooperative interaction. The choice should be not to code it as play, but, instead, to put it into the cooperative participation category.

This rather loose word usage has implications for accurately charting the frequencies of different forms of interactions and play, separately, across ontogeny. This becomes a problem when scholars attempt to summarize time spent in social play, relative to other forms of social behavior, from others' research. Furthermore, if we use these estimates to make inferences about the function of different forms of interaction and play, our figures will probably inflate the importance of play. Specifically, if we assume that there is a correspondence between the cost of an activity (in terms of time or caloric expenditure in play) and its function, then our inferences are bound to be incorrect because our estimates of *play* are incorrect. In the case of all of children's behavior being categorized as play, then estimates of its importance will be inflated.

Cases of social pretense, rather than other forms of social play, are probably the least ambiguous to consider, given the probability that in social interactions, children must communicate their playful intentions so that their peers will understand them and can then response in kind; if they do not do this, play will not be initiated or maintained at a social level (Pellegrini, 1982). The same behavioral cues are available to researchers observing children, often using Rubin's adapted Smilansky-Parten matrix.

In an effort to specify the social and cognitive dimensions of this matrix, Jane Perlmutter and I (Pellegrini & Perlmutter, 1987) factor-analyzed the behaviors of preschool children observed in their classrooms during "free play periods" for three five-minute periods across a four-week period. Children's behaviors were all subordinated to the Smilansky-Parten matrix categories, and three factors emerged: 1) dramatic/constructive factor, 2) a solitary factor, and 3) a functional/constructive factor. We interpreted these results in terms of children's behavior being organized in terms of: make-believe (either dramatic or with objects, reflected in Factor 1); exploratory/constructive behavior with objects, which was not pretend (reflected in Factor 3), and social/non-social behaviors, where dramatic and constructive interaction was typically social (reflected in Factor 2). In the chapter on pretend play I will discuss both social and nonsocial forms of pretend play more thoroughly, but in this chapter, I will limit my discussion of social play to R&T and sexual play. Specifically, in order to proffer some clarity, I will first use ethologists' definition of social play, as R&T (playfighting) and sexual play (playful mounting). While the former has been addressed in developmental and child psychology, the latter has not generally been addressed. Instead, sexual play has more frequently been examined in the older, psychoanalytically oriented literature (e.g., Isaacs, 1972). Social pretend play is also almost unanimously considered a form of children's social play by developmental psychologists, in some cases to the exclusion of other forms of social play (e.g., Garvey, 1990). I will, however, give more in-depth consideration to social pretend in the pretend play chapter.

Sexual play has been widely discussed in the nonhuman play literature. For example, Serge Pellis (Pellis & Pellis, 2006; Pellis et al., in press) has documented sex play among rodents as involving mounting and licking behaviors and as probably learning important reproductive behaviors to be used at maturity. Descriptions of sex play among children are very scarce indeed and most often within the psychoanalytical literature as part of discussions of the origins of love and reflecting "libidinal development" (e.g., Isaacs, 1972). An example, from Susan Isaacs' classic work in the genre has, for example, Harold and George undressing Paul in a play sandpit. They were " 'looking at his tummy' (they said)" (p. 143). In fact they had undone the front of his "knickers" (i.e., underwear). Later they were observed chasing another child to "undress" him as well. In another example, more clearly reflecting what Isaacs sees as children's interests in their parents' sexual activities, a child, says, while fashioning a long and "penis-like" piece of modeling clay: "Somebody's climbing up the lady's ah – ah house" (p. 143).

Exceptions to a psychoanalytical analyses of sex play have been advanced more recently by Lamb and Coakley (1993) and Thorne and Luria (1986). Both of these studies, interestingly, suggest that cross-sex play in some ways prepares children for adults' roles, though some of those roles are less than positive. The Lamb and Coakley study was interesting to the extent that it proffered a typology of what constitutes sex play. Using a retrospective, anonymous survey technique, they sampled females at an all-women's college and asked them, first, to describe a sex game they recalled having played as children, and then prompted them to write with: "I remember...:" They were also asked to rate the clarity of their memory of the story on a scale from foggy to crystal and derived the following categories, as displayed in Table 7.1.

Table 7.1   Forms of sex play

Normal Category	Examples (% Mentioned)
Playing doctor	Pretending to be doctor or nurse where clothes are removed and/or genitals are examined (16.3%)
Exposure	Exposing body parts without pretending (15.3%)
Experiments in stimulation	Physical contact, especially genitalia (14.3%)
Kissing	Kissing (6.1%)
Fantasy sex play	Physical contact, especially genitalia, but with Pretend (29.6)
Other	Sex between dolls, sexual talk (18.4%)

As can be seen in the table, most of the sex games involved some form of imitation of adult sex and exploring genitalia, and fit quite well into our definitions of exploration and play. With that said, this is a very delicate, and in some quarters probably forbidden, topic with young children. And for good reason—sex play can be dangerous and coercive (Thorne & Luria, 1986). In many cases recollections of arousal (26%) or excitement (43%) were reported (Lamb & Coakley, 1993).

So why are these categories considered "normal"? Rightfully, I think, Lamb and Coakley consider *normal* as "what typically occurs" among children. The frequency of recollections of sex play in this sample certainly fits this criterion, especially when we consider that this sort of study is likely to underestimate frequency of occurrence, even though respondents were anonymous. With this said, it really is important that research examine this topic.

WHAT IS R&T?

To my knowledge R&T was first used in the social and behavioral sciences by Harlow (1962) in his discussion of the social play of rhesus monkeys, where R&T resembled "playfighting." As noted above, in preschool children this often takes the form of "superhero play" where quasi-agonistic behaviors are embedded in a fantasy theme. These forms of play are similar to what Saltz, Dixon, and Johnson (1976), in their seminal paper, labeled "thematic fantasy play."

Based on Harlow's work, and on the subsequent work with children by Blurton Jones (1972), R&T has been characterized by positive affect, or a "play face" (as displayed in the photo of the chimp and the young boy in Chapter 2), high-energy behaviors, exaggerated movements, and soft, openhanded hits or kicks. The play faces of the juvenile child and chimpanzee clearly signal that the intent of these acts is playful, *not* aggressive. The Exaggerated movements further help signal the playful, not aggressive, intent to other players.

Such signaling is crucial in playfighting so that the overture is not treated as aggression. As in any form of social communication, the message sender must send an unambiguous message: that this is play. Using a multifaceted message, such as a combination of play face, exaggerated movements, and an announcement: "I'm the Viper!" should maximize uptake. The recipient of the message also must attend to these cues and correctly interpret them. As noted in our earlier discussion of definitions, some children do not accurately attend to these cues (Pellegrini, 1988). Furthermore, children who know each other well, such as friends, are less likely to misinterpret overtures than children who are only acquaintances (Humphreys & Smith, 1987; Smith, Smees, & Pellegrini, 2004).

In terms of structure, R&T is typically characterized by reciprocal role-taking and self-handicapping. That is, in R&T, players change roles so that they alternate between dominant and subordinate; for example, alternating between being on top and on bottom and between being the aggressor and being the victim. In cases where play involves unequal partners (such as a father and his son), the bigger and stronger typically self-handicaps. For example, a father may fall on the floor, allowing his son to be on top; or in a chasing bout, where the faster person slows or staggers, allowing the slower player to catch-up. This latter form of self- handicapping is readily observable among squirrels playing chase: As they chase each other, the faster, more facile squirrel will inevitably outpace the slower animal. The self-handicapping takes the form of the faster squirrel then coming closer to the slow animal so as to encourage the slower animal to continue the play. Self-handicapping probably maximizes players' motivation to sustain play by minimizing the boredom associated with limited role enactment.

Empirically, it is unclear to what extent individuals self-handicap and reciprocate advantageous roles in R&T, though it is assumed that they do (Symons, 1978). Fagen (1981) recognized the fact that results can be mixed, with playfighting sometimes escalating into aggression, be it due to an "honest mistake," where a child accidentally hits another too hard. Alternatively, individuals can "cheat," where they exploit the perceived playful tenor of R&T for their own ends.

That players reciprocate roles and self-handicap has led to the so-called 50:50 rule, whereby in playfighting each animal gains advantage in about 50% of the contests (Altman, 1962). The implication of the 50:50 is that play is "fair" and cooperative to the extent that no individual has unfair advantage over the other and that the play bouts themselves are mechanisms by which individuals in group establish group cohesion—one of the primary, hypothesized, benefits of social play (e.g., Fagen, 1981).

On the other hand, if the 50:50 is not followed, and some players unfairly exploit the playful tenor of R&T for their own advantage, or "cheat" as Fagen (1981) has labeled it, individuals may be using R&T to access or maintain some resource. In this case, R&T would be used as a venue to learn and refine fighting skills—another commonly hypothesized benefit of R&T (Smith, 1982). Playfighting, to be motivating to players, should, however, combine elements of *both* cooperation (following the 50:50 rule) and competition (not following the rule) (Pellis, Pellis, & Reinhart, in press). It may be the unpredictability associated with the competitive aspect of R&T is very important in sustaining social play (Pellis et al., in press; Pellegrini, Dupuis, & Smith, 2007; Špinka, Newberry, & Bekoff, 2001). Consequently, it is important to document the extent to which the 50:50 rule is followed and under what conditions.

In two studies testing the efficacy of the 50:50 rule, the results have been equivocal. First, Bauer and Smuts (2007) studied a convenience sample of domesticated dogs and found no support for the rule. Their results should be interpreted very cautiously, however, because of the extreme limitations with the sampling techniques. Specifically, the observations of dyads of dogs did not control for or manipulate the breed, sex, physical size, or socialization histories of the dogs. These numerous confounds clearly limit unambiguous statement about the social behavior of these animals.

Serge Pellis and colleagues (in press) proposed that the 50:50 rule should be violated in situations where social dominance is unclear, such as in the early stages of group formation. It is well known that when groups of individual children are initially assembled, whether it be the start of a school year in preschool classrooms (Pellegrini et al., 2007; Roseth, Pellegrini, Bohn, Van Ryzin, & Vance, 2007; Strayer, 1980) or as youngsters make the transition from primary school to middle school classrooms (Pellegrini & Long, 2002), rates of aggression increase until social dominance relationships are established, and then decrease. By extension, during early adolescence when social groups and dominance are in a state of flux due to changing schools and rapidly changing body size, boys' R&T tends to relate to aggression and social dominance (Pellegrini, 1995; 2002; 2003). For example, R&T among adolescent boys is likely to escalate to aggression (Pellegrini, 1995); this does not occur during childhood in stable groups (Pellegrini, 1988). Correspondingly, R&T is also considered playful by young children when they are interviewed. For example, in cases where children were shown videotaped R&T and aggressive bouts, they clearly differentiated between the two and consider R&T playful (e.g., Costabile, Smith, Matheson, Aston, Hunter, & Boulton, 1991; Pellegrini, 1988; Smith, Hunter, Carvalho, & Costabile, 1992).

One of the interesting features of R&T is that, with development, its function seems to change. That is, during the juvenile period it is, for most children, related to peer affiliation and cooperative interaction, but during adolescence it relates to aggression and seems to serve a dominance purpose. I, however, following de Waal (1982), suggest that social dominance, in the end, relates to group cohesion. Specifically, after social dominance relationships are established, rates of aggression decrease (e.g., Pellegrini & Long, 2002; Pellegrini et al., 2007) and group cohesion, in the form of cooperation, increases (Pellegrini & Bartini, 2001). This seems to be the case for both human and nonhuman primates (Fagen, 1981). R&T also seems to be more important for males than females. Sexual selection theory (Darwin, 1871) accounts for this difference. Further sexually selection theory provides reasonable, and testable, explanations for the developmental contexts in which R&T develops.

Antecedents to R&T: Sexually Segregated Groups as a Socialization Context

Males and females are very different physically, and these differences have implications for social behavior. As noted earlier, male groups are physically more vigorous than female groups, and it is probably this difference that is responsible for sexual segregation in childhood (Pellegrini, 2004; Pellegrini, Long, et al., 2007). By way of brief review, sex segregation begins at around three years of age and peaks at around eight (Maccoby, 1998), and declines in early adolescence (Pellegrini & Long, 2003; 2007). It is in these segregated groups that R&T develops and is related to adult male sexual roles (Pellegrini, 2004).

At root, ultimate explanations for social segregation can be derived from sexual selection (Darwin, 1871) and parental investment (Trivers, 1972) theories, which posit that males, because they invest less in parenting, are the more competitive of the two sexes in their quest for mates. These differences should lead to males' exhibiting more vigorous, or energetic, behaviors and enacting competitive and physically aggressive social roles, including R&T.

Further, and following a life history perspective, different levels of physical activity and social interaction are also important for males' and females' physical conditioning as juveniles. I have argued that males' early bias toward physically vigorous and rough behavior benefits them in terms of motor training, by interacting with each other (Pellegrini, 2004; Pellegrini, Long, et al., 2007). Motor training benefits, in turn, are related to both their immediate skeletal and muscular development and cardiovascular fitness, as well as to later adult reproductive social roles. Generally, females avoid these active behaviors and interact with each other because they find vigorous behavior, especially in the presence of males, to be aversive and possibly dangerous. In segregated groups, males and females learn and practice, possibly through observational learning and reinforcement (Boyd & Richerson, 1985), the social roles associated being an adult male or female.

Exposure to androgens prenatally is probably a proximate mechanism by which selection pressure is exerted on the initial sex differences in physical activity (Archer & Lloyd, 2002). Data from natural experiments suggest that females exposed to abnormally high levels of prenatal androgens are more similar to male than to non-exposed females, which supports this claim (Berenbaum & Hines, 1992; Hines & Kaufman, 1994). This difference may be responsible, in part, for females' finding males' energetic behavior aversive.

A very early difference in activity preference helps explain males' preference for high-energy behaviors. For example, Kujawki and Bower (1993) demonstrated that infants used body movements to discriminate between boys and girls. Further, Campbell, Shirley, and Crook (2000) conducted a longitudinal experiment with infants at three, nine, and eighteen months of age, using a visual preference paradigm, showing video clips of male typical activities (e.g., chasing, wrestling, climbing, jumping) and female typical activities (e.g., doll play, pat-a-cake, whispering, drawing). They found that male, compared to female, nine-month-olds preferred the male activities.

Males are also reinforced for expressing their physical activity in competitive and dominance-related roles, in the form of R&T and aggression, often by their fathers and later by their male peers. For example, fathers of young males spend significantly more time with their sons than with their daughters (Parke & Suomi, 1981), thus providing same-sex models. During this time, fathers often engage in R&T and other forms of vigorous play with their sons (MacDonald & Parke, 1986).

Sex Differences in R&T

There are robust sex differences in the time and energy costs associated with the R&T of many animals (Meaney et al., 1985), including human juveniles in both industrialized and non-industrialized countries (Whiting & Edwards, 1973). Similar to some samples of chimpanzees (e.g., Nadler & Braggio, 1974), human male juveniles exhibit R&T at higher rates than females, and these rough and competitive behaviors are exhibited by males in their sexually segregated peer groups (Pellegrini, 2004). More specific to the human case, Whiting and Edwards present survey data (indicating that sex differences existed but not including the actual rate of behavior) for children 3–6 years and 7–11 years of age in six cultures, including the United States. Among 3–6-year-olds, the males exhibited R&T more than girls in four of the six cultures, and in five of the six cultures for the 7–11-year-olds. Their data showed that 3–6-year-old American girls engaged in R&T more than boys. DiPietro (1981) and Pellegrini (1989) found the opposite among American children of this age. For example, Pellegrini observed elementary school children on their school playground during their recess periods and found that, for 5-year-olds, boys' R&T was four times greater than girls' and for 7.5- and 9-year-olds, three and two times greater, respectively. In terms of the total behavioral budget of outdoor behavior, boys' R&T accounted for 14% of all their behavior and girls' R&T was 7%.

Similar trends have been observed in other work with both primary school and middle school students in both America and England. For example, year-long observations of eight-year-olds on their English and American school playgrounds found that males engaged in R&T at a rate three times that of females: in 6.5% of the behavior scans compared to 1.9% for females (Blatchford et al., 2003). Similarly, in a group of 13-year-old American middle school students, males' ($M = .91$/focal sample) R&T was close to double that of females ($M = .55$/focal sample) and males initiated R&T with other males ($M = 1.48$) more than they initiated R&T with females ($M = .32$), and at more than double the rate that females initiated R&T with other females ($M = .65$) (Pellegrini, 2003). In short, the sex differences in human juveniles' R&T are robust. Given these differences in resources expended in R&T, there should be corresponding differences in benefits associated for boy's and girls' R&T.

The Development and Possible Functions of R&T

In this section I document the function of R&T from childhood through adolescence, first by specifying the amount of time and energy spent in R&T. Based on one measure of "cost," time budget information, I will make inferences about the function (or benefits) of play. Using cost-benefit analyses to make inferences about function is a standard tool of behavioral ecologists (e.g., Krebs & McCleery, 1984).

Interestingly, the estimated costs for nonhuman and human animals are similar. Specifically, the animal literature suggests that the caloric expense of play is modest, accounting for between 2.5% and 10% of the total energy budget

(Fagen, 1981 for a general review; Martin, 1982, for an experimental study of cats). An estimate of caloric cost of primary school children's locomotor play, of which R&T is a component, is similar, at 2.5% (Pellegrini et al., 1998), and as shown above, the caloric cost of play for males is greater than for females.

Also as noted earlier, *function* for psychologists is typically defined in terms of beneficial consequence (Hinde, 1980) and this consequence can be either deferred or immediate. A deferred-benefit view of play is the commonly held view of play in developmental psychology that benefits of play during childhood are reaped later in life. It reconciles the logical conundrum posed when one defines plays in terms of its being "purposeless" and being more concerned with means than with ends, while at the same time assigning functional importance to play. A deferred-benefits argument for play solves the problem of how a behavior can be both purposeless and functional. Such a view would involve, for example, R&T in childhood predicting fighting skills during adulthood. R&T during the juvenile and adolescent periods could also have immediate benefits; for example, if it predicted cardiovascular health during each period, or social cohesion. The extent to which R&T will have immediate or deferred benefit relates to associated costs.

Costs

Time budgets of R&T are even less common than studies of other forms of play. Most of what we know has been cobbled together from a variety of studies that included R&T and related forms of play, such as locomotor play and exercise play, in studies of children in preschools, daycare centers, primary schools (most of these data come from observations on the playground at recess), and a few at home. The full details of and references to these studies can be found in Pellegrini and Smith (1998). The data clearly show that R&T follows the typical play developmental, inverted-U, curve, as illustrated in Figure 7.2.

During the preschool period, we see R&T accounting for about 4% of all behavior, peaking during the primary school years at around 10%, and declining

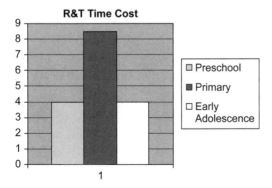

Figure 7.2   Cost in time of R&T

again in early adolescence to around 4%. These data, like the time and caloric costs documented in the animal literature, suggest that the time costs associated with R&T are modest.

In summary, it seems that R&T accounts for a modest portion of children's behavioral budgets, yet it assumes a more important role for boys than girls. Thus, we expect that R&T should have an immediate benefit in boys' development.

Benefits of R&T

R&T probably has both immediate and deferred benefits.

Physical Training

Because some forms of R&T are physically vigorous, they probably relate to children's strength and fitness, an immediate function (Bekoff, 1988). As most of us are aware, physical fitness is a fleeting phenomenon. We stay fit only as long as we keep exercising. During the juvenile period, most children are given the opportunity to engage in physically vigorous R&T during their school recess period, five days a week for nine months a year. As Bekoff (1988) has pointed out, besides the duration of youngsters' R&T is it also important to examine the intensity of these behaviors. So, for example, short but intense bursts of activity associated with certain forms of playfighting, not unlike the "interval training" used by endurance athletes, is beneficial to cardiovascular fitness.

Emotional Encoding, Decoding, and Regulation

An important dimension of social skill is the ability to encode and decode social signals. Successful encoding and decoding of messages, such as "This is play," is necessary if play is to be successfully initiated and maintained (G. Bateson, 1972; Bekoff, 1995). Behaviors that send the message "This is play" are typically exaggerated, compared to more functional counterparts (Biben & Suomi, 1993); for example, playfighting, compared to real fighting, might be characterized by an open mouth, hunched shoulders, and rhythmic movement of the hands.

Research by Parke and colleagues indicates that the ability to encode and decode play signals can originate in vigorous play between parents (primarily fathers) and their children (primarily sons) beginning in infancy and continuing throughout childhood (Carson et al., 1993; Parke, Cassidy, Burks, Carson, & Boyum, 1992). Parke and colleagues found the amount of time spent in vigorous play bouts to be positively related to preschool children's ability to decode emotional expressions, such as happy, sad, angry, scared, and neutral (Parke et al., 1992). Furthermore, children's expression of emotional states was also related positively to bout length (Parke et al., 1992). Involvement in R&T with peers, expressed in terms of proportion of total behavioral output, has also been found to relate to primary school children's ability to decode play signals (Pellegrini, 1988). It may thus be the case that parent–child play provides the groundwork for children's ability to encode and decode emotions, with this ability later being used in physical activity play with peers.

That social play should relate to emotional regulation dates back at least to Harlow (Harlow & Harlow, 1965; Suomi & Harlow, 1972), who suggested that the R&T that rhesus monkeys engaged in with their mothers and their peers probably enabled them to moderate their emotional responses to ambiguous, socially provocative behaviors. For example, while a player might witness an "honest mistake" in R&T, such as one player accidentally hitting too hard, the target juvenile, through experience in play and familiarity with this peer, recognizes it is this probably a mistake because it is embedded in a play bout, and consequently inhibits his aggressive response.

There is more recent comparative theory and evidence to suggest that social play enables individuals to regulate their emotional states (Pellis & Pellis, 2006). Specifically, and consistent with one of the major premises of this book, a number of researchers (Pellegrini, Dupuis, & Smith, 2007; Pellis & Pellis, 2006; Špinka et al., 2001) posit that one of the motivating factors in play generally, and social play specifically, is its unpredictability. Recall the earlier discussion in this chapter where it was noted that this unpredictability presented itself in the competitive dimension of social play. Will I win or will I lose?

This uncertainty, however, is moderated by the fact that play typically occurs among very similar and often familiar individuals. Consequently, while there is uncertainty of outcomes in play, there is a modicum of safety; thus children are willing take chances and risks in this context. Children who engage in social play, per this argument, should be less fearful of uncertainty in the play context and behaviorally more flexible in responding to novel events, relative to less playful contexts (Pellegrini et al., 2007; Špinka et al., 2001).

Social Cohesion

R&T may also have immediate social affiliation/cohesion benefits for boys during childhood, though some experimental comparative results with meerkats do not support this conclusion (Sharpe, 2005). Most basically, R&T typically occurs in sexually segregated male groups that typified by high activity and rough behavior (Fabes, Martin, & Hanish, 2003; Pellegrini, Long, et al., 2007). One hypothesis, the behavioral compatibility hypothesis, holds that children's sex-segregated groups are held together by the similarity of children's behavior. That most boys enjoy R&T and most girls do not may be reason enough for them to bind as a group (Pellegrini, Long, et al., 2007).

Furthermore, it is important to note that R&T and aggression are negatively and non-significantly related for most primary school boys ($r = -.13$, ns) (Pellegrini, 1988). Also, in terms of behaviors immediately following R&T, it does not lead to aggression and group dispersal. Instead, it leads to continued affiliation, in the form of games with rules, at a greater-than-chance probability (Pellegrini, 1988). This should not be surprising, because it typically occurs between friends (Humphreys & Smith, 1987; Smith, Smees, & Pellegrini, 2004), and boys who engage in R&T tend to be popular ($r = .36, p < .01$) and have a varied repertoire for solving social problems ($r = .31, p < .05$) (Pellegrini, 1989). As argued earlier in this chapter, it may be the case that R&T affords opportunities, through role reciprocation and self-handicapping perhaps, to learn and practice a variety of social strategies for initiating and maintaining social interaction with peers, and the boys who have a varied repertoire in R&T also have a varied repertoire to solve social problems (Pellegrini, 1993).

Fighting Skills

The most traditional view in the animal and human literature (Smith, 1982) is that R&T functions to provide safe practice for fighting (and possibly hunting) skills that will be useful in later life. This hypothesis would be consistent with the strong sex difference observed, if one assumes that fighting and hunting skills were and are more characteristically male activities (Boulton & Smith, 1992). It does not, however, predict the age curve for R&T, because "safe" practice of such skills might be especially important in adolescence, when R&T declines. Also, there is little or no direct evidence linking R&T to fighting or hunting skills, in either the animal or the human literature. Finally, this hypothesis does not predict the age changes in "cheating" observed in human R&T.

Players "cheat" when they violate the rules of play by manipulating the non-serious tenor of the activity for their own, exploitive ends. I do not dismiss this argument. Indeed, I suspect that it may be a phylogenetically prior function in some ecologies with some remaining relevance for younger children. As noted earlier in this chapter, R&T may relate to real fighting in those situations where social dominance is dependent on direct, confrontational forms of aggression in contests for relatively scarce resources. In cases where resources are abundant, competition is more likely to resemble a scramble, rather than a contest, and social dominance may be likely to involve cooperative behaviors. From this view R&T would be related to social cohesion and social competence.

Social Dominance

Social dominance is typically conceptualized in terms of individuals' differential access to resources. The most dominant individuals have the most immediate access to resources. Early work on social dominance by ethologists (e.g., see Francis, 1988, for a review of this issue in the animal literature) and child developmentalists (e.g., McGrew, 1972; Pettit, Bakshi, Dodge, & Coie, 1990; Sluckin & Smith, 1977) stressed the role of aggression. For example, some researchers equated dominance with sociometrically nominated "toughness" (e.g., Sluckin & Smith, 1977), while others included the frequency of observed aggressive behaviors as a component of social dominance (e.g., Pettit et al., 1990). In such cases, toughness and aggression was typically used to define social dominance without reference to resource control. As Vaughn and Santos (2007), among many others (e.g., Bernstein, 1981; Francis, 1988), have pointed out, aggression and social dominance are different constructs.

More in line with ethological studies, the centrality of resource control, and behavioral variation in different ecological conditions (Crook, 1970; 1989), social dominance has been defined in terms of dyadic contests and group structure (Hinde, 1978). Dyadic contests, and the resulting social relationships, are defined in terms of winners and losers in resource contests. Using those dyadic comparisons of individuals' encounters, group-level dominance hierarchies are constructed (e.g., Sluckin & Smith, 1977; Strayer, 1980; Vaughn & Waters, 1981). For example, two children are observed in their preschool, each trying to get on one swing. Child A pushes B, and A gains access to the swing. In this instance, A would be coded the winner and B the loser. These sorts of dyadic encounters can be used to determine *dominance relationships*. In documenting dyadic contests in the study of social dominance, it is essential that social behavior be tied to successful or unsuccessful resource control, as social dominance is, at root, concerned with accessing and controlling resources (Charlesworth, 1988; Dunbar, 1988; Hinde, 1978). In cases where the frequency of individuals' aggressive behaviors alone or initiated attempts alone are used as a metric, without reference to the efficacy of these behaviors in controlling resources, aggression, *not* social dominance, is being documented (Vaughn & Santos, 2007).

Furthermore, it is important to keep social dominance *relationships* distinct from social dominance *rank* as the former reflects a dyadic relationship and the latter reflects an individual's place in a larger group (Hinde, 1976). The total number of dyadic contest wins, entered into a dominance matrix, is typically used to determine *rank*, or an individual's status in relation to the larger group. For example, A defeats B and B defeats C. The hierarchy would be A > B > C and assumed to be transitive. Thus, B is unlikely to challenge A and C unlikely to challenge B, each knowing that they would probably be defeated. Based on these comparisons, individuals are rank-ordered in the group.

From this view, different, but complementary, behavioral strategies may be used to achieve dominance relationships and dominance rank. For example, R&T could be used to establish and maintain social dominance when individuals' play is more competitive than cooperative; that is, when they violated the 50:50 rule (Pellis et al., in press).

Cheating at R&T, or exploiting its playful tenor, is more likely to occur in contest, rather than scramble, resources competition (Pellegrini et al., 2007). The most basic form of competition is a *scramble competition*. In a pure scramble situation, and one under "ideal free conditions," individuals are free to go where they please; they all have equal knowledge, and each contestant gets some share of a resource (Parker, 2000). Any form of queuing for a resource is an example of scramble competition. Individuals in a supermarket, for example, can go to any checkout line; each person gets the resource—getting checked –out—eventually. Use of an expensive strategy, such as aggression or cheating at R&T, in this situation where access to resources is guaranteed, clearly is more costly than it is beneficial for an individual.

Cases where two individuals confront each other for a resource are *contest competitions*. More exactly, contest competition is typified by direct, dyadic contests for resources where there are clear winners and losers. In "pure contests," winners take all, if they choose. In such cases, resources are more valuable than in the scramble case and thus more likely to be accessed by aggression and cheating at R&T.

Second, the playful tenor of R&T may be violated when the group dominance structure is unsettled. As noted above, the R&T used to serve a dominance function is most likely to occur in cases where the self-handicapping, or the 50:50 rule, is violated. Indeed, Symons (1978) was critical of the hypothesis that R&T is related to dominance because he assumed that the 50:50 rule is followed. While there are no studies, to my knowledge, of children's and adolescents' following, or not following, the 50:50 rule, the ethnographic record provides illustrations of its being violated. Specifically, Sluckin's (1981) in-depth study of British five- to nine-year-old children's behavior and perceptions of their lives in the school playground provide examples of R&T being used to deceive and manipulate peers. The work of Oswald and colleagues (Oswald, Krappmann, Chowduri, and Salisch, 1987) in Germany with children aged six to ten years also found instances of hurtfulness in the play of the older children in this age range. In my own work among primary school children, however, the vast majority of the cases supported the 50:50 rule, as there was a very low probability of R&T escalating into aggression.

With this said, children's R&T occurs in symmetrical groups, or with children of similar dominance status, and many children say they can determine their own as well as peers' strength from these encounters (Smith, Hunter, Carvalho, & Costabile, 1992)—even though the 50:50 rule appears to be followed. R&T tends to occur between friends (Humphreys & Smith, 1987; Smith & Lewis, 1985) and in groups of three to four children (Pellegrini, 1993); these findings indicate that it is a safe and relatively visible venue to test and exhibit one's physical strength. Thus, through R&T, children can, in an indirect way, assess their own strength and that of others; in this way they prepare for dominance encounters through the primary school period.

The idea that R&T is related to establishing and maintaining dominance status is also consistent with arguments from design. Males often use quasi-agonistic displays (e.g., soft or no-contact kicks and punches, light pushes) in the service of dominance. Very similar behaviors are also displayed in R&T (Blurton Jones, 1972), but these behaviors are embedded in a non-serious context: Kicks and punches do not make contact, and if they do, they are soft; players are smiling; and they often handicap themselves (e.g., let the player on the bottom of a pile get on top).

The picture is much less ambiguous in early adolescence. Neill (1976, p. 219) was the first to suggest that adolescent boys' R&T might be used to establish dominance. His factor-analytic study of 12- to 13-year-old boys' playground behavior found that R&T and aggression often co-occurred. Neill stated that R&T might be a "means of asserting or maintaining dominance; once a weaker boy has registered distress the bond can be maintained by the fight taking a more playful form, but if he does not do so at the start of the fight, the stronger boy may increase the intensity of the fight until he does."

This age change in the function of R&T received some support from Humphreys and Smith (1987). They found that at 11 years, but not at 7 and 9 years, dominance was a factor in partner choice in R&T. When the younger children engaged in R&T, they did so in symmetrical groups, or with peers of similar dominance status; among the older children, dominant youngsters initiated R&T with less dominant youngsters, or in asymmetrical groups.

Results from a study by Pellegrini (1995) shed further light on this age trend. In a longitudinal study of adolescent boys, I found that asymmetrical choices for R&T were observed during the first year of middle school (12 years), but not the second (13 years). Additionally, I (Pellegrini, 1995) found that observed R&T and aggression were significantly and positively interrelated in the sixth grade ($r = .29$); in the second year of that study the correlation was positive but not significant ($r = .12$). The sequential probability of R&T leading to aggression was significant in the sixth, but not in seventh grade. Observed R&T was, however, significantly and positively related to peer-rated dominance in both sixth and seventh grades ($r = .43$ and $r = 31$, respectively). Further, sixth-grade R&T predicted seventh-grade dominance ($r = .39$, $p < .01$) (Pellegrini, 1995). This pattern is consistent with the hypothesis that R&T and aggression are used in the initial phases of group formation to establish social dominance; once dominance is established, the relationship between R&T and aggression is attenuated.

In more recent study of early adolescent males (Pellegrini, 2003), and consistent with the dominance hypothesis, boys' R&T was more frequently intra-sexual than inter-sexual, as indicated in Figure 7.3.

Boys engage in R&T with other boys, not with girls, to establish and maintain status in male groups. Consistent with this argument, observed frequency of R&T for adolescent boys was significantly and positively correlated with observed aggression ($r = .31$) and peer-rated dominance ($r = .25$).

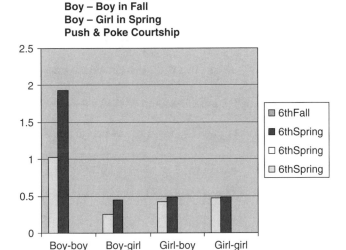

Figure 7.3   Changing target of R&T

Sexual Behavior

With the passage of time across the first year of middle school, one can see the decrease in boy–boy R&T, corresponding to the stabilizing of dominance relationships. At this point we can see an increase in boy–girl R&T. That is, boy–girl R&T, though relatively infrequent, increased from fall to spring of the school year. This occurrence can also be interpreted in terms of adolescents' nascent heterosexual relationships.

In terms of ultimate functions, I examined the extent to which R&T and dominance related to dating. I asked girls to nominate boys to a hypothetical part, and results suggested that dominance was related to that measure in both sixth and seventh grades, as indicated by the correlation coefficients in Table 7.2.

These data clearly show that as male peer groups became less sexually segregated and dominance increased, dating popularity also increased (Pellegrini & Long, 2003). Similar results have been reported by Bukowski and colleagues (Bukowski, Sippola, & Newcomb, 2000).

Furthermore, it may be that inter-sexual R&T is a form of "push and poke" courtship (Maccoby, 1998; Schofield, 1981), whereby boys and girls are using playful and ambiguous behaviors, such as R&T, to initiate heterosexual interaction. These acts are sufficiently ambiguous that if the initiator is rebuffed he or she would not lose face among his or her peers. It could be put off as merely being playful. If, on the other hand, the behavior is reciprocated, successful heterosexual interaction is initiated. Thus, where male–male R&T is related to aggression and dominance, male–female R&T seems playful.

To more directly test this hypothesis, and using the methodology Peter Smith and I developed earlier (Smith et al., 2004), we videotaped males and females engaging in R&T (Pellegrini, 2003) and showed the films to boys and girls who were participants in those events they were viewing and to their classmates who were not participating in the R&T bouts. If my hypothesis was correct there should be participant/nonparticipant differences within each sex. That is, male participants should see the bout as aggressive and contentious as they were experienced at R&T as adolescents. Male nonparticipants, because they did not have R&T experience at that point, should see the bouts as playful, as they were during childhood. Female participants, on the other hand, should see the bouts as playful, not aggressive, because they were experiencing R&T in the context of playful push and poke courtship. Nonparticipating females, on the other hand, have little experience in these matters and see R&T as aggressive. The results, as displayed in Table 7.3 below, generally support these predictions.

Table 7.2   Correlations between segregation and dominance and dating popularity

Dating	6th Fall	6th Spring	7th Fall	7th Spring
Segregation	−0.15(54)	−0.30* (43)	−0.11(69)	−0.24(37)
Dominance	0.07(46)	0.34** (59)	0.42** (64)	0.46** (64)

$*p < .05$ $**p < .01$.

Table 7.3   Descriptive statistics for responses* to interview questions by sex by participation status

	Participant				Nonparticipant				Differences
	Male		Female		Male		Female		
M	SD	M	SD	M	SD	M	SD		

Interview Questions									
Why are you doing it?									
Play									
.73	1.15	1.65	.98	2.53	1.42	1.14	1.15		Male Nonparticipant>Male Part.
Retaliate									
1.26	1.34	1.90	1.33	.60	.87	2.42	1.71		Male Part.>Male Nonparticipant Female Nonparticipant >Female Part.
Is it fun?									
Yes									
3.30	1.34	3.55	1.82	3.96	.126	2.85	1.45		Female Part.>Nonparticipant; Male Nonparticipant>Participant
No									
1.07	1.29	1.00	1.33	1.00	.86	1.66	1.06		
Are you trying to hurt him/hurt?									
Yes									
.50	.86	.10	.30	.46	.69	.47	.74		Male Part.>Nonparticipant; Female Nonparticipant>Participant
No									
4.26	1.21	5.25	1.61	5.00	.90	4.90	1.37		Male Nonparticipant>Participant Female Part.>Nonparticipant

*Scores are frequencies of responses/the number of individuals in each category.

In summary, there seem to be two possible functions of R&T during childhood. First, it may be primarily a competitive construct where children exploit peers and practice their fighting skills. Second, it may be a primarily a cooperative affair where children learn social skills, which in turn serve group cohesion. It may be, however, that these two options are complementary rather than mutually exclusive. Specifically, I suggest that R&T, even if it co-occurs with aggression, could in fact relate to group cohesion if it is used in the context of *establishing* a dominance relationship. This would be the case under the following conditions: R&T is used in contests in the initial stages of group formation, as social dominance relationships are being sorted out.

Specifically, it is well documented that with children (Pellegrini et al., 2007; Roseth et al., 2007) and adolescents (Pellegrini and Long, 2002), rates of different forms of aggression increase, and with time and as social dominance relationships as stabilized, aggression decreases. Illustrative patterns are displayed in Figures 7.4 and 7.5.

If R&T were to serve a dominance function, one would expect rates of cheating at R&T to parallel the trajectories of aggression. It should be high when dominance is being sorted out and decline after it is established.

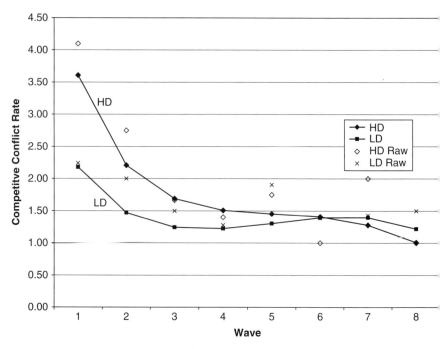

Figure 7.4   Predicted competitive conflict trajectories by social dominance

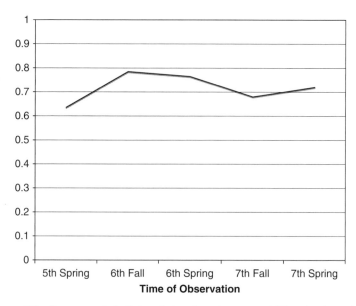

Figure 7.5   Decrement in bullying during the primary to middle school transition

CONCLUSIONS

To conclude this chapter I have documented the difficulty of differentiating social play between children and adults and between peers from other social, but nonplayful behaviors. Therefore, students of social play should be especially vigilant in reviewing the literatures in this area. The most common danger associated with conflating nonplay and play social interaction is that rates of play typically get inflated, thus exaggerating the putative benefits of social play.

Even with these limitations in mind, there is reasonably good evidence, especially that drawn from the comparative literature, for the importance of social play in children's learning the social skills necessary to negotiate childhood and, later, adulthood. Generally, and consistent with the experimental, comparative work, it is probably the case that juveniles' engaging in social play with parents lays an important foundation for subsequent play and more general social interaction and social competence with peers. In cases of a deprived maternal-child relationship, juveniles can gain these skills later by playing with younger peers.

Peer social play probably helps children learn and practice a variety of important social skills, such as the ability to encode and decode social and emotional cues, how to take turns, and how to inhibit impulsive and aggressive responses to provocative social initiatives. Therefore, it is probably important to afford children the opportunity to learn and practice these skills in peer play, rather than in the context of explicitly being taught social skills and "values education" by teachers. Unlike didactic forms of interaction, such as explicitly teaching values, play is motivating for children: They enjoy doing it, and consequently they are willing to take the time to learn the necessary skills to sustain social play.

8

Children's Use of Objects in Exploration, in Play, and as Tools

The various ways that objects are used by nonhuman (McGrew, 1992; Ramsey & McGrew, 2005; Tomasello & Call, 1997) and human juveniles (Piaget, 1962; Power, 2000; Rubin, Fein, & Vandenberg, 1983) have been subjected to a considerable amount of theoretical and empirical attention across a number of different disciplines. Concerning the development of humans' use of and play with objects, Piaget's (1970) theory suggests that children's cognitive development is rooted in their sensorimotor interactions with objects. In this theory, individual children's actions with objects result in basic representations of these actions and objects. These representations, in turn, are important bases for subsequent development. Piaget's sensorimotor theory has also been applied to the use of objects in nonhuman primates (monkeys: Parker, 1977; apes: Hallock & Worobey, 1984). Furthermore and by extension, one school of thought holds that human cognition evolved in the context of apes' manipulation and use of objects and tools (see Tomasello & Call, 1997, for a review). Many of us have seen images of apes using pieces of grass to "fish" for termites, for example.

The basic idea in these Piagetian accounts is that through repeated interactions with objects, individuals construct representations for those objects and their associated action schemas. Object permanence, or the ability to form and keep in mind a representation of an object when it is not perceptually present, is hypothesized to be the result of this sort of repeated experience with object manipulations and neurological maturation. Evidence for these representations is based on children's ability to continue to search for a desired object after it disappears from view, such as when it has been covered. Before object permanence, children assume a covered object has disappeared.

These object-based representations, in turn, become less dependent upon children's actions on objects as children are capable of manipulating the representations themselves, independently of the objects, with the onset of operational thought. As suggested by this Piagetian approach, the predominant view until relatively recently has been that intelligence develops, both ontogenetically and phylogenetically, in the context of solitary individuals interacting with objects. This view persisted even though there were numerous observations, especially involving young children, that interactions with objects actually do take place in a social context, and that children spend considerable time observing others using objects (see Rubin et al., 1983; Tomasello, 1999; and Tomasello and Call, 1997, for reviews).

The importance of social interaction for the evolution of intelligence began with the observations of Jolly (1966) and the theorizing of Humphrey (1976), who suggested that social interactions between conspecifics, not solitary object manipulation, may be responsible for the evolution of primate intelligence. Juvenile chimpanzees, for example, learn to use objects in the presence an adult.

Highlighting the importance of social experience in mental representation, there are examples of infants' mental representations of conspecifics well before they have any experience manipulating objects. For example Andrew Meltzoff and his colleagues (e.g., Meltzoff, 1988; Meltzoff and Borton, 1979; Meltzoff and Moore, 1977, 1992) have shown how human infants, and in some cases neonates, imitate adults' facial expressions and unusual movements. This very early ability to form mental representations and imitate others seems to be specific to human models. In other words, there is a very early bias in humans toward attending to other social actors, and this evidence suggests that social interactions probably mediate the young child's interactions with objects to impact cognitive development.

The importance of social interaction to human and nonhuman primates' representational thought and to their representations of conspecifics and objects been examined in a number of carefully crafted experiments by Mike Tomasello (e.g., 1999; Tomasello and Call, 1997) and colleagues in Leipzig. Specifically, they have demonstrated that nonhuman primates (typically chimpanzees) are capable of understanding social relationships in which they are not involved. For example, individual A can observe two conspecifics fighting and recognize a winner, B, and a loser, C, in a contest. This level of recognition, in turn, influences how A will interact with both A and C. More specifically relevant to interactions with objects, both humans and apes also can understand antecedent-consequence relationships involving an individual and an object, such as an individual using a rock to smash a nut. Only humans, however, seem able to recognize the causal mediation between external events. Specifically, only humans are capable of recognizing that the actor has an intent to smash the nut and is using the rock to that end. Furthermore, children may imitate that behavior to solve a similar problem. Children understand what adults may intend to do with objects and will try to produce similar actions to achieve similar ends. Chimpanzees, on the other hand, do not "imitate" in the sense that they recognize the model's intent.

Instead, they seem to emulate the solution in which the object is used—that is, using a rock in some way, not only the specific way they observed it being used—to access the meat in the nut. That is, they attend to the results produced by the object on the nut, not the intention of using it to access the meat.

Unfortunately, however, the extant child developmental literature on object uses pays only limited attention to the ways that different types of object are used in a variety of social as well nonsocial contexts (though see Flynn & Whiten, 2008). Correspondingly, the different ways that children interact with objects are often labeled under the umbrella term "play." As with other aspects of play, children's interactions with objects are not uniformly play, in the strict sense of the word. My goal in this chapter is to describe the different forms of object use (i.e., exploration, construction, play, and tool use) in childhood and then establish time budgets, where data exist, for each of these forms of object use. Following the theoretical orientation of this book, I will link the time expenditures in each activity to possible functions.

Different Forms of Object Use in Childhood

Surprisingly, there is very little descriptive information about the different ways that children use objects, including playing with objects, in the child development literature. The exception to this is where objects are studied in relation to children's pretend play. For example, children's ability to use an empty tea cup to have a pretend cup of tea, or to use that cup for a hat, has been studied (Tomasello, Siriano, & Rochat, 1999) in the context of children's ability to use socially shared symbols. This material is discussed in the chapter on pretend play.

More commonly in the child development literature, where efforts have been made to address the different types of object use and play exhibited by children, researchers have typically conflated object play with different forms of objects use, not unlike the confounding of social play and peer interaction discussion in the preceding chapter. Specifically, much of the study of children's interactions with objects during childhood has been influenced by Smilansky's (1968) adaptation of Piaget's (1962) theory of play and the ways that she categorized behaviors directed at objects. In her influential monograph, she included "functional play" and "constructive play" as categories to account for children's interactions with objects. Functional play, which was similar to Piaget's (1962) notion of practice play, is characteristic of the sensorimotor period of children's development where they interact with objects to gain mastery. These non–goal-oriented actions with objects, according to Piaget (1962), result from children's pleasure in mastering action-based routines.

"Constructive play," according to Smilansky, has the child learning the "various uses of play materials" and the "building" of something (1968, p. 6). Ironically, perhaps, much of what we know about children's interactions with objects is subsumed under research on "constructive play." I say ironically, because construction, according to Piaget (1962), was not considered to be play. According to Piaget, on whom Smilansky based her work, construction is more concerned with the end product of activity—the construction *per se*—while play is more concerned with the activity, or means, than with the end and consequently is not play *per se* (Piaget, 1962; Rubin, Fein, & Vandenberg, 1983; Smith et al., 1986). An example of construction is displayed in Figure 8.1.

Smilansky's categories of "play," as discussed earlier, were expanded into a heuristic for describing the social (solitary, parallel, and interactive) and cognitive (functional, constructive, and dramatic/pretense) dimensions of play by Ken Rubin and colleagues (Rubin et al., 1976; Rubin, Watson, & Jambor, 1978). In this scheme, Rubin and colleagues considered constructive "play" as involving manipulation of objects to create something. This scheme has been used to generate massive and valuable amounts of descriptive data on the ways that young children use objects (summarized in Rubin et al., 1983). Rubin and colleagues (Rubin et al., 1983) rightfully questioned the validity of "constructive play" as a category because of its incongruity with Piagetian theory: "Constructive play might be viewed as belonging to some other coding schemes" (p. 727). Despite these qualifications, little effort has been made to differentiate construction from play with objects and other forms of object use.

The descriptive data generated by the Smilansky model are, at the same time, both valuable and limited. They are valuable to the extent that they provide very general descriptions of children's object use. They are limited, however, to the extent that the category "constructive play" is probably too gross a category to offer guidance as to the role of "play" objects in children's cognitive development. The above definition given by Smilansky, and subsequently used by Rubin (Rubin et al., 1976; 1978), includes a diverse constellation of goal-directed and non–goal-directed uses of objects. For example, using blocks to build steps might

Figure 8.1   Contruction (Photo: A. Pellegrini)

be considered constructive play. The same act, however, though coded as constructive, might actually be considered "tool use" if a child uses the steps to enhance his or her reach (Amant & Horton, 2008).

The loss of descriptive information by using "constructive play" defined according to the Smilansky model, to include much of children's interactions with objects, has implications for our understanding, not only of the development of the various ways that children use objects, but also of the functional importance of those interactions with objects. That is, exploration of objects, play with objects, construction, and using objects as tools probably have different developmental histories (e.g., different age-related trajectories) as well as different outcomes (e.g., consequences). For example, constructive play, as defined in Rubin's adaptation of Smilansky's categories, does not show age-related changes (at least from the ages of three to five years) when children are observed in their preschool classrooms (Rubin et al., 1978). That constructive play does not follow the typical inverted-U developmental curve of play is further evidence that it probably has different antecedents of play and is not *play* in the strict sense that *play* is more means- than ends-oriented. In terms of function, I will illustrate below how these forms of object use have different consequences.

Play with objects, following the definition of play advanced in this book, is probably pretend play in many cases. Furthermore, using objects in pretend initially entails that children are simulating someone else's use of those objects. With experience, children learn to have other, more abstract, objects represent another object. For example, they can have a pencil representing a hammer, in the context of mother–child interaction. With young children in this context, mothers typically mark instances of pretend by smiling or vocalization (Lillard, 2006; Tomasello, 1999). From these sorts of experiences, children come to recognize adults' intentions toward objects, and indeed toward people, and imitate adults' uses of objects (Tomasello, 1999).

Very young children recognize that objects can be used in a pretend mode, such using an empty cup to drink pretend tea or, as shown in the photograph below, pretending to drive a toy car. As noted, many scholars interpret these early playful uses of objects as simulations, rather than representations of others' intentions (Harris, 1991; Lillard, 2006; Tomasello, 1999). When they start to use objects not functionally related to a pretend act, such as using a cup for a hat or a pencil for a hammer, however, they probably are doing so because they recognize the intention behind using such an object to represent something else. This develops in the context of parent–child interactions (Lillards, 2006; Tomasello, 1999).

Relative to this sort of play with objects, exploration and tool use are different still (Hutt, 1966). *Exploration* is the behavior exhibited when individuals first encounter objects; they explore their properties and attributes, as illustrated in the illustration below, in Figure 8.3. Through exploration, children find out that objects, for example, are flat or rounded, long or short, used for drinking or for covering one's head. These attributes and the ways that they observe others utilizing them, in turn, are related to children's play with those objects. Below, in Figures 8.2 and 8.3, we see that exploration can also be solitary or social.

Figure 8.2 Social exploration (Photo: A. Pellegrini)

Figure 8.3 Solitary exploration (Photo: A. Pellegrini)

The interpersonal processes associated with children exploring objects are also important. Typically, infants' and young children's interest in objects is stimulated when they are interacting with or observing adults using objects. When adults handle objects, for example, children, in turn, become interested in those objects; for example, they may pick up the objects, examine them, and learn about them, a process labeled *stimulus enhancement* (Tomasello, 1999; Tomasello & Call, 1997). Relatedly, in emulation, infants or young children observe adults handling objects in an unexpected way, such as using a knife as a screwdriver, and they thereby discover uses for those objects they might not have discovered on their own (Tomasello, 1999; Tomasello & Call, 1997). In such cases, children recognize the correspondence between action and the change in the environment.

Exploration shows developmental change microgenetically, as it increases with the presentation of a new object and then decreases (Burghardt, 2005; Hutt, 1966). Exploration also changes with age, decreasing during childhood (Henderson and Moore, 1979) and is necessary for play with objects (Hutt, 1966). These trends are consistent with a view that the processes involved in exploring, stimulus enhancement, and emulation are precursors to the processes used in play with objects and imitation.

Regarding *tool use*, age trends too are evidenced with skills increasing from infancy through early childhood (Connolly & Dalgleish, 1989; Connolly & Elliot, 1972). Studies of tool use in childhood also show increases in facility with age, but they are drawn almost solely from performance on experimental tasks (e.g., Bates, Carlson-Luden, & Bretherton, 1980; Flynn & Whiten, 2008). Developmental descriptions of children's use of objects in children's everyday worlds, encompassing exploration, play, construction, and tool use, are sorely lacking (Power, 2000).

One clear exception to this is the comparative work of Mike Tomasello and colleagues, where they have compared the tool use of chimpanzees and young children. According to Tomasello (1999), tool use, like exploration and play with objects, is influenced by the social context. Indeed, it probably is learned and develops in a social context. Specifically, tool use probably begins with children imitating a significant adult. For example, a child could imitate using a pipe cleaner to push a pea down a narrow tube. In order for a behavior to be imitated, and not emulated, for example, the child must recognize and produce the behavior another has performed as well as its effect on an object. The child must also recognize the relationship between the behavior and the goal; that is to say, the child must recognize that the behavior is intentional (Tomasello & Call, 1997). This recognition is also the basis of using objects in pretend play as socially negotiated symbols, as noted above. Chimpanzees do not imitate experimenters' use of tools, in this sense. Instead, they emulate their use of tools by using the tool to effect change in the environment without imitation.

With these distinctions among different forms of object use in mind, it is important to try to cobble together a picture of their uses by children. Naturalistic, time-budget descriptions of children's tool use are unfortunately lacking, even though they are very important for a number of reasons. First, they would complement the age-related descriptions of toddlers' (Chen & Seigler, 2000) and children's tool use in contrived studies (Smitsman & Bonger, 2002; Vandenberg, 1980; van Leeuwen, Smitman, & van Leeuwen, 1994). Furthermore, descriptions of preschoolers' use of tools in their everyday niches would be an important complement to the descriptions of infants' and toddlers' tool use provided by Connolly (Connolly & Dalgleish, 1989; Connolly & Elliot, 1972). Time-budget studies also provide a basis for understanding possible functions of behaviors. Following behavioral ecological theory, behaviors where benefits are greater than costs should be favored by natural selection.

A behavioral ecological model for the specific conditions under which sophisticated object use, such as tool use, develop in primates has been advanced by Carel van Schaik, a biological anthropologist, and his colleagues (van Schaik, Deaner, & Merrill, 1999). They, like Vauclair (1984) and Tomasello and Call (1997), posit that tool use evolved in primates in the context of foraging (e.g., extracting) for food. Consequently, an important dimension of their model for the evolution of tool use should include an examination of different foraging, or extracting, niches. Specifically, when food is encased in some matrix, such as nut meat in shells or termites in mounds, tool use would afford opportunities to use tools to extract the food.

Next, relatively high levels of manual dexterity and manipulative skill are necessary to use or make a tool to extract the food; apes have this level of motor skill (van Schaik et al., 1999). Third, they must be intelligent. By this it is meant that animals are able to explore materials in order to discover their attributes. Next, animals should explore the objects or tools as a way to gain insight, or discover different ways that the objects can be used to solve a foraging problem in much the same way that the chimpanzee, Sultan, used sticks as a tool to reach bananas in Köhler's (1925) famous work. Again, apes have these requisite skills. A number of species of monkeys, such as capuchins and baboons, also show interest in objects. The interest in objects expressed by these species, as well as by apes, is related to the variety of their diets and, in some cases, the need to use objects in extractive foraging (Tomasello & Call, 1997).

Another important dimension of "intelligence" is the ability to relate one object to another object, a strategy necessary for using objects as tools. The ability to relate one object to another is a hallmark of Piaget's tertiary schemes, or Stage 5 of his sensorimotor stages (Tomasello & Call, 1997). Human infants, relative to chimpanzees and bonobos, spend more time doing this: 12%, 5%, and 0%, respectively (Tomasello & Call, 1997). Furthermore, adult chimpanzees organize objects in relation to each other in rather unsophisticated ways. For instance, when given a series of five nesting cups, the chimpanzees tended to only nest two cups—a smaller in a larger.

But ecological/foraging conditions alone are not sufficient to stimulate tool use. For example, van Schaik and colleagues point out that in one sample of orangutans (in Gunung Palang, Borneo), adult males ate *Neesis* seeds, which are embedded in irritant hairs that pierce the skin when the fruit skin is broken without using tools. It has been suggested that the lack of a social model using tools to eat these seeds as well as the lack of a more social orientation are responsible for the lack of tool use (van Schaik et al., 1999).

In the wild, most nonhuman primates are not interested in manipulating objects (Tomasello & Call, 1997), though there is some anecdotal evidence of it, such as the case of a gorilla using a stick to determine the depth of a stream while crossing it (Breuer, Ndoundou-Hockemba, & Fishlock, 2005). When nonhuman primates are reared in captivity by humans, the differences between humans and monkeys and apes diminish considerably. So, interest in objects and subsequent ability to use objects as tools is probably a result of emulating humans' actions on objects in social contexts. For example, in a context rich in objects and individuals using them, apes can observe humans manipulating and using objects to solve problems. The frequency of these models probably affects the degree to which they spread among a group of individuals, be they human or nonhuman primates.

Further evidence from Brian Hare in Tomasello's lab, in the form of the emotion/reactivity hypothesis (Hare, Brown, Williamson, & Tomasello, 2002; Hare, Call, & Tomasello, 2005), suggests that the process of domestication results in gregarious animals, like humans and domesticated dogs, not only being socially outgoing but also mediating their fear and aggressive behaviors so that they will cooperate, rather than compete, with conspecifics. A cooperative orientation results in these animals being able to share meaning in their communications, and eventually intentionality.

The Importance of the Time Budget Study of Children's Use of Objects

Time spent in different types of activities with objects during childhood can be framed in this study in terms of a behavioral ecology theory advanced by van Schaik and colleagues. From this position, descriptions of the "costs" associated with an activity serve as an indicator of its importance, or function. As noted earlier, high costs, relative to benefits, correspond to high benefits; and low costs, relative to benefits, usually (though not always) correspond to low benefits (Caro, 1988; Martin & Caro, 1985). Costs are typically documented in terms of the resources (time, energy, and risk of injury and death) expended to acquire or learn a skill. Time in an activity is typically expressed as the portion of the total time budget spent in that activity (Martin, 1982), and energy is typically expressed in terms of caloric expenditure in that activity relative to the entire caloric budget (Pellegrini, Horvat, & Huberty, 1998).

The logic of this level of analysis is as follows. Learning and acquiring specific skills involve different trade-offs between costs and benefits, and individuals tend to adopt the most "efficient," or optimal, strategies to solve problems across ontogeny (Krebs & Davies, 1997). For example, in learning to use tools, trade-offs must be made between different opportunities (e.g., playing with objects vs. observational learning) in light of the finite amount of time and calories available. From this view, there should be a correspondence between time budgets and the benefits associated with expenditures in each activity: Time spent in different types of activity use should relate positively to using those objects to solve problems. This level of analysis has proven to be useful in documenting the role of certain forms of play in children's development. For example, and as will be demonstrated in the discussion of locomotor play, caloric cost of children's locomotor play tends to be "moderate," accounting for about 5% of the time and energy during childhood (Pellegrini et al., 1998), and this level of cost corresponds to moderate benefits of play (Martin & Caro, 1985).

Correspondingly, time spent in different forms of object use should predict children's ability to use objects and tools in a variety of ways. However, the experimental studies examining the role of interaction with objects and subsequent use of objects to solve problems have employed very brief periods of object interaction, usually ten minutes or less (e.g., Dansky & Silverman, 1973; 1975; Smith & Simon, 1984; Sylva, Bruner, & Genova, 1972). It seems rather questionable that training children for ten minutes would have anything more than a transitory effect, if that. A more valid test of function would be to use total time spent in different forms of object and tool use across a long duration of time, such as observing children in a classroom across a whole school year to predict tool use facility. In other words, observing children's uses of objects and tools across a relatively long time frame should provide a valid sample of their facility with objects, relative to their being assigned to different objects experiences for ten minutes.

This sort of long-term observational strategy has been effectively, and admirably, employed by Bock (1999; 2005) in the area of object play and tool use, in his ethnographic work among the Okavango Delta people (Botswana). Specifically, using an extensive corpus of direct behavioral observation, he described the development of different forms of object play and tool use for boys and girls from birth through 18 years of age. Playful tool use took the form of play pounding, where children, usually girls, would take a stick, reed, or mortar and pound dirt. This activity is similar to the grain-processing work in which women engage. Indeed, groups of young girls often initiated this task close to adult women actually engaging in the task. Bock also designed an experimental task where girls' grain-processing efficiency was assessed.

Bock's results indicated that boys engaged in more object play than girls. Additionally, boys' object play followed an inverted-U curve, typical of the development of other forms of play (Martin & Caro, 1985; Power, 2000), accounting for 0.11 of the observations at 0–3 years, 0.17 at 4–6, and 0.03 at 7–9 years. For girls, an inverted-U curve was also observed for object play, but the peak was at a later age: 0.04 at 0–3 years, 0.08 at 4–6 years, 0.11 at 7–9 years, 0.15 at 10–12 years, and zero at 13–15 years. The trajectory for play pounding for girls paralleled object play: 0.05, 0.16, 0.17, 0.22, and zero, respectively.

Other ethnographic and ethological studies of tool use have been conducted with a particular eye on sex differences (Power, 2000). Examples of this sort of activity involve girls using sticks in domestic tasks, like cooking, while boys are using tools as weapons in pretend play. These examples have even been observed in the human foraging literature (see Gosso, Otta, Morais, Ribeiro, & Bussab, 2005). For example, forager boys (in the Amazon) more than girls, are frequently seen playing with bows and arrows, and sling-shots. Similarly, the forager literature supports the idea that girls more frequently than boys make tools associated with gathering. For example, making baskets out of palm leaves is another common form of play among the Parakanã girls from Pará State (see Gosso et al., 2005). Indeed, this activity was observed exclusively among girls. Examples of these Amazonian forgers' object use in are displayed in Figures 8.4–8.6.

Describing the various forms of object use (i.e., exploration, play, construction, and tool use) should also help clarify inconsistent and confusing gender differences reported in the child developmental literature. For example, in most of

Figure 8.4   Foraging children weaving (Photo: G. Gossi)

Figure 8.5   Foraging children cooking (Photo: G. Gossi)

the studies concerned with object use, using the Smilansky-Parten matrix, it is reported that females engage in constructive play more than males (Johnson & Erlsher, 1981; Johnson, Erlsher, & Bell, 1980; Rubin et al., 1976; Rubin et al., 1978). However, boys' constructions tend to be more complex than girls' (Erickson, 1977; see Rubin et al., 1983, for a summary), and boys, relative to girls, tend to be more facile with objects as indicated by their performance on the block-design portion of the Wechsler Preschool and Primary Scale of Intelligence (Caldera et al., 1989). Describing the time spent using objects in construction, exploration, play, and tool use should clarify this confusion by presenting descriptive information on boys' and girls' object use for each of these categories, if observed across a relatively long time span.

To make more direct functional inferences about children's observed uses of objects, we could also examine the extent to which each of these observed categories predicts children's ability to use objects to solve "convergent problems" (i.e., lure-retrieval tasks) and "divergent problems" (i.e., associative fluency). Both types of problems have been examined extensively in the child development literature. While more detail on method will be provide below, I provide a general picture of the tasks.

In one type of convergent task, Gredlein, Bjorklund, and Hicking (2003) presented children with an assembled tool (a hoe) and two components of tools (a rake head and the rake handle), similar to those displayed below. They were asked to use the objects to retrieve a lure.

In a second type of convergent task, modeled after Köhler (1925) and Kathy Sylva and colleagues (Sylva, Bruner, & Genova, 1976), children can be presented with disassembled components of a tool that has to be assembled in order to retrieve the lure, such as the dinosaur in Figure 8.7.

It is also is important to note that this is both a tool *construction* and a tool *use* task, not a use task alone. In this distinction, the tool construction task may be more accurately considered a measure of creativity, rather than the ability to imitate how others use an already constructed tool. This sort of task has been used extensively in the child development literature (e.g., Simon & Smith, 1983, 1985; Vandenberg, 1980), though the results of Sylva and colleagues have not generally been replicated. Specifically, the classic study of Sylva and colleagues (1976) found that preschool children's play with objects in an experimental setting related to their subsequent ability to construct a tool used to retrieve a lure. Other researchers, however, have not replicated these results (Simon & Smith, 1983; 1984; Vandenberg, 1980). An example of objects used in tool construction tasks is illustrated by the Tinker Toy–like objects presented in Figure 8.7.

Using objects in divergent problem-solving situations, or tasks for which there is no one correct answer, is also very common in the child development literature (Sutton-Smith, 1966). Specifically, Dansky and Silverman's (1973; 1975) frequently cited studies examined the effects of "play" with objects on children's associative fluency, or creative uses for objects. In the first study, Dansky and Silverman (1973) provided children with conventional, but novel, objects. In one condition they were asked to play with the objects; in others they

Figure 8.6   Foraging children playing with bows and arrows (Photo: G. Gossi)

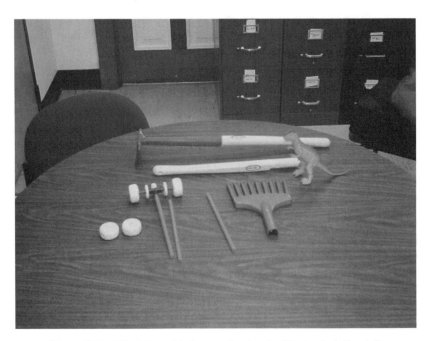

Figure 8.7   "Tools" used in lure retrieval tasks (Photo: A. Pellegrini)

observed an adult manipulating the objects or were exposed to a control condition. These sessions lasted less than ten minutes. Children were then asked to list all the uses possible for one of the objects to which they were exposed. For example, creative uses for a matchbox might include using it as a pretend boat.

They found that children in the play condition generated the greatest number of creative responses, relative to children in the other conditions.

In the second experiment by Dansky and Silverman (1975), children were assigned to similar conditions to those in the first experiment, but then asked to generate creative uses for objects with which they did *not* interact. In other words, the researchers were examining the extent to which the "play set" from the experimental condition generalized to new objects. Again, they found that children in the play condition, relative to the other conditions, were the most creative. They argued that these effects were due to an induced "play set," a temporary, creative orientation to objects presented.

While being widely cited, these studies of associative fluency, like the Sylva and colleagues study, do not replicate when double-blind procedures are used (Smith & Whitney, 1987). The results, then, were probably due to experimenter bias. As noted earlier, these studies also suffered from very limited experimental treatments. Furthermore, and especially in light of the limited time of the treatment and relative unfamiliarity of the experimental props, children may have been more likely to have been exploring the objects, not playing with them.

With all this said, one could rightfully question the efficacy of an experimental treatment of ten minutes or so on children's behavior. That the experimental literature on object play and problem-solving has not consistently shown effects may be more due to these very limited treatments than to the lack of efficacy of the role of play or exploration with objects. A more valid approach to documenting the role of object play and exploration in tool use would involve documenting the time children spend in different types of object use across a relatively long period of time in their natural ecologies, and then regressing those values on to children's performance in different object use tasks (Pellegrini & Gustafson, 2005). This larger corpus of observations should provide a more robust indicator of children's facility with objects, relative to the relatively short-term studies cited above.

Time Spent Using Objects by Preschoolers and Possible Functions

Kathy Gustafson and I (Pellegrini & Gustafson, 2005) conducted this type of study in the Shirley Moore Nursery School at the University of Minnesota across one academic year. Observations were conducted three afternoons per week for one entire school year. Observations used in data collection, however, followed a period of extensive training and time spent in classrooms so that children could become habituated to the researcher's presence.

Classrooms were organized around a variety of activity centers and play areas that were equipped with a wide assortment of play materials such as blocks; dress-up clothes; stuffed animals; dolls; trucks; musical instruments; puzzles; board games; clay; materials for painting, writing, drawing, and cutting; water tables; sand tables; book areas; computers (installed with age-relevant software programs), and printers. The playground area, where children were also observed, included a large sand area; a large climbing apparatus; and swings, as well as an assortment of tricycles, toy wagons, and shovels. Classrooms also had adjacent observation booths from which all indoor observations were conducted. Outdoor observations were conducted while standing on the side of the playground area.

Observations consisted of one-minute focal child sampling with continuous recording (Pellegrini, 2004) during periods of free play. We were especially interested in four dimensions of the focal child's behavior with objects: Exploration, Play, Construction, and Tool Use. Descriptions not involving objects were coded as Other so that we could establish the time spent in different forms of object use compared with all other behavior observed. Descriptions of each of the four categories and nine subcategories are provided in Table 8.1.

Children were also asked to participate in three types of object-use tasks (two convergent and one divergent tool tasks).

The first convergent tool retrieval task involved selecting a tool with which to retrieve a toy dinosaur that had been placed out of reach of the student. The materials for the first task consisted of three potential retrieval tools: a plastic toy hoe (25 inches long and 5 inches wide), a plastic rake head without a handle (10½ inches long and six inches wide), and a plastic toy rake handle without the rake head (17½ inches long). A plastic toy dinosaur (7 inches long and 3 inches high) was used as the item to be retrieved. A picture of these tools is displayed above in Figure 8.7.

In this task, children were told: "In this game I want you to figure out a way to use these things, or one of them, to get the dinosaur at the other end of the table. You can use these things in any way to get the dinosaur. You cannot get out of your seat, however. Take your time and try. Go ahead and let's play the game." Children were given a series of hints if they could not perform the task.

Table 8.1   Object use categories and tool use subcategories

Object Use	Explanation and Example
Exploration	"What can it do?" Flat or negative affect. Sniff; squeeze; shake; rotate, bring to eyes; drop
Play	"What can I do with it?" Positive affect. Pretending (e.g., cues in language or gestures)
Construction	Building something that is end-oriented (not play)
Tool Use	Using an object as a means to an end; to get something done
Reach	Extend reach; rake; insert and probe; stack and climb
Weapon	Throw; brandish; wave; threaten with
Body Aid	Support self (e.g., using an object as a crutch)
Pour/Wipe	Control liquids (e.g., using an object to pour liquid)
Bang	Using an object to make a noise; crashing, or slamming an object for the sake of making noise
Empty/Fill/Dig/ Poke	Using an object to fill or empty containers; or using an object to jab or prod
Art/Write	Using an object to write, draw, paint, etc.
Transport/Carry	Use an object to transport or carry something; or transporting, carrying, or holding an object
Throw/Kick	Throwing or kicking an object (but not as a weapon)

Specifically, children were first told: "Why don't you try reaching with one of these things?" Next they were told: "Why don't you try this?" (The experimenter pointed at the connected rake).

In the second convergent task, children were asked to *construct* a tool and then use that tool to retrieve a toy. Children were presented with Tinker Toy parts and told: "In this game I want you to figure out a way to use these things to get the dinosaur. You can use these things in any way you want to get the dinosaur. You cannot get out of your seat, however. Go ahead, take your time and try." The hints were as follows: "Can you think of a way to use some of these things? Can you try using the round yellow pieces and the sticks to help you? Can you try using the round yellow pieces and the sticks together to help you? Can you put one stick into each end of the yellow round piece to make a longer stick? I will hold a stick. Can you put the round yellow piece on the end of it? Can you use the other sticks and round yellow pieces to make it longer?" A picture of these tools is also displayed above in Figure 8.7.

The following dimensions of each child's performance were scored: the total time (in seconds) needed by the child to use one or more of the objects to successfully retrieve the dinosaur; the number of hints provided to the child by the experimenter while completing the task; and the number of swipes (e.g., attempts to use one or more of the objects to retrieve the dinosaur). The hints were provided in a sequential order but in ways that were appropriate to the phase of the task in which the child was engaged. The hints also provided the child with gradually more specific help in accomplishing the second task. Specifically, the hints consisted of the following: 1) Can you think of a way to use some of these things to get the dinosaur? 2) Can you try using a round piece to help you? 3) Can you try using the round pieces and the sticks together to help you? 4) Can you put one stick into each end of the round piece to make a longer stick? 5) I will hold this stick. (The experimenter picked up a stick for the child.) Can you put the round piece on the end of it? 6) Can you use the other sticks and round pieces to make it longer? 7) (The experimenter connected the pieces for the child and had him/her use the experimenter-constructed pieces to retrieve the dinosaur.)

The third task was a divergent problem-solving task—associative fluency— and involved asking children to generate novel uses for one of three common household objects (Dansky & Silverman, 1973; 1975; Wallach, 1970). One of the following objects was placed on the table in front of the child: a paper cup, a plastic spoon, or a marker (in counterbalanced order). We analyzed only the novel uses, defined as those that reflected an unusual or atypical way of using the targeted object.

After each child had completed these three tasks, the Wechsler Preschool and Primary Scales of Intelligence, Object Design Test (WPPSI), was given. Following the directions of the WPPSI subtest, the child was asked to use a set of colored blocks to reproduce up to 14 different block patterns presented to them one at a time by the examiner. Two attempts were allowed to reproduce each design. Scores were based on the number block designs reproduced correctly, the number of block designs reproduced correctly on the first attempt, and (on selected designs) the number of block design patterns completed correctly within a specified time limit. At the completion of the test, each child's Block Design raw score was converted to a Block Design scaled score, using a table provided in the WPPSI manual.

Boys' and Girls' Uses of Objects

Descriptive statistics for frequency of occurrence of boys' and girls' different use of objects are displayed in Table 8.2. As can be seen, the rates of occurrence for play and tool use were similar, approximately one per observation. Total tool use and play accounted for 24% and 26%, respectively, of all observed behavior, with boys engaging in each form of behavior more than girls. From these descriptive data we conclude that tool use, like play, occurs at a moderate to high level during children's play time in nursery school. More generally, these data indicate that exploration, construction, play with objects, and tool use, relative to other behavior, accounted for more than half of the children's observed behavior.

Furthermore, these relatively high figures probably reflect the enriched nursery school environment in which these children were observed. The classrooms and the playground were equipped with various and numerous objects and tools with which children were encouraged to play. For example, the playground had rakes, shovels, and wheelbarrows for children to use. Similarly, the classrooms were also object-rich, with blocks, sorting and water tables, puzzles, etc. In order to gain a wider understanding of the time spent interacting with objects, we still need to know how children use objects throughout their whole day, in and out of school. For example, when children are observed in everyday contexts (Bock, 1999), the time budgets are lower (c. 16%–17% at peak).

Sex differences in observed uses of objects were also examined. As can be seen from Table 8.2, the difference favoring females for construction is consistent with extant research (Rubin et al., 1983). Girls' uses of objects in construction often took the form of doing puzzles and art activities, all relatively sedentary activities. Boys, on the other hand, used objects in play and marginally more as tools. Boys' play with objects was often embedded in the context of fantasy play, where objects were used to enact superhero themes, consistent with the early finding of Saltz, Dixon, and Johnson (1977). Also consistent with the ethnographic literature, we found that males, more than females, tended to use objects

Table 8.2   Descriptive statistics for object use by sex (N = 35)

Category	Males (n = 18)		Females (n = 17)		T-stat	p-value
	M	SD	M	SD		
Explore	0.11	.15	0.005	.007	−1.40	.16
Play	1.40	.52	0.96	.50	−2.55	.01
Construction	0.50	.40	0.98	.40	2.91	.006
Total Tool	1.21	.62	0.97	.41	−1.32	.19
Other Behavior	1.68	.67	1.66	.47	.083	.93

Table 8.3   Inter-correlations between measures of object uses* (N = 35)

	2	3	4	5
Explore 1	−.007	−.04	−.20	.13
Play 2		−.36*	−.07	.05
Construction 3			.05	.01
Tool 4				.24
Age 5				

as weapons (Bock, 2005; Gosso et al., 2005). The photograph below illustrates Amazonian foraging boys playing with bows and arrows, in preparation for their adult role as hunters.

We were also concerned in this study with the construct validity of the four categories of object use (i.e., exploration, play with objects, construction, and tool use) as they are typically conflated in the child development literature. To this end, we examined the inter-correlations, displayed in Table 8.3, between each dimension of object use observed among these children.

Results from these analyses reinforce the importance of differentiating children's uses of objects. Specifically, only one of the seven inter-correlations between these measures was significant (play and construction), and the correlation was negative; measures of exploration, construction, and tool use were not significantly inter-correlated with play.

Consistent with Piaget's formulations, construction and play were negatively inter-correlated. And consistent with Hutt, exploration and play were independent. Total tool use was not related to play, exploration, or construction. In short, each of these categories is distinct.

Using Objects as Tools to Solve Convergent and Divergent Problems

Another dimension of the developmental histories of each construct relates to the beneficial consequences of each category of object use. To this end, we examined the predictive relationships between each form of object use and performance on a divergent problem-solving task (associative fluency) and two convergent problem-solving tasks (connected and unconnected lure-retrieval tasks) with objects. As part of these analyses, children's spatial intelligence was statistically controlled so that inferences could be made about the role of object use in problem solving, independent of spatial intelligence.

First, regarding sex differences, no significant differences were observed in any of the three tasks, though the directions favored the females in the connected and associative fluency tasks. The lack of sex differences for both convergent (both the tool tasks) and divergent problem-solving (associative fluency) tasks are consistent with earlier work (Pepler & Ross, 1981). Descriptive statistics for these analyses are displayed in Table 8.4.

Performance on individual tasks did not relate to performance on the other tasks. Within-task performance, however, was correlated (time and hints for the

Table 8.4   Descriptive statistics for objects used to solve problems by sex (N = 20)

Category	Males (n = 10)		Females (n = 10)			
	M	SD	M	SD	T-stat (df = 18)	p-value
Assoc. Fluency	3.10	2.38	5.00	4.42	1.19	.24
Connected Retrieval Task						
Time (in secs)	33.70	35.48	27.50	22.09	−.46	.64
Hints	1.50	.85	1.30	.48	−.64	.52
Unconnected Retrieval Task						
Time (in secs)	102.00	73.20	138.20	114.91	.84	.41
Hints	2.20	1.23	3.80	2.90	1.60	.12

connected and unconnected retrieval tasks). Simply, the correlation between time and hints is probably due to the fact that the more time taken to solve each retrieval problem, the more hints the children received.

The predictive relations between observed object uses and performance on the associative fluency task and on the connected and unconnected lure-retrieval tasks revealed that neither observed play nor exploration predicted problem solving on any of the three tasks. That exploration was a very low-occurrence behavior may be partially responsible for these results. A combination of the age of the children as well as their familiarity with the objects is probably responsible for these results. Specifically, when one considers that exploration is more typical of infants and toddlers than of preschoolers (Belsky & Most, 1981), and that children were observed interacting with the same objects across time, it is not surprising that low levels of exploration were observed.

In terms of the lack of relationship between play with objects and performance on any of the problem-solving tasks, as displayed in Table 8.5 and 8.6, the current results would seem to question the often-trumpeted value of play for both convergent and divergent problem-solving tasks with objects.

This is similar to the argument made by Smith and colleagues in reference to the questionable role of play in lure-retrieval performance (Simon & Smith, 1983; 1985) and associative fluency (Smith & Whitney, 1987).

In the future it would be important to examine both social and solitary dimensions of object use and how each relates to performance outcomes, such as those reported

Table 8.5   Inter-correlations between uses of objects to solve problems (N = 20)

	2	3	4	5
Associative Fluency 1	.08	.07	−.13	.02
Connected Time 2		.89**	.001	.30
Connected Hint 3			−.10	.12
UnConnected Time 4				.74**
UnConnected Hint 5				

** p < 01

Table 8.6   Partial correlations between observed object use and performance on using objects as tools, controlling for spatial intelligence (N = 20)

	Performance Associative Fluency	Connected Time	Connected Hint	Unconnected Time	Unconnected Hint
Object Use					
Explore	0.04	−0.21	−0.21	−0.16	−0.38
Play	−0.18	0.35	0.33	0.10	−0.15
Total Tool	−0.34	−0.01	0.12	−0.32	−0.45*
Construct	0.52*	−0.45*	−0.46*	−0.30	−0.06

$Df = 16 * p < .05$

here. For example, Fagen (1981) has suggested, using hypothetical models, that animals' solitary play with objects, rather than social play, should facilitate creativity. This, he suggests, is due to the primacy of individual's genetic fitness. From this view, creative uses of objects observed by conspecifics in social contexts could reduce the creative individual's fitness in relation to the observers if the observers use those strategies to maximize their fitness, not that of the creative individual.

In contrast, it may be the case, for example, that playing with objects in groups, more than solitary object play, maximizes creative responses. In social, rather than solitary, contexts, children have the opportunity to observe a variety of models using objects in numerous ways. The more varied experience, in turn, should relate to enhanced performance in using objects in convergent and divergent tasks. An interesting test of these two hypotheses could involve observing siblings (who share genes) in social and solitary object play contexts to compare which of the two situations elicits more creative uses of objects and which is the better predictor of creativity in a variety of tasks.

Construction and tool use differentially predicted performance on the problem-solving tasks. More specifically, construction was a significant predictor of associative fluency and performance on both dimensions of the connected tool retrieval task, but it did not predict performance on the unconnected task: Tool use predicted one dimension of performance on the connected tasks (number of hints).

The unconnected task was more difficult than the connected task, as indicated by the differences in time and hints needed to solve each. The time needed to complete the unconnected task was greater by a factor of four than the connected task, and more than double the number of hints was needed.

The different patterns for connected and unconnected tasks merit further discussion. First, as displayed in Table 8.5, performance on one task was not related to performance on the other, though measures of performance within each task were interrelated. Second, the connected task was less demanding than the unconnected task, as evidenced by the difference in time needed to solve each problem. Third, the magnitudes of the correlations between observed tool use and performance on the unconnected task were higher than on the connected task. The pattern for observed construction was the opposite: Correlations were higher (in two of the three cases) between time in construction and performance on the connected compared to the unconnected tasks. With regard to the unconnected tool task, it is probably the case that the specific skills needed to solve the problem took more time and practice than those needed in the easier, connected task.

Interestingly, the more time spent in two subcategories of tool use, *banging* and *weapon*, related to more time and hints needed to solve the connected problem. Indeed, the magnitudes of the correlations for the weapon subcategory were especially high. The weapon subcategory was also significantly related to the play category, suggesting that children who used weapons as tools also engaged in fantasy. In our observations, there were no cases of girls using tools as weapons, thus this was a male phenomenon.

It would be interesting to examine the extent to which the weapon subcategory related to a more closely related task, such as throwing an object at a target. Males' use of tools as weapons may relate to tool use task, but with a different sort of task. Specifically, boys' use of objects as weapons may predict performance on a task where they throw an object at a target. Consistent with this view, sex differences on children's performance on target tasks (favoring males and girls with high levels of androgen relative to control girls) but not on mental rotation tasks have been reported (Hines, Fane, Pasterski, Mathews, Conway, & Brook, 2003).

Why did time spent in construction predict both performance on the divergent problem and the connected convergent problem? Construction is an "ends"-oriented behavioral category. In the process of constructing, children typically coordinate means toward some end product. This set of skills was sufficient to solve the simpler, connected, retrieval task and the associative fluency task, but less effective with the more complex, unconnected, retrieval task. For the latter task, a more diverse and specific set of skills, reflected in the total tool category, was necessary to solve the unconnected task.

CONCLUSION

Data on their uses of objects in exploration, play with objects, construction, and tool use. The distinction among these categories is an important one as, to my knowledge, they have not been differentiated in the child development literature on children's play. These categories are distinct, and they should be treated as such, as they have different developmental histories and different implications for using objects to solve problems. With all of this said, much more work is needed, however, particularly observational work documenting the time spent in different sorts of object use.

The anthropological work of John Bock (1999; 2005) among pastoral people of Botswana provides some guidance here. Females' tool use, for example, was assessed in the processing of grain—a task they were expected to perform as adults. Perhaps a female-oriented task could involve using a stick to locate a stimulus (such as a fruit or vegetable) embedded in a complex field of other stimuli. Similarly, a male-oriented task, such as the ability to saw accurately a piece of wood or their ability to throw a stick at a target might be more likely to reveal sex differences on task performance.

It should also be apparent from the discussions in this chapter that much more attention needs to be paid to the social context with which children use objects. It is important to know, for example, the ways that mothers interact with their children and peers interact with each other in different forms of object use. While we do have detailed information on these social processes around using objects in pretend play and to a much lesser degree, exploration, we do not have much information at all on tool use and tool invention.

9

Locomotor Play

In this chapter I examine locomotor play. Interestingly, this form of play has received wide and deep attention from behavioral biologists (e.g., Bekoff & Byers, 1981; Fagen, 1981) and comparative psychologists (Povinelli & Cant, 1995) but very little attention from developmental psychologists, with the notable exception of Pellegrini and Smith (1998). For example, in the only chapter dedicated to play in *A Handbook of Child Psychology*, Rubin, Fein, and Vandenberg (1983) made no mention of it, and instead talked primarily about functional and pretend play, in addition to "constructive" play.

This limitation may reflect deep-seated biases towards the study of specific forms of play, to the exclusion of other forms. Specifically, there is a long tradition of a cognitive bias in the study of play, perhaps due to the long-lasting impact of Piaget's theory of development on the field, and the consequential study of pretend play. Recall, when Peter Smith and Ralph Vollstedt (1985) asked adults to rate critical aspects of play, fantasy was the most important defining characteristic. Correspondingly, the current resurgence in the study of play is due in part to the study of pretend play and its role in children's theory of mind (Harris, 1990; 2005; Lillard, 1993; 1998; 2002).

This is an interesting state of affairs given our current state of knowledge regarding definitions and putative functions of play. Specifically, locomotor play has been clearly defined in terms of exaggerated and nonfunctional behaviors and behavioral sequences as displayed in Figure 9.1 (Fagen, 1981). Furthermore, functional attributes of locomotor play, both immediate and deferred, have been proffered by scholars from a variety of disciplines, including zoology (Byers, 1998; Byers & Walker, 1995; Stamps, 1995) and psychology (Pellegrini

Figure 9.1   Exaggerated movement (Photo: A. Pellegrini)

& Smith, 1998; Povenelli & Cant, 1995). From this position, it seems that many psychologists have ignored one of the most common forms of play, as well as some basic theoretical and definitional assumptions regarding the functions of play.

Locomotor play has a vigorous physical component, and thus it may variously be called *physical activity play* (Pellegrini & Smith, 1998) or, more commonly *locomotor play* (Bekoff & Byers, 1981). Indeed, much of children's physical activity can be seen as playful in the sense that it is minimally constrained by adult demands, involves novel forms and sequences of motor behaviors and routines, and is accompanied by positive affect.

Adults, however, often show some ambivalence toward children's high levels of physical activity. This ambivalence is reflected in over-diagnosed cases of attention deficit, hyperactive disorder, or ADHD, (British Psychological Society Working Party, 2005) in boys. Children who are physically active can pose challenges for care-givers; one common alternative to addressing the problem is to medicate the child to make him less active (Pellegrini & Horvat, 1995). This bias may also be reflected in the relative paucity of research on children's physical activity generally (Pellegrini & Smith, 1993; 1998; Welsh & Labbé, 1994), and on locomotor play (Pellegrini & Smith, 1998), more specifically. Yet physical activity may be important, not only for physical development, but also perhaps for cognitive performance following activity, and even for aspects of social organization and social skills. Physical activity play may, in some senses, matter psychologically.

In this chapter I discuss the definition of locomotor play in human and nonhuman juveniles, as well as ontogenetic and sex trends. I will also examine locomotor play in terms of antecedents (hormonal and socialization events) and function.

WHAT IS LOCOMOTOR PLAY?

As noted in the definitional chapter, both child developmentalists and ethologists agree that players, typically children or juveniles, are concerned with means more than ends. Furthermore, play activity appears to be "purposeless," or to occur for its own sake, and, perhaps, be enjoyable (Martin & Caro, 1985; Rubin et al., 1983). Locomotor play, like other forms of play, is also multidimensional and may involve symbolic activity, as in the case of boys enacting a superhero theme involving running, chasing, and playfighting. The activity may also be social or solitary, but the distinguishing behavioral features are a playful context, combined with what Simons-Morton et al. (1990) describe as moderate to vigorous physical activity, such that metabolic activity is well above resting metabolic rate. Examples of locomotor play include running, climbing, chasing, and swinging.

Because of this multidimensionality, the way that any form of play is classified is not always clear cut. In this book, unlike in my earlier work (Pellegrini & Smith, 1998), however, I no longer consider playfighting, or rough-and-tumble play (R&T), primarily a type of locomotor play. Instead R&T was treated as a form of social play, as it has been by behavioral biologists (e.g., Fagen, 1981; Lewis, 2005; Martin & Caro, 1985) and anthropologists (Fry, 2005). Like most forms of play, R&T is multifaceted and can have object, locomotor, and social dimensions, yet it is primarily social. Furthermore, I label the form of play under discussion in this chapter *locomotor play*, not *physical activity*, as I have in the past (Pellegrini & Smith, 1998). This re-labeling is an effort to keep labels in the human and behavioral biology literatures consistent and minimize confusion in the literature. In what follows I first describe locomotor play in terms of its ontogeny, with examples from both the human and nonhuman literature, with corresponding sex differences, because these may indicate different types of physical activity play that may have different functional significance (Byers & Walker, 1995).

Age and Sex Trends in Locomotor Play

Play, as noted repeatedly in this book, follows an inverted-U developmental course, and locomotor play is no different: It begins in early infancy, peaks during childhood, then declines during adolescence, and declines rapidly in adulthood, following my definition of play (Byers & Walker, 1995; Fagen, 1981; Rubin et al., 1983). Some scholars, such as Brian Sutton-Smith (1997), would disagree, as they consider activities such as vigorous sport to be play. As will be discussed in the later chapter on games, sports and games are not "play" in the sense that they are both governed, for the most part, by *a priori* rules. In this view, the trends in locomotor play in humans appear to show two successive peaks, reflecting three types of play, probably with different functions. These are designated as 1) rhythmic stereotypies and 2) exercise play. Each is discussed in turn.

Rhythmic Stereotypies

Although most studies in the infancy literature relate to the ontogeny of symbolic play with parents (e.g., Bornstein & Tamis-LeMonda, 1995) and sensorimotor exploration and play (e.g., Ruff & Saltarelli, 1993), there is limited evidence documenting infants' locomotor play. Most notably, the late Esther Thelen's (1979; 1980) longitudinal study of infants' "rhythmical stereotypies" during the first year of life provides basic and important descriptive information. Rhythmical stereotypic behaviors are similar to my definition of locomotor play to the extent that they are gross motor movements, "and it is difficult to ascribe goal or purpose to those movements" (Thelen, 1979, p. 699); examples include body rocking and foot kicking. The onset of these behaviors is probably controlled by general neuromuscular maturation.

Stereotypic behaviors tend to peak during the midpoint of the first year of life: at six months, some infants spend as much as 40% of a one-hour observational period in stereotypic behavior (Thelen, 1980). After this point, the behaviors gradually disappear from normal children's behavioral repertoires (Thelen, 1979). Throughout the first year of life, infants spend 5.2% of their time in stereotypic behaviors (Thelen, 1980). Some early parent–infant interactions probably provide other locomotor play opportunities. For example, Roopnarine, Hooper, Ahmeduzzaman, and Pollack's (1993) examination of play between parents and one-year-old infants in India suggests that locomotor play, such as tossing the infant in the air and bouncing on the knee, accounted for 13% of all play, whereas object play accounted for 80%. Similarly low rates of American parent–infant locomotor play (or vestibular stimulation) were reported by Thelen (1980).

Regarding sex differences, none are reported in the incidence of rhythmic stereotypies. Specifically, Thelen (1980) compared rates for ten male and ten female infants; these averaged 35.1 and 34.4 bouts per hour, respectively, a very small and insignificant difference.

Exercise Play

By "exercise play" I mean gross locomotor movements in the context of play, such as swinging, jumping or climbing, and splashing and swimming. The distinguishing feature of this play is its physical vigor: it may or may not be social, but the distinctively specialized social form of R&T was discussed in the chapter on social play. Exercise play in this sense can start at the end of the first year, and it can be solitary or with parents or peers. In fact, much of the research on parent–infant play does not distinguish between exercise play and R&T, but appears to be describing "rough physical play" (Carson, Burks, & Parke, 1993; Roopnarine et al., 1993), which I considered under R&T. Low rates of American parent–infant physical play have been reported by MacDonald and Parke (1986), with rates peaking at around four years of age. A few cases of infant exercise play without parents have been reported. Konner (1972), for example, reported that the !Kung, a one-time Botswana foraging group, encouraged infants to chase after and catch large insects. In many cultures, ranging from model

Figure 9.2   Exercise play among forager children (Photo: G. Gossi)

industrialized societies to foragers, exercise play is often typified by positive affect and, in some cases such as illustrated below, involves learning important skills, such as swimming as displayed in Figure 9.2.

As we move to the preschool period, greater incidences of exercise play are reported, though, as was the case in infancy, most of the peer play literature for this period focuses on pretend play, not physical activity play. Furthermore, where the latter is reported, it is often in the form of R&T, which tends to co-occur with pretend during this period (Pellegrini & Perlmutter, 1987; Smith, 1973; Smith & Connolly, 1980). In a few studies, "gross motor" play other than R&T is reported, sometimes occurring alone, sometimes with peers (rather than with parents).

Exercise play *per se* increases from the toddler to the preschool period and then declines during the primary school years, with a likely peak at around four to five years (Eaton & Yu, 1989; Routh, Schroeder, & O'Tuama, 1974). Specifically, for two-year-olds, Rosenthal (1994) reports that it accounts for about 7% of behavior observed in daycare settings. For children two to four years of age, Field (1994) reports physical activity play accounting for 10% of all daycare behavior. Similarly, Bloch's (1989) observations of children in a Senegal fishing village found that gross motor activities accounted for 11% and 13% of children's play in the home at two to four years of age and five to six years of age, respectively.

In two ethological studies in British nursery schools, using a variety of samples, McGrew (1972) and Smith and Connolly (1980) observed children's behavior at a microanalytical level. In McGrew's sample, with a mean age of 49.2 months, approximately 20% of children's activity was physically vigorous, such as run, flee, wrestle, chase, jump, push and pull, lift, and climb. Similarly, in Smith and Connolly's (1980) sample, with a mean age of 43.3 months, vigorous activities, such as run, chase, and climb (but also including R&T), accounted for 21% of their behavior.

As children move into primary school, a decline in physical activity is witnessed, perhaps due to the fact that they are spending more time in an environment—school—which discourages, rather than encourages, physical activity. For children aged six to ten years, "exercise play" accounted for only 13% of all outdoor behavior observed during school recess periods (Pellegrini, 1990). This relative decrease in play might be underestimated, however, because the primary school observations occurred on school playgrounds, rather than in classrooms, unlike most studies of preschoolers; the relative spatial density of classrooms, compared to playgrounds, inhibits gross motor activity (Smith & Connolly, 1980).

It will be important for our later argument for the functions of locomotor play to demonstrate that during the preschool and primary school years children engage in substantial amounts of exercise play. Blatchford (1996) described the general levels of English primary school children's activity on the school playground and found that most (60% of the children) are engaged in some form of physically active play or games during their daily break times, which lasted between 65 and 75 minutes.

What about physical activity outside the school context? Simons-Morton and colleagues (1990) studied children aged nine and ten years, using children's self-reported frequency of moderate to vigorous physical activity (MVPA), that includes play and nonplay forms of physical activity, over three days. Major sources of MVPA were running, walking fast, games and sports, and cycling. MVPAs generally were slightly more common before or after school (2.3/day) than during school (1.6/day). Throughout the whole day, most children engaged in one or two long (>10 min.) MVPAs per day. In general, then, exercise, and possibly exercise play, is quite common in early and middle childhood, and appears to peak in the preschool and early primary grades, although more evidence is certainly needed to clarify exactly when the age peak occurs.

Sex differences in exercise play suggest that males tend to engage in exercise play at higher rates than females. Eaton and Enns's (1986) meta-analysis of 90 studies of sex differences in motor activity level reported a significant difference in favor of males, with the effect size tending to increase from infancy to mid-adolescence. Part of this sex difference may be due to differential maturation rates. Eaton and Yu (1989) found that relative maturity (percent of estimated adult height attained) interacted with sex, being negatively related to activity level, with girls being both less active and more physically mature than boys. As will be discussed below, these differences in physical activity probably form an important basis for the existence of segregated sex peer groups which begin during the preschool period and wane in early adolescence (Maccoby, 1998; Pellegrini, 2004; Pellegrini, Long, Roseth, Bohn, & Van Ryzin, 2007).

Summary of Age and Sex Trends

In summary, forms of locomotor play are quite common in childhood. In primary schools, most children engage in active play during their daily break times.

Furthermore, levels of physical activity play are moderate for most children when they are out of school. An analysis of age trends suggests three successive inverted-U curves describing two different forms of locomotor play. Rhythmic stereotypies peak in infancy at around six months of age, and sex differences have been observed. Exercise play peaks during the preschool years, accounting for up to 20% of observed school recess behavior, and declines during the primary school years, accounting for about 13% of observed behavior; males, more than females, engage in exercise play. I postulate that these successive age peaks reflect different forms of play with different functions.

Males exceed females in frequency of locomotor play among many other mammalian species as well (Meaney, Stewart, & Beatty, 1985; Smith, 1982).

Antecedents to Sex Differences

Hormonal Influences

Sex differences appear to be absent in rhythmical stereotypies, but appreciable for exercise play. Hypotheses about the functions of play must take into account such sex differences and the causation of such differences. Hormonal influences on play have been implicated in sex differences in vigorous physical activity. Hormonal influences typically center around the effects of endogenous and exogenous androgens on neural organization and behavior (Meaney et al., 1985). Normal exposure to androgens during fetal development predisposes boys, more than girls, toward physical activity. Excessive amounts of these male hormones are hypothesized to "masculinize" females' play (Collaer & Hines, 1995; Hines, 1982; Hines, Fane, Pasterski, Mathews, Conway, & Brooks, 2003; Hines & Kaufman, 1994). The experimental literature involving mice, rats, hamsters, and monkeys supports the androgenization hypothesis (Collaer & Hines, 1995; Quadagno, Briscoe, & Quadagno, 1977). For obvious ethical reasons, the effects of androgens on human behavior can only be studied through natural experiments, where fetuses receive abnormally high levels of these male hormones because of genetic defects (e.g., Congenital Adrenal Hyperplasia [CAH]) or difficulties during pregnancy (e.g., where mothers take synthetic progestins).

Most human studies of CAH support the androgenization hypothesis. These studies typically have used questionnaire methodology to ask parents or children about their preferences for various activities, including physically active sports. The frequently cited research of Money and colleagues (e.g., Money & Ehrhardt, 1972) has shown that androgenized girls are more "tomboyish": They prefer male activities more than do non-androgenized girls. Using observations of toy preferences in CAH children compared to controls, Berenbaum and Snyder (1995) found that CAH girls showed greater preference for boys' toys and activities.

Socialization Effects

Socialization interacts with hormonal events in the expression of behavioral sex differences (Ehrhardt, 1984; Fabes, 1994; Maccoby, 1986; Meaney et al., 1985;

Quadagno et al., 1977). Beginning with interactions with their parents, boys and girls are socialized into different, and often segregated, worlds that tend to reinforce these gender differences (Maccoby, 1986; 1998; Meaney et al., 1985; Pellegrini, 2004; Pellegrini et al., 2007). For example, fathers spend more time with their sons than with their daughters (Parke & Suomi, 1981), and when with their sons, they engage in physically vigorous play (Carson et al., 1993; MacDonald, 1993; MacDonald & Parke, 1986). That girls are more closely supervised by parents and teachers (Fagot, 1974; 1994) may further inhibit their physically vigorous behavior (Maccoby, 1986). In the section on sex segregation, I will discuss the implications of different levels of physically vigorous behavior on children's segregated peer groups.

Functions of Locomotor Play

For almost a century, the dominant view in child development (Groos, 1898; 1901) has been that play has deferred benefits. That is, during the period of extended childhood, children engage in play to learn and practice the skills necessary to be functioning adult members of society. This assumption is based on the long-maintained emphasis among child developmentalists on developmental continuity (Bateson, 1981; Gomendio, 1988; Kagan, 1971). Bateson's (1981) metaphor for the deferred-benefit view of play is "scaffolding": Play functions in skill assembly, and then is disassembled when the skill is mastered.

Alternatively, play may be viewed, not as an incomplete or imperfect version of adult behavior, but as having immediate benefits during childhood. This "metamorphic" view (Bateson, 1981) posits that play and its consequences are unique to the niche of childhood, and that later benefits are not necessary for its explanation (Bjorklund & Green, 1992; Gomendio, 1988; Pellegrini, Horvat, & Huberty, 1998). This view is consistent with recent discussions suggesting that play occurs at specific periods during which development may be modified (Byers & Walker, 1995; Thelen, 1979). Accordingly, the previously discussed age distribution of locomotor activity play may be useful in evaluating functional hypotheses.

Different forms and dimensions of locomotor play may serve specific developmental functions (Gomendio, 1988; Smith, 1982). I discuss the function(s) of locomotor play, considering the age trends and sex differences summarized above. I also consider both the dimension of locomotor physical activity itself and the dimension of social participation that distinguishes exercise play from R&T. Although some authors list up to 30 possible functions for play (Baldwin & Baldwin, 1977), certain functions (physical training, cognitive, and social) are most commonly advanced.

As a first step in establishing the functional importance of locomotor play during childhood, I present evidence from a small number of play-deprivation studies, either natural or experimental. These suggest that a lack of opportunity to engage in physical activity play leads to compensation later, concluding that play is of functional benefit.

The use of deprivation study to determine the effects of locomotor play has a long and interesting history in the animal literature. Rather than relying on some variant of surplus energy theory, the assumption behind play-deprivation studies is that immature organism will, after deprivation, attempt to compensate for lost opportunities to exercise during deprivation. Deprivation studies, and especially social play-deprivation studies (Einon, Morgan, & Kibbler, 1978) are, however, often plagued with methodological confounders, such as play deprivation being confounded with other sorts of deprivation. For example, trying to deprive an animal of social play also typically deprives that animal of social interaction, so we do not know what is affecting behavior—the lack of social play or the lack of more general social interaction. Locomotor play-deprivation studies are, however, less prone to this problem because locomotion can be eliminated rather easily; thus we can have relative confident in these results. Most notably, Müller-Schwarze (1968) deprived deer fawns of exercise for a prolonged period and then observed their locomotor play after release. Consistent with the prediction, deer were more active after the deprivation than before.

In Thelen's (1980) study of rhythmic stereotypies in the first year of life, infants who engaged in spontaneous physical activities frequently when given the opportunity were those observed to receive less vestibular stimulation from caregivers and those who were more often restricted in natural movements (e.g., placed in infant seats). Thelen (1980, p. 148) concluded that "deprivation of active as well as passive movement may . . . promote stereotypy."

Three sets of field experiments have looked at deprivation of locomotor play during childhood. Peter Smith and Theresa Hagan (1980) studied English preschool children (three to four years old) who were deprived of vigorous exercise by varying the amount of time they remained in their classrooms engaged in sedentary seatwork. After deprivation periods, they played outdoors. On the long, compared to short, deprivation days, children's play was more vigorous in the immediate post-deprivation period.

Utilizing a similar deprivation paradigm with American primary school children (five to nine years old), Pellegrini and colleagues (Pellegrini & Davis, 1993; Pellegrini, Huberty, & Jones, 1995) replicated Smith and Hagan's results: Children in long, compared to short, deprivation periods engaged in higher levels of physical activity. Deprivation, however, predictably interacted with sex of the children; boys, more than girls, were especially active after long deprivation.

These results support the following generalization: If children are deprived of opportunities for locomotor play, they will, when given the opportunity to play, engage in more intense and sustained bouts of locomotor play than they would have done if not so deprived. This generalization, in turn, suggests that locomotor play is serving some developmental function(s) such that a lack of it leads to compensation. It may be the case that deprivation of locomotor play during the juvenile period is especially important because this is a time when the skeletal, muscular, and neural systems are developing, and practice in the form of exercise is necessary for normal development. If individuals are deprived of that opportunity, they may over-compensate later, when given opportunity to exercise.

In the remainder of this section, I first consider physical training (and related) functions of rhythmical stereotypies and of exercise play. I then examine possible cognitive functions of exercise play. Lastly, I examine socialization effects of a dimension of exercise play, children's levels of physical activity upon their segregation into same-sex peer groups.

Physical Training

Both rhythmic stereotypies and exercise play seem to have physical training benefits. First, rhythmic stereotypies, such as waving the arms and kicking, peak at around six months of age. The onset of these actions is probably controlled by general maturational processes, which correspond to neuromuscular maturation (Field, Ting, & Shuman, 1979). Thelen (1979), in her naturalistic longitudinal study of infants' rhythmic stereotypies, suggests that this is a sensitive period in neuromuscular development, similar to the argument of Byers and Walker (1995). Her functional inferences about physical activities are based on the systematic onset of specific behaviors and their co-occurrence with milestones of motor development.

Thelen found that the individual behaviors appeared during a restricted period; onset was not randomly distributed. This pattern, she argued, is indicative of neuromuscular maturation. To support this claim further, she presented significant correlations between the age of onset of stereotypic groups (e.g., legs, arms, hands, and knees) and the age of passing items from the Bayley Scales of Infant Development reflecting neuromuscular, not cognitive, development. Rhythmic movements of given body systems appear to increase just before the infant achieves voluntary control of that system.

It could be postulated that infants' rhythmic stereotypies are primarily functional for the immediate benefits of improving control of specific motor patterns. The correspondence between the ages at which these movements occur and cerebral development suggests that, initially, rhythmic stereotypies may be manifestations of immature sensorimotor integration. Play may modify or eliminate irrelevant synapse formations; with maturation, these patterns are used in more goal-directed ways (Byers & Walker, 1995; Thelen, 1979). Such a hypothesis is consistent with the lack of sex differences in these behaviors, because there is no reason to suppose that control of motor patterns at this very basic level of generality is more important for boys than for girls.

With the onset of locomotion, another developmental course may begin, as evidenced by the correspondence between exercise play and muscle differentiation, strength, and endurance. Brownlee (1954) was the first to propose that animal play was related to juvenile muscle development. Fagen (1976) extended this argument by proposing deferred benefits of exercise play for motor training: specifically, muscle strength, general cardiopulmonary functioning, and metabolic capacity. He suggested that the forms of exercise play, often involving varied, interrupted, and repeated use of muscle groups, as well as whole-body activities, would be well suited to these deferred benefits. Byers and Walker (1995), in a thorough review of the animal play and motor training literatures, evaluated the issue of immediate or deferred benefits of exercise play for three aspects of motor training: endurance, strength, and skill and economy of movement. They suggest that exercise play may improve skill and economy of movement due to the effects of exercise on muscle fiber differentiation and cerebellar synaptogenesis. They present developmental data from house mice, rats, cats, and giraffes and conclude that physical activity in the juvenile period, beginning in the early postnatal period and declining at mid-lactation, is a sensitive period in the development of these functions. Exercise play during this period has a lasting effect on subsequent economy and skill of movement.

In human juveniles, exercise play may help shape the muscle fibers used in later physically vigorous activities. This could improve the economy and skill of movement along the lines suggested by Byers and Walker in other species, although we know of no direct evidence for this. The evidence suggests, however, that endurance and strength may be developed through sustained exercise bouts. The age course of exercise play also corresponds to the growth of arm and leg muscles and bones during the preschool period (Tanner, 1970). Consistent with this claim, an experimental, longitudinal study of children documented the relationship between one form of exercise play—jumping—and bone mineral content (Gunter et al., 2008). Exercise play during the school years and beyond might continue to benefit muscle and bone remodeling and strength and endurance training; physiological effects have been observed into adulthood in numerous species (Byers & Walker, 1995).

Byers and Walker (1995, p. 29) were skeptical that exercise play functions to support strength or endurance. They concluded that, "in many species, it is unlikely that play is a form of endurance or strength training because play bouts are too brief to prompt such benefits of exercise." They suggested that children would need to engage in daily bouts of exercise play lasting one hour, four to five days per week, to increase endurance significantly. But based on previous data from research on preschool and primary school children's playtime and activities out of school, I postulate that children at these ages may well engage in exercise play at levels meeting these criteria. Ethological studies of preschool children discussed above show that 20% of children's behavior during free-play periods, usually lasting the whole morning, was classified as vigorous (McGrew, 1972; Smith & Connolly, 1980). Although some primary school children's play opportunities may be more limited, due to school regimens, their recess periods, typically accounting for 20 to 60 minutes per day in American schools and 65 to 75 minutes per day in English primary schools (Blatchford, 1996), are also characterized by exercise play (Blatchford, 1996; Pellegrini, 1990). These activities are supplemented by activities in other contexts, as children usually engage in more than two physically vigorous activities daily outside of school (Simons-Morton et al., 1990).

Additional evidence for the role of locomotor play and endurance training comes from comparisons of athletes and non-athletes. Although we recognize the limitations of these comparisons for making functional inferences, they do provide some evidence in a very restricted literature. This evidence supports the hypothesis that children who habitually engage in vigorous games and sports show immediate benefits in terms of being fitter than children who do not. Smoll and Schutz (1985) studied 3,000 students in British Columbia aged 9, 13, and 17 years. Athletes emerged as significantly fitter than non-athletes on all physical fitness tests. This was true for both boys and girls. Differences between athletes and non-athletes were small at 9 years, but increased substantially by 13 and 17 years. This would be consistent with physical training effects of such participation, although other explanations—such as selective participation and dropout—are also possible.

Relatedly, Lussier and Buskirk (1977) examined the effects of a 12-week endurance training program (distance running) on 8- to 12-year-old boys and girls. Training decreased heart rate during sub-maximal workloads and increased maximum oxygen uptake. Other studies of endurance training have had positive immediate results, and reviews concur (e.g., Rowland, 1985; Simons-Morton, O'Hara, Simons-Morton, & Parcel, 1987) in concluding that regular, high-intensity training can improve cardiorespiratory functioning.

The evidence presented thus far suggests that children are given opportunities for exercise play that are probably adequate for endurance training; but before firm conclusions are made, even for the preschool and primary school periods, more research is needed to document the intensity and duration of exercise play. Furthermore, we do not know, beyond the period of childhood, the extent to which vigorous physical activities are playful, *per se*, or not. This remains an important task for future research.

In summary, exercise play, in the preschool years especially, seems frequent enough to serve an immediate function of strength and endurance training. It may also improve skill and economy of movement, although specific evidence for this is lacking. This hypothesized set of functions is consistent with the age curve for exercise play (Tanner, 1970). More intriguing is its relationship to the sex difference observed. Strength training at least would be more important for males in the "environment of evolutionary adaptedness" for fighting and hunting skills (e.g., Boulton & Smith, 1992); however, it could also be argued that endurance training is equally or more important for females (for gathering activities). Although very speculative at present, such hypotheses could lead to more differentiated predictions concerning gender differences in types of exercise play, analogous to Silverman and Eals's (1992) differentiation of types of spatial ability in relation to gender differences.

Three other functional hypotheses regarding the physical component of exercise play can be taken from the animal literature; these are the fat-reduction hypothesis, the thermoregulation hypothesis, and foraging and escape-route learning. Initial studies of physical activity play in children were theoretically framed in variants of Spencer's Surplus Energy theory (1898), in which such play was seen as a way of dissipating energy surplus to bodily requirements. Although little logical or empirical support currently exists for this theory (Burghardt, 1984; 1988; 2005; Smith, 1982; Smith & Hagan, 1980), Barber (1991) develops a variant of the argument. He suggests that energy is not usually in short supply for young mammals, and that play prevents obesity by ensuring that "surplus" energy is not stored as unnecessary fat. In particular, some young animals may need to consume large amounts of food to get enough protein, and play can "burn off" the excess requirements. In addition, play, by generating heat, may provide a defense against cold exposure.

These postulated functions could be applied to human children as well as to other young mammals. The childhood period, which involves high rates and levels of physical activity play, also corresponds negatively to gains in fat (Tanner, 1970, p. 86). That is, after nine months of age, when play involving locomotion is increasing, fat gain has a negative velocity until six to eight years of age. Although these age trends are consistent with Barber's hypothesis applied to human children, sex differences are not; there seems no reason to suppose that fat reduction should be more important for boys in the preschool years.

The vigorous dimension of exercise play may also serve an immediate function in relation to thermoregulation—the ability of individuals to regulate their body temperatures (Burghardt, 1988). According to this hypothesis, children would engage in exercise play, which expends stored caloric energy, to raise their body temperature when the ambient temperature is low (Barber, 1991). The empirical record provides some support for this claim. Studies of outdoor play have found that exercise play is increased by cool ambient temperatures for preschool (Smith & Hagan, 1980) and primary school children (Pellegrini et al., 1995), and low levels of exercise play are observed in tropical climates (Cullumbine, 1950). Whereas exercise play might be used by children to raise body temperature, nonplayful physical activity is another way that human beings of all ages (and other mammals; Barber, 1991) can raise their body temperatures in cold climates. Therefore, these benefits are not limited to childhood. In addition, this hypothesis does not explain the specific age course of exercise play, nor does it explain the sex difference found. We hypothesize that thermoregulation is an incidental benefit of exercise play, and that thermoregulation, when important, can also be achieved by other means as far as humans are concerned.

In summary, exercise play may function primarily to develop physical strength, endurance and economy of movement. There is also some evidence to support the fat-reduction theory; and thermoregulation is postulated to be an incidental benefit of exercise play. I next examine possible cognitive functions for locomotor play.

Cognitive Effects of Locomotor Play?

Less obvious, and more equivocal, than the likely benefits of exercise play for physical development are possible effects on psychological, and especially cognitive, factors. The role of locomotor play in nonhuman animals' foraging and escape-route learning has been advanced by Judith Stamps (1995). Stamps suggests that when juveniles are placed in novel environments, their rates of time and energy spent playing increases, relative to being situated in familiar contexts. The result of this investment in play seems to take the form of animals' discovering and refining routes to be used to forage for food and for escape from predators. For example, in the course of playing, birds fly around their home arenas and discover the most efficient routes to escape from a pursuing predator. To my knowledge there is no evidence for the role of locomotor play on children's knowledge of their environments. This sort of research might not only examine the role of play in knowing the local landscape but also perhaps assessing the role of play in children's ability to negotiate their way through those environments. The research on human locomotor play and cognitive performance, instead, has been mostly concerned with performance on more general cognitive tasks, such as school performance. Here I review whether engaging in exercise play has proximal consequences for cognitive performance. Effects on cognitive tasks might be expected from several theoretical viewpoints; however, these theories link any cognitive benefits to outcomes one step removed from exercise play *per se*; namely, arousal breaks from cognitive tasks, and sense of mastery or well-being.

First, exercise play can lead to heightened arousal, which might influence performance following the inverted-U hypothesis (Tomporowski & Ellis, 1986). That is, moderate levels of arousal lead to better performance than do higher or lower levels. Alternatively, increased arousal may lead to a narrowing of attention to core task components (Easterbrook, 1959). Second, exercise play might, by breaking up cognitive tasks, provide spaced or distributed practice rather than massed practice (Ebinghaus, 1885/1964; James, 1901). In another version of this approach, stemming from the cognitive immaturity hypothesis (Bjorklund & Pellegrini, 2002), the specifically playful nature of the break could be considered important. Relatedly, effects on performance, possibly mediated by breaks and enhanced attention, might be dependent upon enhanced feelings of mastery, or of well-being, after exercise play.

Unfortunately, much of the available research on exercise and cognitive performance is on adults. Tomporowski and Ellis (1986) provided a comprehensive review of 27 such studies directly linking exercise intervention—only some of which can be defined as exercise play—to cognitive performance. They considered effects of different types of exercise (short or long duration; anaerobic or aerobic) on cognitive tasks given during or after the exercise.

The pattern of findings is conflicting. The only consistent trends emerged from studies of brief, high-intensity anaerobic exercise (hand dynamometer, or weight-pulling); here, moderate levels of muscular exertion usually improved cognitive task performance assessed during the exercise (e.g., participants would grip a hand dynamometer in each hand and recall nonsense syllables). This generally inconclusive pattern of findings may be due both to inconsistencies across studies and to confounding factors, such as different levels of participants' motivation to participate or different initial levels of physical fitness.

Although information on children is limited, a large-scale study of the benefits of guided physical activity (physical education classes) on children's school performance was conducted by Shephard and colleagues (1983; Vollé et al., 1982). As part of the Trois Rivières project in Canada, entire primary school classrooms (grades two through six) received an additional five hours of physical education per week; control classrooms received no physical education. Teachers apparently were aware of children's condition assignments, but the influence of teacher bias was minimized by the administration of independent, province-wide examinations. The academic performance of children in the experimental group was superior to that of the control children. The authors suggest that the benefits shown in this project may have been due either to arousal caused by the enhanced exercise or by shortening of class work time (and hence "spaced practice") by inserting physical education classes (Shephard, 1983).

The latter interpretation is consistent with Stevenson and Lee's interpretation (1990) of achievement in Japanese, Taiwanese, and American schools. They suggested that the frequent breaks between periods of intense work in Japanese schools (usually ten minutes every hour) maximize children's cognitive performance. That children's task vigilance increases when the time spent on the task is distributed, rather than massed, is a consistent finding in the animal and human learning literatures (Dempster, 1988). The massed versus distributed practice literature consistently shows few differences across ages from preschool to old age (Dempster, 1988). Individual differences in children, such as "distractibility" or "activity" levels, may mediate the effectiveness of distributed practice regimens, however, and should be addressed in future research.

It thus remains questionable whether it is exercise play *per se*, rather than just a break from sustained classroom work, that is responsible for any increased cognitive performance. More will be said about the cognitive implications of children's exercise play in the chapter on the educational implications of play. Briefly, there I will discuss a series of experiments with primary school children, where I and my colleagues (Pellegrini et al., 1995) examined the relationship between the level of physical activity in exercise play on the school playground during recess, and subsequent attention to standardized classroom tasks.

Perhaps more encouraging, and an area for future research, is the experimental evidence for the role of locomotor play in learning due to increased synaptic and neurotransmission in mice engaging in voluntary, play-like exercise, relative to controls (Van Praag, Shubert, Zhao, & Gage, 2005). Specifically, young and aged mice were housed with or without a running wheel and injected with bromoeoxyurdine or retrovirus to label newborn cells. After one month, learning was assessed, and the aged, experimental mice showed faster learning and better retention than controls. Furthermore, running enhanced fine morphology of new neurons of both young and aged mice, suggesting that locomotor play has both immediate and deferred benefits in mice. While there are obvious limitations to the application of this work to the human case, it provides some guidance. Perhaps we should be looking at the effects of locomotor play on neural organization across ontogeny, rather than its effects on only learning.

Social Effects of Locomotor Play

Physical activity generally and locomotor play more specifically have important effects on children's social behavior, primarily by affecting the composition of their peer groups. As discussed in Chapter 6, beginning early in the preschool years (at around two to three years of age) sex differences in physical activity and locomotor play bias children to spend most of their time with same-sex peers, in sex-segregated groups (e.g., Fagot, 1994; Legault & Strayer, 1990; Maccoby, 1998; Pellegrini, 2004; Pellegrini et al., 2007; Pitcher & Schultz, 1983). This pattern continues through the preschool (Fabes, 1994) and into the early adolescent years, at which point it wanes, especially in contexts encouraging

integration (Pellegrini & Long, 2003; 2007). Sex segregation is a robust phenomenon across non-industrialized human societies (Bock, 2005; Condon, 1987;
Whiting & Edwards, 1973). For example, in Whiting and Edwards' (1973)
study of ten cultures, young children (four to five years of age) spent most of
their time in segregated groups. It is in these segregated groups that children
probably learn socially prescribed social roles for males and females.

Such cross-cultural, and indeed cross-vertebrate species findings (e.g.,
Ruckstuhl, 1998; Ruckstuhl & Neuhaus, 2002; 2005) have led child developmentalists to acknowledge the "interactive," but unspecified, roles of biology and
socialization in determining sex segregation. The level of generality in stating
that segregation is due to some unspecified interaction between biology and
socialization is hardly useful in generating theory-driven hypotheses (see
Bateson, 1987 for a discussion). Biology and socialization certainly interact to
influence children's sex segregation and behavior, but we need theory to guide us
as to what interacts with what in order to generate and test specific hypotheses.
Sexual selection theory (Clutton-Brock, 1983; Darwin, 1871) is one such theory
of sex differences in behavior, which enables us to generate testable hypotheses
regarding sex segregation (Pellegrini, 2004).

Also as discussed in Chapter 6, early activity biases children to interact with
compatible peers, but socialization pressures also force boys to interact with boys
and high-activity girls to segregate among themselves, separate from other girls
(Pellegrini, Long, et al., 2007). An extensive corpus of observational data was
collected on children's physical activity and sex segregation across much of a
school year with minimal sampling and observer biases. Documentation of boys'
and girls' differing levels of physical activity in the behaviors characterizing
males' and females' groups in naturalistic conditions was based on the work of
Pellegrini and colleagues (Pellegrini et al., 1998). Specifically, Pellegrini and
colleagues (1998) conducted a series of field experiments with primary school
children and established the construct validity of an observational rating scale to
assess physical activity and caloric expenditure by relating these behavioral
ratings to concurrent assays of aggregated heart rate and actometer readings.

A number of important methodological points made in that study must be
considered when examining the role of physical activity in sex-role-stereotypic
behaviors such as locomotor play and physical activity. First, sex differences in
activity need to be documented using objective, mechanical, recording devices
(i.e., actometers and heart-rate monitors). Objective measures such as these
minimize biases associated with male and female observers scoring boys' and
girls' activity. That active behavior is assumed to be more male than female
may lead to observer bias (March & Hanlon, 2004). Second, extant research
examining the role of physical activity in sex segregation has used likert-like
observational ratings of children's activity with limited validity. For example,
Maccoby and Jacklin (1987) used a seven-point scale (1–7) and Fabes, Martin,
and Hamish (2003) used a four point scale (1–4), and neither presented validity
information on these scales. Similarly, Serbin and colleagues (Serbin et al., 1994)
used teacher ratings of toddlers' activity and disruptive behavior, thus conflating
the two. The metric for physical activity used in our research was derived from a

measure documenting caloric expenditure (Eaton, Enns, & Pressé, 1987) and has established construct validity (Pellegrini et al., 1998). This validity insures that physical activity, in terms of a continuous measure of caloric expenditure, is actually being measured.

Third, our observations (Pellegrini et al.,1998; 2007), were conducted in multiple classrooms across relatively long time intervals and consequently are probably more representative of individuals' behavior than some earlier work on the role of physical activity in children's sex segregation. By contrast, much previous work in this area (the work of Martin & Fabes, 2001, is an exception), which minimized the role of physical activity in sex segregation (summarized in Maccoby, 1998), relied on numerous observations conducted within a very limited time period. More specifically, Maccoby's observations with preschoolers were limited to six seven-minute observations, all of which were all conducted in *one* day. Furthermore, observations of older children (6.5 years) were limited to 71 ten-second observations, also all collected in *one* day. Indeed, Maccoby and Jacklin (1987) themselves acknowledge that failure to find an effect for physical activity on segregation may have been due to these methodological limitations.

Consistent with this concern, a recent meta-analysis on sex differences in physical activity demonstrated that limited numbers of observations attenuate sex differences in activity (Campbell & Eaton, 1999). Correspondingly, aggregating multiple observations collected during one day probably resulted in interdependent observational data. The dependency is due to the fact that contiguous observations (i.e., observations within each seven-minute sampling interval and within one day) tend to be more interrelated than separate observations each day, being collected across a number of different days (e.g., Smith, 1985), thus further limiting the generalizability of the behavioral sample. By contrast, sampling behavior across a broader time frame, as in our research, yields a more representative and valid sample of behavior. In short, much of the extant research on the role of physical activity in sex segregation has a very limited sampling base that may result in null findings for the role of physical activity in sex segregation.

CONCLUSIONS

In light of the relative paucity of research in the area of locomotor play, directions for future research on the nature of such play and its hypothesized benefits in physical, cognitive, and social domains are recommended. There is a need for more descriptive data on the forms of locomotor activity play and their age trends throughout childhood and adolescence. The reviews by Byers and Walker (1995) and Pellegrini and Smith (1998) show the importance of age trends in examining functional hypotheses. Yet, for exercise play especially, data are scanty. Although one can be reasonably confident of the inverted-U curve with age, we cannot be confident that the peak is at four to five years as we have assumed. Also, different types of exercise play may peak at different ages, and the developmental course may be different for boys and girls. Sex differences in exercise play are more intriguing with respect to functional hypotheses. Conceivably, these differences may be more complex and differentiated than previously thought, as Silverman and Eals (1992) found in the domain of spatial ability; for example, sex differences might be different for aspects of exercise play relevant to strength as opposed to those relevant to endurance.

The benefits of exercise play for two dimensions of motor training—strength and endurance—should be immediate and occur across the life span. By "immediate" we mean that strength and endurance will result from repeated activity bouts, usually across the span of a number of weeks (Byers & Walker, 1995). However, we need more information on duration, frequency, and intensity of physical exercise of both the playful and nonplayful variety from infancy through adulthood, and the correspondence between these data and measures of immediate and sustained fitness. To test the hypothesis that exercise play relates to bone remodeling and physical endurance and strength, as measured by decreased heart rate during exercise or VO_2Max (the maximum rate of oxygen uptake during exercise), we need to measure the separate contributions of nonplayful and playful vigorous activity to physiological measures of endurance and strength.

I have suggested that locomotor play has two forms: rhythmic stereotypies and exercise play. These forms have different age distributions and possibly different functions. Exercise play probably has immediate beneficial consequences for children's motor training. This is consistent with evolutionary reasoning as well as with the evidence, and it might be hypothesized to be the earliest ultimate function for exercise play in mammals. There may be additional benefits of fat reduction and thermoregulation, which we hypothesize to be incidental.

Locomotor play deserves greater attention from psychologists. In general, our conclusions have been strongly tempered by the insufficiency of available evidence. What evidence there is has not infrequently come from areas such as sports science, rather than psychology, with a consequent neglect of psychological variables. There is scope for considerable conceptual rethinking in the area; in particular, the usual stress on deferred rather than immediate benefits of play deserves reevaluation.

Even if benefits of locomotor play are more immediate than deferred, they may still be important. There are public health implications for the role of locomotor play for the physical fitness of children growing up in a modern industrial society. Children have limited opportunities for physical activity, due to shortage of play spaces, dangerous neighborhoods, and the increased demands of formal schooling. That children seem to "need" physical activity is supported by the rebound effects observed in deprivation studies. The evidence suggests that if children are deprived of locomotor play for long periods of time, their health, in terms of cardiovascular and physical fitness, may suffer.

10

Pretend Play

"Our games didn't end up with the bell; they ran from recreation period to recreation period under the chestnut trees and around the single-storey lavatory building we called the piss hut. We fought. The piss hut, which was next to the gym, was the Toledo Alcázar. True, the event had taken place the year before, but in our school boy dreams the Falangists were still heroically defending the walls, the Reds storming in vain. Part of the reason for the latter's failure lay in our lack of enthusiasm: nobody wanted to be a Red, myself included. All of us considered ourselves stalwart supporters of General Franco. In the end, a few of the older boys had us draw lots, and I, never suspecting the future significance of the draw, was one of the several first-year boys who drew Red. Clearly, the future starts making itself felt in the school yard." (Grass, 1999, p. 94)

This quote is a brief recollection of the pretend play of the ten-year-old Günter Grass, a Nobel laureate for literature, in his schoolyard play in 1937. Like many students of play, Grass considers childhood pretending important for the roles enacted in adulthood. For this reason, perhaps, pretend play is arguably the most thoroughly studied aspect of human play behavior. Indeed, pretense is often used as *the* defining attribute of play. For example, Ken Rubin and colleagues (Rubin, Fein, & Vandenberg, 1983) included it as one of their dispositional criteria for play, along with intrinsic motivation, means over ends, not being exploratory or instrumental, freedom from external rule, and active engagement. This bias towards pretend play was reinforced by an empirical interview study conducted by Peter Smith and Ralph Vollstedt (1985). In that study, they showed video-clips of children's behavior to English adults, including those well trained in child psychology as well as educated lay people, and asked them to categorize the behaviors as playful or not and then to give reasons for their choices. The subjects mentioned pretend as *the* most important attribute in their categorizing a behavior as playful.

The importance of pretend play in conceptions of play, more generally, is not limited to the educated lay public, like those in the Smith and Vollstedt study. Some of the most influential theorists in the field of human development have also concentrated on this form of play. For example, Freudian theory (e.g., Freud, 1940; Peller, 1952; 1954) has been concerned with pretend, especially as it related to "wish fulfillment." In pretend, according to this view, individuals are able to express ideas that are unacceptable or disturbing in reality, but in pretend play are not forbidden. This notion of pretend play as being motivated by wish fulfillment is also fundamental to Vygotsky's (1967) theory of play. Of course, Piaget's (1962) interest in play also centered on pretend play.

In terms of defining pretend play and recognizing it, as distinct from other forms of play, is not as problematic as differentiating play from nonplay more generally. This is probably due to the fact that pretense, especially when it is social, is often accompanied by language marking the interactions explicitly as play or pretend, such as "Let's pretend" or "I'll be the Dad and you the Mom." With that said, defining pretense is not free from controversy.

The remainder of this chapter will be organized as follows. First, I will proffer a definition of pretend play. As part of this section, I will specify how four components of pretending (decontextualized behavior, self–other relations, sequential combinations, and object substitution) change from infancy through early childhood (Fein & Apfel, 1979; McCune-Nicolich & Fenson, 1984; Nicolich, 1977; Watson & Fisher, 1977; 1980). Second, I will discuss adult–child pretend play. As with other forms of play, the beginning of children's pretense has important roots in interaction with adults generally, and mothers specifically. Third, I address the progression from solitary to social pretending with peers. In the fourth section I address the purported beneficial consequence of pretend play. Lastly, I will address the degree to which pretend play is unique to humans.

WHAT IS PRETEND PLAY?

Pretend play has been variously labeled as symbolic play, make-believe play, and in some cases sociodramatic play, typically when a social role, such as a pretend doctor, is enacted. As with many aspects of children's development, Piaget (1962) made very important contributions to the study of children's pretend play. For Piaget, play was an activity where assimilation dominated accommodation. In Piaget's view of pretend play, children subordinated the outside world to their inner schema. For example, a child sees a doll and subordinates the doll's identity to his or her own and calls it "My baby."

With regard to "symbolic" play specifically, Piaget suggested symbolization begins with deferred imitation. In such cases, children have ideas or representations of an action or a person, and they later try to reproduce it. Symbolic play is an extension of this representational process where children recognize that one thing stands for another. Piaget labeled this the "semiotic function." Through repeated engagement in pretend play, children practice substituting one thing for another, and this practice of having one thing represent another and separating the symbol, or the signifier, from what it represents, or the signified, is important for children's more general representational competence. Other examples of early representational competence include learning that words represent objects or people. Simply put, pretense involves substitutions where one thing represents something else.

Furthermore, and like other, more general definitions of play, symbolic actions are decontextualized; that is, they are taken out of their functional context. For example, children's pretend eating is taken out of the context of a real meal. Correspondingly, it is assumed that the child recognizes that these pretend acts are in fact detached and different from their functional counterparts.

Interestingly, Mitchell (2006), who is concerned primarily with pretend play, but in nonhuman animals, also defines pretending in terms of an animal's knowing that an action is unrelated to the current reality. However, and importantly for the implications to the study of nonhuman animals' play, Mitchell does not think that play needs to be explicitly representational. Indeed, pretend maybe a form of imitation, again not unlike Piaget's discussion of the origins of children's play actions and vocalizations. Importantly, these criteria do not differentiate play from deception, where one animal may act as if it is hurt by limping, when in fact it is not hurt, so that a conspecific will not attack it.

Correspondingly, instances of animals' self-handicapping, as was discussed in the social play chapter, also might fit into the definition of pretend play. For example, by slowing down in a game of chase (self-handicapping), animals, it can be argued, are engaging in reciprocal role-taking and implicitly taking other animals' perspectives (e.g., Rosenberg, 1990).

While many scholars have followed Piaget's general definition of pretend play, others consider his definition to be too general and undifferentiated (McCune-Nicolich & Fenson, 1984). Notably, Lillard (1994) proffers six criteria that must be met before an act would be considered pretense: A pretender, a reality, a mental representation that is projected onto the reality, and an awareness and intention on the part of the pretender. These representational criteria are stringent and perhaps controversial standards to be met for pretense. For example, some students of human development and play, especially as it relates to theory of mind research, agree that children may enact fantasy roles, but disagree on the extent to which these enactments entail representations.

It seems that some pretend play, especially the pretending of very young children, is more limited, in the sense that they are only reenacting others' behaviors. Correspondingly, it is also recognized that the very young children engaging in these early forms of pretense are not necessarily representing each other in the sense that they are representing others' intentions and other mental states. This view is consistent with Paul Harris's (1991) position on pretend play. Harris posits that young children initially "simulate" the actions of others in their pretend play and that this early form of pretend does not involve young children's representing the mental states of their co-players. Instead, pretend play, in Harris's view, has the young child enacting a pretend world through the repeated simulation of a variety of roles they observe around them.

Initially, young children assume that their thoughts and beliefs about these enactments are the same as their playmates'. Repeated social interactions in pretend play with peers are central to this model, because children, after repeated interactions where viewpoints between players clash, come to recognize that their peers sometimes do not share the same view of a scenario that is being enacted. This typically occurs by the time children are about three years of age. At this point, children put their own beliefs and desires about the scenario aside and try to imagine the beliefs and desires of their peers. With this accomplished, children will go back to their original simulation and try to understand it from the points of view of their peers. In the early phases of this process, children's understanding of others' simulations is a mixture of their imagined views of their peers and their own egocentric perspective. For example, children realize that they and their peers share different views of a real and pretend apple. By four or five years of age children can understand that they have different beliefs from others with respect to two mutually exclusive objects. Correspondingly, understanding others' points of views depends on the accuracy of children's simulations. With repeated social encounters in pretend play, children's simulations of others become more accurate.

In short, defining pretend play as having one thing representing something or someone is too simple. While rudimentary forms of pretending do not necessarily involve mental representation *per se* and may be observed in nonhumans, "higher" forms of pretending necessitate explicit mental representation and seem to be unique to humans. In one view (e.g., Alexander, 1989; Harris, 1991), social interactions are especially important in the evolution of humans' ability to mentally represent others' mental states. Alexander (1989) further speculates that social pretend play allows individuals to hypothesize, expand, and internalize a variety of social, physical, and intellectual scenarios that are useful in cooperative and competitive bouts with peers. These different levels of representation are evident in the development of the four components of pretend play.

Decontextualized Behavior and Self–Other Relations

Decontextualized behaviors involve taking a familiar or functional behavior, such as drinking from a cup or eating with a fork, and using a close variant of that behavior in a different, and nonfunctional, context. So, a child might take an empty cup and "drink" from it, as if it actually contained liquid, or use a fork and pretend to eat from an empty plate. This sort of activity has been observed in children interacting with replica toys at around 12 months of age (Fein & Apfel, 1979). Seemingly similar types of decontextualized behavior have been observed with nonhuman primates. For example, bonobos trained to use symbols in the lab of Savage-Rumbaugh and McDonald (1988) were observed in what was described as pretend eating.

Clearly, these behaviors are rooted in observed activities and their associated objects, and it has been suggested (e.g., Rubin et al., 1983) that such decontextualized actions are "scripted" behaviors (Schank & Ableson, 1977). That is, children's memory for the events and actions they represent in pretend are organized in terms of the functional and temporal contexts in which they were actually observed, not as isolated states. As such, the way that these events are remembered resembles a scripted story, or narrative (Galda, 1984; Wolf & Grollman, 1982). So, drinking from a cup is remembered as an activity embedded in the larger context of mealtime with a beginning, characters interacting in time, and perhaps even an ending. From this perspective, early pretend actions are rooted in their larger social behavioral context.

As children become aware that their acts are representational and abstracted from their real context, they enrich their enactments (McCune-Nicolich, 1981). For example, drinking behaviors from pretend cups are embellished with slurping sounds. Next, children's decontextualized behaviors become less reliant on their bodily actions and then directed at something or someone else, an indicator of self–other relation. For example, a child may offer his or her mother a "drink" from an empty cup. At about 12 months, approximately 81% of the infants' pretend acts were self-directed; 31% were mother-directed, and 19% were directed at a doll (Fein & Apfel, 1979; Rubin et al., 1983).

Self-directed pretend behaviors decrease from this point and are replaced in frequency by other-directed pretend (Belsky & Most, 1981; Fein & Apfel, 1979; Rubin et al., 1983). Specifically, at about 15 to 20 months of age, young children begin to direct their pretending away from themselves and toward play objects, such as dolls, or, less commonly, another person, such as their mothers (Fein & Apfel, 1979; Rubin et al., 1983). Initially, infants treat objects as passive recipients, such as a child feeding a doll, but with time they begin to treat the objects as if they were acting, too; self-directed pretend tends to disappear by this time (Rubin et al., 1983; Watson & Fischer, 1977). It is probably the case that repeatedly engaging in play with objects and other social actors, and in conjunction with increased social cognitive sophistication, enables young children treat dolls as animate beings. It is doubtful, however, that a two-year-old child has a representation of the doll as an animate being in the sense discussed above. It is more likely the case that these behaviors are "simulations" of familiar behavioral scripts that these children have observed.

Substitute Objects

The ability to substitute one object for another is a hallmark of pretending and one also considered crucial in Vygotsky's (1967) theory of pretend play (Fein, 1979; Harris, 2006). For Piaget, as noted above, the ability to substitute one object for another was just another step en route to more general representational competence. Indeed, Piaget considered instances where young children transformed the identity of a functional object into a pretend object to be an example of pre-rational, autistic thought, not dissimilar to psychoanalytic notion of wish fulfillment and free association (Harris, 2006; Piaget, 1962).

Object substitutions in pretend play were also discussed by Vygotsky (1967), but unlike Piaget he viewed these transformations in a more positive light (Harris, 2006). Specifically, Vygotsky assigned importance to children's ability to transform the identity of one object to another in play because this ability was seen as central to children's ability to separate a symbol from its referent and eventually to use an arbitrary representational system, such as writing. In writing, an arbitrary sign, in the form of a word such as *car*, represents a concrete entity. Furthermore, and as will be discussed later in this chapter, for Vygotsky the ability to engage in pretend transformations does not disappear from a person's cognitive repertoire once they become adult, rational thinkers. Instead, representing and imagining fantastic scenarios are used in various adult enterprises, such as art and science.

With these disagreements in mind, both theorists agree that with age, children's object substitutions should become more abstract, and the empirical record supports these claims. Specifically, between 14 and 19 months of age, children's use of realistic objects, such as replica toys, in pretend increases (Fein & Apfel, 1979; Rubin et al., 1983; Watson & Fischer, 1977; 1980). By 19 months of age, however, the use of more abstract, substitute objects for play props, such as a folded up towel representing a baby, increases (Fein, 1975; Rubin et al., 1983; Watson & Fischer, 1997); by two years of age, 75% of the children in one study (Watson & Fischer, 1977) used this level of abstract substitution.

Greta Fein included a more demanding criterion for substitution in her study of children's pretend, comparing single substitutions (e.g., a real cup is used to feed a doll represented by a block) and double substitutions (where neither the cup nor the doll are realistic). In this case, 70% of the children (at 24 months of age) pretended under the single substitution condition and 33% under the double substitution condition. Fein also reported that it seemed more difficult for children to execute double substitutions using functionally ambiguous objects, such as blocks for cups, than when using props whose function is explicit but conflicting to the proposed use in pretend, such as using a car for a cup (Rubin et al., 1983; Watson & Fischer, 1980).

Related to the functional ambiguity of objects used in pretend, I (Pellegrini, 1987) conducted an experimental study with four- and five-year-olds to examine the degree to which children's pretend, generally, was dependent on the functional explicitness of play props. Specifically, I coded "object transformations," like the cases where children's pretend play themes were dependent on the props' definitions, such as using a toy stethoscope to a doll's heart; and "ideational transformations," where play themes were not dependent on the presence of an object. For example, children could use language to define a situation, such as, "This is my doctor's office," or a role, such as "I'll be the nurse." In these cases children were using language to define a play theme or social role, not an object.

Procedurally, these university preschool children were observed in laboratory playrooms interacting on two occasions with relatively realistic play props (e.g., doctors' kits, dolls, blankets, and pill bottles) and interacting on two occasions with functionally ambiguous play props (e.g., pieces of styrofoam in various shapes, pipe cleaners, as well as wooden and plastic blocks). First, I found that there were no age differences between four- and five-year-olds in their uses of object or ideational transformations: thus, and consistent with Fein and Apfel's (1979) earlier work, children, by the time they reach four years of age, are quite capable of engaging in pretend play, independently of the functional explicitness of the play props.

With that said, children were more likely to use object transformations, especially substitutions, with the ambiguous than with the more realistic props.

For example, children might pick up a block and say, "This is my car." It also appeared, though there is only anecdotal evidence to support this claim, that children's pretend play object substitutions were related to the attributes of the props they used. For example, the shape of a block roughly resembles a car. The U-shape pieces of styrofoam were used on more than one occasion as a hat. This interpretation is also consistent with the view expressed in the earlier discussion of definitions of play, that play may be preceded by exploration because in exploration children discover objects' attributes and it is these attributes that form a basis for subsequent pretending.

I also found that boys, more than girls, were likely to transform the objects in the ambiguous contexts. This sex difference is consistent with a wide body of research (summarized in Rubin et al., 1983) suggesting that boys, relative to girls, are both more likely to play with blocks and other constructive type props, and when they do their play is also more sophisticated. This is probably due to the fact that socialization and hormonal events bias boys to interact with these sorts of props and the large-motor behaviors that accompany this sort of interaction (Archer & Lloyd, 2002; Maccoby, 1998).

In short, children's decontextualized pretend culminates, in the late preschool years, when they are consciously aware that their action is pretense, by using language to frame their pretend themes; for example, "this towel is my baby." Children embed these individual pretend play transformations into larger, coherent themes that roughly resemble scripted events from which they were derived.

Sequential Combinations

With increased experience and corresponding social, cognitive, and linguistic sophistication, children's enactments become more elaborate. By this I mean that individual pretend behaviors are woven into a series of interrelated themes. These themes, in many ways, resemble stories, or narratives (Galda, 1984). For example, a child may pretend to feed a doll, "burp" it, and then put it down for a nap (McCune-Nicolich, 1981; Pellegrini, 1985; Wolf & Grollman, 1982). It is probably the case, as suggested above, that pretend play themes are derived from children's memories of and participation in everyday events, such as dinner time, bathing, or interacting with mother. Such events are remembered in "scripted" form (Nelson, 1986; Nelson & Gruendel, 1979). That temporally and causally motivated scripts resemble narratives is probably responsible for the narrative structure of children's sequentially organized pretend play.

Also as noted in the preceding section, there is an age progression from play that is dependent upon functionally explicit props, such as replica toys, to play that is relatively independent of explicit props. Furthermore, this age trend is moderated by the types of props with which children interact. The ambiguity of play props is, in turn, related to age trends observed with children's ability to weave individual play transformations into coherent themes. Specifically, in one experimental study I (Pellegrini, 1985) was concerned with the effects of explicitly "scripted play" props (i.e., dolls, blankets, pill bottles, and doctor's kits) and functionally ambiguous props (i.e., variously shaped and sized pieces of styrofoam and pipe cleaner shapes) on the elaboration of sequential enactments, where "elaboration" was defined in terms of the degree of integration of enacted narrative themes. The elaborations ranged from single enactments, such as covering a doll with a blanket, to at least four interrelated enactments (e.g., covering the doll with a blanket, patting it and singing it a lullaby, kissing it good night, and listening to its heart). As noted above, children were observed in same-sex dyads, playing twice each with the two sets of props.

Result showed, not surprisingly, that with age (four to five years of age) children's sequential enactments became more elaborated. Interestingly, however, age did interact with play props such that there were no age differences observed on the less elaborated levels of sequential themed behavior, but there was an age difference observed at the highest level. Specifically, for the highest level of sequencing, five year olds' enactments, relative to four year olds', were more elaborated with the functionally ambiguous props.

This finding suggests that only the older children had the cognitive and linguistic facility necessary to sustain interrelated sequential themes using ambiguous props. To do so not only requires children to use language to unambiguously define the meaning of a prop that has no apparent function, but it also requires the ability and willingness to recognize the beliefs and intentions of their playmate so that they can clarify any ambiguity (Pellegrini, 1982). For example, Child A may hold out a piece of styrofoam and say, "Do you like him?" Child B may not know who "him" is and ask, "Who's 'him'?" Child A then would clarify with "He's our new dog. Charlie."

In short, children enacted interrelated themes of pretend play by four years of age, indicative of their explicit awareness of the representation nature of their pretend. This level of skill seems to be supported by the explicitness of the props, however. Only by five years of age did children have the social cognitive and linguistic resources necessary to unambiguously represent their intentions and beliefs in such a way that their interactions could be coordinated with a peer across an extended play theme.

While not studied extensively, individual differences in how preschoolers pretend with objects and integrate them into larger themes, as well as in more general forms of symbolization, have been reported by a group of researchers associated with Harvard's Project Zero (e.g., Wolf, Davidson, Davis, Walters, Hodges, & Scripp, 1988). With specific reference to pretend play of young children, Dennie Wolf and Howard Gardner (1978) have observed two types of play styles: "Patterners" and "Dramatists." Patterners, generally, expressed interest in the object world and organized objects and information presented to them into patterns, such as building structures with blocks. Dramatists, on the other hand, were more interested in their social worlds and attended to what others did, felt, thought, and interacted with others; for example, assigning pretend roles to blocks as family characters. In terms of the pretend play of these two types of children, they differed according to bases for transforming or renaming objects in pretend, ability to replay past experiences, and ability to deal with imaginary objects.

Regarding renaming objects, Patterners renamed objects based on their physical attributes. For example, a spoon could be used as a pretend ice cream cone.

Dramatists would rename any object to fit a pretend theme, independent of the object's attributes. In terms of replaying familiar experiences, Patterners were reluctant reenacters, while Dramatists did it frequently and in relatively sophisticated ways. Correspondingly, patterners seemed uncomfortable with the imaginary world, while dramatists engaged in imaginative activities from an early age.

These individual differences are especially important to keep in mind when making recommendations about educational experiences for children. Dramatic reenactments may not be optimal for all children. Individuals often take different routes to becoming competent, what systems theorists label *equifinality* (Bertalanffy, 1968). There are multiple routes to competence, often mediated by the interface between individual levels variables and one's ecological niche.

It should be clear at this point that the initiation and maintenance of social pretend play is heavily dependent on children's use of oral language; the ambiguities inherent in pretend necessitate verbal explication. With this in mind I will return to this topic, after I discuss children's move from solitary to social pretend play.

MOVING FROM SOLITARY TO SOCIAL PRETEND PLAY

As just described, the frequency and complexity of children's pretend play increases across the preschool and early primary school period and moves, for most children, from solitary to social, and declines at the end of this period, to be replaced by games with rules, at least according to Piaget's (1962) theory. As we

Figure 10.1   Solitary pretend play (Photo: A. Pellegrini)

have seen with the Günter Grass quote at the start of this chapter and as I will discuss later in this chapter, the view that pretend virtually disappears from children's, and indeed adolescents' and adults', behavioral repertoires has only equivocal support (Harris, 2006; Lillard & Sorensen, no date; Sutton-Smith, 1997).

In this section I will address the progression of children's pretend play from a solitary to a social mode. Much of the empirical evidence for this change is derived from Ken Rubin's nesting (summarized in Rubin et al., 1983) of the cognitive "play" categories presented by Sara Smilansky (1968) as functional, constructive, dramatic, and games with rules, with an adapted version of the social participation categories proffered by Mildred Parten (1932): solitary, parallel, and interactive participation. Recall that, in the earlier chapter on social play, I suggested some limitations with this model. The one limitation that was especially problematic from my point of view was how researchers using the system tended to subordinate all of children's behavior into one of these categories, whether the behavior was play or not, according to most standard psychological definitions. The result of this practice, of course, is that estimates of children's time budgets in play are inflated. These inflated values have implications, not only for our descriptions of the course of different forms of play, but also for our inferences regarding the functional value of different forms of play.

This limitation, however, is minimized when it is used to categorize children's pretend, and especially social pretend, for the simple reason that the "playful" criteria of the behaviors being observed are more explicit in pretending than in other forms of play. More specifically, in pretend play, children often mark their intentions with explicit, verbal announcements of role assignments and object transformations. In the case of solitary pretend, these explicit markers are less common, but children often use sound effects to accompany their typically exaggerated actions, such as the sounds of a truck as they are pushing it. Thus, I will rely heavily on data generated using Rubin's matrix to describe the occurrence of both solitary and social pretend play.

One caveat is necessary, however. I will consider instances of parallel behavior as social rather than solitary. Recall from the chapter on social play that parallel interaction involves children next to each other engaging in similar activities but not interacting directly. The judgment that parallel interaction is social, rather than nonsocial, is based on the argument that children engage in parallel behavior as an act of social proximity or affiliation. They choose social proximity, rather than separation, and this strategy is often followed by social interaction (Bakeman & Brownlee, 1980; Smith, 1978).

I will use an adult example to illustrate the point. Imagine you are at a cocktail party and you know very few people there, yet you want to interact with some of them to get to know them. A common strategy to achieve that end is to approach a small group of people already interacting in a circle, and as you approach you will notice that the group, quite literally, will open up: People will change their posture, make face-to-face contact with you, and in the process make physical space for you in the group. It is now up to you to make the next social move, such as a greeting.

The point of this example is that children too use a similar strategy to enter a group. Very young children have a relatively limited verbal repertoire to initiate and maintain social interaction, so they may rely on engagement in the same activity in close social proximity to peers in the initial phases of group formation. Of course children who do not go beyond the parallel strategy may have problems with the social information processing and consequently may be excluded from future social interaction.

Solitary Pretend Play

Solitary behavior generally, and solitary play specifically, have been studied extensively by Ken Rubin and his colleagues (e.g., 1982; Rubin & Coplan, 1998) and more recently by Rob Coplan, a former student of Rubin's (e.g., Coplan et al., 2004; Coplan & Rubin, 1998). Coplan and Rubin (1998) make an important distinction among solitary passive behavior, solitary activity behavior, and reticent behavior. Solitary passive behavior is characterized by exploratory behaviors with objectives, and thus it probably should not be considered to be play in many cases. Reticent children engage in onlooker behavior, such as looking at other children playing, or are unoccupied; again, this is not play. Solitary active behavior, while infrequent, includes repeated sensorimotor actions or solitary dramatic play as displayed in Figure 10.1, and thus is of interest to us in this section of the chapter.

In naturalistic observation of preschoolers, typically conducted in university laboratory school, solitary pretend behaviors account for 1% to 5% of all play behavior (Rubin et al., 1983). We do not know, however, the ratio of solitary pretend play to other, *nonplay* forms of behavior, perhaps because play was not systematically differentiated from non-play by researchers using this matrix. What we do know, however, is that the degree to which children's play is nonsocial or social depends on a number of classroom contextual variables.

Specifically, children in classrooms usually self-select themselves into social contexts and activity centers that will either support or dampen their social/ nonsocial pretend play. For example, in my early research, a negative correlation was observed between the number of teachers in a classroom (and in university classrooms the number can range from one to five or more) and children's solitary pretend play, suggesting that teachers may have intervened when children were playing alone (Pellegrini, 1984). Furthermore, there was a negative correlation between the number of children in an activity center and solitary pretend play (Pellegrini & Perlmutter, 1989), suggesting, again, that physical proximity to peers maximizes the likelihood of social interaction. Similarly, children were more likely to exhibit social pretend in "housekeeping/dramatic" centers. It makes sense that children too would recognize these social demands and choose those contexts supporting the form of interactions they want.

In order to understand the effects of these contexts, independent of children's self-selection into different social and materials contexts, we assigned them to experimental play conditions, described earlier in this chapter, of constructive, ambiguous props, and pretend-oriented, doctor-theme, props (Pellegrini & Perlmutter, 1989). Interestingly, we found that there was neither an age-related effect among these four- and five-year-olds' solitary pretend play nor a context effect, though solitary dramatic play was observed very infrequently (4% of all observed behavior) and probably due to the experimental contexts. Specifically, children were observed in relatively small and familiar experimental rooms with another, familiar same-sex child and no adult; so there was an expectation that they would interact socially. With that said, the 4% figure is consistent with the 1% to 5% reported by Rubin and colleagues (1983) in their review of naturalistic studies. Social pretend, by contrast, accounted for 33% of children's observed behavior in our experimental observations.

Social Pretend Play

The Beginnings of Social Pretend Play

The transition from solitary to social pretend play is a hallmark of the preschool period, reflecting children's relatively sophisticated social cognitive and linguistic development. As suggested above, because social pretend play involves, by definition, the communication and coordination of abstract meaning between people, the possibility for ambiguity and the subsequent breakdown of social interaction around a pretend theme is relatively high. This state of affairs is why social pretend play has been afforded such an important role in the ontogeny of children's theory of mind (e.g., Leslie, 1987). With both social pretend and theory of mind, children are concerned with others' intents and beliefs. Also in both theory of mind and social pretend play research, the role of a close adult–child relationship, such as the mother–child relationship, is central to children's developing ability to understanding others' intentions (Howes, 1992; Tomasello & Call, 1997).

There is also a very good biological reason for mothers to spend time in joint interaction with their infants and children. Mothers are "motivated" to spend time and energy on their offspring because they represent a major genetic investment. Her offspring contain 50% of her genes, and the mother wants to maximize the survival and reproduction of her offspring, and her genes (Trivers, 1972). Therefore, mothers not only invest in protecting and provisioning their offspring, but also in tutoring them in the skills necessary to maximize the offspring's survival and reproduction. Mother–child playful interactions are part of this process (Bjorklund, 2006).

The offspring, too, have an interest in maintaining a close relationship with their mothers, providing their mothers are responsive to their needs. That is, offspring depend on mothers for protection and provisioning, and they try to maximize the resources they extract from their mothers (Trivers, 1974). This dynamic relationship of interdependence is enacted in the mother–child attachment relationship. This relationship is developed in social pretend play and forms an important base of children's representations of other social relationships. This developmental progression has been documented in a series of studies by Carolee Howes (1992) and her students. According to Howes, children's social pretend with mothers begins at around 12 to 15 months of age when children take pretend play actions outside their functional context (i.e., decontextualization), such as pretending to drink from an empty cup. In a mother–child interaction context, mothers will structure pretend scenarios to maximize children's participation (Lillard, 2006), because the child is now capable of responding to its mother's pretend initiations, often by watching, complying with, and imitating those acts. To maximize children's participation, mothers monitor their children's behavior closely, being particularly vigilant around pretend behavior; they look at children closely and smile after children's pretend play acts (Lillard, 2006). In this way children learn to recognize pretend play actions as distinct from non-pretend interactions, and they also come to realize the value of this sort of behavior in social interactions. Mothers may also "correct" a child's inappropriate response. For example, if a child does not respond to the offer of a cup of tea, the mother might ask, "Aren't you thirsty?"

By contrast, if this same decontextualized play act were initiated in the presence of a peer, there would be a lower likelihood that it would elicit a response. If there was a response from a peer, however, it would probably take the form of the peer looking or smiling at the child, or imitating the action (Howes, 1992), not extending it as done by the mother. In other words, peer play partners are expressing an interest in the play initiation, but they may not have the skills to extend the interaction more explicitly like adults do. Even if this rather low level of interest is expressed, however, children come to recognize that pretend acts have social value (i.e., they are reinforced) and will be likely to continue.

Between 16 to 24 months of age, and as discussed above, children's pretend play acts become yet more decontextualized, to the extent that they are no longer centered on the child: Children's pretend acts can be directed at another person (Howes, 1992; Nicoloch, 1977; Watson & Fischer, 1977). In the presence of a peer, children of this age are more likely than younger children to try to enlist each other in pretending, and if successful, to enact, or imitate, pretend acts similar to the initiation (Howes, 1992), though children's relatively low social cognitive and linguistic skills limit the degree to which pretend play can be extended beyond this rudimentary level. For example, Child A may initiate a pretend act in the presence of Child B, such as moving a car around the floor saying "Brrmmmmmmmm." Child A looks at Child B when this is completed and recruits Child B by handing over the toy car, and Child B then moves it across the floor, too (Howes, 1992).

By the end of their second year of life, children's pretend play acts become more integrated into longer behavioral scripts with both their mothers and their peers. In the mother–child dyad, it is not infrequently the case that the child initiates a script, such as changing a doll's diaper. Mother typically supports and extends these actions with prompts more for detailed enactments; for example, "Do we have more diapers?" "How do you know she needs to be changed?" Finally, at the end of this period, mothers encourage children's independent pretend play (Howes, 1992).

In the peer context at the end of the second year, children's pretend becomes more coordinated in enacting scripts (Howes, 1992). Peers tend to enact the same themes and comment on each other's contributions to themes, often by directing each other's play. In fact, at around three years of age, children's comments on the management of pretend play with their peers are actually more frequent than those dedicated to pretend *per se* (Sachs, Goldman, & Chaille, 1984). More will be said about the language used to coordinate pretend play later in this chapter. Suffice it to say for now, that the roots of peer social pretend play run deep into the mother–child relationship. Mothers, at least those in modern industrialized societies, seem to deliberately teach their infants to differentiate pretend from non-pretend behavior, teach them to extend their play themes, and generally, reinforce children's pretend enactments.

Current evidence (e.g., Lillard, 2006) suggests that mothers, or a more competent playmate, actually guide children's play to higher levels, consistent with Vygotsky's notion of the zone of proximal development. In this view, adults try to maximize children's participation in interaction by being responsive to children's levels of play. More specifically, if children are faltering in play, adults will then pose a relatively simple comment, such as "What's in the cup?" If children are responding adequately, they will pose more demanding comments, such as, "Are there any treats to go with the tea?"

Vygotksy's theory of adult–child interactions is also important for the descriptions of how very young children come to understand the mental states of others, proffered by both Angeline Lillard (2006) and Mike Tomasello (1995; Tomasello, Kruger, & Ratner, 1993; Tomasello & Call, 1998). In Tomasello's view, infants' interactions with their mothers resemble basic forms of conversations. Children and mothers engage in joint interaction where they each direct the other's attention using vocalizations and gestures. That infants check to see if mothers are responding to their efforts to direct attention suggests that they, the infants, are beginning to view others as intentional agents.

Important for the development of young children's symbolization-processing involved in both pretend play and language is the realization that their imitations of adults' actions and language can be used to solve social problems. Thus, they recognize that adults are using gestures and vocalizations to get something done (i.e., recognizing adults' intentions), and they use those same strategies to attain a goal. Children come to realize that adults use symbols, language, and gestures to direct their attention. Tomasello and colleagues (Tomasello et al., 1993) label this *cultural learning*. Correspondingly, by the second year of life, children recognize adults' intentionality when adults use objects in fantastic, or pretend ways. Continued experiences with adults and peers extend children's ability to understand that others have different views of situations and symbols than they do.

These descriptions of mother–child interaction in pretend play are also similar, at a general level, to that proffered by attachment theory, such that securely attached children and their mothers interact in a synchronous fashion. The evolutionary roots of attachment theory, of course, provide an explanation to the motivation question. Mothers and children alike are motivated to maximize children's survival. Building on this, I suggest a more differentiated, behavioral ecological, explanation for mothers' willingness to invest in her children. Recall, mothers would be more willing to invest in their children, and consequently spend more time interacting with their children and at more intensive levels, in ecologies that are relative abundant. In this sort of niche it pays off, in terms of inclusive fitness, to invest more resources in fewer children (Belsky, Steinberg, & Draper, 1991). In less abundant and more severe ecologies, mothers try to maximize fitness by investing less in individual children and maximizing the number of offspring. The result of each of these strategies translates into children being securely and insecurely attached, respectively. Each attachment style, in turn, impacts the ways in which children interact with their peers.

Social Pretend with Peers

Children's pretend play with their peers is characteristic of the preschool period, and increases in frequency from three to five years of age (Pellegrini & Perlmutter, 1989; Rubin et al., 1983). Observations of children in university preschool classrooms suggest that children's pretend usually occurs in "fantasy corners" or housekeeping areas (Pellegrini, 1984; Pellegrini & Perlmutter, 1989). The two explanations for these findings are that the play props elicit the observed form of play. Alternatively, children may select themselves into areas that support fantasy and act accordingly.

In the experimental study described above conducted by Jane Perlmutter and me (Pellegrini & Perlmutter, 1989), where children in same-sex and mixed-sex dyads were randomly assigned to contexts containing functionally explicit or functionally ambiguous, the explicit props elicited more pretend, generally, as well as more social pretend, than the ambiguous props. These findings replicate the earlier findings of Pulaski (1970; 1973). There are also consistent sex-differences in social pretend play where girls engage in pretend more frequently than boys and their pretend is more complex (Garvey, 1990; Pellegrini & Perlmutter, 1989). Importantly, these findings are robust even in studying involving poor African American children (McLoyd, 1980; 1981).

Again, our research shows that boys and girls differentially select themselves into play areas that support their preferred mode of play. Girls, generally, prefer to play with domestic role oriented props, such as housekeeping and dress up props, and boys prefer to play with props supporting large motor movement, such as blocks and trucks and to play out of doors (Garvey, 1990; Pellegrini & Perlmutter, 1989; Rubin et al., 1983). When boys and girls are playing with preferred props, the themes of their fantasy play typically relate to those props and corresponding sex differences in themes: Boys fantasy is more action-oriented and quasi-aggressive, or what Eli Saltz and colleagues (Saltz, Dixon, & Johnson, 1977) labeled "thematic fantasy play". Girls' fantasy with their preferred objects is more-domestically oriented and "dramatic" (Saltz et al., 1977). When boys and girls are observed in both naturalistic and experimental settings these findings replicate (Pellegrini & Perlmutter, 1989). It also seems to be the case that as preschool-age children get older, they become more aware of the sex role expectations associated with their play with different props. Specifically, we found that as girls got *older* their play with the male preferred props in experimental settings was *less* sophisticated than that of *younger* girls. Clearly they are learning to exhibit sex role consistent behavior by five years of age (Pellegrini & Perlmutter, 1989).

Briefly, social role theory posits that social roles in society have different levels of status. In modern industrial societies male roles are typically higher status than female roles. By extension, children's play with male- and female-preferred play props should reflect this bias. This bias is especially pronounced when boys and girls, in mixed-sex dyads, interact with male- or female-preferred play props. In our experimental work we found boys dominated girls in these contexts, by talking more, initiating more topics, issuing more commands. Girls, by contrast, imitated more and asked for help more. In short, sex differences in play are moderated by the sex of children's play partners and the props with which they are interacting.

It is also very important to note that children's social ecology affects their social pretend play. Not surprisingly the number of peers present is positively correlated with children's social pretend (Pellegrini, 1984; Pellegrini & Perlmutter, 1989). Children obviously need peers with whom to play if their play is to be social. By contrast, and perhaps surprisingly, children's pretend is often inhibited when too many adults are present. I say surprisingly because folk wisdom states that it is good to have lots of adults in preschool classrooms, perhaps as a reaction to the unfortunate reality of many understaffed preschools. University preschools have the opposite problem. Often there are too many adults in the classroom, often a head teacher, an assistant, and an aid- plus one or two student teachers! In separate studies at the University of Georgia Lab School, we found a negative correlation between number of adults present in a play area and the frequency and sophistication of children's social pretend (Pellegrini, 1983; 1984; Pellegrini & Perlmutter, 1989).

Why might this be the case? Piaget's (1965; 1970) explanation for the different role of peers and adults in children's social and cognitive development is a likely candidate. Briefly, Piaget suggested that when children interact with each other, they are more likely to disagree with each other, relative to their interactions with adults. Indeed, minimal adult presence was listed by Rubin and colleagues (Rubin et al., 1983) as part of their contextual definition of play. Adults are viewed by children as authorities, thus inhibiting disagreement. Disagreements, or dis-equilibrations, are important for Piaget because they are motivators of change. For example, some children may have a concept that only boys, and not girls, can play at being doctors. In play, a boy may have a girl partner and she wants to play the doctor role, thus causing dis-equilibration in the boy's concept. In order for play to continue the boy must assimilate this new information, and thus enriching, or causing an accommodation, the earlier concepts of males, females, and doctors.

This inhibitory effect of adult presence is also surprising in light of our earlier discussion of the role of adults, generally, and mothers, specifically on very young children's pretend. Recall, we noted that Vygotsky's notion of the zone of proximal development had adults maximizing children's exhibition of competence by providing the necessary support so that children could participate in the tasks at hand. So, why is that note the case with preschool children's pretend play?

I think there are two reasons. First, by the time children are three years of age they are capable of initiating and sustaining pretend (e.g., Fein & Stork, 1981), thus they do not need adults to scaffold their play. Second, the nature of the task, pretend play, is such that children seemingly want to maximize the unpredictable, as I discussed in the social play chapter, and peers are better at doing this than are adults. For example, adults are excellent tutors, even in the late preschool and primary school years, for cognitively convergent tasks, such as planning the best route to a store, while peers are better are more divergent tasks (Ellis & Rogoff, 1986; Tudge & Rogoff, 1989).

Even with this said, there is a persistent belief among many play researchers and educators that some children, especially lower socioeconomic status children, need adult guidance, or tuition, in order to maintain social pretend play. This assumption can be traced back to the work of the Israeli psychologist Sara Smilansky (1968; 1971). In her very influential work with lower social economic status Israeli children, she suggested that they were not capable of maintaining pretend play with peers because of their inadequate language skills and the inability to take their peers' points of view. From this position, poor children needed to be trained in how to engage pretend play (labeled sociodramtic play by Smilansky) with their peers.

This claim also stimulated a very vocal, and sometimes vitriolic, debate of the perceived deficits vs. the differences of poor children's social and cognitive abilities relative to middle class children (see McLoyd, 1982 for a very well argued critique of the deficit position). The subsequent research stimulated by Smilansky for the most part, demonstrated that preschool children, from three years of age on, do not need adults to support their play (see Fein & Stork, 1981; McLoyd, 1982; Pellegrini, 1984).

The other implication of Smilansky's claims was that it stimulated massive amounts of "play training" studies (see Rubin et al., 1983 for a review). Implications from the results of these training studies were also used to make claims about the role of play in children's social, cognitive, and linguistic development (see Smith, 1988). As Peter Smith pointed out, this research conflated the effects of play with adult tuition in play. That is, children were not only playing but they were being coached by adults to play, so the effects of play alone were confounded with the adults' input (Smith & Syddall, 1978; see also Rubin, 1980).

I set out to correct this limitation in my own research with a group of poor, primarily Africa American primary school children (grades kindergarten and 1st grade) in rural Georgia (Pellegrini, 1984). In this experimental study I tried to identify those aspects of social pretend play that were effective in facilitating children's comprehension of the storied they enacted, with particular emphasis on teasing out the effects of adult tuition in comparison with peer play on children's pretend play. To this end, I formed four groups of four children (two boys and two girls). In all conditions children were read stories on three occasions: Little Red Cap; The Three Billy Goats Gruff; Three Little Bears. In the "full condition" children were asked to enact the story they had just heard and were exposed to all components of the play training regimen: Adult coaching, verbalization about the story, peer disagreement-compromise in pretend play.

In the second condition, the peer play condition, children enacted the stories as in the "full condition", but without adult direction. In the third condition, the assimilation/accommodation condition, after being each read each story, individual children were asked to first retell the story. After all children in their groups had done this, each child was then asked how his/her story was different from and similar to each of their peers' stories. In this condition, children verbally represented the stories and assimilated and accommodated to their peers' versions of the stories without fantasy, so we could judge its relative impact.

The fourth condition was a control condition. After being read each story children were asked to draw pictures about the story, without talking to their peers. Thus in this condition, we had children mentally representing the stories, through art, but not interacting with peers or adults. Children in all conditions were asked both to orally recall each of the stories and to answer a series of story comprehension questions immediately after the treatments and again one week later.

Results revealed that there were no differences between the full condition and the peer play condition on the immediate measures and each of them was more effective than the conflict/resolution condition. The latter condition, however, was more effective than the two play conditions in maintaining children's story knowledge. These results support the idea that poor children, like their middle class counterparts, too can maintain play without adult guidance, similar to the claims made by Greta Fein with younger children (Fein & Stork, 1981). Furthermore, the peer disagreement and agreement cycle that typified children's social pretend with peers is crucial in their long term learning. The diminishing role of pretend per se, may be due to the age of these children, almost six and seven years of age. Perhaps with younger children, fantasy, in addition to the assimilation/accommodation characteristic of peer interaction would make a greater contribution.

Different configurations of child-child social fantasy: Siblings. Peer relationships, like mother–child relationships, however, are not all "created equal" when it comes to facilitating children's social and cognitive decentering in play. Generally, there are two sets of variables that are relevant to peer groups and children's social pretend play: Close relationships and diverse social contacts. Close peer relationships, such as sibling and friendship relationships, like the mother–child relationship, may facilitate prolonged and rather sophisticated pretend play because of the trust and familiarity characteristic of these relationships.

Sibling relationships are characterized not only by familiarity, but also of a kin relationship. Recall that the notion of inclusive fitness states that individuals try to maximize the survival and reproduction of their offspring and kin, relative to nonkin, with the implication being that individuals will be more cooperative and altruistic with kin, relative to non-kin, and close kin, relative to distant kin. From this position siblings' play should be more cooperative and less aggressive, relative to the play of nonkin. Furthermore, if there is conflict, reconciliation should be more common between siblings, relative to nonkin. Before you start thinking of how you and siblings played and that my description does not reflect that reality, consider the following. The characterization that I presented reflects general, group level means- Not individual cases. That is, siblings as a group, tend to play more cooperatively, relative to nonkin.

Judy Dunn's (Dunn & Kendrick, 1982) observations conducted in the homes of her Cambridge, England families illustrate this point. She shows that while there is consistency in siblings' play behavior with each other, there is also variation. Specifically, she found that in some families siblings often played together harmoniously, and the older sibling frequently helped care for the child. In these cases, the younger sibling often imitated the older child. These siblings did not often exhibit aggression toward each other. In other families, older children were aggressive toward their younger and the latter did not imitate the former.

Play between siblings did, however, provide older children with opportunities to explore aspect of their "self". Dunn and Kendrick give an example of siblings in pretend play and an older sibling taking on the role of a younger child. The fictional younger child does not comply with a request made by his mother because he was "only a baby"! Similarly, when older siblings play with a parent they explore their gender by taking on the gender of their younger sibling.

The play experiences of siblings, in turn, seem to affect children's play with nonkin, suggesting that the inclusive fitness argument can be complemented with a social learning dimension. Specifically, the play styles of siblings influence the choice of peer playmates (Sutton-Smith & Rosenberg, 1970). For example, older siblings prefer to play with younger peers and younger siblings prefer to play with older peers. A similar picture emerges with regard to sex. The play styles of children with opposite sex siblings have been categorized as "tomboyish" or "sissyish", respectively, of girls with male siblings and boys with female siblings. Thus, it seems that children prefer playmates who share similar styles of interaction. This phenomenon of behavioral compatibility, labeled as "homophilly", is also the basis of friendship between peers (Hartup, 1996; Kandell, 1978).

Different configurations of child-child social fantasy: Friends. The importance of friendships as close relationships for children, and their characteristic concordance, I posit, is rooted in the ways in which cooperation and altruism evolved in humans. Recall, the earlier discussion of how trust, cooperation, and altruism was more likely to occur among kin, relative to nonkin. It was probably the case that early human societies were comprised of small groups of individuals who shared a kin bond. As these small, kin-based social groups became larger and less concentrated with kin, individuals' in stable groups who shared a common history continued to cooperative with each other, much like groups composed of kin. This explanation is consistent with the explanation for the evolution and cooperation and reciprocal altruism (Axelrod & Hamilton, 1981; Trivers, 1971).

Friendship has been defined as a reciprocal relationship and is often measured by having children nominate peers they consider to be friends; friends are those who reciprocally nominate each other (Hartup, 1996). In the early childhood, friendship is typically influenced by propinquity, or the degree to which children are in close physical proximity and share interests in common activities (Hartup, 1996), not unlike siblings (Sutton-Smith & Rosenberg, 1970). Thus, two children who ride to school on the same bus, share the same classroom, and both like vigorous playground games are more likely to become friends, relative to children who don not share the same classroom and activities.

Friendship, once it is established, results in children maintaining close proximity and when separated friends become distressed, not unlike an attachment relationship (Hartup, 1983). From this position, friends trust each and work hard to maintain their relationship. The implication of this mutual trust and investment is that friends, relative to nonfriends, are more willing to disagree and conflict with each other but they also are more likely to reconcile (Hartup, Laursen, Stewart, & Eastenson, 1988; Pellegrini, Galda, Bartini, & Charak, 1997).

These conflict-resolution cycles in friendship, in turn, lead children to reflect on their emotional state, as evidenced by their using words such as sad, happy, and naughty (Pellegrini et al., 1997). It may be, following Bruner (1986), that encoding emotion words after a conflict helps to "cool" one's emotions and thus enables children to reflect on the mental and linguistic processes, as evidenced by their encoding mental terms such as think, easy, hard, and linguistic terms, such as talk, say, tell. The use of the "meta" terms, in turn, enables individuals to clarify play roles, for example, Doctors can't say poo poo, and thus enable the play theme to be sustained.

The extant literature on social pretend play supports these claims of the facilitative role of children's friendship (e.g., Howes, 1992; Pellegrini et al., 1997; Roopnarine & Field, 1984). Friends, relative to acquaintances, have longer and more concordant play bouts and like the play between siblings, involve relatively high levels of self-disclosure. Indeed, friends' pretend play, similar to that of siblings' play, involves fantasy themes centering around self disclosure, such as gender roles and parents' divorce. Howes (1992) suggests that similar concerns and fears may be an important basis for preschool children's friendships and subsequent pretend play.

Different configurations of child-child social fantasy: Close vs diverse. There is, however, an alternative view of the type of peer group composition that maximizes the maintenance of children's pretend play. This view posits that rather than close relationships, such as friendships and sibling relationships, exposure to a varied group of peers, with whom children have little shared experience, maximizes the types of language that are important to pretend play. This position has been advanced by Basil Bernstein (1960; 1971; 1972), an English sociologist of education.

Basil's Bernstein's theory was advanced in the early 1960's and concerned primarily with social class differences in socialization experiences that lead to children's differential levels of language production and eventually school performance. While social class, in the end, is not important to the argument presented here, the impact of different social roles enacted in the various socialization contexts sometimes associated with social class is important. Bernstein posited that some groups (English working class) were more socially insolated and parochial than others (English middle class) and as a result shared a common set of experiences and beliefs. As a result of this shared background, the communication style of this more "restricted" group did not have to verbally explicate meaning in conversation in order to make themselves understood by each other. Their shared knowledge did not necessitate, for example, that they define pronouns, or use logical arguments to convince others of the efficacy of a belief, thus an absence of causal and temporal conjunctions.

This "restricted code", to use Bernstein's label, works very well in contexts where individuals share knowledge or a physical context. Think, for example, when you give directions to a location to someone with whom you share knowledge of an area, such as a neighbor or spouse. You can be very well understood even when you are relatively vague. This strategy will not work, however, with someone who is not familiar with the area. In such cases you must verbally explicate even the smallest details, such as street names and orientation. Bernstein suggested that when individuals lived in environments characterized by a variety of social roles, rules, and orientations they needed to be verbally explicit in order to be understood.

So which position is more effective in maximizing explicit language and social fantasy, the close or the diverse peer group experience? Ted Melhuish, now at Birkbeck College, London University, and I set out to answer this question while we were both at Cardiff University with a group of Cardiff, Wales primary school children (5 ½ year olds) in two experiment (Pellegrini, Melhuish, Jones, Trojanowska, & Gilden, 2002). In the first experiment dyads of previously unacquainted, same-sex children were assigned to one of two conditions. In the first, unfamiliar/varied condition, individuals were paired with a different, previously unfamiliar peer in four separate observations. In the second, unfamiliar/acquaintance condition, initially unfamiliar children interacted with the same peer across all four observations. In both conditions, children were read a book (a different narrative each time) by an experimenter and after the reading, they were given toys, paper, crayons, and pen and told to play/draw/write about the story that was just read to them. We measured the use of verbally explicit language, including talk about talk and talk about mental states and emotions in each condition.

First, we found that for the unfamiliar/acquaintance condition, relative to the other condition, that children's language about language and language about emotions increased across time. This suggests that the formerly unacquainted children established a relationship, with time, and the language they used reflected their willingness to talk about emotions and also to reflect upon the verbal processes by which they interacted.

In the second experiment, we used the same design with similar age Cardiff children and compared friendship dyads with an unfamiliar/acquaintance condition, like the second condition used in the first experiment. While friends used both more emotion terms and language about language than the other group, these differences decreased significantly with time, supporting the hypothesis that the children in the unfamiliar/acquaintance condition established a relationship with time, not unlike a friendship. So, the verdict seems to be in: Friends maximize children's talk about language in pretend play and this seems to be due to the fact that friends provide emotional support for each other.

The general picture I have sketched here is of pretend play becoming more social and more complex with age. After beginning in the context of mother–child interaction at around 1½ – two years of age, pretend more social and peaks in the preschool years, around five years of age. During the preschool years pretend become more dependent on children's use of rather sophisticated forms of language, which will be addressed in the next section, in order for it to be sustained.

The Language of How Social Pretend with Peers Gets Done

As I have discussed, the ability to initiate and maintain pretend play with a peer requires a fair amount of social cognitive as well as verbal facility. Most basically, children must be willing and able to take the perspective of their peers so that they can then enlist their linguistic skills to explicate the meaning of their play themes so that they are mutually understood. To this end, children must have the ability to verbally explicate what it is they mean so that it is understandable to a peer.

Interestingly, children seem to acquire these skills while interacting with peers in pretend (e.g., Burns & Brainerd, 1979; Pellegrini, 1986), thus the relation between social pretend and explicit language is dynamic in the sense that they influence each other. The ambiguity inherent in pretend play, where there is little correspondence between the meaning of an object or a role in play and its real meaning necessitates that children verbally explicate meaning. As children gain practice using the "imaginative function" of language (Halliday, 1969–1970), their pretend becomes more sophisticated and is maintained for a longer duration as the themes become more sophisticated and less dependent upon objects.

In the earliest forms of social pretend children will initiate a pretend play bout with a peer and if their partners lack adequate linguistic skills the latter will merely repeat the overture, rather than expanding it, as a way of acknowledging and reinforcing the social overture (Pellegrini, 1982). As children gain linguistic sophistication, the use repetitions to maintain play decreases and expansions increase (Keenan, 1974; Pellegrini, 1982). So Child A initiates a pretend play bout asking: Wanna play cook? Child B expands this by saying Let's have tacos.

Even in the case of relatively mature children, the play overture must be clear if play is to progress. If the overture is ambiguous, the responder may still repeat the overture, but the repetition will have a questioning intonation and typically, it is clarified by the initiator (Pellegrini, 1982). In cases of ambiguity or disagreement, which are very common in social pretend, children spend a fair amount of time "out of the play frame", negotiating meaning (Sachs et al., 1984). Indeed, it has been suggested that more time is spent out of frame, negotiating and clarifying meaning, than in frame, playing (Sachs et al., 1984).

The language surrounding these negotiations is characterized explicated meaning. Not only do children explicate their feelings, in emotional terms, thoughts, in mental terms, language processes, in linguistic terms, but they also frame their arguments by using causal and temporal conjunctions. For example, girls can be doctors "'cause my Momma's one!" Furthermore, and also as discussed earlier in this chapter, in order to minimize ambiguity, children explicitly define their pronouns and embellish their nouns with adjectives (Pellegrini, 1982; 1986). These design features of the language used in social pretend, as will be discussed in the chapter addressing the educational implications of play, are similar to the design features of school-based literacy (Bernstein, 1960; Halliday, 1969–1970; Heath, 1983; Pellegrini & Galda, 1993).

Pretend Play Beyond Childhood?

The proposition that pretend play declines in early childhood and disappears from individuals' behavioral repertoires in middle childhood and adulthood is treated as a truism by many researchers and theoreticians. Indeed, it is a basic tenet of Piaget's (1962) theory of play. Recall, pretend play for Piaget is indicative of young children's autistic thought- something to be grown out of and replaced by logical thought (see Harris, 2006).

Vygotsky's (1962; 1967) theory, by contrast, suggests that pretend play, as a form of symbolic representation, is just the beginning of individuals' ability to imagine alternative realities, such as day dreaming, speculating, creative endeavors, and hypothesizing. And, from this view, it should not disappear with the appearance of logical thought. The quotation at the very beginning of this chapter from Günter Grass's childhood recollections clearly show examples of pretend in the play of 10 year old boys.

This level of anecdotal evidence might rightfully be criticized as lacking the necessary scientific rigor to establish the existence of pretend in childhood. As we will see, however, they are indeed consistent with current research. Specifically, Angeline Lillard and her student Laura Sorensen (no date) conducted two studies supporting the claim that pretend continues well into childhood. In the first study, they asked undergraduates to complete a retrospective questionnaire about childhood pretend and when and why it had stopped. Most students reported that they had played until they were 10 and 11 years of age, like the young Günter Grass, and others reported it continuing until they were 15 years of age. Examples of later pretend included conversation with a National Hockey League star, pretend with Barbie dolls, and even in intimate relations as an adult.

When asked to recollect why they had stopped pretending, most students said that they had shifted their interests to school, sports, and social activities. From these results, Piaget's claim that games replace pretend was supported, but at a later age. In the second experiment Lillard and Sorenson asked parents of children ages five through 14 years of age to keep diaries of children's daily activities, including fantasy, across a one week period. They found that 100% of the five to seven years olds pretended during the week and 75% of the eight to nine year olds did. These findings are consistent with the literature on imaginary friends, which persist well into primary school (Lillard, 2006; Taylor, Carlson, Maring, Gerow, & Charley, 2004).

Functions and Benefits of Pretend Play

Putative functions and benefits of pretend play are legion. Pretend play has been given hallowed status among educators and psychologists, and done so relatively uncritically. Peter Smith (1988) has discussed phenomenon in his description of the "play ethos". The underlying rationale for many of these claims is derived from Piaget's equilibration theory which the conflicts and resolutions associated with social pretend spur social cognitive development. From the perspective of Piaget's structural theory, the assimilation/accommodation/equilibration cycles characteristic of social pretend play should affect all aspects of children's social and cognitive development.

In this section I will review, first, correlational studies examining the relations between pretend play and specific criterion variables. Then, I will examine experimental studies were children of different ages were exposed to various types of play training regimens. By way of clarification, and perhaps warning, it should be noted that most of the studies reviewed suffered from a variety of serious methodological limitations, most notably experimenter bias.

Correlational Studies

Language and literacy. I will begin with a description of studies examining the relations between children's social pretend play and oral language and early literary measures. This discussion will be some what abbreviated as many of these findings are also reported in the chapter on the educational implications of play.

I begin with an early study I conducted to examine the relation between the observed play behavior of kindergarteners and their performance on the Metropolitan Readiness Test (MRT). I (Pellegrini, 1980) found that children who engaged in social pretend, relative to constructive and functional play scored the highest. This study, however, was limited in numerous ways. Firstly, experimenter bias was not controlled. Second, the correlations were contemporaneous so we do not know the directionality of the relations. It could have been, for example, that children high on the skills assessed by the MRT tended to engage in social pretend. Additionally, a third, mediator, variable may have been responsible for the relations. For example, it could be that the correlation between social play and MRT performance was really due to the fact that these children were verbally facile. Verbal facility is certainly correlated with both social pretend and MRT scores and if those correlations are controlled, the relation between social play and MRT performance may attenuate to non-significance.

In a follow-up study Lee Galda and I (Pellegrini & Galda, 1991) examined different forms of social pretend in preschool children at the University of Georgia preschool and their subsequent relations to measures of emergent reading and writing. In this longitudinal study, in which verbal IQ was controlled, the level of abstraction in children's pretend (object or ideational transformations) predicted children's early writing performance. Furthermore, children's use of meta-linguistic language in pretend predicted their subsequent reading. While experimenter bias still limits these findings, that they were replicated by another group of researchers, in a different part of the country (Dickinson & Moreton, 1991). These findings support the hypothesis that the ambiguity of trying negotiate meaning in social pretend affords opportunities to verbally explicate meaning and become adept at manipulation different symbolic systems.

Creativity and role-taking. Relations between children's social pretend and their creativity has a long and enduring history. This hypothesis stems from the view that in pretend, children are creating "alternative worlds" and are thus creative. In support of this claim, significant bivariate, contemporaneous correlations between children's social pretend and creativity (measured by children's ability to generate alternate uses for standard objects) have been reported by a number of researchers (e.g., Dansky, 1980; Johnson, 1976). It should be noted, again, that these contemporaneous correlations are subject to numerous alternative interpretations, such as directionality of "effects" (if there are any) and possible mediators, as well as experimenter bias effects.

Engaging in social pretend necessitates children to decenter socially and cognitively. Consistent with this argument, Rubin and Maoni (1975) found, in a study of Canadian preschoolers, that observed pretend play correlated contemporaneously with spatial perspective taking. In another study of Canadian preschoolers, but one in which children's age and IQ were statistically controlled, Jennifer Connolly (1980, cited in Rubin et al., 1983), found that social pretend still correlated with social competence and peer popularity.

In short, the evidence for a relation between social pretend and creativity is weak but the relations with role taking is stronger.

Theory of mind. Children's ability to take the perspective of someone else is not dissimilar from their ability to understand others' beliefs and intentions, or theory of mind. Related to this point, Alexander (1989) noted that social pretend play is probably adaptive, in the biological sense, because it enables individuals to construct and internalize a variety of social scenarios which, in turn, would be useful for social interaction in both cooperative and competitive encounters.

The evidence supporting the relations between pretend play and theory of mind is equivocal, however. Peter Smith (2006) reviewed nine correlational studies examining the relation between pretend and theory of mind, with verbal ability or intelligence statistically controlled, and of the 46 correlation coefficients reported, only 14 were statistically significant. Note, I did not include the measures of imaginary companions or impersonation reported by Smith (2006), as they are distinct from pretend play. The correlations that were the highest (e.g., .49) were between joint pretend and joint proposals in play and theory of mind. These findings are consistent with the idea that coordination of one's behavior in relation to someone else's should afford opportunity to decenter and reflect on others' behaviors, thoughts and beliefs, in relation to one's own. On the whole, the evidence is rather sketchy and experimental evidence would certainly make for a more convincing case.

Experimental Studies

Arguably, the most influential experimental study examining the effects of social pretend play on children's social, cognitive, and linguistic development was Sara Smilansky's (1968) work in Israel with economically disadvantaged preschoolers and kindergarteners. In Smilansky's work, she trained children to engage in what she called "sociodramatic play", which had the following components: Verbal interaction among children, pretend in regard to objects and roles, sustained interaction, and adult tutoring in play. Adults took either a play role or tutored in the play frame. This model of play was found to be an effective facilitator of children's sustained sociodramatic play.

Subsequent studies by Eli Saltz and his students (Saltz, Dixon, & Johnson, 1977; Saltz & Johnson, 1974) were also very influential partially because they extended and clarified the meaning of "sociodramatic play". For Saltz and colleagues, sociodramatic play was play relating to realistic, sometimes, domestic themes, such as home life, or occupations, such as a fireman, or a solider. By contrast, thematic fantasy play was play related to more fantastic themes, such as superheroes. Saltz and colleagues argued that the latter involved higher levels of mental representation because they involved more fantastic and less realistic themes. Saltz and colleagues (1977) found that play intervention facilitated a number of outcomes, such as impulse control and language production and language reception. Like Smilansky, and most of the other pretend play training studies, except for Pellegrini (1984), the studies had adults tutoring children in various forms of social pretend, and thus conflated play with adult tuition. Furthermore, all of these studies did not control for experimenter bias.

Keeping these limitations in mind, the results of these studies, and many others, provided equivocal support for the claim that play training facilitates social pretend play, as well as a variety of social, cognitive, and linguistic outcomes (See Rubin et al., 1983; Smith, 2005 for summaries of these studies). As noted earlier in this chapter, adult tuition does not seem to play as especially important role in these effects (Pellegrini, 1984). It is also very important to note that the findings of the effectiveness of pretend play training is inconsistent across this wide and varied array of studies. These inconsistencies are due, in part, to the great variety of the participants in these studies in terms of the ages and social economic status of the children. Adding further to this diversity, the various play training regimens were defined, implemented, and monitored in a number of different ways, thus making comparison difficult (Rubin et al., 1983). Add to these issues, there was the almost constant methodological limitation associated with experimenter bias. As was discussed in the chapter on object play, when experimenter bias is controlled some very well documented effects of play, on associative fluency (Dansky & Silverman, 1973; 1975) and using objects to solve problems (Sylva, Bruner, & Genoa, 1976), do not replicate (Simon & Smith, 1983; 1985; Smith & Whitney, 1987; Vandenberg, 1980).

The above described work, in many ways represents the Old View of the role of pretend play in children's development. It basically tested Piagetian-based tenets for the role of symbolic representation and decentration on development. The "New View" for the role of pretend play relates to its affect on theory of mind. It might be argued that that this new period began with Leslie's (1987) influential paper on the role of pretense and representation and theory of mind in *Psychological Review*. In this paper Leslie argued that the representational skills exhibited in pretend, where things and people represented other things and roles, was an early indicator of the sorts of skills necessary to represent others' beliefs and intentions indicative of theory of mind. As noted above, the correlational evidence for a relation between pretend play and theory of mind is equivocal.

In one direct experimental test between pretend play training and theory of mind, Dockett (1998, cited in Smith, 2005) trained four year old Australian children for three weeks in sociodramatic play and compared their performance on a variety of theory of mind task to a control group, who experienced only the regular curriculum. Children in the play group scored higher, relative to the comparison group, on theory of mind tasks at the post test and again three weeks later. On the whole, the link between pretend and theory of mind remains rather tenuous as indicated, primarily, by the correlational results. More experimental work is needed to replicate Dockett's findings but this work must follow experimental rigor (i.e., following double blind procedures). The theory justifications are clearly there to guide such efforts.

Experimental studies examining the role of pretend in children's ability to speculate about propositions that appear to be false and relevant to theory of mind have been carried out by Paul Harris (2006) and colleagues (Dias & Harris, 1988; 1990). They suggest, provocatively, that preschoolers' engagement in pretend play enables them to speculate about propositions that appear to be empirically false, to suppose that they are true, and to work out the implications. Specifically, by framing scenarios in a pretend frame, Harris and colleagues argue, children, from as young as two years of age, are able to speculate about possible implications. For example in Harris and Dias (1988), four and five year olds were told the following: All fish live in trees. Tot is a fish. Does Tot live in the water? In the pretend condition, children were first invited to think in terms of a distant planet, and told in a story-like dramatic way. In the control condition, children were given these sorts of reasoning problems with no pretend cues. Results revealed that children in the pretend condition could suspend their initial empirical bias and make the correct logical conclusions based on the information presented, insights implicated in theory of mind.

Harris and colleagues suggest that through imagination, from childhood through adulthood, individuals are able to suspend reality, imagine alternate scenarios and apply them to current circumstances. An interesting example of how the pretend of a school boy influenced his adult artistic expression comes, again, from Günter Grass (2006). In his 2006 memoir he repeatedly refers to the importance of childhood pretend and imagination for his later work as both a writer and a graphic artist:

"What far-off spaces was the grimacing youngster inhabiting without leaving the classroom? In what direction was he spooling his thread? As a rule, I was moving backward in time, ravenously hungry for the bloody entrails of history and mad about Pitch-Dark Ages or the Baroque interim of a was lasting thirty years" (p. 30).

Do Nonhuman Animals Engage in Pretend Play?

There is some evidence, admittedly controversial, that nonhuman primates also engage in pretend play. There are numerous reports of home-reared (enculturated) chimpanzees seemingly, engaging in elaborate symbolic play (e.g., Hayes, 1951; Jensvold & Fouts, 1993; Gardner & Gardner, 1971; Temerlin, 1975). For example, Washoe, a chimpanzee trained successfully to use American Sign Language, was observed bathing, soaping, and drying her dolls (Gardner &

Gardner, 1971) and another language-trained chimpanzee signed to her dolls (Temerlin, 1975).There are also several observations of wild chimpanzees displaying behavior that has been interpreted as fantasy play (for example, treating a log as a baby, see Wrangham & Peterson, 1996). Such observations in wild apes are rare, and observations in enculturated apes, although presumably reflecting symbolic representation, are open to a wide variety of alternative explanations (Gómez, & Martín-Andrade, 2005). For example, these sorts of pretend enactments quite easily could be fit into the category of simulations, as described by Paul Harris. From this view, these enactments are just that, and not metarepresentational activities.

Richer, or more generous, interpretations of nonhuman animals' "pretend" have been proffered, however, and its relation to fantasy and theory of mind. First, by way of having adequate cognitive capacity to have a theory of mind, Bekoff (1997) notes that great apes have a relatively high encephalization quotient (the ratio of actual brain size to body size expected from a regression equation for the relationship between brain size and body size). Consequently, they may have the cognitive capacity required for fantasy.

Second, recent research reported by Hare, Call, and Tomasello (2001), suggests that chimpanzees do seem to recognize that conspecifics may have different perspectives on events and objects but again, they do not seem to recognize others' intent. In experiments involving chimpanzees' ability to take a conspecific's perspective in a food seeking task, chimps could recognize that others see things differently than they do. This view of others enables them to predict and influence conspecifics' behavior in novel situations. Recognition of others' intent, as we have discussed, is crucial to some views of representational thought.

These are the sorts of skills described above in the most rudimentary forms of children's fantasy play. With this said, both young children and chimpanzees have difficulty recognizing others' mental states and using their knowledge to imagine what others might see in novel situations. From this view, they do not have a theory of mind, even though they recognize that others see the same objects in different way from them, and vice versa. This skill is clearly relevant in acquiring resources, such as food.

The sorts of play described above are consistent with the view that play is simulation or action based, and seems consistent with descriptions of 2- to three-year-old human children's fantasy. These interactions do not depend on having a theory of others' minds, but do depend on limited perspective taking skills, of the sort that chimpanzees seem to have in some contexts (Hare et al., 2001). Animals take behaviors from functional contexts (e.g., behaviors used in a real fight context) and simulate them in social play contexts. Their sustained and playful interactions are evidence that animals recognize that these behaviors have different aims from these same behaviors in serious contexts (Rosenberg, 1990).

Furthermore, that animals use "metacommunicative" play signals (Bekoff, 1977) as a way that to announce to others that "This is play," suggests that animals also recognize that conspecifics may have a view of the situation that is different from theirs. Nonhuman and human primates alike use play faces to mark the beginning of a bout much in the same way, using exaggerated movements and voices. Additionally, animals use play signals to clarify possible ambiguity, or "honest mistakes", in play (Fagen, 1981). Play markers, such as bows or play faces, reliably follow play behaviors that might be misinterpreted as too rough and possibly aggressive. Following these markers (or behavioral "punctuations"), animals reliably resume play (Bekoff, 1997).

These aspects of play enable animals to learn and practice the use of social signals. In this sort of social play, they encode and decode play signals so that they can manage social interactions with conspecifics. It is during these social interactions with conspecifics that animals, human and nonhuman primates alike, learn and practice the social skills necessary to function in social groups (Suomi & Harlow, 1972).

However, fantasy play in humans beyond its rudimentary stages involves more than social role substitution. For example, Bering (2001) proposes that symbolic play be differentiated between *feature-dependent make-believe,* in which imaginative behavior is directed toward an object that resembles another object (e.g., a child treating a shoe as if it were a telephone or Washoe bathing her doll as if it were a baby), and *true symbolic play,* in which individuals follow social scripts in the absence of any perceptually eliciting stimuli while in the context of play. There is some evidence that most of the fantasy play of human children until nearly their third birthday can best be described as feature-dependent make-believe, and that it not until this time that children's fantasy play begins to clearly involve mental representations of objects that are perceptually dissimilar from the objects they purport to represent (Ungerer, Zelazo, Kearsley, & O'Leary, 1981). Bering (2001) further argues that the incidence of fantasy play observed in great apes reflects only feature-dependent make-believe and does not require advanced forms of symbolic representation, as is seemingly required for attributing beliefs and knowledge to others (i.e., theory of mind).

I concur, and propose that the fantasy play observed in nonhuman animals may reflect a species-specific adaptation and may not be governed by the same type of cognitive systems as the fantasy play observed in humans (Burghardt, 1999; Pellegrini & Bjorklund, 2004). In other words, the similarity in play likely reflects phenotypically similar, but phylogenetically independent, (convergent) solutions to the problems associated with living in socially complex groups. Because of the nearness of our last shared common ancestor, it seems more likely that the cognitive abilities for feature-dependent make-believe displayed by some great apes may have served as the basis for the evolution of human-like symbolic abilities, such as those seen in true symbolic play.

However, animals' ability to make inferences about the communicative intent of others is facilitated by human culture, as evidenced by the "pretend play" of nonhuman primates noted above, as well as evidence comparing domesticated dogs with wolves (Hare, Brown, Williamson, & Tomasello, 2002). Domestic dogs, because of their extended and close relations with humans across history are especially attuned to human attention and communicative signals, such as facial signals (Call, Bräuer, Kaminski, & Tomasello, 2003). It is probably these cultural experiences, where nonhuman animals are treated as "intentional beings", that is also responsible for enculturated apes exhibiting pretend play (Tomasello & Call, 1998). Thus, culture shapes the phenotypic behavior important in nonhuman animals' social cognition, generally, and pretend play, specifically.

CONCLUSION

In this chapter I have sketched the developmental progression of pretend play, beginning in the mother-infant dyad and moving into the peer realm. It should be very clear that there are distinctive differences between solitary pretend and social pretend with peers. This process begins as mothers and infants interact in pretend play bouts. As described by Lillard, mothers closely monitor children's gestures and vocalizations associated with pretend play. The interplay between mothers' and children's pretend play bouts is similar to the more general process described by Tomasello and colleagues (e.g., Tomasello & Call, 1998; Tomasello et al., 1993) for children's coming to understand that others' intentions are different from their own intentions. Human culture puts a premium socializing not only infants but also domestic animals to view others as intentional agents.

In the pretend play between young preschool peers, children probably think that they and their partners see the world through the same eyes, following Harris' simulation view of pretend. With repeated experiences where points of view do not match, children come to realize that their views differ from those of their peers. Thus, the process of repeated interaction where meaning must be clarified is probably the mechanism responsible for children being able to consider the beliefs and intentions of others.

How does this explanation fit into the larger picture of children's social pretend in its phylogenetic context? It may be the case that the cognitive processes responsible for the evolution of animals' ability to cooperate with each other are crucial to shared intentionality (Hare, Brown, Williamson, & Tomasello, 2002). Through cooperative interaction, initially with a more competent tutor, individuals seem to learn about their own intentions, relative to those of others. From this position, human culture is important in affording opportunities to view others as intentional agents. The extended juvenile period of humans when embedded in the relatively protected and abundant ecologies which characterizes societies where mothers and children play for an extended period enables young children to learn that others have intentional states different from their own and that symbols can signal these different states.

Correspondingly, in cultures with differentiated and complex social roles, knowledge regarding effective practices must be passed from one generation to the next and this is may be done efficiently through some symbolic medium and in the context of mother–child play. Mothers socialize their offspring in joint play into the ways in which knowledge and intentions are communicated via symbolic media, such as gestures, noises, and eventually language. This explanation not only accounts for social cognitive development but also the ways in which they learn socially mediated symbol systems like pretend play and language.

11

The Role of Games

It should be evident from what we have discussed so far in this book that play has received substantial theoretical and empirical attention. By contrast and quite surprisingly, the games that children, adolescents, and adults engage in have received much less attention. I say surprisingly because games, and a specific form of games, sport, occupy a significant portion of adults' time and monetary budgets. Think, for example, of the size of the budgets of the sports programs of American universities, not to mention the amount of time and money spent by Americans on gambling, a form of "gaming"!

Furthermore, at least one influential psychological theorist, Piaget (1965), suggested that games have important implications for children's, and especially boys', social and cognitive development. Correspondingly, there have been repeated calls for more research on games over the last 50 years or more (e.g., Gump & Sutton-Smith, 1953; Hart, 1993; Rubin, Fein, & Vandenberg, 1983; Sutton-Smith, 1973; 1975; Sutton-Smith, Rosenberg, & Morgan, 1963). These calls, however, have largely gone unheeded. Take, for example, a recent edition of a volume in *The Handbook of Child Psychology,* on social and personality development (Eisenberg, 1998), where not a single reference can be found in the subject index to *games* or *games with rules,* down from the rather sparse six references in the 1983 *Handbook* (Hetherington, 1983)!

Similarly to our earlier discussions around definitions of play, so, too, is defining games important. In any discussion of games, it is very important to differentiate games from play because the two sometimes are confused, possibly because they share some design features (Garvey, 1977). For example, both play (e.g., fantasy play) and games (e.g., soccer) are rule-governed. The rules governing games, however, and following Piaget's (1965) formulations, are typically *a priori* and codified, while the rules governing play are flexible, negotiated by players in different ways, and not set in advance. For example, in a play episode where two children are pretending to cook a meal, they can negotiate rules and roles regarding what is to be cooked (e.g., Let's cook *stew*. No, let's have *cake*), how it is to be cooked, and who does it (I want to be the cook now). Once these issues are agreed upon, play behavior follows these rules, until the rules are challenged, at which time the rules are negotiated yet again (Fein, 1981; Garvey, 1977). Indeed, and as was discussed in the chapter on pretend play, more time is typically spent negotiating and renegotiating rules of play than in play *per se* (Garvey, 1977).

Games, on the other hand, are guided by explicit rules that are set in advance, and violation of these rules usually results in some form of sanction, not renegotiation (Garvey, 1977). So, for example, in a game of basketball, a child running with the ball without dribbling would be told by peers to forfeit the ball. As will be discussed below, the distinction between play and games based on the flexibility-of-rules criterion is sometimes not so clear-cut. Some forms of games, played especially by children, seem to implement rules in games rather flexibly.

The two photographs below illustrate pretty clearly dispositional differences between play and games. The specific game, in this case the sport of interscholastic cross-country skiing, is very serious business in the state of Minnesota. Note the grimace and determination on the face of this high school athlete competing in the state championship, indicative of a game, albeit a very serious game, as displayed in Figure 10.1.

In the next picture, Figure 10.2 the same athlete (in the front of the photo) is skiing on the very same trail, but not competing: He out having fun—playing— not concerned about his place in a race but enjoying the activity for itself. This

Figure 11.1   "Game Face" (Photo: A. Pellegrini)

Figure 11.2   "Play Face" (Photo: A. Pellegrini)

should be apparent from his broad smile, and what he is doing can be considered play—not games.

While Piaget's (1965) classic study of games centered on marbles, most of the extant research has examined the games and sport of children and adolescents out of doors, on playgrounds (e.g., Sluckin, 1981), in urban streets (e.g., Goodwin, 1990; Opie & Opie, 1969), and on sporting fields (Fine, 1987). These studies have been carried out by researchers from fields as varied as folklore (Opie & Opie, 1969), sociology (Coleman, 1971; Fine, 1987), and psychology (Sluckin, 1981). Much, though certainly not all, of the research on games on playgrounds has tended to dichotomize games, generally, from other forms of behavior, such as play (Pellegrini, Kato, Blatchford, & Baines, 2002), or games from "goofing around" and tricks (Parrott, 1975). From this viewpoint, behavior in games is defined following Piaget: Children and adolescents following *a priori* rules and behavior in games are compared with behavior in other categories.

One possible reason for the general paucity of research on children's games may be the availability of and access to a research sample of children and adolescents at times when they typically engage in games (i.e., during the primary and secondary school day or after school). Compare the ease with which infants and preschool children can be observed in university laboratory schools and the massive amount of research on the modal forms of play for children of these ages, sensorimotor and fantasy play (Rubin, Fein, & Vandenburg, 1983). Primary and secondary school children, on the other hand, are less accessible for study and offer fewer opportunities for observations of peer interaction, as much of the primary school day is tightly scheduled around regimens of solitary and sedentary academic work (Pellegrini & Blatchford, 2000).

Even with these limitations in mind, the school playground at recess does, however, provide an excellent, if underused, venue for the study of school-age children's peer interaction generally (Boulton & Smith, 1993; Hart, 1993), and games with peers (Boulton, 1992) more specifically. Furthermore, participation in recess is, by most school standards, required for all children; thus, problems associated with self-selection out of recess are minimal. Most important for the purposes of this book is the fact that recess is one of the few places during the mandatory school days where children are free to interact with their peers in various activities, including games, with relatively few restrictions (Boulton & Smith, 1993). It is therefore an ideal venue for studying a relatively large and diverse sample of children and adolescents engaging in activities that they enjoy: games, sports, and interacting with peers.

Correspondingly, observations of children and adolescents on the playground at recess probably yield valid information about their competence because interaction with peers at recess is both motivating and demanding for children (Waters & Sroufe, 1983). That is, children and adolescents typically enjoy recess, games, and sports, and to successfully engage in games and sports requires a fair level of social and cognitive sophistication (Sutton-Smith, 1975). For example, children must know the rules of the games and subordinate their personal views and desires to those rules and to the positions of their peers. That children enjoy these interactions motivates them to exhibit the high levels of competence required to participate in games. Children's behavior in playground games then should provide valid insight into their competence: their ability to get along with a variety of individuals (peer popularity) and to form close relationships (such as friendships).

Interaction with peers, especially around games in a school setting, is an especially interesting developmental task for studying social competence during middle childhood. Engagement in games with peers requires the sorts of social facility (e.g., cooperation, turn-taking, rule-governed behavior) necessary for competence with peers. Participation in games varies from simple turn-taking games, such as tag and chase, to typically more complex games with a variety of roles and rules, such as ball games and verbal games (Borman & Kurdek, 1987; Sutton-Smith, 1973; 1975). Though chase games can be complicated (Finnan, 1982), most are relatively simple. The simplicity of most chase games is reflected in the fact that they have been observed among primary school children at the start of the school year more than at the end (Thorne, 1986). Children also find them "boring" after they have been played repeatedly (Blatchford, 1998).

Ball games, on the other hand, often involve a variety of roles and, consequently, children do not become bored with them very easily (Blatchford, 1998). For example, in basketball, there are forwards, guards, and a center, with each of these having both offensive and defensive roles. Furthermore, there is a wide catalogue of rules governing ball games. Clapping, jump-rope, and hopscotch games, too, have multiple roles, such as jumper and rope spinner, and numerous rules (Opie & Opie, 1969). These clapping and jump-rope games seem to be almost exclusively the province of girls, and in many cases in American schools, especially African American girls (Goodwin, 1990). This may be due, in part, to the fact that girls, relative to boys, are more verbally facile, and verbal facility is required in chanting, hopscotch, and jump-rope games (Goodwin, 1990; Heath,

1983; Janikas, 1993; Lever, 1976; Maccoby, 1998; Thorne, 1986). From this view, less complex games, such as chase, should decrease with time as children mature and learn the rules associated with more sophisticated games. As participation in less complex games decreases, participation in more complex games, such as ball games, should increase.

Games on the Primary School Playground

Documenting the frequency with which children play games generally, and certain games in particular, is an important research goal, though it has not commonly been pursued. From the orientation of this book, documenting the frequency with which individuals engage in games during different periods in development is an indicator of costs expended in that realm and thus provides some insight into the possible function of games in development. A developmental perspective also leads us to posit that the types of games in which children engage should vary with their age. Correspondingly, there should be different benefits associated with games at various points in development. For example, chase games might affect both social affiliation and muscular/skeletal development. By contrast, the games typically requiring the greatest coordination of social, cognitive, and physical skills, such as ball games, might benefit social cognitive sophistication.

In an attempt to document the time that children spend playing different games on the school playground, my colleagues Peter Blatchford, Ed Baines, and I studied children's games on their primary school playgrounds in Minneapolis and London. We were interested, initially, in indexing the frequency with which children engaged in globally defined games on their urban school playgrounds (Blatchford, Baines, & Pellegrini, 2003; Pellegrini et al., 2002; 2004). Games were globally categorized ball games, such as soccer or basketball; chase games, such as tag or "it"; and verbal/jumping games, such as jump-rope or hopscotch games. We also considered the variety of different games children played as well as the variety of children from different ethnic groups with whom they interacted. Children in their first full year of schooling (first grade and its English equivalent) were observed on the school playground during their recess periods throughout the school year; results are displayed in Table 11.1.

Table 11.1   Games played by boys and girls by Time (Pellegrini et al., 2002)

	Time 1		Time 2		Time 3	
	Males	Females	Males	Females	Males	Females
All Games	.41	.13	.30	.10	.52	.16
Chase Games	1.35	1.09	.62	.45	.36	.21
Ball Games	.36	.06	.52	.04	1.39	.19
Verbal Games	.11	.22	.10	.41	.01	.28
Variety Games	.96	.70	.77	.48	.94	.55
Variety Ethnics	.98	1.14	.97	1.32	1.00	1.34

Consistent with the idea that the types of games children participated in would change with their age and gender, we found, first, regarding gender, boys engaged in more games and in a greater variety of different games than girls did. This gender difference probably reflects the fact that boys are more physically active than girls as a result of both hormonal and socialization events (Hines & Kaufman, 1994; Maccoby, 1998), as was noted in the earlier discussion of sex segregation and social play. When boys are put into a context that affords opportunities for physically vigorous activity, such as an outdoor playground at recess, predicable and robust gender differences are observed (Harper & Sanders, 1975).

Girls, by contrast, were more frequently observed in verbal games, such as jump-rope chanting and clapping games. This, as suggested earlier, probably reflects girls' greater verbal facility, relative to boys. This finding is also consistent with ethnographic studies of children from a variety of ethnic groups (e.g., Goodwin, 1990; Heath, 1983; Lever, 1976; Thorne, 1986; 1993). While this finding has been replicated by a variety of research teams with different theoretical and methodological orientations, it should be noted that all studies, including our own, had relatively small samples. Thus, the generalizability of these findings is still limited.

We also found that gender differences became greater as time passed during the school year. Specifically, no significant gender differences were found in the relative frequency of total games during the first part of the school year, but they became apparent by the end of the year. Boys engaged in more games and in a greater variety of games at the end of the year, relative to the beginning. Girls' participation in games remained flat across the year. These results confirm the socialization expectation that the playground is a venue that affords males opportunities to engage in locomotor and competitive activities. Correspondingly, as girls become socialized to stereotypical sex roles, they are learning not to participate in activities typically deemed to be in the male sphere and inappropriate for females.

Even in light of these stereotypes, it may be very important to examine individual differences in boys' and girls' participation in different types of games, such as girls' jump-rope and chanting games and boys' vigorous ball games. This level of analysis could provide insight into the transaction between biological dimensions of behavior, such as temperament, and socialization forces, such as sex-role stereotyping. It may be, as argued in earlier chapters, that individual differences in girls, such as activity level, result in different levels of social and game participation. Recall from this discussion on the role of physical activity in children's sex segregation where we found that highly active girls, and all boys, started off playing by among themselves. Following from this argument, it may be that when most girls participate in games, they engage in chanting games, while more physically active girls engage in jump-rope games, first with boys, because they, too, are more physically active than most of their female peers.

Chase games, as expected, decreased throughout the year, and ball games increased. Similarly, Thorne's (1986) ethnographic study of primary school children in Michigan playgrounds also found that chase games tended to be observed at the start of the school year and decreased as the year progressed. Chase games may have declined with time because of the relative simplicity of these games. The simplest variants of chase games involve only the most basic rules: chase and be chased. The simplicity of chase games is further evidenced by the fact that most simple variations are commonly observed even in very young preschool children (Pellegrini & Smith, 1998). Many of these games require little background knowledge or negotiations about interpretations; thus children can interact with each other in these games from the very earliest phases of social group formation. With repetition, chase, unlike ball, games become boring to children of this age (Blatchford, 1998) and are dropped out of the children's daily game repertoires.

Furthermore, and more interestingly, it may be the case that children used chase games as opening gambits in initiating interaction with new and unfamiliar peers and as bases for playing new and more complex games, like ball games. Specifically, the simple chase games may have also served as "scaffolds" for subsequent social interaction between initially unfamiliar peers. We use the term *scaffold* as it has been used in studies of play (Bateson, 1981). That is, a scaffolding behavior is used in the early developmental history of another, more complex, behavior. When that stage of development has been reached, the scaffold is disassembled and disappears (Bateson, 1981). Simple games can act as scaffolds for more complex forms of social interaction during phases of interaction when peers are not familiar with each other. That is, knowledge of relatively simple and routine games is probably shared by many children. These routines serve as a way that they can interact with each other when they have limited social skills and are not familiar with each other. With social cognitive development and familiarity with rules of games, simple games declined and are replaced by more complex forms of social interaction. Similar arguments for the role of simple and routinized behavioral scripts in learning more complex skills have been made by Corsaro (1985) for young children's social competence, and by Snow (1989) for children's language learning. Familiarity among peers also contributes to the increase in complex games such as ball games, relative to simpler games, across time. Familiar peers, more than unfamiliar peers, engage in more sophisticated and cooperative forms of interaction from infancy through adolescence (e.g., Brody, Graziano, & Musser, 1983; Hartup, 1983).

Rules of the Games

The level of description of the games that I have offered thus far is admittedly undifferentiated. Indeed, it may be that merely coding behavior, globally, as a verbal game versus a ball game versus chase, for example, is too gross to detect girls' engagement in games. Perhaps if we had used more fine-tuned coding and recording strategies (such as coding game complexity using audio-video recording devices), sex differences in the observational data would have been less robust. This explanation is not, however, consistent with Goodwin's (1990) ethnographic study of African American urban children. Using more microanalytic ethnographic techniques, Goodwin too found that boys played games more frequently than girls. Additionally, Thorne's (1993) ethnographic research also found boys engaging in chase more frequently than girls.

Clearly more detailed work is need to make more refined statements about game "complexity" and "rule-governed behavior" and the ways such variation is observed across time and is related to function. One sort of detailed description of the progression from "simple" to "complex" games has been provided by the Israeli psychologist Rivka Eiferman (1973). As part of an impressive, large-scale study of games on Israeli school playgrounds, Eiferman (e.g., 1970; 1971; 1979) has shown how children negotiate rules as they are engaged in games. In this study, Eiferman classified the different types of rules used in children's playground games and suggested that there are two macro-level categories of rules: instructions and regulations. Instructions are can be used by participants to guide each other in their conduct in games. Instructions are more like a set of explicit strategies used to participate in games, thus they are not necessary in order to participate in games.

As for the regulations of games, knowledge of those regulations is necessary to participate in the games, and they seem to be closer to what we typically consider "rules of the game." Eiferman (1973) suggests there are four types of game regulations: requirements, prohibitions, rules of permission, and meta-rules. *Requirements* are the basic rules of conduct for games and, as such, dictate individuals' conduct in games. An example of a requirement might be that in a game of hide and seek, individuals must count to 100 before beginning their search. Requirements are the types of rules most frequently studied, according to Eiferman (1973).

Prohibitions, by contrast, specify what may not be done in games. For example, in basketball, individuals may not step on the boundary lines. If they do, they are "out of bounds." Thus, with both requirements and prohibitions, when there is an infraction, there is usually some sort of sanction, such as having to forfeit the ball or a turn. A less stringent set of regulations is the rules of *permission*. Where requirements and prohibitions are typically mandatory, rules of permission are much more flexibly enforced. So, for example, in a game of hide and seek, the seeker may chose to count more or less loudly. In the first case, the hiders are more aware of the time they have to hide than in the second case. Utilization of different sets of rules may vary according to the age and sophistication of those engaged in the game. For example, the "loud" rule may be used to enable younger or less experienced individuals to participate in the game.

Similarly, *meta-rules* enable individuals to introduce flexibility to the rules of games, and in most cases these meta-rules take precedent over more established rules. For example, in a game of touch football, a meta-rule might state that two-hand tags only count if they are above the waist. This meta-rule might replace the more general rule that two-hand tags count if they are placed anywhere on the body. Like rules of permission, meta-rules enable youngsters to introduce different levels of complexity into the games. In the case of using the meta-rule of tags above the waist, the game is made more difficult. By contrast, a meta-rule of one-hand tags' replacing two-hand tags would make the game less difficult. Therefore, different meta-rules can be introduced to accommodate participants at different levels of game facility. Consistent with this generalization, Eiferman (1973) found that rule of permission and meta-rules were found more frequently in the games of children six to ten years of age than in those of children ten to fourteen years of age, suggesting that youngsters introduce flexibility into games in order to include young players.

Children's knowledge of rules of games and knowledge of how they and their peers follow, or do not follow, rules, by the time they are in primary school is also important in their development and presentation of themselves. That is, and from a social interactionist perspective (Cooley, 1902; Fine, 1981; Mead, 1934), the degree to which children and adolescents choose to follow rules of games is a way that they manage the social impressions of themselves that they convey to peers. They can send a message to their peers of being competent and strong, or relatively incompetent and weak, by the ways that they follow rules of the game. Peers, in turn, may treat them according to this presented self. For example, children may purposefully appear to struggle with rules of a game or a skill at enacting the game with the hope that peers will perceive them as incompetent—a perceived weakness that might later be exploited in a game. Furthermore, some flexibility in rule interpretation may be afforded to friends, relative to non-friends, as a way to send a message of confirmation of friendship.

Participation in Games and Competence in School

From this analysis it should be clear that children's and adolescents' participation in games, at various levels, involves a rather sophisticated suite of social cognitive strategies. Consequently, engaging in games should be beneficial to participants, either in terms of practicing extant skills and strategies or in the learning of new ones.

Earlier in this book we discussed the hypothesis, rooted in Vygotskiian (1967) theory, that children exhibit higher levels of competence in play than in more realistic behavior. This idea is based on the two propositions that play is motivating (that is, children want to participate in it because they enjoy it) and demanding (that is, it requires social and cognitive sophistication to participate in it). A similar argument has also been made for the role of games. Specifically, the noted educational sociologist James Coleman (1971) suggested almost 40 years ago that games could be used as an educational tool because they were both motivating and demanding. Coleman noted, in his study of high school students in Illinois, that the organization of high school academic work is such that it minimizes youngsters' attention. By contrast, he posited, students' efforts in some extracurricular activities, such as clubs and sport, maximizes engagement. He suggested that educators might want to include some dimensions of games into the school curriculum to motivate students who otherwise might not be motivated to achieve in school academics.

Coleman's arguments are strikingly similar to those made for the role of play in education and development more generally. He posits that the intrinsically motivating dimension of games absorbs youngsters in the activity. Furthermore, the active role that individuals take in games, like play, results in their recognizing the relationship between their efforts and the outcome of the game. The recognition that effort, not some inborn trait, is responsible for one's achievement is crucial to one's educational success (Eccles, Wigfield, & Schiefele, 1998).

Facility at games can be gauged in a number of different ways. Eiferman (1970) suggested that youngsters' facility at game playing could be indexed by the size of the group playing the game: The larger the group, the more complex the game and the more skill necessary to participate in and lead in that game. Her data from a large-scale study of playground games involving 100,000 Israeli school children supported her hypothesis: Group size in games generally increased with age, and socio-economic status.

This idea of game leadership, or facility, is similar to that developed by Peter Blatchford, Ed Baines, and me in studies of children's games on their primary school playgrounds in Minneapolis and London, where we defined leadership in terms of the number of children in the focal child's immediate peer group (Blatchford, Baines, & Pellegrini, 2003; Pellegrini et al., 2002). This idea of facility is derived from the ethologically oriented work on leadership and dominance (Chance, 1976; Vaughn & Waters, 1981). Dominance, as discussed earlier, is an ethological construct indicative of an individual's status in a social group. Dominance, as discussed earlier, is typically achieved by a combination of pro-social and assertive strategies (Pellegrini & Bartini, 2001; Pellegrini, Roseth et al., 2007) with an aim toward accessing some resource, such as access to a toy or a piece of playground equipment. Peer groups have dominance hierarchies that range from most to least dominant where most-dominant individuals are leaders and are sought after and attended to.

Children may want to be around leaders for a number of reasons. For example, by affiliating with leaders, youngsters may learn valuable social skills from or form alliances with leaders. Alliances with leaders can also protect more vulnerable children from bullying and victimization (e.g., Hodges & Perry, 1999; Pellegrini, 2002). Thus, the number of individuals surrounding an individual is an observational indicator of leadership status.

Competence for children at games on the school playground, especially during primary school, can also be conceptualized in terms of forming and maintaining peer networks (e.g., being liked by peers and having friends) and adhering to group norms within organized peer groups (such as playing games with rules with peers) as well as adjusting to the demands of school (Sroufe, Egelund, & Carlson, 1999). This definition is derived from developmental theory suggesting that competence is defined differently at different ages (Bjorklund & Pellegrini, 2000), and competence can be represented by corresponding "developmental tasks" (Waters & Sroufe, 1983), such as games with peers in a school setting. Additionally, social engagement with peers in games during the school day, at recess, should be indicative of one's efficacy in one dimension of early schooling. Specifically, in both the very early primary grades and at recess, children's social competence with peers and learning to follow rules is stressed. In later grades the classroom climate is characterized by much less peer interaction (Pellegrini & Blatchford, 2000).

In our research on the games of children, we examined the extent to which game leadership predicted children's adjustment to school as well as their social competence. This work followed from the assumption presented by Coleman that games are an important developmental task for children, especially boys, entering

Table 11.2   Correlations between measures of game facility

Teacher Rated Games 4	2	3	4
Observed Games 1	.60**	.29*	.24*
Group Size 2		.32**	.28**
Peer Noms Sports 3			.35**

$*p < .05 ** p < .01$

primary school. In this work we defined game facility as the aggregate of a variety of measures: peer nominations of being good at games and sport, teacher ratings of being good in games and sport, and behavioral observations of the relative frequency of children's engagement in total games and the average size of their playgroups during games across the first two-thirds of the year. Adjustment to school was defined as an aggregate of self-reports (e.g., "I'm happy when I'm at school") and teacher ratings of children (e.g., "Good at games"). Social competence was defined in terms of peer nominations of being liked and having friends. Aggregates, as discussed throughout this book, are used so as to maximize construct validity (Cronbach, 1971; Rushton, Brainerd, & Pressley, 1983).

The correlation coefficients presented below, in Table 11.2, confirm the importance of a number of assumptions. First, the significant correlation between group size and both teacher-rated and peer-nominated competence at games confirms the validity of using group size as a proxy for competence, following Eiferman (1970).

We also found that children's, but especially boys', game facility predicted both adjustment to school and social competence. This is consistent with the theoretical assumption that the social rules and roles that children learn in games with their peers on the school playground predict competence with their peers and in adjusting to the first grade. Both niches are similar to the extent that they encourage rule-governed behavior and cooperative interaction with peers. As children progress through school, however, the similarities between the playground and the classroom diminish.

While these results do reinforce earlier research where children's peer relations in school predicted school success (e.g., Ladd & Price, 1987) they also extended the importance of games and schooling to low-income children. It is well known that children, and again boys especially, from economically disadvantaged groups have difficulty adjusting to and succeeding in school (e.g., Heath, 1983). Our work demonstrates that success in one part of the first grade school day (games at recess) can predict more general school adjustment. The mechanism by which this happens, however, is not clearly understood.

We also examined inter-ethnic interaction on the playground across the school year, as this type of social interaction is an indicator of individuals' social competence in the sorts of diverse groups that typify most American and European inner city schools. The level of ethnic variety in playgroups did not, however, vary by either time or gender. It is probably the case, following Contact Theory, that desegregation may actually entrench segregation unless existing stereotypes are changed (Allport, 1954). This seems to be especially true when children are placed and observed in unstructured settings, such as the recess period.

A basic aim of school desegregation in the United States has been to provide opportunities for students from diverse backgrounds to interact with each other in integrated schools, resulting in fading racial divides (see Schofield, 1981 for a discussion). The extent to which this ideal corresponds to the empirical record is, however, questionable. In a study of an American middle school, Schofield (1981) observed youngsters at various venues and found that peer groups were by and large segregated. Similar results were reported by Boulton and Smith (1993) in their observational study of a group of ethnically diverse primary school children on playgrounds in the north of England.

With this said, it is very important to examine the effectiveness of policies that foster inter-ethnic interaction. Research with adolescents, for example, has shown that school policy can enhance cross-ethnic group interaction (Schofield, 1981). While it is clearly difficult to accomplish, it is very important to try to do. As part of these efforts, however, we should also examine the maintenance of effects of these programs in that these biases, though they are less persistent than sexual segregation biases, can be very difficult to change without adult-provided structure and support (Maccoby, 1998; Serbin, Tonick, & Stemglanz, 1977).

CONCLUSIONS

In this chapter I made a brief foray into the realm of children's and adolescents' games. As noted, this area is incredibly under-researched. That games are so under-studied yet so interesting and important to children, adolescents, and adults should be a message to the research community: This is an important topic. If there is doubt, consider the billions of dollars spent in the "gaming" (i.e., gambling) industry, state and national lotteries, and sport at both professional and college levels. From this perspective it is imperative to study games, and indeed sport, in order to understand the contexts in which individuals actually develop.

The extant orientation in studying children and adolescents among many researchers seems to be one where individuals are studied in places where we as researchers have easy access for relatively brief periods of time (Bronfenbrenner, 1979; Wright, 1960). In this mode, we study students in classrooms interacting with teachers more than we study students interacting with parents or peers in their natural habitats using prospective, longitudinal designs (McCall, 1977). As noted above in the discussion on social interactionist theories, advanced at the turn of the nineteenth to twentieth century, the peer context is an especially important one as this orientation has not decreased during the past 100 years.

By implication, the games in which children and youth spend much of their free time are important contexts to study. In the best possible world, of course, the study of games in the peer cultured would be best examined in the broader contests of children in community contexts (Eccles & Roeser, 2005). In short,

I think we are missing something very important, as theory and limited empirical data suggest. Children and adolescents seem to learn and practice very important social cognitive skills in peer groups. We do not study these phenomena in correspondence to their importance, at least to their importance to the participants. Indeed, in some contexts, such as many school settings, policy is aimed at restricting students' access to the very contexts, such as the school recess period, where these skills develop.

A central assumption of this book has been that social interactions with both adults and peers are central to the developmental processes. That is, peer-related activities enable youngsters to explore their interests and developing sense of self. Providing positive and motivating peer-related activities at the start of youngsters' middle school experiences, for example, could help to socialize their school and achievement orientations (Eccles et al., 1998). Certain types of games and sports may have especially positive effects for a number of reasons.

Specifically, research suggests that engaging in certain types of organized peer activities, such as track and field, are positively associated with a number of social outcome measures of adjustment (e.g., Mahoney, Larson, Eccles, & Lord, 2005). Engaging in sports, specifically, seems to help youngsters make the difficult transition from primary to secondary school by providing a network of supportive peers and adults (Eccles & Roeser, 2005). This is similar to the argument I made earlier in this chapter where children's facility with games on the school playground at recess was predictive of their adjustment to the first year of school.

Additionally, however, extracurricular activities generally, and some sports and games specifically, afford peer interactions in relatively safe, healthy, and achievement-oriented contexts (Mahoney et al., 2005). The nature of the peer relationships in many sports also provides additional value, to the extent that being on a team provides youngsters with a sense of belonging and a supportive network. Unlike gangs, which also provide a sense of belonging and a supportive network, some organized sport and games do this in the context of positive social norms.

If we take endurance sports, such cross-country running or Nordic skiing for example, the benefits of participation are clear. Performance in these sports is seriously hampered by drug use, such as tobacco and alcohol. Furthermore, endurance training is a year-round activity, so participation involves youngsters in training for long, sustained periods. Participation in these activities is also often associated with parental participation, thus maintaining the important link among children, parents, peers, and school. Youngsters who run and ski often have parents who do the same. Thus, a connection between youngsters and their parents is maintained, as are the connections with school and peer networks. Youngsters continue to participate in these activities with their parents as well as their peers, and their parents also attend formal and informal contests.

An especially interesting dimension of the endurance sports is the relatively equal status afforded to male and female athletes. In Nordic skiing, males and females not only train together as a team but their high school state meets are also held together. In one study of high school athletes, girls who participated in track and cross-country running, relative to other sports, were least likely to belong to antisocial peer groups and most likely to belong to an academic peer group (Barber et al., 2005). Correspondingly, endurance athletics, with its stress on training and nutrition, should have the added benefits of helping girls maintain a healthy body image during a time when early adolescent girls are at risk of developing unhealthy eating and exercise habits.

Lastly, excellence in many sports and games generally, and endurance sports specifically, is related to commitment to a training regimen and to the recognition that one's performance is directly related to one's training. Sports and games afford opportunities for skill building (Mahoney et al., 2005). Interestingly, academic excellence is also related to the recognition that achievement is a result of one's own effort, not just an "inborn" talent (Eccles et al., 1998). As a result, the peer ethos on these teams tends to value hard work in both sport and academics. If students "buy into" the ethos of the sport and the team, they are also buying into academic success and correlated healthy behaviors. For example, of the Nordic skiers on recent Minneapolis Southwest High School teams, the vast majority of students were enrolled in the academically selective and demanding International Baccalaureate (IB) program, and relatively high numbers were also National Merit Scholars.

While the picture I have painted thus far is perhaps consistent with an ideal, and in some ways reminiscent of Mathew Arnold's view of sport at Rugby School as immortalized in *Tom Brown's School Days* (Hughes, 1895), there is always the other face of sport and games—the one too often portrayed by many professional and some amateur athletes whose participation is characterized by cheating, showboating, and intentionally trying to injure other players. Clearly, youngsters, families, schools, and society, more generally, would all be well served if sports, games, and extracurricular activities were conceptualized along the lines of embedding these activities in a broader context of positive youth development.

12

The Role of Play in Education

This school is only good for those who want to learn from books. You'll loose your sense of purpose .... Walk in single file out of the classroom, down the stairs, and into the playground.
—Paul McCartney, *Liverpool Oratorio*

The quotes by the Headmaster in Paul McCartney's *Liverpool Oratorio* and the quote in Chapter 10 by Günter Grass (1999), the Noble laureate in literature, represent contrasting views of the roles of play and the playground experience in children's lives. McCartney's view is probably the dominant view of schooling in the industrialized world. School, for most, comprises "The Three R's"—reading, writing, and 'rithmatic. Play does not seem to belong among this traditional trinity of schooling. After all, in it, in playing, children are more concerned with the means, or the process, than the end product. Schooling is concerned with end products, with test results a paradigm case of this orientation!

Grass, on the other hand, presents a view of play and childhood as a clandestine world of fantasy themes, reminiscent of Sutton-Smith's portrayal (1987; 1990; 1997) of children's playground behavior. The roles enacted in the playground, for Grass, had important implications for life.

Against this backdrop of equivocal pulls for and against play in school, a number of efforts have been made to fit play into school curricula, especially in the preschool years. Much of this effort stemmed from the influence of Piagetian theory on education. Being primarily concerned with cognitive development, Piaget's views of development and play have been linked by a number of psychologist and educators (Smilansky, 1968) to children's cognitive development and academic performance in school (Saltz & Johnson, 1974; Saltz, Dixon,

& Johnson, 1977). For example, in the classic "play training" studies done by Eli Saltz and his students, children's intelligence quotient (IQ) was an outcome measure for indexing the effects of play. Having teachers guide children's play with an eye toward improving their IQ or academic achievement fit nicely into the *zeitgeist* where the impact of early education programs, such as Head Start, was IQ and achievement, the *sine qua non* of an educational program's effectiveness (Zigler & Trickett, 1978). In keeping with this academic orientation, in the first section of this chapter, I examine the role of pretend play on one aspect of academic achievement, early literacy.

There was, however, widespread criticism of such narrow reliance on outcome measures to judge the efficacy of educational programs, as long ago as the 1970s. Ed Zigler was one of the earliest, most vocal and most persuasive voices in this debate against such a narrow view of educational program impact (Zigler & Trickett, 1978; Zigler & Bishop-Josef, 2006). Zigler, a professor emeritus of psychology at Yale and one of the founding fathers of Head Start, has argued eloquently for at least 30 years to broaden the criteria against which children should be evaluated, and, instead, advanced the construct of social competence as an educational outcome measure. From this view, not only would children's cognitive facilities be assessed, but also their social skills with peers, their hygiene, school attendance and tardiness, etc., would be considered measures of the "whole child."

Using social competence, rather than narrower constructs such as IQ or scholastic achievement, makes sense from a number of perspectives. First, children's social and cognitive status are significantly interrelated. For example, children with poor social skills tend to do poorly in school and drop out more than do those with better social skills (Coie & Dodge, 1998). To ignore this interrelationship is clearly a sin of omission. Furthermore, using a variety of interrelated measures of a construct increases its validity (Cronbach, 1970; Rushton, Brainerd, & Pressley, 1983).

This more catholic definition of educational attainment is also consistent with the putative benefits of play. It followed from Zigler's critique (Zigler & Trickett, 1978) that basic psychological research examining the role of play in both social and cognitive outcomes measures flourished in the late 1970s through the 1980s (summarized in Rubin, Fein, & Vandenberg, 1983). These studies, both correlational and experimental, were often framed primarily in terms of Piaget's theory and constructed what Peter Smith (1988) labeled the "play ethos." The play ethos was a "mindset" whereby researchers and educators saw play as all good for all children—despite what the data told us, and the data did not always convey unequivocally good news. For example, Smith (Smith & Syddall, 1978), early on, pointed out that most of the experiments where children were trained in pretend play typically confounded adults' tutoring a child in play with play itself (though see Pellegrini, 1984). Furthermore, and as noted above, some important, and frequently cited results, such as the effect of play on problem-solving (Sylva, Bruner, & Genova, 1976) and the effect of play on creativity (Dansky & Silverman, 1973; 1975) were not replicated when double-blind procedures were used (Simon & Smith, 1983; 1985; Smith & Whitney, 1987). Interestingly, the efficacy of play in facilitating some of these outcomes is still cited from these studies—more than 20 years after they were not replicated (e.g., Berk, Mann, & Ogan, 2006)! Clearly, the way forward is to have the best science guide school practices. Where the data are positive, they should be implemented; where not positive, we should say so. If we as psychologists do not take the lead, the bad evidence will drive out the good, and the case for play in school will be driven out, too.

In keeping with the importance of children's social competence as an educational outcome, I examine the ways that children's experiences on the playground during their school recess period related to educational outcomes in the second part of this chapter.

Early Examinations of Pretend Play and Early Literacy

An especially active research area over the past 20 years has been the role of play, and again primarily pretend play, on children's early literacy development. Attempts to link pretend play to literacy development have been especially prolific in early education (e.g., Bellin & Singer, 2006; Christie & Roskos, 2007). Though the study of the interrelations between pretend play and literacy dates back to the early 1970s (e.g., Wolfgang, 1974), most of the work in this area has appeared in the last 20 years. This latter corpus of research will be reviewed in terms of the ways that it informs us about the developmental processes involved in pretend play and literacy and about the related issue of teaching young children. We begin with a brief review of early research on pretend play and literacy to set the historical context.

Conceptual Links Between Pretend Play and Early Literacy

The early work on play and literacy was generally typified by a Piagetian theoretical orientation and a definition of literacy according to standardized achievement measures of reading and writing (e.g., Pellegrini, 1980; Wolfgang, 1974). The aspect of play examined was primarily pretend play, in which a child has a signifier represent something else, a "signified." As part of this process, children used objects or language in the symbolization process; for example, a doll could represent a baby. More abstractly, children could execute symbolic transformations independently of objects, such as using language in redefining a situation: "Let this be the doctor's *office*." Generally, children are capable of pretending by 24 months of age (Lillard, Nishida, Massaro, Vaish, & Ma, 2007) and making both object-dependent and object-independent, or ideational, transformations by the time they are three years of age (Rubin et al., 1983).

Piagetian researchers took the position that pretend play is essentially an assimilative activity that reflects a more general level of children's semiotic, or representational, functioning. That is, pretend play involves a dominance of assimilation over accommodation to the extent that the child is "transforming reality in its own manner without submitting that transformation to the criterion of objective fact" (Piaget, 1963, p. 111). Furthermore, and to borrow from the

Laboratory of Comparative Human Cognition's (LCHC) (1983) description of Piagetian research, cognition in this tradition is conceptualized as a central processing metaphor. While more will be said about these processes below, suffice it to say for now that the central processing metaphor applied to pretend play–literacy suggests that facility in pretend play reflects a more general symbolic, cognitive facility. In this view, pretend play should be related to literacy, as well as to other aspects of cognition, because they all are realizations of similar underlying cognitive processes. In short, Piaget's conception of cognition suggests that children within specific stages think of various aspects of their world in a similar fashion.

Another characteristic of this early research is that pretend play was not differentiated according to its many dimensions. Pretend play behavior was often classified as part of Smilansky's (1968) adaptation of Piaget's levels of play: functional, constructive, dramatic (or pretend), and games-with-rules (Takhvar & Smith, 1990). Methodologically, children's behavior was typically coded according to a variant of Smilansky's model and then related to some standardized measure of reading and/or writing. If dramatic play accounted for more variance in measures of literacy than "lower," less symbolic forms of play, then the Piagetian hypothesis was supported. Pretend play, despite having many components, most of which are shared with other, non-play, forms of interaction, was seen as important in children's literacy development. It was assumed that the symbolic component in the observed behavior, though it was not measured specifically, was responsible for gains in literacy.

As noted above, educational impact in the early 1970s was typically defined narrowly, in terms of cognition, typically assessed on standardized, by norm-referenced, achievement measures. The same was true for early literacy, where it was assessed by norm-referenced measures of reading and writing (e.g., Pellegrini, 1980). Research in this earlier psychometric tradition did, however, seem to support the Piagetian hypothesis (Lovinger, 1974; Pellegrini, 1980; Wolfgang, 1974). That significant relationships were found between pretend play and standardized measures of reading and writing was probably a result of many things, despite the problems with the definitions of play and measures of literacy. Specifically, in the studies cited above, relationships between children's pretending and reading and writing could have been mediated by more general measures of the linguistic and cognitive competence. Though all researchers, myself included (Pellegrini, 1980), made their genuflections to the use of correlation methods and to not making statements about causality, the ball began to roll. Play was beginning to be seen as a major component in the development of young children's literacy.

With this said, during this period, developmental and educational psychologists were also beginning to highlight the non-developmental nature of most standardized tests (e.g., Kohlberg & Mayer, 1972). Specifically, most norm-referenced achievement measures of reading and writing were theoretically rooted in the notion that learning is the process of adding discrete parts to form a cognitive whole. That is, children's literacy was based on an adult conception of reading, where component parts, such as recognizing letters and words, were broken down into component parts. In this view of literacy, children's status as readers and writers was represented by their progress along a continuum of this adult standard of reading. Children's reading was thus viewed as quantitatively, not qualitatively, different from adults' reading.

Marie Clay (1972), the late New Zealand psychologist, was at the vanguard of a new, "emergent literacy" view of reading and writing. She viewed literacy as a whole suite of behaviors that were specific to school-based literacy. For example, children were assessed on the degree to which they recognized that words, not pictures, were being read, and that reading progressed from left to right. Correspondingly and perhaps more basically, developmentally oriented researchers were also beginning to be concerned with the oral language roots of literacy (Heath, 1983; Olson, 1977; Snow, 1983). These researchers, like the prescient, and late, English sociologist of education Basil Bernstein (1960; 1971), recognized similarities in the design features of school-based literacy events and certain forms of oral language and how this form of oral language may represent a form of emergent literacy for preschoolers. More will be said about how what has been labeled *literate language* generated in play relates to early literacy.

Suffice it to say for now that researchers started to view literacy for young children in terms of literate language and as something qualitatively different from the literacy of adults. Furthermore, many of these same researchers were also viewing literacy as something very specific to Western models of literacy (Scribner & Cole, 1978), a notion consistent with a Vygotskiian idea of situation-specific cognition (Laboratory of Comparative Human Cognition [LCHC], 1983) and not something driven by a central cognitive processing mechanism, more akin to a Piagetian model. As will be discussed below, each of these models makes different predictions for the relationship between play and literacy, even though they are both "developmental."

Over the last 20 years, a number of researchers have examined the connection between pretend play and literacy development. These researchers, for the most part, have been motivated by Vygotskyan and Piagetian theories. First, I will examine the roles of Vygotskiian and Piagetian theory in recent studies of pretend play and literacy development. Next, studies that attempt to determine the developmental and causal roles of play in literacy from Piagetian and Vygotskiian perspectives will be discussed. I will, however, only review longitudinal and experimental studies, because only in such designs do we find the antecedent-consequence relationships that are necessary, but not sufficient, to imply causality. Lastly, I will explore the implications of this research for teaching and research in literacy.

Interestingly, in many, if not most, studies of pretend play and literacy (e.g., Pellegrini & Galda, 1991; Morrow, 1990; Neuman & Roskos, 1991; 1992; Schrader, 1990) both Piagetian and Vygotskiian theories are referred to as providing the theoretical orientation of the studies. The implication of these simultaneous references to Piaget and Vygotsky is that the two theories make similar assumptions about the role of symbolic play in the development of children's literacy. While it is implied that the two theories view pretend play as driving the child's symbol-making competence in similar ways, little or no exposition of the specific ways that these theories relate to the issues at hand is undertaken. Where it is undertaken, it is stated that the representational competence in pretend play should predict other forms of representational competence, such as reading and writing.

While there are similarities between the two theorists, my reading of Vygotsky's (1967) and Piaget's theories (1932; 1967; 1970; 1974; 1983) and the contributions of their interpreters, such as the LCHC (1983), Bruner (Bruner & Bornstein, 1989), and Rogoff (Tudge & Rogoff, 1989), lead me to question their equivalence on the relationship of pretend play and literacy. While I also recognize that exposition of similarities between the theories may help us better understand children, it is also important to foreground and discuss the differences between the theories.

THE IMPORTANCE OF THEORETICAL CLARITY: SPECIFYING THE PRETEND PLAY–LITERACY LINK

As Kohlberg and Mayer (1972) noted a number of years ago, the issue of theory in relation to school curriculum and assessment is not trivial. At the risk of stating the obvious, theory should be the guide in determining what we consider relevant in what it is we teach, how we teach it, and how it gets assessed (see also Cazden, 1975). If, for example, Piagetian theory is invoked, we should be looking for homogeneity across representational media, and pretend play, reading, writing, oral language, and other dimensions of cognition, like numeracy, should be interrelated. A Vygotskiian perspective, on the other hand, would have play serving a functional role in areas like writing. The representational nature of play, where one object functions as another object, should be related for young children to other socially defined first-order symbol systems, like drawing and early writing, but not reading, a second-order symbol system (Vygotsky, 1983). Generally, the first set of studies, reviewed in the next section, are longitudinal in design and follow a Vygotskiian orientation; those in the second, experimental, set are more Piagetian.

Longitudinal Relations

The influence of pretend play on literacy has been conceptualized in at least two different ways. First, several researchers, primarily interested in the play of preschool children, have studied the relationship between pretend play and the accompanying aspects of oral language that are thought to be early manifestations of literacy, or what might be labeled "literate language." Part of this argument is that in pretend play children use the same form of language used in school-based literacy events and thus become facile with the components of school-based literacy (Heath, 1983; Galda, 1984; Pellegrini, 1985). Both literate language and social pretend play involve the conveyance of meaning unambiguously. Researchers in this group generally take a developmental view of literacy. That is, rather than conceptualizing literacy only as children's ability to read and write, they take the view that specific aspects of preschool and primary-school children's oral language and school-based literacy share features, such as narrative structure and decontextualized texts. These studies also typically follow a Vygotskiian orientation in that they generally examine separately the relations among oral language, play, and literacy, and they explain literacy in terms of reading and writing separately.

Specifically, preschool children's abilities to tell and comprehend stories and use oral language that minimally relies upon context and shared assumption, or what has been variously labeled as *elaborated code*, by Basil Bernstein (1960; 1971), *cohesive text*, by Halliday and Hasan (1976), *literate language*, by David Olson (1977), and *decontextualized language*, by Catherine Snow (1982). This linguistic register is hypothesized to be an important precursor to school-based literacy to the extent that in both cases children are maximizing their use of language and minimizing their use of context and shared knowledge assumptions to convey and decode meaning. Indeed, some scholars consider the use of "literate language" to be evidence of literacy in young children (Scollon & Scollon, 1981). Thus, the language of pretend play can be considered "literate" to the extent that it shares design features with school-based literacy events, like reading and writing and the oral language surrounding them (Bernstein, 1960; 1971; Heath, 1983; Pellegrini, 1985; Scollon & Scollon, 1981; Wolf & Pusch, 1985).

The English linguist Michael Halliday (1978) noted, more than 30 years ago, that the imaginative function of language used during pretend play was realized with such text explication features as anaphora, where pronouns were linguistically defined, and the use of causal and temporal conjunctions, both hallmarks of literate language. Later empirical work illustrated Halliday's point clearly. Children engaging in pretend play, as compared to other forms of play and peer interaction, use more cohesive oral language; this has been shown in naturalistic studies of preschool children's play (Pellegrini, 1982; 1985; Wolf & Pusch, 1985) and experimental studies of kindergarten children (Pellegrini, 1984).

Additionally, preschool children's pretend play is characterized by the narrative structures that typify many school-based literacy events (Galda, 1984; Guttman & Frederiksen, 1985; Heath, 1983; Neuman & Roskos, 1992; Pellegrini, 1985; Nicolopoulou, McDowell, & Brockmeyer, 2006; Sachs, Goldman, & Chaille, 1985). Cochran-Smith (1984) has made a similar argument in her discussions of story time and literacy. In short, certain kinds of language that characterize pretend play and story time are thought to be important to early literacy to the extent that they share design features, such as narrative structure and the use of decontextualized language, with school-based literacy events.

While it is important to describe similarity in design features between children's oral language in pretend play and subsequent literacy events, it is also important to establish more direct, empirical links between the two in order to convincingly make a developmental argument. This is generally done using longitudinal research designs where empirical relations are tested between theoretically relevant aspects of oral language at point 1 and measures of literacy at point 2, while simultaneously controlling possible mediators such as verbal IQ.

This approach has been taken by Heath (1983), Pellegrini and Galda (1998; Galda, Pellegrini, & Cox, 1989; Pellegrini, Galda, Dresden, & Cox, 1991), Dickinson and Moreton (1991), and Wolf (Wolf & Pusch, 1985). The classic work of Shirley Heath (1983) shows the ways that different language and pretend play patterns during the preschool period differentially affect children's subsequent school-based literacy. Similar findings have been reported by Wolf and Pusch (1985).

Subsequently, Lee Galda and I (Pellegrini & Galda, 1989; 1991) and Dickinson and Moreton (1991) examined the longitudinal relations between specific aspects of language and pretend play and school-based literacy from the preschool period to the primary-school period. These were two different research teams working independently of each other with very different samples, yet they arrived at similar conclusions. Pellegrini and Galda (Galda et al., 1989; Pellegrini et al., 1991) made naturalistic observations in the University of Georgia laboratory preschool classrooms of children's pretend play and language over two years; various measures of "emergent" reading and writing, as well as measures of vocabulary status, were administered.

Similarly, David Dickinson and Moreton (1991) also observed preschool children, of mixed socioeconomic status, in the context of their preschool environments, in the northeastern United States, and predicted their literacy in kindergarten. They, too, obtained measures of play and language as well as a battery of standardized measures of emergent literacy and language. Furthermore, Dickinson and Moreton, like Pellegrini and Galda, used conservative statistical methods to control for alternate sources of variance in their predictions. Consequently, the extent to which the findings from these separate studies converge provides an interesting example of replication.

The Pellegrini and Galda studies themselves had replication samples built into their research designs, using their own modified versions of emergent reading and writing measures and Clay's Concepts About Print measure with two cohorts of children. Pellegrini and Galda found that reading and writing were statistically independent of each other when the Peabody Picture Vocabulary Test (PPVT) was statistically controlled. Such control is important if the variance due to the theoretically important variables (i.e., symbolic transformations and linguistic verbs) is to be identified. Furthermore, the different developmental trajectories of reading and writing were illustrated when it was found that three-and-a-half-year-old children's use of symbolic transformations in play (e.g., having a pen represent a sword or transforming oneself into a "doctor"), predicted writing but not reading at five years (Galda et al., 1989; Pellegrini et al., 1991).

These findings were explained in terms of Vygotsky's theory, wherein both writing and pretend play for preschoolers are examples of first-order symbolization: Both involve symbols representing objects rather than words, and both are more graphic than linguistic systems for young children. Reading (on both an adaptation of an emergent reading scale and Clay's Concepts About Print), on the other hand, was predicted by children's ability to "go meta" on their linguistic system by using linguistic verbs, such as *say, talk,* and *write.* The ability to talk about *language* predicted reading. In short, reading was a second-order symbolization process in that the written word represented the spoken word, which represented objects or actions.

The longitudinal work of Dickinson and Moreton (1991) tells a very similar story. As noted above, their research found that three-year-old children's time spent in talk during symbolic play with their peers related to a standardized vocabulary measure at five years of age and was a significant predictor of a reading-related measure, knowledge of print. Thus, the pretend play of preschoolers and the oral language surrounding it are relatively good predictors of reading-related measures of literacy in kindergarten. These findings are especially robust because the alternate sources of variance were controlled.

Results from both the Pellegrini and Galda and the Dickinson and Moreton studies seem to be inconsistent with one aspect of Vygotsky's theory. Adults in both these studies seemed to inhibit aspects of children's pretend play and language use. In preschool classrooms the presence of adults seems to inhibit children's pretend play and uses of a variety of functions of oral language (Pellegrini, 1983; 1984). Dickinson and Moreton (1991) have extended this finding with regard to preschoolers' vocabulary development and print knowledge (Dickinson & Moreton, 1991).

It could be argued that with children of this age (three to five years of age) adults suppress children's exhibition of competence in pretend play because when children and adults interact, adults do most of the work, such as initiating interaction and repairing breakdowns. In peer contexts, children must negotiate these areas themselves, and this negotiation itself is probably the context in which literate language is generated. When children are negotiating meaning and role assignment, among other things in pretend play, they must make themselves clear, as what it is they are doing or proposing to do is not, by definition, related to their immediate, real world. Thus, to be understood they must explicate meaning by linguistically defining roles and prop definitions. In cases where the meaning is clear but there is disagreement about who enacts a specific role, for example, children must convince their peers of their position, and this usually involves using meta-linguistic terms (e.g., "Doctors don't say that") and a variety of conjunctions to organize their arguments (e.g., "I wanna do that 'cause you were the doctor the last time") (Pellegrini, 1985).

It must be stressed, however, that these differential adult–child effects are probably specific to the pretend play context with relatively older preschoolers. With younger children, adults facilitate their pretend play and oral language (Pellegrini, 1983; Slade, 1987). While adults seem to inhibit young children's fantasy, they clearly enhance other aspects of children's development (e.g., Ellis & Rogoff, 1986; Rogoff, Göncü, Mistry, & Mosier,1993).

The research efforts discussed above are interesting for at least two reasons. First, and most important, they used longitudinal designs where relatively large corpora of oral language and pretend play were collected and related to theoretically consistent measures of early literacy. The Pellegrini and Galda and Dickinson and Moreton studies are also interesting to the extent that they attempted to identify the contributions of theoretically relevant variables to literacy. In these studies, this meant looking at relevant aspects of pretend play and controlling variables, like vocabulary, that might be correlated with play and literacy. Controlling for alternative sources of variance, like some more general measure of ability or adult guidance in play, is clearly important if we want to make statements about play *per se*.

Experimental Relations

While longitudinal approaches to the study of pretend play and literacy development have a variety of strengths, they also can leave the nagging suspicion that there is some hidden mediator responsible for the relationship between x and y. Internally valid, true experiments, on the other hand, eliminate this possibility, and thus we can move closer to understanding the effect of one variable on another. The problem with such approaches, of course, is that they typically take place in contrived settings and consequently tell us about the way some variables *can* affect others; they may not tell us much about the ways that these variables *actually* affect development (McCall, 1977); naturalistic, longitudinal designs, of the sort just described, do that. While this is a well-recognized problem of experimental research, experimental studies have provided important insights into the relative effectiveness of different aspects of play. Furthermore, the extent to which results from experimental and naturalistic studies converge or diverge is important in terms of replication of findings.

Bronfenbrenner (1979) suggested that ecologically valid experiments would result in our having the best of both worlds: data derived from children observed in experimentally manipulated, yet meaningful and familiar settings. The issue of ecological validity is particularly important in the study of children, and especially of children in school settings. Like Bronfenbrenner (1979), I acknowledge that experiments in child development and education should be ecologically valid to the extent that they present children with demands, props, and peers that resemble their everyday ecology. It is incumbent on researchers choosing experimental designs to illustrate, as explicated by Bronfenbrenner in his Proposition G, the ecological validity of their experiments. While this has been done in some areas of children's symbolic play (Pellegrini & Perlmutter, 1989), it has not been done in the specific area of pretend play and literacy. In the experimental studies to be reviewed below, tests of ecological validity were not conducted. To do so would have required empirical demonstrations that the same or similar children, in their classrooms and in the experimental contexts, experienced similar demand characteristics, such as enacting teacher-read stories, group composition factors, and play props.

The experimental studies to be reviewed below can loosely be classified as part of a Piagetian tradition in developmental psychology examining the effects of the play on children's general social cognitive development (e.g., Saltz et al., 1977; Smilansky, 1968). For example, some of these studies manipulated peer interaction and conceptual conflict, and conceptual conflict was basic to Piaget's (1970) equilibration theory and related to the importance of peers in the social environment.

These studies diverge, however, from Piagetian theory in some basic ways. First, the early (e.g., Saltz et al., 1977) as well as later (e.g., Bellen & Singer, 2006) studies have adults guiding children's pretend play; the later studies, however, have *both* peer and adult pretend-play conditions. Second, adults provided children with themes around which to play. In some cases adults also acted as co-players, and in others, as directors. While one might argue that providing children with stories to play around is not "play" in the sense that the children are not choosing the theme of their play, I do not see this as qualitatively different from environmental intervention designs that try to guide play themes by providing props that are familiar or unfamiliar (e.g., Bellen & Singer, 2006; Neuman & Roskos, 1992). Children in schools are often asked to enact certain play themes after stories or assigned to play areas with teacher-specified themes. Clearly, this is an interesting issue, worthy of a test of ecological validity.

In what follows, I first review studies of the effects of children's pretend play on the ability to produce and comprehend stories. Next, I review research that manipulated play environments to affect children's literate language.

In a series of experimental studies, I (Pellegrini, 1984b; Pellegrini & Galda, 1982) and Steve Silvern and Peter Williamson (Silvern, Taylor, Williamson, Surbeck, & Kelley, 1986; Williamson & Silvern, 1991) examined the effects of playful reenactment of stories on the story comprehension of children in the early primary-school years. At the most general level, these studies found pretend play to be effective for preschool children rather than older children; that is, more effective than various comparison groups, for kindergarten, but not older, children. Furthermore, the presence of adults tutoring children in play did not affect their story comprehension or production. These findings are consistent with one aspect of Piaget's theory and also replicate some of the research reviewed above regarding the role of adults in play. More specifically, children, by the time they are three years old, do not seem to need adults to help them play; they are very capable of carrying on themselves. Second, and also consistent with Piaget, pretend play seems to serve a developmental function during the preschool period, and its influence, consistent with developmental theory, wanes as children progress through primary school.

My 1984 study was the first experimental effort to "unpack" the components of one type of pretend play—pretend about fantasy characters, or "thematic fantasy play," as labeled by Saltz and colleagues (1977), in relation to the effect of these components on one aspect of literacy, story comprehension. I (Pellegrini,1984) found that the conceptual conflict typical of *both* realistic peer interaction and pretend play with peers (i.e., explicating similarities and differences between viewpoints), or what Williamson and Silvern (1991) call *metaplay,* was more important than other components, such as verbalization during play and symbolic reenactment (make-believe in regard to objects, roles, and situations). Thus, and consistent with Piaget's theory, pretend play *per se* had minimal effects on primary-school children's story comprehension. Rather, the language of conceptual conflict accompanying peer interaction, in and out of pretend play, was important to literacy as measured by immediate, maintained, and generalized story comprehension assessment. These studies did not, however, examine the extent to which the pretend play had an effect on children's writing.

It was argued by both Pellegrini (1984b) and Williamson and Silvern (1991) that certain forms of language that occur during peer pretend play, not symbolic transformations themselves, were important in children's story comprehension. Symbolic enactment thus seems to be assimilative and, as such, minimally related to literacy (Piaget, 1932). Talk around conflicts and talk about talk, or "metaplay," to use Silvern and Williamson's label, is more accommodative and seems to be important for learning to produce and understand stories. Like the more naturalistic work with preschoolers discussed above, the results from these experimental studies showed that the oral language of pretend play, not the symbolization process as such, served a causal function in one dimension of early literacy—story comprehension.

Pretend play may be especially important in early literacy to the extent that it helps children go "meta" on their surroundings. By going meta, children are using language to reflect on language. It may be that pretend play, following the experimental work of Garvey (1987; 1990) and Dunn's (1988) in-home observations, is a particularly good context, though certainly not a unique context, for children to engage in the conflict-resolution process that results in using language to talk about language. Pretend play gives rise to conflict because of its inherent ambiguity; things in fantasy are not, by definition, what they are in reality. These conflicts and subsequent negotiations are out of the fantasy frame, thus the importance of non-fantasy talk around conflict resolution. Furthermore, in pretend play, children usually interact with children they consider friends (Hartup, 1983). With friends, compared to non-friends, children are more likely to disagree and then compromise (Hartup, 1983). In order to resolve the conflicts and clarify the ambiguity, children must use language to talk about language.

In short, the experimental studies suggest that pretend play *per se* seems to have minimal effects on one aspect of children's early literacy—story comprehension—during the primary school years. These effects for pretend play on story comprehension are virtually nonexistent by the time children enter second grade. What does seem to be important for this important dimension of literacy are verbal interaction and conceptual conflict, which occur with, but are separate from, pretend play. These types of conflict result in children's using language to talk about language; this is important for story comprehension. These results are similar to those presented in the longitudinal studies discussed above. For both preschool and elementary-school children, then, verbalizations in which children used language to talk about language predicted aspects of reading.

To conclude this section, the extant research suggests the following picture for preschool children. Reading and writing seem to start off as different things, with the former having roots in the oral language and conflict characteristic of peer play, while the latter has its roots in the interrelated symbolic processes of peer play. That peer interaction is important during the preschool period in no way should minimize the earlier, potent effects of adult relationships. During the primary school years, pretend *per se* becomes less important than the oral language used to negotiate play themes.

The Pretend Play and Early Literacy Connection: Implications for Schooling

Some of the implications of the research discussed above are rather clear-cut, especially in light of the consistency of the findings, across research teams and using very different methodologies. Perhaps mostly clearly, the language surrounding the pretend play of young children is important for reading-related aspects of early literacy. The symbolic-transformation component of pretend play, other the other hand, seems important for the early writing of preschool children. Furthermore, research with older elementary school children has shown that playful language interactions between upper elementary school peers during writing sessions may be important for writing development (Daiute, 1990). With this said, however, there is certainly less research on the pretend play/writing connection than on the play/early reading connection.

Another implication relates to the differential effects of pretend play according to children's age. Pretend play is typical behavior for preschool-age children, as originally proposed by Piaget, and seems to help them develop the representational skills necessary in writing. Furthermore, the language that characterizes pretend play enables children to use language to talk about language; this seems to be important for early reading. That pretend play contributes to literacy beyond the preschool period is not supported by the evidence, though anecdotes, such as the one provided by Günter Grass at the beginning of this chapter, and theorizing by Harris (2007) and Vygotsky (1971), suggest that pretend play is certainly important for subsequent creative endeavors.

Of course, none of this is to say that pretend play is bad. Behaviors associated with pretend play, such as talk about talk, seem to be the prime movers in the development towards reading. Peer interaction activities among children who are familiar with each other, either in the symbolic or the realistic mode, may be effective ways to stimulate the forms of metalanguage and metacognition that relate to literacy. Theory and research also make the point clearly that pretend play seems to serve this function during the preschool and very early primary-school years. Thus, pretend play as a curricular strategy is age-specific.

The literature on play environments and literate language has educational implications as well. A number of researchers in this area have shown that when children go into an area designed by adults to elicit pretend play, they do use literate behavior and language (Morrow, 1990; Neuman & Roskos, 1991; 1992; Pellegrini, 1982; 1983). It would be interesting to relate this environmental approach to the differential roles taken by peers and adults in play centers.

The role of the adult, or teacher, in this mix is an interesting and often controversial one. The overwhelming evidence, both from theory and from the empirical record, suggests that adult presence typically interferes with specific aspects of children's pretend play and certain aspects of oral language production.

Adults, on the other hand, are more effective tutors than peers when a specific skill must be learned, such as errand planning or classification tasks (Ellis & Rogoff, 1986; Tudge & Rogoff, 1989) or knowledge about print (Dickinson & Moreton, 1991). In short, adults and peers seem to do different things. Again, this should not be surprising. Much more research, however, is needed on the differential roles of peers and adults.

In a related issue, the effectiveness of peer interaction and adult–child interaction probably also varies according to other, more macro-level variables, such as environmental resources available to children and families, and individual differences typifying children and their families. For example, for families and schools with adequate resources, parents and teachers have time to interact individually with and teach their children. In situations where resources are scarce, parents and teachers spend more of their time securing resources and less time interacting with individual children. In such cases, other children, such as siblings and peers, do the teaching. A study of pretend play that considers these factors would be very important, not only for the research community, but also for teachers designing classrooms.

A related implication concerns the very nature of social interaction and cognition. The work of two Dutch psychologists, Adriana Bus and Marinus van IJzendoom (1988), is particularly interesting in this regard. In their examination of mother–child book-reading events, they found that children's attachment status, or the quality of the social-emotional relationship between mothers and children, is predictive of maternal teaching styles while reading. They, along with others (e.g., Matas, Arende, & Sroufe, 1978), argue that such important relationships provide the basis for subsequent social cognitive development. Researchers should now begin to look at social relationships other than the mother–child dyad, particularly in light of the fact that children spend much more of their time interacting with people other than their mothers (Rogoff, 1991). Dunn's work with siblings (1988) has gone a long way in this direction. It seems to us that we now need to look at specific social groupings around specific activities.

In our own work with children in another form of close relationship, friendships (Pellegrini & Galda, 1998; Pellegrini, Melhuish, Jones, Trojanowska, & Gilden, 2002), we found that young children who were paired with a friend, rather than with acquaintances and a variety of unfamiliar peers, generated more literate oral language, which, in turn, predicted their status on Clay's Concepts About Print test. These relations were, however, mediated by peer conflicts and resolutions. That is, friends disagreed with each other more than other groups but they also resolved their disagreements more frequently.

A final implication of work in this area is what *has not* been covered. Specifically, the whole notion of different individual developmental pathways has been little addressed. It is a well-recognized proposition from systems theory (Bertalanffy, 1968) that organisms take different pathways to attain similar goals. Martin and Caro (1985) have suggested that researchers in the area of play often fall into the trap of thinking that play is the only route to a specific outcome, such as literacy, and that if one does not play in a specific way, one does not attain the goal. The work of Howard Gardner (1980), Dennie Wolf (Wolf et al., 1988), and their respective colleagues is particularly instructive here. They document individual differences not only in forms of play but also in forms of literacy. We as researchers and teachers must come to realize that different types of children learn in different ways, and that structural views of development and teaching, which minimize or ignore individual differences, are doomed to fall short as individuals often take different routes to competence. While play offers one route to competence for many children, there probably are other, equally effective routes.

THE PLACE OF RECESS IN SCHOOLS

In this section I discuss the role of recess in children's school performance. While not all of the behavior that children exhibit during recess is play in the ways we have defined it, much of it is. Furthermore, it is one of the few places that we can readily observe primary school children's interactions with their peers. Thus, much of what is observed on the school playground at recess is social and locomotor play and games (Pellegrini, 2005). Unlike the case of preschool children's pretend play and its social cognitive implications for education, very little research has been conducted on children's behavior at recess generally, and the implications of these behaviors for education (for exceptions see my earlier reviews: Pellegrini, 2005; Pellegrini & Smith, 1993).

This state of affairs is surprising, as the psychologist and educator interested in peer relations during middle childhood is hard-pressed to find a venue to observe naturally occurring peer interactions. Yet, one of the few, yet under-studied, places that this can be done with relative efficiency is on the school playground during the recess period (Hart, 1993). The recess period is similar to free play time for preschool children to the extent that in both places we have a relatively large sample of children, located in one place, engaging in spontaneous and minimally directed peer interactions. Furthermore, in both places children develop and learn important social and motor skills.

In light of this it is interesting that the school recess period is currently being drastically eliminated or cut from the school day across the United States, Canada, and the United Kingdom (Pellegrini, 2005). The typically stated reason for this policy is that recess is counter-productive to traditional educational aims. For example, it is often stated that having recess takes time away from teaching more basic skills in an already very limited and crowded school day. Thus, one solution often proffered for these time constraints is to limit recess time and reallocate that time to instruction, on the assumption that this will maximize school performance.

One of the reasons for this assault on recess may be the perception that what goes on during the recess period is "play" and perceived further as not adding anything important to educational outcomes. Certainly if play is defined from contextual perspective, much of what is observed on the playground at recess could be considered play. After all, the playground is a playful context—by definition. This judgment is reinforced by the fact that children are individuals on the school playground at recess, and by some definitions the behavior of juveniles is play.

In this section I will not differentiate the various sorts of behaviors that occur on the playground, some of which are clearly not play. I will, however, argue that the recess period actually maximizes social and cognitive dimensions of school performance. Furthermore, the recess period affords opportunities for children to learn and develop skills associated with two key dimensions of social competence in middle childhood (Waters & Sroufe, 1983): peer relations and adjustment to full-day, formal schooling. First, however, I will provide an historical backdrop on the place of recess in American and English schools.

Documentation of the place of recess in the school day is very spotty, possibly reflecting the low regard for recess in both the school and academic community. One early "national survey" was conducted by the National Association of Elementary School Principals (NAESP) in 1989. This survey was sent to the state superintendents of education of all 50 states plus the District of Columbia. Responses from 47 states were received. Results indicated that "recess," in some form, was held in 90% of the cases; and of those cases, 96% had one or two recess periods daily. In 75% of the cases, recess lasted from fifteen to twenty minutes each. Importantly, we do not know the form that recess took. It could have been a physical education class or a more traditional free play period on the playground. Data from this survey should be interpreted very cautiously, given the limitations associated with the selectiveness of the sample and the unknown psychometric properties of the survey.

In 1999, another survey was conducted, this time by the U. S. Department of Education and only data on kindergarteners were available (see Pellegrini, 2005). At this point, 71% of American kindergartens reported having recess; 14.6% and 6.7% had, respectively, recess three or four times per week, and 7.7% had no recess period. In terms of recess duration, 27% of the respondents said they had thirty minutes of recess, 67.4% had sixteen to thirty minutes, and 6% had less than fifteen minutes. Interestingly, children attending private kindergartens were twice as likely (i.e., 48%) to have recess as those attending public kindergartens (22%). This last finding parallels a more general finding across all the primary grades: Children above the poverty level were granted almost twice the amount of time in the school day for recess (7%) as those from below the poverty level (4%) (Roth, Brooks-Gunn, & Linver, 2003). It may be that middle-class parents recognize the importance of recess and insist that their kids get it.

There is also a trend in the United Kingdom for recess to be diminished, and the motivations appear similar to those at work in the United States—concern with achievement. In a well-designed, nationally representative survey of recess, or "break time" as it is called in England, Peter Blatchford (Blatchford & Sumpner, 1998) asked abut changes in recess across the five years between 1990/1991–1995–1996. He found that 38% and 35% of junior and secondary schools, respectively, had reduced duration of the lunchtime recess break, and 26% of the infant schools reported reductions. Similarly, reductions were reported for the afternoon recess period: 12%, 27%, and 14% of infant, junior, and secondary schools, respectively, reported the elimination of that recess period!

These data clearly indicate that recess holds a marginal place in the school curriculum. In the next sections, I will present data suggesting that recess time actually helps students develop socially, adjust to school, and learn, in the traditional sense.

Recess and Classroom Achievement

In this section I explore the relations between children's recess behavior, some of which is play, and traditional measures of classroom performance. I was initially guided in my work in this area by my earlier research on the relationship between pretend play and early literacy. Recall, in that work, I showed that specific types of oral language used by preschoolers with their peers accurately predicted their early literacy status. I suggest that the competence used in social interaction with peers is related to skills and strategies tapped by traditional measures of achievement. The added benefit of observing children on the playground at recess, relative to more tradition assessment contexts, is that they are highly motivated to exhibit these strategies because they enjoy the processes associated with using them. In this section I explore the idea of play as a context for assessment that was introduced in the preceding chapters. I argue that the playground may provide an interesting assessment venue for young children because the interaction among peers there is cognitively and socially very demanding and at the same time very motivating for children. This combination should lead to children's exhibiting higher levels of competence than on traditional achievement tests.

The specific types of social interaction on the playground that I examined here are related to the behavioral attributes related to social and object use: peer interaction, adult-directed behavior, and object use. Play tends to be self-directed, rather than adult-guided, and, correspondingly, a number of studies have demonstrated that, when given free choice in a play environment, children who choose to interact with peers are more sophisticated, on a number of social-cognitive measures, than children who chose to interact with adults (e.g., Harper & Huie, 1985; Pellegrini, 1984; Pellegrini & Perlmutter, 1989; Wright, 1980).

These findings are consistent with Piagetian (1970) theory, which suggests that the disequilibration characteristic of peer interaction facilitates development, whereas the typically unilateral interaction characteristic of adult–child interaction inhibits development. That is, when children interact with peers rather than adults, they are more likely to disagree with each other. When peers disagree, they are confronted with points of view other than their own. If they want the interaction to continue, which they usually do, they must incorporate (or *accommodate*, to use Piaget's term) their peers' points of view into a compromised form of interaction. In short, to engage in sustained social interaction with peers requires a fair amount of social (e.g., cooperation, perspective taking) and cognitive (e.g., ability to communicate clearly) skill. By comparison, when interacting with an adult, the adult will often take over some of this difficult work if the child is having problems (Pellegrini, 1984; Vygotsky, 1978). Furthermore, children do not tend to question adults as they are typically socialized not to question or challenge grownups.

Interaction with peers in schools may be particularly important as children are making the kindergarten to first-grade transition. My initial research in this area was a reaction against a law in the State of Georgia (where I lived at the time) requiring kindergarten children to pass a standardized paper and pencil test in order to be promoted to first grade. My intention was to show, once again, that standardized achievement and aptitude measures alone have limited explanatory and predictive power for young children. Ed Ziegler and Penelope Trickett (1978) made this point over 30 years ago in service of a similar cause; i.e., to argue against over-reliance on standardized measures of cognition such as IQ tests, and in favor of measures of social competence, to assess the impact of early intervention programs like Head Start. I also hoped to use these analyses to show legislators and people in the state departments of education, like Georgia, that their view of children and ways to study them is much too limited.

How Well Does Kindergartners' Playground Behavior Predict End of First-Grade Achievement?

In this section I demonstrate that what children do on the playground as kindergarteners (i.e., object play, peer interaction, and adult-directed behavior) is a valid predictor of their first-grade academic achievement, as measured by the Georgia Criterion References Test (GCRT) while taking their kindergarten achievement into consideration.

The results from this research, as displayed in Figure 12.1, first of all, suggest that the kindergarten Metropolitan Readiness Test did indeed predict first-grade academic achievement, followed by adults present (a significant negative predictor), objects manipulated, and peers present (Pellegrini, 1992). However, and most importantly for our discussion of the point of recess, the behavioral measures collected while children were on the playground at recess were more predictive of first-grade achievement, even after kindergarten achievement was statistically controlled! The important point here is that what kids do on the playground accounts for a statistically significant, and unique, portion of the variation (40%) beyond what standardized tests tell us.

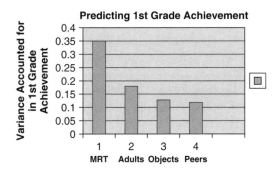

Figure 12.1   (Pellegrini, 1992)

It was interesting that kindergarten achievement as measured by the Metropolitan Achievement Test, while a significant predictor, left a significant portion of first-graders' achievement unexplained. Again, this finding supports the criticisms of Ziegler and Trickett (1978) that standardized measures of children's cognition have limited predictive value. Significantly more variance in first-grade achievement is accounted for when children's behavior in a naturalistic and motivating environment is considered.

I caution, however, that test scores, though limited in their predictive powers, should not be totally disregarded, as they did indeed account for a statistically significant portion of the variance in first-grade achievement. Getting rid of tests totally, or "throwing the baby out with the bath water", would limit our understanding of a very complex phenomenon, school achievement.

Another important aspect of the results relates to the developmental nature of the findings. During this period of developmental flux (Kagan, 1971; White, 1966), aspects of children's object use and peer relationships predicted more traditional aspects of school achievement. To illustrate, the object-use measure was a positive predictor of achievement. This was a measure of children manipulating sticks, logs, and stones on the playground. It should not be surprising that the cognitive demands of such manipulative activity should predict performance on a test with a mathematical thinking component; indeed, object use was a positive, significant predictor of performance on the math portion of the GCRT. Recall in the chapter on object play, that children's construction was a reliable predictor of using objects to solve convergent problems, such as making a tool to retrieve a lure.

Also recall that I made a similar argument earlier in this chapter for the role of pretend play in early literacy. Literacy, for preschool and kindergarten children, is different than it is for adults. For young children, literacy seems to take the form of using and understanding explicit oral language. Similarly, a relationship between object manipulation and early numeracy is certainly consistent with Piagetian theory (1983) and the curricular advice of Constance Kamii and Rheta DeVries (1978), and more recently by Herb Ginsberg (2006). These scholars suggest that logico-mathematical thought has its developmental roots in object manipulation. Caution must be exercised, however, when interpreting such a correlation. Specifically, just because two things are related does not mean that one causes the other. For example, it could be that children's logico-mathematical thought caused them to play with objects, not vice versa.

Furthermore, we also found that peer interaction in kindergarten was a positive and significant predictor of first-grade achievement, while adult-directed behavior during kindergarten was negatively and significantly related to first-grade achievement. That is, the more frequently children interacted their peers at recess, the higher they scored on the GCRT. By contrast, the more children interacted with adults, the lower they scored! Children who chose to initiate and maintain contact with adults in a play arena, rather than peers, may have lacked the social skills to interact with their peers. Again, this finding is similar to that presented in the pretend play/literacy section and in the more general social competence literature showing that when young children choose to interact with teachers, compared to peers, in play-oriented contexts, teachers do most of the work of maintaining interaction (Harper & Huie, 1985; Wright, 1980).

In comparison, when children interact with peers, they must use their own social competence to initiate and sustain interaction (Piaget, 1965). When we observed children with adults, the adults were more likely to be talking than children. Consistent with the Piagetian argument, when children and adults were together on the playground, adults talked and children listened. On the other hand, when children were in the presence of peers, their likelihood of talking, compared to not talking, was beyond chance. It is also important to note that the amount of peer talk was positively related to achievement (i.e., the more one talked with peers, the higher the achievement).

To conclude this section, I have demonstrated that observations of children at recess are an excellent venue to examine children's competence because interaction with peers at recess is both motivating and demanding for children. These findings are further supported by the research in the chapter on games where we found that, for children in their first year of full-time schooling, their facility at game-playing on the playground during the school recess period predicted their end-of-year social competence, where social competence is defined rather globally as children's adjustment to the various developmental tasks, such as developing control of one's emotions, learning to make friends, and adjusting to school across the lifespan (Waters & Sroufe, 1983). In the early primary school years, children engage in games on the playground, rather than the more traditional forms of play, such as pretend, like preschool children (Piaget, 1970; Pellegrini et al., 2002).

Recess and Attention in the Classroom

In this section I address what may be a more proximal effect of recess on children's cognitive performance in school, by examining the experimentally manipulated effect of varying recess timing regimens on children's attention to controlled classroom tasks. Attention is a measure that is consistent with theories suggesting that breaks from concentrated schoolwork should maximize performance. Following the notion of massed versus distributed practice (Ebbinghaus, 1885; James, 1901), children should be less attentive to classroom tasks during longer, compared to shorter, seat work periods (e.g., Stevenson & Lee, 1990). Briefly, massed versus distributed posits that individual performance is maximized when efforts are "distributed" across number of trials, rather than "massed" into fewer trails. For example, a child given a total of 100 spelling words to memorize will do better if he studies the words in ten separate ten-minute sessions rather than in two fifty-minute sessions. Following Stevenson and Lee's (1990) anecdotal attributions of the role of recess in Asian children's school achievement, we designed a series of experiments to test the effects of recess breaks on children's classroom behavior after recess. In the studies reported below, attention and inattention were measured in terms of children's looking/ not looking at either their seat work or, in cases when the teacher was reading to them, at the teacher. Additionally, children's fidgeting and listlessness was also coded as a measure of *in*attention while children did their seat work. While this measure of attention was less differentiated than others, such as skin conductivity or heart rate, it was practical for research conducted in functioning classrooms. Furthermore, this measure is an important indicator of more general school achievement (Johnson, McGue, & Iacano, 2005).

The effects of recess timing on children's attention to classroom work was examined following the design used by Smith and Hagan (1980), where *recess timing* was defined as the amount of time *before* recess that children are forced to be sedentary (or are deprived of social and locomotor play) and attend to class work. This type of regimen typifies most primary school classrooms (Minuchin & Shapiro, 1983). The school in which this research was conducted allowed the researchers to manipulate the times that children went out for recess as well as children's seat work before and after recess.

The children enrolled in this public elementary school were from varied socioeconomic and ethnic backgrounds. In all of the cases, the children in each of the grades were systematically exposed to different schedules for recess timing. On counter-balanced days they went out to recess either at 10:00 a.m. or at 10:30 a.m. The first study, to our knowledge, to address directly this issue of outdoor recess activity and post-recess attention found that third-grade children's attention before recess was lower than it was after recess, especially for boys, thus suggesting that recess facilitated attention (Pellegrini & Davis, 1993).

Those findings, however, were limited to the extent that we did not control the pre- and post-recess task used to assess children's attention. That is, the results may have been confounded by the fact that children's attention and inattention were related to the gender role stereotypicality of the tasks they worked on. Specifically, in the Pellegrini and Davis (1993) study, children's class work often involved listening to a story. Because the researchers did not systematically manipulate or control the stories read, it may have been the case that some of the stories read were more preferred by girls, thereby maximizing their attention to the task and minimizing boys'. Given this state of affairs, the resulting attention data may have been due to the effects of recess, the stereotypicality of the task, or both. In the next series of experiments this confounding factor was removed by systematically varying gender-preference of tasks before and after recess: In some cases they were read female-preferred stories (with female characters), and in other cases male-preferred stories (with male characters).

In Experiment 1 of a new series of experiments, the effects of outdoor recess timing on the classroom behavior of boys and girls in kindergarten (~ five years old), grade two (~ seven years old), and grade four (~ nine years old) were examined (Pellegrini, Huberty, & Jones, 1995). As in all experiments in this series, recess timing varied by thirty minutes. Children's attention or inattention was assessed before and after recess on male-preferred and female-preferred books.

In Experiment 1, the pre-recess results supported the suppositions of Stevenson and Lee (1990), who proposed that children are less attentive during long, compared to short, work periods. That is, children were generally less inattentive after recess than before recess, and younger children, relative to older children,

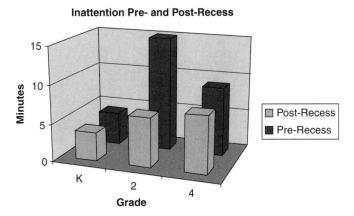

Figure 12.2   Inattention pre- and post-recess

were more inattentive. For example, fourth-grade children's mean attention scores were greater during the short deprivation time, relative to the long deprivation time. Figure 12.2 displays the pre-recess and post-recess *inattention* for grades K, two, and four. Note that at each grade level the children were more *inattentive* before than after recess.

Furthermore, it was found that boys' and girls' attention was influenced by the gender-role stereotypicality of the story. For example, fourth-grade boys in the long-deprivation condition were more attentive to male-preferred stories and less attentive to female-preferred stories, while the pattern was reversed for the girls. This finding is consistent with the extant literature on gender preference for stories (e.g., Monson & Sebesta, 1991).

Results from this experiment should be interpreted cautiously, primarily because of the small sample size (20 children per grade and 10 children per sex within each grade) and because there was only one classroom at each grade level. Replication is clearly needed to assure that the results are not aberrant (Lykken, 1968), especially when the results have implications for school policy.

To this end, in a new experiment, Experiment 2, second- and fourth-graders (one classroom for each grade) were studied in the same school as in Experiment 1. The results from Experiment 2, similar to those from Experiment 1, revealed that children's task attention is affected by recess timing, and that timing interacted with dimensions of the task as well as children's age and gender. Children generally, but especially second-graders, were more attentive after recess. In Figure 12.3, the pre- and post-recess inattention scores are displayed.

In Experiment 3, students in two fourth-grade classrooms were studied and the same recess timing paradigm was employed. The recess period was indoors, however. The same experiment was conducted with two separate, intact classrooms. Such a design was chosen because of the relatively small samples involved in each classroom. This procedure minimizes the probability of obtaining aberrant results if similar results are obtained in both samples—thus

Inattention Pre- and Post-Recess

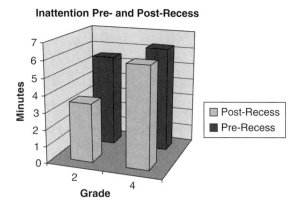

Figure 12.3   Inattention pre- and post-recess

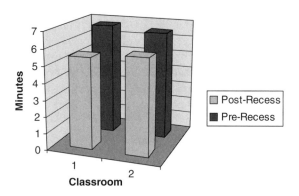

Figure 12.4   Inattention pre- and post-recess

replicating each other. The results from this experiment are similar to those from other experiments: Attention was greater after the recess period than it was before the break in classroom 2. The result from the indoor recess study was similar to the outdoors results—Children are generally more attentive to classroom work after recess than before. Whether recess is indoors or outdoors does not seem to matter. In Figure 12.4, these results are displayed with pre-recess and post-recess scores of inattention for the two classrooms.

The message from this research is clear. Breaks between periods of intense work seem to maximize children's attention to their class work. More speculatively, it is probably this increased attention that is partially responsible for the positive relations between recess and performance on achievement tests (Pellegrini, 1992; 2005). What we really still need to know, however, is the effect of different recess regimens on attention. A first step in this direction was already presented, as we found that indoor recess periods, like outdoor periods, seemed to be effective facilitators of children's attention to class work. This result is consistent with mass versus distributed practice as the mechanism responsible for the effects of recess on attention. From this view, the nature of the break is less important than having a break *per se*. To more thoroughly examine this hypothesis, researchers should examine different types of breaks after periods of intense cognitive work. For example, does watching a short video or listening to music for a short period facilitate attention? Furthermore, do these effects vary with age? Researchers should also consider the possibility that different aspects of recess regimens should have different optima for different outcome measures (Bateson, personal communication, July, 2005). Frequent well-timed breaks may enhance attention, while social dimensions of the recess period are probably more important for social competence and more general school adjustment.

Bjorklund's cognitive immaturity hypothesis provides some general guidance here (Bjorklund & Pellegrini, 2000; 2002). The theory suggests that breaks for preschool and young primary school children should be "playful" and unstructured. Providing time for children to interact with peers or materials on their own terms—that is, with minimal adult direction—should maximize their attention to subsequent tasks. With older children and adults, merely providing breaks between periods of intense work might suffice to maximize attention. The research on massed versus distributed practice with adults supports this view.

Another crucial aspect of the recess period that needs further research is the duration of the recess period. Should it be 10 minutes, 20 minutes, 30 minutes, etc.? We simply do not know. Answers to this question have obvious implications for school policy and scheduling. We explored the issue of recess duration with a sample of preschool children (ages four to five years) (Holmes, Pellegrini, and Schmidt, unpublished data). Procedurally, children had "circle time" and were read a story before recess. Then they went outdoors for recess periods of 10, 20, or 30 minutes. When they returned to their classrooms, they again sat in a circle and listened to a story read to them by their teachers. Attention was recorded and coded for whether the child was gazing in the direction of the book or the teacher reading the book.

Consistent with earlier work with older, primary school children reported above, attention was greater following the recess period, and girls were more attentive than boys to classroom tasks in all conditions. Thus it seems reasonable to conclude that recess breaks help children attend to classroom tasks.

Regarding the differing durations of recess periods, we found that attention to classroom tasks was greatest following the 20- and 10-minute outdoor play periods, whereas the 30-minute period resulted in higher rates of inattention. These findings are consistent with anecdotal evidence from the United Kingdom, where children become bored with recess after too long a period, and thus longer periods may become counterproductive (Blatchford, 1998). This work needs to be replicated, as it represents only one short-term study with a relatively small sample. The duration of the recess periods is clearly important, as it is one of the persistent questions posed to us by parents and teachers. How long should the recess be? Should its duration vary with children's age? Clearly at this point we only have hints, and are not sure.

CONCLUSIONS

Theories and data presented in this chapter provide support for the positive role of recess in the school curriculum. While it is very difficult to predicting young children's achievement, I suggest that assessing children in contexts that are simultaneously motivating and socially and cognitively demanding will maximize the likelihood of eliciting children's competence. The use of any single measure, and especially standardized tests with young children, limits our understanding of a very complex process. Even when tests are reliable predictors of achievement for older children, they often are not especially motivating for young children and probably underestimate competence (see Messick, 1983). The school recess period may be one such venue where children exhibit their maximally complex social and cognitive processes. I have presented data demonstrating that kindergarten and first-grade children's recess behaviors, respectively, predicted academic achievement and adjustment to school.

At another and perhaps more basic level, providing breaks over the course of the instructional day facilitates primary school children's attention to classroom tasks. That these results were obtained using well-controlled field experiments (e.g., recess-deprivation periods and classroom attention tasks were experimentally manipulated) and replicated a number of times by different groups of researchers, should provide confidence in the findings.

Additionally, the studies reported above demonstrated the effects of both indoor and outdoor recess periods on attention. These studies provide insight into the role of a relatively sedentary break period on subsequent attention. From a policy perspective, educators sometimes use indoor recess as an alternative to outdoor breaks. This may be due to the fact that teachers or playground supervisors are reluctant to go outdoors during inclement weather or they may be sensitive to the possibility of lawsuits related to injuries on playground equipment. Our results provide support for the efficacy of indoor breaks.

The results presented here support the anecdotal evidence from Taiwanese and Japanese schools suggesting that, in order to maintain high levels of attention, children need frequent breaks in the course of the day (Stevenson and Lee, 1990). According to Stevenson and Lee (1990) Asian schools provide frequent breaks across a relatively long school day. These breaks, they suggest, are related to children's school performance. Also as noted above, English children have frequent recess period in their school day, but the durations of these periods, too, have been eroding (Blatchford, 1998). However, in England, as in the United States, what children do in the playground at recess has "educational value" to the extent that children's participation in games predicts school adjustment and social competence (Pellegrini et al., 2002; Blatchford et al., 2003). This evidence should inform policy and be used to guide policymakers and politicians seeking to diminish or eliminate recess from the school curriculum.

American children's school days and school years should be lengthened, to more closely approximate the experiences of children in Asia and Europe. Such a policy would bring the total number of hours American children attend school in a year closer to that of other countries in the world. This increase should have the corresponding benefit of increasing achievement. Longer school days and years—*in conjunction with frequent breaks*—should accomplish this. Additionally, a longer school day and year would ensure that children have a safe place while their parents are at work. Children would be in school, learning and interacting with their peers, rather at home, unsupervised, or in expensive after-school care.

While recess periods alone seem to be important, it is also important to let children interact on their own terms with peers. Providing children with a physical education class as a substitute for recess does not serve the same purpose (Pellegrini, 2005; Council on Physical Education for Children, 2001). This conclusion is supported on a number of fronts. First, and at the level of theory, both the cognitive immaturity hypothesis and massed versus distributed practice theory suggest that, after periods of intense instruction, children need breaks from this instruction. A physical education class is another form of instruction and thus would not provide the sort of break needed to maximize instruction. Furthermore, physical education classes typically do not provide the variety of rich opportunities for peer interaction that recess does. The research presented above pointed to the importance of peer interaction for both social and cognitive outcomes. The importance of physical education for classroom attention is typically predicated on the idea that children "need to blow off steam" after periods of work, and the vigorous activity associated with physical education should serve this purpose. However, the idea of "blowing off steam" is rooted in Surplus Energy Theory—an invalid nineteenth- century theory (Evans & Pellegrini, 1997).

With all these positive words, I must stress that the data presented here are very limited indeed and in need of extension. A number of years ago I wrote a grant proposal to the US Department of Education to study the effects of different recess regimens of school achievement. The proposal, to understate the case, was not positively received. One reviewer suggested that my Dean be notified of the sorts of things I intended to study and be sanctioned! The climate seems a bit more positive now, but it is still an uphill battle.

13

Conclusion: What's It All Mean?

Writing the concluding chapter in a book can be, and often is, an exercise in redundancies—a mere repetition of what has already been said. I will try not to fall into that trap. Instead, I will try to bring order to what is in many ways a rather disordered field. Based on these suggestions I will make some policy-oriented recommendations for the place of play in children's lives.

Half Full or Half Empty?

As I have noted thorough this book, the place of play in human development has been a very controversial one. Indeed, when different opinions of play are voiced, one wonders if they can be talking about the same phenomenon. I will take examples from the scientific and educational communities to illustrate this point. First, the noted evolutionary biologist E. O. Wilson (1975) anointed play as one of the most important topics for sociobiologists to study. Similarly, some quarters of the developmental psychology community have come to close sanctifying play, considering it a necessary experience for children, without which serious social emotional damage will be done (e.g., Singer et al., 2006). Relatedly, it has been researched by some of the most notable psychologists in the field such as Jerome Bruner (1972), Harry Harlow (1962), Jean Piaget (1962), Brian Sutton-Smith (1999), and L. S. Vygotsky (1967).

By contrast with the same scientific community, the topic has been virtually ignored by an influential segment of developmental psychologists for the past half century. H. Schlosberg (1947), for example, saw the topic as irrelevant and unworthy of study. As if taking their cue from Schlosberg, the six editors of *The Handbook of Child Psychology*, from 1946 to present, have included only one chapter on play (Rubin et al., 1983). Similarly, a segment of the evolutionary biology community is skeptical of the value of play, suggesting that it has no function (Sharpe, 2005), and when its value is conceded, its putative function is thought to be minimal (Martin & Caro, 1985).

In early and primary education, too, opinions regarding the importance of play are bimodal. Some educational organizations, such as the National Association for the Education of Young Children (1992), list play experiences as crucial for healthy early education and development. Edward Zigler (Zigler & Bishop-Josef, 2006), a founding father of Head Start, advocates including play in the education of young children. At the other end of the spectrum, children's play experiences are being diminished or eliminated altogether in many primary schools in North America and Britain (Pellegrini, 2005). Specifically, the opportunity to play, in the form of recess periods during the school day, has become marginalized and eliminated from the curriculum of many primary schools across North America and Britain (Pellegrini, 2005).

This level of discord, especially within disciplines, is reason to pause. Why is it that very well-respected scholars, for the most part, come to such different conclusions? In this chapter, I will address this issue, suggesting that differences in how play is defined and the ways in which function is conceptualized lead to misunderstanding.

Differences in Definition

The way that a construct is defined is, to state the obvious, important. For example, inconsistency in defining and labeling a construct across different research teams makes any integration of a field nearly impossible (e.g., Bem, 1995). As I noted in the very first chapter of this book, perhaps most problematic in terms of defining play in the child development literature is that the term *play* is often used too casually; it is frequently used to label most forms of children's social and non-social behavior, regardless of whether it is play or not. From this point of view, all that children do, especially with each other, is considered "play" (Martin & Caro, 1985). For example, Mildred Parten (1932) in her seminal work on categorizing children's social participation labeled as solitary *play*, parallel *play*, and cooperative *play* (all my emphasis) forms of peer interaction that might not be play, according to many operational definitions. Labeling these forms of social behavior as categories of play has continued into the present day (e.g., Martin & Fabes, 2001, p. 431; Rubin, Bukowski, & Parker, 1998, p. 635).

Some might argue that I am making this much too complicated and that we really do not need a "formal" definition of play because most people "recognize it when they see it." Indeed, the claim that most people recognize play when they see it, yet it is so difficult to define, is a common prologue to many discussions of defining play (e.g., Burghardt, 2005; Martin & Caro, 1985). In fact, there are many cases in which they do not accurately "recognize when they see it"! There have been empirical studies of the ways that children (Smith, Smees, & Pellegrini, 2005; Smith & Vollstedt, 1983), youth (Pellegrini, 2005), and adults (Smith et al., 2005) categorize behaviors as "play" or "non-play," and there is disagreement, especially regarding ambiguous, provocative forms of play such as rough-and-tumble play and sexual play. These findings suggest that some level of definitional consensus is necessary.

None of this is to say that explicit efforts have not been made to define play operationally (Wilson, 1975), but they have been very difficult and akin to encountering a "hornets' nest," according to some (Bekoff & Byers, 1981). Robert Fagen (1981), in his seminal volume *Animal Play Behavior*, has a five-page appendix listing definitions of play. In the child development literature, a list of play attributes is also offered by Rubin, Fein, and Vandenberg (1983) in their *Handbook of Child Psychology* chapter on play. Specifically, they defined play according to observable behaviors (functional, symbolic, and games), dispositional attributes (intrinsic motivation, attention to means over ends, differentiation between play and exploration, relationship to instrumental behavior, freedom from external rules, and active engagement), and context (familiarity, free choice, minimal adult intrusion, and stress-free). Rubin and colleagues suggested that behaviors be not categorized dichotomously, as either play or not play, but instead along a continuum, from more to less playful, depending on the number of criteria met. This procedure implicitly assumes that all attributes all equal. From this viewpoint, a behavior meeting four criteria (e.g., free choice, stress-free, attention to means, and minimal adult intrusion) should be more playful than a behavior meeting three (e.g., free choice, non-instrumental, and attention to means). The four-criteria behavior could be a child taking a nap, while the three-criteria behavior could be a child using a pencil as a rocket ship. Most observers would consider the second, not the first, example to be play, despite the difference in the number of criteria met.

Indeed, some child psychologists (e.g., McCune & Fenson, 1984; Smith & Vollstedt, 1985) and educated lay observers (Smith & Vollstedt, 1985) consider pretend, or symbolic, play to be a paradigm case of play. Consequently, one default rule for defining play would be to categorize only fantasy as play. This is an inadequate solution in that children engage in other forms of play, such as object, locomotor, and social play, that might not have a fantasy dimension, yet it is still play. In the case of object play, for example, hitting a hollow block with a stick, seemingly for the joy of the different sounds made, would be playing with the object, but not fantasy. In the locomotor case, swinging from a tree branch can certainly be considered play, just as children's play wrestling is social play without fantasy.

A more principled approach has been advanced by Gordon Burghardt (1984; 2005), a longtime student of play and the difficulties associated with defining it. He suggests that there are five core criteria, all of which must be present, for a behavior to be categorized as play. They include: the behavior must be voluntary, observed in a "relaxed field"; the behavior is not functional in the observed context; the behaviors are repeated but the behavioral elements are exaggerated, segmented, and nonsequential in relation to the functional variant of the behavior.

A *relaxed field* is one where the individual is safe, healthy, and well fed. Furthermore, the child should choose to voluntarily engage in some social, locomotor, fantasy, or object-directed activity that is not directly or immediately functional, such as engaging in a wrestling bout whose function is not to hurt or defeat his or her peer. The nature and sequence of these behaviors would not resemble those in a functional context. For example, the child would use an exaggerated voice and exaggerated stepping movements to approach a peer— like a pretend monster perhaps—and in the course of wrestling, the dominant and subordinate "combatants" would switch roles. These criteria can be realized in the four domains of play: locomotor (e.g., rolling down a hill), object (e.g., piling blocks in different configurations), social (e.g., play fighting), and pretend (e.g., enacting domestic roles). Furthermore, each of these domains, with the obvious exception of social play, can be either social or solitary.

In short, the voluntary component of play provides the motivation necessary for children to persevere at an activity, trying out a variety of behavioral routines where the means over ends, nonfunctional criteria mean that children are not concerned with doing something "right." The consequence of behaviors meeting all these criteria means that play behaviors are typically more variable than their more instrumental versions in terms of exaggeration, sequencing, and segmentation. In this definition, children are not enacting associated behavioral routines in ways that are mere copies of the functional activity. In other words, play behaviors are not imperfect attempts to copy, or accommodate to, functional behaviors, but are instead creative, or behaviorally flexible, encounters with the world (see Piaget, 1966; Sutton-Smith, 1966, debate on this point). The behavioral-flexibility characteristic of play, I suggest, is the main function of play.

Functions of Play

The variety of ways that "function" is defined in relation to the benefits associated with play can further add to the confusion over the importance of play. Specifically, in both the animal and human play literatures, the putative functions of play are legend. For example, some students of children's play (e.g., Singer et al., 2006) posit that children's play has benefits for a wide variety of social, emotional, and cognitive areas. Correspondingly, two primatologists, Baldwin and Baldwin (1977), have listed 30 possible functions of play.

The critical reader may at this point be asking: How can play be so important in children's lives when one of its necessary definitional criteria is that is non-functional? This logical conundrum can be solved by assuming that play behavior is not immediately functional during the juvenile period, when it is observed; instead, its benefits are deferred to maturity (Martin & Caro, 1985). This deferred benefit, or scaffolding, view of play assumes that play is used during development to assemble a skill, and when that skill is mastered, the scaffold, or the need for play, is removed and no longer necessary (Bateson, 1976; 1981). Most child developmental theories of play (Groos, 1901; Piaget, 1962; Vygotsky, 1967) take this deferred-benefits position. For example, the social symbolic role-playing of preschoolers is thought to be an imperfect attempt by children to understand their appropriate adult roles.

By contrast, a metamorphic view of play (Bateson, 1981) holds that play has immediate benefits, reaped during childhood. From this position, what children do is not an imperfect variant of adult behavior but germane and adaptive to the period of childhood (Bjorklund & Green, 1992). Play during childhood helps the child negotiate the demands of that period. For example, social symbolic play may increase children's efficacy in social interactions with their peers. If their exhibition of new behaviors were dependent on relatively accurate approximations of mature behavior—they would view themselves as failures and interact with the world minimally. This difference in when benefits of play appear will have an obvious impact on our judgments about the importance of play. In Table 13.1 I present a heuristic for examining immediate and deferred benefits of the four forms of play.

What is Functional?

"Function" has numerous meanings (Hinde, 1980). For developmental psychologists, function is often equivalent to having beneficial consequences; for example, locomotor play is an antecedent to increased bone density (Gunter, Baxter-Jones, Mirwald, Almstedt, Fuchs, Durski, & Snow, 2008). On the other hand, function for ethologists is often equated with adaptive utility and fitness (Burghardt, 2005); for example, locomotor play might result in increased body size, chances of survival, social dominance, and eventually reproductive fitness (Pellegrini, 2008). Even though fitness may be an "ultimate" function of play, it is important to recognize that during an individual's life history, there are different tasks germane to those periods that are necessary to master so that the individual can survive, mature, and eventually reproduce.

From this definition of function, it is assumed that natural selection operates on all periods of development, not only adulthood. Life history theory suggests that the trade-offs between the costs (i.e., in terms of time and calories expended in play and risks of injury and to survivorship) and benefits associated with play be examined in relation to individuals' growth and maintenance, in addition to reproductive success at different periods in development (Stearns, 1992).

Table 13.1   A heuristic for studying "Functions" of play

	Immediate	Deferred
Locomotor	Cardiovascular fitness	Muscle/skeletal differentiation
	Bone density	Cerebellar synaptogenesis
Object	Fine motor control	Tool use
Social	Social cohesion	Social skills
	Efficacy	
Symbolic	Wish fulfillment	Hypothetical scenarios
	Language/TOM	

Furthermore, it is assumed that if there are costs associated with a behavior or strategy, it probably has been naturally selected and has utility (Martin & Caro, 1985): If play costs are high, then benefits should also be high. If costs are low, then benefits, too, should be low.

In keeping with the notion that play is heterogeneous, there are different levels of costs for different forms of play across ontogeny. For example, survivorship costs of some forms of social play are relatively high, where time and caloric costs of social play for those same animals are low to moderate (e.g., Harcourt, 1991a, b). Similarly, in humans, there appear to be a high survivorship costs to locomotor play in childhood, relative to adulthood, as evidenced by the co-occurrence of deaths and injury in apparently "playful" contexts, such as bicycling and swimming (National Vital Statistics—Mortality Rates, 2006). Caloric costs of children's locomotor play, on the other hand, are low to moderate (Pellegrini et al., 1998).

While extant data documenting deferred benefits of play are scarce (Martin & Caro, 1985; Pellegrini, in press), there are data documenting relations between different forms of play and immediate benefits. Specifically, locomotor play relates to increased bone density (Gunter et al., 2008), social play to social dominance (Pellegrini, 2008), and symbolic play to theory of mind (e.g., Smith, 2005) and early literacy (Pellegrini and Galda, 1993). Deferred benefits, where they have been documented, include cerebellar synaptogenesis for locomotor play in some nonhuman animals (Byers & Walker, 1995). A proposed, but empirically unsupported, deferred benefit of children's symbolic play is the ability to think hypothetically as an adult (Alexander, 1989; Harris, 2006).

More speculatively, it may be that play serves both immediate and deferred benefits by increasing behavioral and cognitive flexibility. As noted above, the means over ends and nonfunctional definitional criteria of play should result in behavioral and cognitive flexibility. Scholars from psychology (e.g., Bruner, 1972; Sutton-Smith, 1966; 1967) and biology (e.g., Bateson, 2005; Burghardt, 2005; Fagen, 1981; Špinka et al., 2001) have posited links between play and creative responses to the environment for over 40 years. The gist of these associated hypotheses is that in the safe context of play, characteristic of species with an extended juvenile period, animals place themselves into unconventional and often disorienting positions. These novel situations afford opportunities to experiment with a variety of behavioral and cognitive routines and generate novel, and possibly adaptive, responses. With repeated play experiences, individuals become facile at enlisting these processes, and thus they become more accessible in times of need, such as during an emergency (Stamps, 1995).

Because play affords opportunities for the generation of new responses to novel environments, it is an excellent candidate for behavior affecting evolutionary processes, or what Pat Bateson (2006) call the "adaptability" driver. The importance of play in impacting evolution relates to its being a relatively low-cost way that to develop alternative responses to new and challenging environments (Bateson, 2005). A low-cost strategy is one that has low risk and is likely to be incorporated into the behavioral repertoire and eventually into the genotype.

This is not to say that adults cannot also learn and develop alternative strategies, but it is probably less costly, and consequently more likely to spread through the population, if it is accomplished through play in childhood (Bateson, 2005; Burghardt, 2005). Organisms, especially complex ones like humans, are sensitive to environmental perturbations early in development, and novel behavioral responses to these environments lead them to develop new, and more flexible, phenotypes, than less flexible conspecifics. That play during periods of immaturity is less costly than other strategies during other periods of development is predicated on organisms' being well-provisioned and protected for a period of prolonged immaturity. These conditions afford opportunities to develop novel behaviors early in ontogeny and these new behaviors, in turn, influence subsequent development (Burghardt, 2005). The ease (and low cost) with which these novel behaviors are acquired should result in their being expressed as a result of mutation (Bateson, 2005). For example, Suomi (2005) has demonstrated how social play of juvenile rhesus monkeys interacts with their genotype to impact future ontogenetic, and possibly phylogenetic, development.

Innovative behaviors associated with play during the juvenile period should be especially prone to this process because of the adult protection and provisioning associated with play during the juvenile period (Bjorklund, 2006). Later periods in development are not typically characterized by this level of protection and provisioning (Burghardt, 2005).

Research and Policy Implications

More research into children's and youth's play is needed, especially the sort that documents how much time is spent in each form of play during the periods of early and middle childhood. It is quite surprising that we know so little about how much time and energy is spent in play, as well as other behaviors, outside of the university nursery school. I am certainly not the first to make this indictment—it has been made repeatedly for the last 50 years in our field (Bronfenbrenner & Crouter, 1983; McCall, 1977; Wright, 1960). While our knowledge of children's pretend play, even at home (Haight & Miller, 1993), is adequate, we still know very little about other forms of play. Take object play. What we know about this category is typically lumped into a very general category called "constructive play," which many do not consider play at all (Pellegrini, 2005; Piaget, 1962; Rubin, Fein, & Vandenberg, 1983; Smith, 1988).

Also, at the level of description, we know surprisingly little about children's and youth's sexual play, a dimension of social pay (though see Lamb & Coakley, 1993; Pellegrini, 2005; Thorne & Luria, 1986), even though more than one-half of those sampled in one retrospective survey reported having engaged in this form of "play" (Lamb & Coakley, 1993). The line between "play" and abuse, especially when initiators are older, is crucial to understand.

Lastly, future research in play should consider both immediate and deferred benefits. While the difficulty associated with tracking deferred benefits is obvious, these benefits are worth pursuing.

So what are the policy implications of this discussion of varying definitions and functions of play? First, and perhaps most importantly, we should take care to label a behavior as *play* when it fits explicated definitions of the construct. By my definition, all that children do is not play. Nor is it play when we tell children that we're going to "play" a phonemic awareness game and have them sing scripted letter–sound correspondences. In play, by my definition at least, children must be more concerned with the means of an activity, such as recombining different sounds in a variety of orders, rather than the ends of the activity, such as making the correct sound for a specified letter (see Cazden, 1974, for an interesting example of play with language).

Correspondingly, our educational policy needs to be guided by empirical relations between specific forms of play and specific outcomes. As noted above, there are data to support the view that play in all four areas predicts, albeit modestly, a variety of outcomes. With this said, there is a real danger that some advocates of play for children will be overzealous in their beneficial attributions of play. While this is understandable in an educational environment that is trying to minimize children's play-related activities, such as the school recess periods, this position also jeopardizes the possibility of future inclusion of play. Policy-makers and parents will associate the advocacy of play with overblown claims. To paraphrase Sir Thomas Gresham: The bad evidence will drive out the good evidence. If advocates of play stick to realistic readings of the data—it will be included in curriculum.

References

Ainsworth, M. D. S. (1973). The development of mother–infant attachment. In B. Caldwell and H. Ricciutti (eds.), *Review of child development research*, Vol. 3 (pp. 1–94). Chicago: University of Chicago Press.

Alexander, R. D. (1989). Evolution of the human psyche. In P. Mellers and C. Stringer (eds.), *The human revolution: Behavioural and biological perspectives on the origins of modern humans* (pp. 455–513). Princeton, N.J.: Princeton University Press.

Alexander, R. D., Hoogland, J. L., Howard, R. D., Noonan, K. M., and Sherman, P. W. (1979). Sexual dimorphisms and breeding systems in pinnipeds, ungulates, primates, and humans. In N. A. Chagnon and W. Irons (eds.), *Evolutionary biology and human social behavior* (pp. 402–435). North Scituate, Mass.: Duxbury Press.

Allport, G. M. (1954). *The nature of prejudice*. Cambridge, Mass.: Addison-Wesley.

Altmann, S. A. (1962). Social behavior of anthropoid primates: Analysis of recent concepts. In E. L. Bliss (ed.), *Roots of behavior* (pp. 277–285). New York: Harper.

Altringham, J., and Senior, P. (2002: September). Sexual segregation in bats. Paper presented at the Workshop in Sexual Segregation, Department of Zoology, Cambridge University, Cambridge, U.K.

Amant, R. S., and Horton, T. E. (2008). Revising the definition of animal tool use. *Animal Behaviour*, 75: 1199–1208.

Applebaum, M., and McCall, R. (1983). Design and analysis in developmental psychology. In W. Kessen (ed.), *Handbook of child psychology*, Vol. 1 (pp. 415–476). New York: Wiley.

Archer, J. (1992). *Ethology and human development*. Hemel Hempstead, U.K.: Harvester Wheatsheaf.

Archer, J., and Lloyd, B. (2002). *Sex and gender* (2nd edition). London: Cambridge University Press.

Arnett, J. (1992). Reckless behavior in adolescence: A developmental perspective. *Developmental Review*, 12: 339–373.

Axelrod, R., and Hamilton, W. (1981). The evolution of cooperation. *Science*, 211: 1390–1396.

Bakeman, R., and Brownlee, J. (1980). The strategic use of parallel play: A sequential analysis. *Child Development*, 51: 873–878.

Bakeman, R., and Gottman, J. (1986). *Observing interactions: An introduction to sequential analysis*. New York: Cambridge University Press.

Baldwin, J., and Baldwin, J. (1978). Reinforcement theories of exploration, play, and psychosocial growth. In E. O. Smith (ed.), *Social play in primates* (pp. 231–253). New York: Academic Press.

Baldwin, J. M. (1896). A new factor in evolution. *American Naturalist*, 30: 441–451; 536–553.

Bandura, A. (1986). *Social foundations of thought and action: A social cognitive theory*. Englewood Cliffs, N.J.: Prentice Hall.

Barber, N. (1991). Play and energy regulation in mammals. The Quarterly Review of Biology, 66: 129–147.

Barlow, G. W. (1989). Has sociobiology killed ethology or revitalized it? In P. P. G. Bateson and P. Klopfer (eds.), *Perspectives in ethology*, Vol. 8 (pp. 1–45). London: Plenum.

Bateman, A. J. (1948). Intra-sexual selection in *Drosophilia*. *Heredity*, 2: 349–368.

Bates, E. (1979). *The emergence of symbols: Cognition and communication in infancy*. New York: Academic Press.

Bates, E., Carlson-Luden, V., and Bretherton, I. (1980). Perceptual aspects of tool use in infancy. *Infant Behavior and Development*, 3: 127–140.

Bateson, P. P. G. (1964). An effect of imprinting on the perceptual development of domestic chicks. *Nature*, 202: 421–422.

Bateson, P. P. G. (1976). Specificity and the origins of behavior. In J. Rosenblatt, R. Hinde, E. Shaw, and C. Beer (eds.), *Advances in the study of behavior*, Vol. 6 (pp. 1–20). New York: Academic.

Bateson, P. P. G. (1978). How behavior develops. In P. Bateson and L. Klopfer (eds.), *Perspectives in ethology*, Vol. 5 (pp. 55–66). New York: Academic.

Bateson, P. P. G. (1981). Discontinuities in development and changes in the organization of play in cats. In K. Immelmann, G. Barlow, L. Petrinovich, and M. Main (eds.), *Behavioral development* (pp. 281–295). New York: Cambridge University Press.

Bateson, P. P. G. (1987). Biological approaches to the study of behavioural development. International *Journal of Behavioral Development*, 10: 1–22.

Bateson, P. P. G. (1988). The active role of behaviour in evolution. In M.-W. Ho and S. W. Fox (eds.), *Evolutionary processes and metaphors* (pp. 191–207). London: Wiley.

Bateson, P. P. G. (2003). The promise of behavioural biology. *Animal Behaviour*, 65: 11–17.

Bateson, P. P. G. (2005). Play and its role in the development of great apes and humans. In A. D. Pellegrini and P. K. Smith (eds.), *The nature of play: Great apes and humans* (pp. 13–26). New York: Guilford.

Bateson, P. P. G. (2006). The adaptability driver: Links between behaviour and evolution. *Biological Theory: Integrating Development, Evolution, and Cognition*, 1: 342–345.

Bateson, P. P. G., and Martin, P. (1999). *Design for a life: How behaviour develops*. London: Jonathan Cape.

Bateson, G. (1972). *Steps to an ecology of mind*. San Francisco: Chandler.

Bauer, E. B., and Smuts, B. A. (2007). Cooperation and competition during dyadic play in domestic dogs, *Canis familiaris*. *Animal Behaviour*, 73: 489–499.

Bekoff, M. (1977). Social communication in canids: Evidence for the evolution of a stereotyped mammalian display. *Science*, 197: 1097–1099.

Bekoff, M. (1978). Social play: Structure, function and the evolution of a co-operative social behavior. In G. M. Burghardt and M. Bekoff (eds.), *The development of behavior: Comparative and evolutionary aspects* (pp. 367–383). New York: Garland.

Bekoff, M. (1988). Social play and physical training: When "not enough" may be plenty. *Ethology*, 80: 330–333.

Bekoff, M. (1988). Motor training and physical fitness: Possible short-and long-term influences on the development of individual differences in behavior. *Developmental Psychobiology*, 21: 601–612.

Bekoff, M. (1995). Play signals as punctuation: The structure of social play in canids. *Behaviour*, 132: 419–429.

Bekoff, M. (1995). Playing with play: What can we learn about cognition, negotiation, and evolution. In D. Cummins and C. Allen (eds.), *The evolution of mind* (pp. 162–182). New York: Oxford University Press.

Bekoff, M. (1997). Playing with play: What can we learn about cognition, negotiation, and evolution. In D. Cummins and C. Allen (eds.), *The evolution of mind* (pp. 162–182). New York: Oxford University Press.

Bekoff, M., and Byers, J. A. (1981). A critical re-analysis of the ontogeny and phylogcny of mammalian social and locomotor play. In K. Immelmann, G. Barlow, L. Petronovich, and M. Main (eds.), *Behavioural development* (pp. 296–337). Cambridge: Cambridge University Press.

Bekoff, M., and Byers, J. A. (1992). Time, energy, and play. *Animal Behavior*, 44: 981–982.

Bellin, H. F., and Singer, D. G. (2006). My magic story car: Video-based play intervention to strengthen emergent literacy of at-risk preschoolers. In D. Singer, R. M. Golinkoff, and K. Hirsch-Pasek (2006) (eds.), *Play = Learning* (pp. 101–123). New York: Oxford University Press.

Belsky, J. (2001). Developmental Risks (Still) Associated with Early Child Care. *Journal of Child Psychology and Psychiatry,* 42: 845–859.

Belsky, J. (2003). The Politicized Science of Day Care: A Personal and Professional Odyssey. *Family Policy Review*, 1: 23–40.

Belsky, J. (2005). Differential susceptibility to rearing influence: An evolutionary hypothesis and some evidence. In B. J. Ellis and D. F. Bjorklund (eds.), *Origins of the social mind: Evolutionary psychology and child development* (pp. 139–163). New York: Guilford.

Belsky, J., and Most, R. (1981). From exploration to play: A cross-sectional study of infant free-play behavior. *Developmental Psychology*, 17: 630–639.

Belsky, J., Steinberg, L., and Draper, P. (1991). Childhood experience, interpersonal development, and reproductive strategy: An evolutionary theory of socialization. *Child Development*, 62: 647–670.

Benedict, R. (1934). *Patterns of culture.* Boston: Houghton Mifflin.

Berenbaum, S. A., and Snyder, E. (1995). Early hormonal influences on childhood sex-typed activity and playmate preferences: Implications for the development of sexual orientation. *Developmental Psychology*, 31: 31–42.

Bering, J. M. (2001). Theistic percepts in other species: Can chimpanzees represent the minds of non-natural agents? *Journal of Cognition and Culture*, 1: 107–137.

Berk, L. E., Mann, T. D., and Ogan, A. T. (2006). Make-believe play: Wellspring for development of self-regulation. In D. Singer, R. M., Golinkoff, and K. Hirsh-Pasek (eds.), *Play = Learning* (pp. 74–100). New York: Oxford University Press.

Berlyne, D. (1960). *Conflict, arousal, and curiosity.* New York: McGraw-Hill.

Berlyne, D. (1966). Curiosity and exploration. *Science*, 153: 25–33.

Berlyne, D. (1970). Children's reasoning and thinking. In P. H. Mussen (ed.), *Carmichael's Manual of Child Psychology*, Vol. 1 (pp. 939–982). New York: Wiley and Sons.

Bernstein, B. (1960). Language and social class. *British Journal of Sociology*, 1: 217–227.
Bernstein, B. (1971). *Class, codes, and control.* Vol. 1. London: Routledge and Kegan Paul.
Bernstein, B. (1972). Social class, language, and socialization. In P. Giglioli (ed.), *Language and social context* (pp. 157–178). Harmondsworth, U.K.: Penguin.
Bernstein, I. (1981). Dominance: The baby and the bathwater. *The Behavioral and Brain Sciences*, 4: 419–457.
Bertalanffy, L. von (1968). *General systems theory.* New York: Braziller.
Bianchi, B., and Bakeman, R. (1978). Sex-typed affiliation preferences observed in preschools: Traditional and open school differences. *Child Development*, 49: 910–912.
Biben, M., and Suomi, S. L. (1993). Lessons from primate play. In K. MacDonald (ed.), *Parent-child play* (pp. 185–196). Albany, N.Y.: State University of New York Press.
Bidell, T. (1988). Vygotsky, Piaget and the dialectic of development. *Human Development*, 31: 329–348.
Bjorklund, D. J. (1978). Negative transfer in children's recall of categorized material. *Journal of Experimental Child Psychology*, 26: 299–307.
Bjorklund, D. F. (2006). Mother knows best: Epigenetic inheritance. Maternal effects, and the evolution of human intelligence. *Developmental Review*, 26: 213–242.
Bjorklund, D. F. and Green, B. L. (1992). The adaptive nature of cognitive immaturity. *American Psychologist*, 47: 46–54.
Bjorklund, D. F., and Pellegrini, A. D. (2000). Child development and evolutionary psychology. *Child Development*, 71: 1687–1708.
Bjorklund, D. F., and Pellegrini, A. D. (2002). *Evolutionary developmental psychology.* Washington, D.C.: American Psychological Association.
Blatchford, P. (1996: October). A national survey of break time in English schools. Paper presented at the annual meetings of the British Educational Research Association, Lancaster.
Blatchford, P. (1989). *Social life in school.* London: Falmer.
Blatchford, P., Baines, and Pellegrini, A. D. (2003). The social context of school playground games: Sex and ethnic differences and changes over time after entry into junior school. *British Journal of Developmental Psychology*, 21: 481–505.
Blatchford, P., and Sumpner, C. (1998). What do we know about break time? Results from a national survey of break time and lunch time in primary and secondary schools. *British Educational Research Journal*, 24: 79–94.
Bloch, M. N. (1989). Young boys' and girls' play in the home and in the community: A cultural ecological framework. In M. N. Bloch and A. D. Pellegrini (eds.), *The ecological context of children's play* (pp. 120–154). Norwood, N.J.: Ablex.
Blurton Jones, N. G. (ed.) (1972). *Ethological studies of child behaviour.* Cambridge: Cambridge University Press (a).
Blurton Jones, N. (1972). Categories of child–child interaction. In N. Blurton Jones (ed.), *Ethological studies of child behaviour* (pp. 97–129). London: Cambridge University Press (b).
Blurton, Jones, N. (1972). Characteristics of ethological studies of human behaviour. In N. Blurton Jones (ed.), *Ethological studies of child behaviour* (pp. 3–33). London: Cambridge University Press (c).
Blurton, Jones, N. (1976). Rough-and-tumble play among nursery school children. In J. Bruner, A. Jolly, and R. Sylva (eds.), *Play—Its role in development and evolution* (pp. 352–63). New York: Basic Body.

Blurton, Jones, N. (1993). The lives of hunter-gatherer children: Effects of parental behavior and parental reproductive strategy. In M. F. Pereira and L. A. Fairbanks (eds.), *Juvenile Primates: Life history, development, and behaviors* (pp. 309–326). New York: Oxford University Press.

Blurton Jones, N. G., Hawkes, K., and O'Connell, J. F. (1997). Why do Hadza children forage? In N. L. Segal, G. E. Weisfeld, and C. C. Weisfeld (eds.), *Uniting psychology and biology: Integrative perspectives on human development* (pp. 279–313). Washington, D.C.: American Psychological Association.

Bock, J. (2005). Farming, foraging, and children's play in the Okavango Delta, Botswana. In A. D. Pellegrini and P. K. Smith (eds.), *The nature of play: Great apes and humans* (pp. 254–284). New York: Guilford.

Borgerhoff Mulder, M., Richerson, P. J., Thornhill, N. W., and Voland, E. (1997). The place of behavioral ecology anthropology in evolutionary social science. In P. Weingart, S. D. Mitchell, P. J. Richerson, and S. Maasen (eds.), *Human by nature: Between biology and the social sciences* (pp. 253–282). Mahwah, N. J.: Erlbaum.

Borman, K. M., and Kurdek, L. A. (1987). Grade and gender differences in and the stability and correlates of the structural complexity of children's playground games. *International Journal of Behavioral Development*, 10: 241–251.

Bornstein, M. H., and Tamis-LeMonda, C. (1995). Parent–child symbolic play: Three theories in search of an effect. *Developmental Review*, 15: 382–400.

Bornstein. M. H. (2007). On the significance of social relationships in the development of children's earliest symbolic play: An ecological perspective. In A. Göncü and S. Gaskins (eds.), *Play and development* (pp. 101–130). Mahwah, N.J.:Erlbaum.

Boulton, M. J. (1991). Partner preference in middle school children's playful fighting and chasing. *Ethology and Sociobiology*, 22: 177–193.

Boulton, M. J. (1992). Participation in playground activities at middle school. *Educational Research*, 34: 167–182.

Boulton, M. J. (1993). Children's ability to distinguish between playful and aggressive fighting: A developmental perspective. *British Journal of Developmental Psychology*, 11: 249–263.

Boulton, M. J., and Smith, P. K. (1990). Affective bias in children's perceptions of dominance relationships. *Child Development*, 61: 221–229.

Boulton, M. J., and Smith, P. K. (1992). The social nature of play-fighting and play chasing: Mechanisms and strategies underlying cooperation and compromise. In J. H. Barkow, L. Cosmides, and J. Tooby (eds.), *The adapted mind* (pp. 429–444). New York and Oxford: Oxford University Press.

Boulton, M., and Smith, P. K. (1993). Ethnic, gender partner, and activity preferences in mixed-race children's social competence develop in the context of interacting with their peers in the U.K.: Playground observations. In C. Hart (ed.), *Children on playgrounds* (pp. 210–238). Albany, N.Y.: State University of New York Press.

Bowlby, J. (1969). *Attachment and Loss*. Vol. I: *Attachment*. New York: Basic Books.

Boyd, R., and Richerson, P. J. (1985). *Culture and the evolutionary process*. Chicago: The University of Chicago Press.

Breuer, T., Ndoundou-Hockemba, and Fishlock, V. (2005). First observations of tool use in wild gorillas. *Public Library of Science Biology*, 3: 2041–2043.

British Psychological Society Working Party (2000). *Attention Deficit/Hyperactivity Disorder: Guidelines and principles for successful multi-agency working*. Leicester, U.K.: Author.

Bronfenbrenner, U. (1973). *Two worlds of childhood: US. and USSR.* New York: Pocket Books.

Bronfenbrenner, U. (1979). *The ecology of human development.* Cambridge, Mass.: Harvard University Press.

Bronfenbrenner, U., and Ceci, S. J. (1994). Nature-nurture reconceptualized in developmental perspective: A bioecological model. *Psychological Review*, 101: 568–586.

Brownlee, A. (1954). Play in domestic cattle: An investigation into its nature. *British Veterinary Journal*, 210: 48–68.

Bruner, J. (1972). The nature and uses of immaturity. *American Psychologist*, 27: 687–708.

Bruner, J. (1986). *Actual minds, possible worlds.* Cambridge. MA.: Harvard University Press.

Bruner, J., and Bornstein, M. (1989). On interaction. In M. Bornstein and J. Bruner (eds.), *Interaction in human development* (pp. 1–16). Hillsdale, N.J.: Erlbaum.

Bruner, J. S., Jolly, A. Sylva, K. (ed.) (1975). *Play—Its role in development and evolution.* New York: Basic Books, Inc.

Bruner, J. and Sherwood, V. (1976). Peekaboo and the learning of role structures. In J. Bruner, A. Jolly, and K. Sylva (eds.), *Play—Its role in development and evolution* (pp. 277–285). New York: Basic Books.

Bukowski, W. M., Sippola, L. A., and Newcomb, A. F. (2000). Variations in patterns of attraction to same- and other-sex peers during early adolescence. *Developmental Psychology*, 36: 147–154.

Burghardt, G. M. (1973). Instinct and innate behavior: Toward an ethological psychology. In J. A. Newton and G. S. Reynolds (eds.), *The study of behavior. Learning, motivation, emotion, and instinct* (pp. 322–400). Glenview, Ill.: Scott, Foresman, and Co.

Burghardt, G. M. (1977). Ontogeny of communication. In T. A. Sebeok (ed.), *How animals communicate* (pp. 71–97). Bloomington: University of Indiana Press.

Burghardt, G. M. (1984). On the origins of play. In P. K. Smith (ed.), *Play in animals and humans* (pp. 5–42). London: Blackwell.

Burghardt, G. M. (1988). Precocity, play, and the ectotherm-endotherm transition. In E. Blass (ed.), *Handbook of behavioral neurobiology*, Vol. 9: (pp. 107–148). New York: Plenum Press.

Burghardt, G. M. (1998). Play. In G. Greenberg and M. M. Haraway (eds.), *Comparative psychology: A handbook* (pp. 725–733). New York: Garland.

Burghardt, G. M. (2001). Play: Attributes and neural substrates. In E. M. Blass (ed.), *Handbook of behavioral neurobiology*, Vol. 13: *Developmental psychobiology, developmental neurobiology and behavioral ecology: Mechanisms and early principles* (pp. 327–366). Kluwer Academic/Plenum, New York.

Burghardt, G. M. (2005). *The genesis of animal play: Testing the limits.* Cambridge, Mass.: MIT Press.

Burghardt, G. M., Layne, D. G., and Konisberg, L. (2000). The genetics of dietary experience in a restricted natural population. *Psychological Science*, 11: 69–72.

Burns, S. M. and Brainerd, G. J. (1979). Effects of constructive and dramatic play on perspective rating in very young children. *Developmental Psychology*, 15: 512–521.

Bus, A., and vanIJzendoorn, M. (1988). Mother-child interaction, attachment, and emergent literacy. *Child Development*, 59: 1262–1272.

Bus, A. G., vanIJzendoorn, M. H., and Pellegrini, A. D. (1995). Joint book reading makes for success in learning to read: A meta-analysis on inter-generational transmission of literacy. *Review of Educational Research*, 65: 1–21.

Buss, D. M. (1989). Sex differences in human mate preferences: Evolutionary hypotheses tested in 37 cultures. *Behavioral and Brain Sciences*, 12: 1–49.

Butterfield, H. (1931/1965). *The Whig interpretation of history*. New York: Norton.

Byers, J. A. (1998). The biology of human play. *Child Development*, 69: 599–600.

Byers, J. A. (1998). Biological effects of locomotor play: Getting into shape or something more specific? In M. Bekoff and J. A. Byers (eds.), *Animal play: Evolutionary, comparative, and ecological perspectives* (pp. 205–220). Cambridge: Cambridge University Press.

Byers, J. A., and Walker, C. (1995). Refining the motor training hypothesis for the evolution of play. *American Naturalist*, 146: 25–40.

Cairns, R. B. (1979). *Social development: The origins and plasticity of interchanges*. San Francisco: Freeman.

Cairns, R. (1983). The emergence of developmental psychology. In W. Kessen (ed.), *Handbook of child psychology*, Vol. 1 (p. 41–102). New York: Wiley.

Caldera, Y. M., Culp, A. M., O'Brien, M., Truglio, R., T., Alvarez, M., and Huston, C. (1999). Children's play preferences, constructive play with blocks, and visual-spatial skills: Are they related? *International Journal of Behavioral Development*, 23: 855–872.

Call, J., Bräuer, J., Kaminski, J., and Tomasello, M. (2003). Domestic dogs (Canis familiaris) are sensitive to the attentional state of humans. *Journal of Comparative Psychology*, 117: 257–263.

Campbell, A. (1999). Staying alive: Evolution, culture, and women's intrasexual aggression. *Behavioral and Brain Sciences*, 22: 203–252.

Campbell, A. (2002). *A mind of her own: The evolutionary psychology of women*. Oxford: Oxford University Press

Campbell, D. W., and Eaton, W. O. (1999). Sex differences in the activity level of infants. *Infant and Child Development*, 8: 1–17.

Carmichael, L. (ed.) (1946). *Manual of child psychology*. New York: Wiley.

Carmichael, L. (ed.) (1954). *Manual of child psychology*, 2nd ed. New York: Wiley.

Caro, T. (1988). Adaptive significance of play: Are we getting closer? *Trends in Ecology and Evolution*, 3: 50–54.

Caro, T. M. (1989). Indirect costs of play: Cheetah cubs reduce maternal hunting success. *Animal Behaviour*, 35: 295–297.

Caro, T. M. (1995). Short-term costs and correlates of play in cheetahs. *Animal Behaviour*, 49: 333–345.

Caro, T. M., and Bateson, P. (1986). Ontogeny and organization of alternative tactics. *Animal Behaviour*, 34: 1483–1499.

Carruthers, P. (2002). Human creativity: Its cognitive basis, its evolution, and its connection with childhood pretence. *British Journal of the Philosophy of Science*, 53: 225–249.

Carson, J., Burks, V., and Parke, R. (1993). Parent-child physical play: Determinants and consequences. In K. MacDonald (ed.), *Parent-child play* (pp. 197–220). Albany, N.Y.: State University of New York Press.

Caspi, A., McClay, J., Moffitt, T. E., Mill, J., Marin, J., Craig, I. W., Taylor, A., and Poulton, R. (2002). Role of genotype in the cycle of violence in maltreated children. *Science*, 297: 851–854.

Caspi, A., and Moffitt, T. E. (2006). Gene-environment interaction research, joining forces with neuroscience. *Nature Reviews Neuroscience*, 7: 583–590.

Cazden, C. B. (1975). Hypercorrection in test responses. *Theory into Practice*, 13: 343–346.

Chance, M. R. A. (1967). Attention structure as a basis for primate rank order. *Man*, 2: 503–518.

Chapman, M. (1986). The structure of exchange: Piaget's sociological theory. *Human Development*, 29: 181–194.

Charlesworth, W. (1988). Resources and resource acquisition during ontogeny. In K. MacDonald (ed.), *Sociobiological perspectives on human development* (pp. 24–77). New York: Springer-Verlag.

Charlesworth, W. R., and Dzur, C. (1987). Gender comparisons of preschoolers' behavior and resource utilization in group problem solving. *Child Development*, 58: 191–200.

Chen, Z., and Siegler, R. S. (2000). Across the great divide: Bridging the gap between understanding of toddlers' and older children's thinking. Monographs of the Society for Research in *Child Development*, 65 (Serial No. 261).

Chisholm J. S. (1996). The evolutionary ecology of attachment organization. *Human Nature*, 7: 1–37.

Chisholm, J. S., Burbank, V. K., Coall, D. A., and Gemmiti, F. (2005). Early stress: Perspectives from developmental evolutionary ecology. In B. J. Ellis and D. F. Bjorklund (eds.), *Origins of the social mind: Evolutionary psychology and child development* (pp. 76–107). New York: Guilford.

Christie, J., and Johnsen, E. P. (1983). The role of play in social-intellectual development. *Review of Educational Research*, 53: 93–115.

Christie, J. and K. Roskos (eds.) (2000), *Play and early literacy*, 2nd ed. Mahwah, N.J.: Erlbaum.

Chomsky, N. (1965). *Aspects of a theory of syntax*. Cambridge, Mass.: MIT Press.

Chomsky, N. (1975). *Reflections on language*. New York: Random House.

Choudhury, J. B. (2002). Non-parametric confidence interval estimation for competing risks analysis: Application to contraceptive data. *Statistics in Medicine*, 21: 1129–1144.

Clark, R. W. (1971). *Einstein. The life and times*. New York: Avon Books.

Clay, M. (1972). *Concepts about print*. Auckland, New Zealand: Heinemann.

Clutton-Brock, T. M. (1983). Selection in relation to sex. In D. S. Bendall (ed.), *Evolution: From molecules to men* (pp. 457–481). London: Cambridge University Press.

Cochran-Smith, M. (1984). *The making of a reader*. Norwood, N.J.: Ablex.

Coie, J. D., and Dodge, K. A. (1998). Aggression and antisocial behavior. In N. Eisenberg (ed.), *Manual of child psychology*, Vol. 3: *Social, emotional, and personality development* (pp. 779–862). New York: Wiley.

Coie, J., Dodge, K., and Coppotelli, H. (1982). Dimensions and types of social status: A cross-age perspective. *Developmental Psychology*, 18: 557–570.

Coleman, J. S. (1971). Learning through games. In E. Avedon and B. Sutton-Smith (eds.), *The study of games* (pp. 322–325). New York: Wiley.

Collaer, M. L., and Hines, M. (1995). Human behavioral sex differences: A role for gonadal hormones during early development. *Psychological Bulletin*, 118: 55–107.

Condon, R. G. (1987). *Inuit youth: Growth and change in the Canadian Arctic*. New Brunswick, N.J.: Rutgers University Press.

Connolly, J. (1980). The relationship between social pretend play and social competence in preschoolers: Correlational and experimental studies. Unpublished doctoral dissertation Concordia University, Montreal.

Connolly, K., and Dalgleish, M. (1989). The emergence of a tool-using skill in infancy. *Developmental Psychology*, 23: 894–912.

Connolly, K., and Elliott, J. (1972). The evolution and ontogeny of hand functions. In N. Blurton Jones (ed.), *Ethological studies of child behaviour* (pp. 329–384). Cambridge: Cambridge University Press.

Conradt, L. (1998). Measuring the degree of sexual segregation in group-living animals. *Journal of Animal Ecology*, 67: 217–226.

Conradt, L. (2005). Definitions, hypotheses, models, and measures in the study of animal segregation. In K. E. Ruckstuhl and P. Neuhaus (eds.), *Sexual segregation in vertebrates: Ecology of the two sexes* (pp. 11–34). Cambridge: Cambridge University Press.

Cooley, C. (1902). *Human nature and the social order.* New York: Charles Scribner.

Coplan, R. J., Gavinski-Molina, M.-H., Lagace-Seguin, D. G. and Wichmann, C. (2001). When girls versus boys play alone: Nonsocial play and adjustment in kindergarten. *Developmental Psychology,* 37: 464–474.

Coplan, R. J., and Rubin, K. H. (1998). Exploring and assessing nonsocial play in the preschool: The development and validation of the Preschool Play Behavior Scale. *Social Development,* 7: 72–91.

Corsaro, W. (1981). Entering the child's world. In J. Green and C. Wallat (eds.), *Ethnography and language in educational settings* (pp. 117–146). Norwood, N.J.: Ablex.

Corsaro, W. A. (1985). *Friendship and peer culture in the early years.* Norwood, N.J.: Ablex Publishing Co.

Cosmides, L. (1989). The logic of social exchange: Has natural selection shaped how humans reason? *Cognition,* 31: 187–276.

Cosmides, L., and Tooby, J. (1987). From evolution to behavior: Evolutionary psychology as the missing link. In J. Dupre (ed.), *The latest on the best: Essays on evolution and optimality* (pp. 277–306). Cambridge, Mass.: MIT Press.

Cosmides, L., and Tooby, J. (1992). Cognitive adaptations for social exchange. In J. H. Barkow, L. Cosmides, and J. Tooby (eds.), *The adapted mind: Evolutionary psychology and the generation of culture* (pp. 163–228). New York: Oxford University Press.

Costabile, A., Smith, P. K., Matheon, L., Aston, J., Hunter, T., and Boulton, M. J. (1991). A cross-national comparison of how children distinguish serious and playful fighting. *Developmental Psychology,* 27: 881–887.

Council on Physical Education for Children (2001). Recess in elementary schools: A position paper from the National Association for Sport and Physical Education. Retrieved September 28, 2000, from http://eric.ed.uiuc.edu/naecs/position/recess play/html.

Cronbach, L. J. (1971). Validity. In R. L. Thorndike (ed.), *Educational measurement* (pp. 443–507). Washington, D.C.: American Council on Education.

Cronk, L. (1991). Human behavioral ecology. *Annual Review of Anthropology,* 20: 25–53.

Crook, J. H. (1970). Social organization and the environment: Aspects of contemporary social ethology. *Animal Behaviour,* 18: 197–209.

Crook, J. H. (1989). Introduction: Socioecological paradigms, evolution and history: Perspectives for the 1990s. In V. S. Standen and R. A. Foley (ed.), *Comparative socioecology: The behavioural ecology of humans and other mammals* (pp. 1–36). Oxford: Blackwell Scientific.

Cross, G., and Walton, J. (2005). *The playful crowd.* New York: Columbia University Press.

Cross, G. (1997). *Kids' stuff: Toys and the changing world of American childhood.* Cambridge: Harvard University Press.

Cross, G. (2004). *The cute and the cool: Wondrous innocence and modern American children's culture.* New York: Oxford University Press.

Cullumbine, H. (1950). Heat production and energy requirements of tropical people. *Journal of Applied Physiology,* 2: 201–210.

Cummings, C. R., Goulding, D., and Bagley, G. (1969). Failure of school physical education to improve cardio-respiratory fitness. *Canadian Medical Association Journal,* 101: 69–73.

Daiute, C. (1990). The role of play in writing development. *Research in the Teaching of English*, 24: 4–7.

Daly, M., and Wilson, M. (1983). *Sex, evolution, and behavior*, 2nd ed. Boston: William Grant.

Dansky, J. (1980). Make-believe: A mediator of the relationship between play and associative fluency. *Child Development*, 51: 576–579.

Dansky, J., and Silverman, I. W. (1973). Effects of play on associative fluency in preschool-age children. *Developmental Psychology*, 9: 38–43.

Dansky, J., and Silverman, I. W. (1975). Play: A general facilitator of associative fluency. *Developmental Psychology*, 11: 104.

Darwin, C. (1859/1958). *The origin of species: By means of natural selection of the preservation of favoured races in the struggle for life*. New York: New American Library.

Darwin, C. (1859/2006). *The origin of species: By means of natural selection of the preservation of favoured races in the struggle for life*. Mineola, New York: Dover Publications, Inc.

Darwin, C. (1871). *The descent of man, and selection in relation to sex*. London: John Murray.

Darwin, C. (1877). Biographical sketch of an infant. *Mind*, 2: 285–294.

Dawkins, R. (1976). *The selfish gene*. New York: Oxford University Press.

Dawkins, R. (1982). *The blind watchmaker*. Essex, England: Longman.

Dempster, F. (1988). The spacing effect. *American Psychologist*, 43: 627–634.

de Waal, F. B. M. (1985). The integration of dominance and social bonding in primates. *Quarterly Review of Biology*, 62: 459–479.

de Waal, F., and Lanting, F. (1997). *Bonobo: The forgotten ape*. Berkeley: University of California Press.

Dewey, J. (1938/1963). *Experience and education*. New York: Collier.

Dias, M., and Harris, P. L. (1988). The effect of make-believe play on deductive reasoning. *British Journal of Developmental Psychology*, 6: 207–221.

Dias, M., and Harris, P. L. (1990). The influence of imagination on reasoning by young children. *British Journal of Developmental Psychology*, 8: 305–318.

Dickinson, D., and Moreton, J. (1991: April). Predicting specific kindergarten literacy skills from three-year-olds' preschool experiences. Paper presented at the biennial meeting of the Society for Research in *Child Development*, Seattle.

DiPietro, J. A. (1981). Rough-and-tumble play: A function of gender. *Developmental Psychology*, 17: 50–58.

Dodge, K. A., and Coie, J. D. (1987). Social information processing factors in reactive and proactive aggression in children's peer groups. *Journal of Personality and Social Psychology*, 53: 1146–1158.

Draper, P. (1972). Social and economic constraints on child life among the !Kung. In R. B. Lee and I. De Vore, I. (eds.) (1976), *Kalahari hunter-gathers* (pp. 199–217). Cambridge, Mass.: Harvard University Press.

Dunbar, R. I. M. (1988). *Primate social systems*. Ithaca, N.Y.: Cornell University Press.

Dunn, J. (1988). *The beginnings of social understanding*. Cambridge, Mass.: Harvard.

Dunn, J., and Kendrick, C. (1982). *Siblings*. Cambridge: Harvard.

Dyson, A. (1983). The role of oral language in early writing processes. *Research in the Teaching of English*, 17: 1–30.

Eagly, A. H. (1987). *Sex differences in social behavior: A social-role interpretation*. Hillsdale, N.J.: Erlbaum.

Eagly, E. A. (1997). Sex differences in social behavior: Comparing social role theory and evolutionary psychology. *American Psychologist*, 52: 1380–1383.

Easterbrook, J. A. (1959). The effect of emotion on cue utilization and the organization of behavior. *Psychological Review*, 66: 183–201.

Eaton, W. C., and Enns, L. R. (1986). Sex differences in human motor activity level. *Psychological Bulletin*, 100: 19–28.

Eaton, W. C., and Keats, J. G. (1982). Peer presence, stress, and sex differences in motor activity of preschoolers. *Developmental Psychology*, 18: 534–540.

Eaton, W. C., and Yu, A, P. (1989). Are sex differences in child motor activity level a function of sex differences in maturational status? *Child Development*, 60: 1005–1011.

Ebbinghaus, H. (1885/1964). *Memory*. New York: Teachers College Press.

Eccles, J. S., Wigfield, A., and Schiefele, U. (1998), Motivation to succeed. In N. Eisenberg (ed.), *Handbook of child psychology*, Vol. 3 (pp. 1017–1096). New York: Wiley.

Eccles, J. S., and Roeser, R. W. (2005). School and community influences on human development. In M. H. Bornstein and M. E. Lamb, M. E. (eds.), *Developmental science: An advanced textbook* (pp. 513–555). Mahwah, N.J.: Lawrence Erlbaum Associates.

Ehrhardt, A. A. (1984). Gender differences: A biosocial perspective. In A. Sondergegger (ed.), *Nebraska symposium on motivation* (pp. 33–50). Lincoln: University of Nebraska Press.

Eibl-Eibesfeldt, I. (1989). *Human ethology*. New York: Aldine de Gruyter.

Eifermann, R. (1970). Cooperativeness and egalitarianism in kibbutz children's games. *Human Relations*, 23: 579–587.

Eiferman, R. (1971). Social play in childhood. In R. Herron and B. Sutton-Smith (eds.), *Child's play*. New York: Wiley.

Eiferman, R. (1973). Rules in games. In A. Elithorn and D. Jones (eds.), *Artificial and human thinking* (pp. 147–161). San Francisco: Jossey Bass.

Eiferman, R. (1978). Games of physical activity. In F. Landry and W. Orban (eds.), *Physical activity and human well-being* (pp. 741–751). Miami, Fla.: Symposium Specialists.

Eiferman, R. (1979). It's child's play. In L. Shears and E. Bower (eds.), *Games in education and development* (pp. 75–102). Springfield, Ill.: Thomas.

Einon, D., Morgan, M., and Kibbler, C. (1978). Brief periods of socialization and later behavior in the rat. *Developmental Psychobiology*, 11: 213–224.

Eisenberg, N. (ed.) (1998). *Manual of child psychology*, Vol. 3: *Social, emotional, and personality development*. New York: Wiley.

Eisenberg, N. (ed.) (2006). *Handbook of child psychology*, Vol. 3: *Social, emotional, and personality development*. New York: Wiley.

Ellis, B. J., and Garber, J. (2000). Psychosocial antecedents of variation in girls' pubertal timing: Maternal depression, stepfather presence, and marital and family stress. *Child Development*, 71: 485–501.

Ellis, S., Rogoff, B. (1986). Problem solving in children's management of instruction. In E. Mueller and C. Cooper (eds.), *Process and outcome in peer relationships* (pp. 301–325). Orlando, Fla.: Academic Press.

Englund, M. M., Levy, A. K., Hyson, D. M., and Sroufe, L. A. (2000). Adolescent social competence: Effectiveness in group settings. *Child Development*, 71: 1049–1060.

Erckmann, W. W. (1983). The evolution of polyandry in shorebirds: An evaluation of hypotheses. In S. K. Wasser (ed.), *Social behavior of female vertebrates* (pp. 113–168). New York: Academic Press.

Erickson, E. H. (1950). *Childhood and society*. New York: Norton.

Erickson, E. H. (1977). *Toys and reason*. New York: Norton.

Erickson, F. (1986). Qualitative methods in research on teaching. M. Wittrock (ed.), *Handbook of research on teaching* (pp. 119–161), New York: Macmillan.

Evans, J., and Pellegrini, A. D. (1997). Surplus Energy theory: An endearing but inadequate justification for break time. *Educational Review*, 49: 229–236.

Fabes, R. A. (1994). Physiological, emotional, and behavioral correlates of gender segregation. In C. Leaper (ed.), *Childhood gender segregation: Causes and consequences* (pp. 19–34). San Francisco: Jossey-Bass.

Fabes, R. A., Martin, C. L., and Hanish, L. D. (2003). Young children's play qualities in same-, other-, and mixed-sex peer groups. *Child Development*, 74: 921–932.

Fabes, R. A., Martin, C. L., Hanish, L. D., Anders, M. C., and Madden-Derdich, D. A. (2003). Early school competence: The roles of sex-segregated play and effort control. *Developmental Psychology*, 39: 848–858.

Fagen, R. (1976). Exercise, play, and physical training in mammals. In P. P. G. Bateson and P. H. Klopfer (eds.), *Perspectives in ethology* Vol. 2: (pp. 189–219). London: Plenum.

Fagen, R. (1981). *Animal play behavior*. New York: Oxford University Press.

Fagot, B. I. (1974). Sex differences in toddlers' behavior and parental reaction. *Developmental Psychology*, 10: 554–558.

Fagot, B. I. (1994). Peer relations and the development of competence in boys and girls. In C. Leaper (ed.), *Childhood gender segregation: Causes and consequences* (pp. 53–66). San Francisco: Jossey-Bass.

Fein, G. G. (1975). A transformation analysis of pretending. *Development Psychology*, 11: 291–296.

Fein, G. (1979). Echoes from the nursery: Piaget, Vygotsky, and the relationship between language and play. In E. Winner and H. Gardner (eds.), *Fact, fiction, and fantasy in childhood* (pp. 1–14). San Francisco: Jossey-Bass.

Fein, G. G. (1981). Pretend play in childhood: An integrative review. *Child Development*, 52: 1095–1118.

Fein, G. G., and Apfel, N. (1979). The development of play: Style, structure, and situation. *Genetic Psychology Monographs*, 99: 231–250.

Fein, G. G., and Fryer, M. G. (1995). Maternal contributions to early symbolic play competence. *Developmental Review*, 15: 367–381.

Fein, G. G., and Fryer, M. G. (1995). When theories don't work, chuck 'em or change 'em. *Developmental Review*, 15: 401–4013.

Fein, G. G., and Stork, L. (1981). Social class effects in integrated preschool classrooms. *Journal of Applied Developmental Psychology*, 2: 267–279.

Fernald, A., and O'Neill, D. K. (1993). Peekaboo across cultures: How mothers and infants play with voices, faces, and expectations. In K. MacDonald (ed.), *Parent–child play* (pp. 259–286). Albany, N.Y.: State University of New York Press.

Field, T. M. (1994). Infant day care facilitates later social behavior and school performance. In E. V. Jacobs and H. Goelman (eds.), *Children's play in child care settings* (pp. 69–84). Albany, N.Y.: State University of New York Press.

Field, T. M., Ting, G., and Shuman, H. H. (1979). The onset of rhythmic activities in normal and high-risk infants. *Developmental Psychobiology*, 12: 97–100.

Fine, G. A. (1981). Friends, impression management, and preadolescent behavior. In S. R. Asher and J. M. Gottman (eds.), *The development of children's friendships* (pp. 29–52). New York: Cambridge University Press.

Fine, G. A. (1987). *With the boys: Little League baseball and preadolescent culture*. Chicago: University of Chicago Press.

Finnan, C. (1982). The ethnography of children's spontaneous play. In G. Spindler (ed.), *Doing the ethnography of schooling* (pp. 355–381). New York: Holt, Rinehart and Winston.

Francis, R. C. (1988). On the relationship between aggression and dominance. *Ethology*, 78: 223–237.

Fischer, K. (1980). A theory of cognitive development. *Psychological Review*, 87: 477–531

Freud, S. (1940). *An outline of psychoanalysis*. New York: Norton.

Fromberg, D., and D. Bergin, D. (eds.) (2006). *Play: From birth through twelve: Contexts, perspectives, and meanings*, 2nd ed. New York: Garland.

Frost, J., and Sanderlin, S. (eds.) (1985). *When children play*. Wheaton, Md.: Association for Childhood Education International.

Fry, D. P. (1987). Difference between play fighting and serious fighting among Zapotec children. *Ethology and Sociobiology*, 8: 285–306.

Fry, D. P. (2005). Rough-and-tumble social play in children. In A. D. Pellegrini and P. K. Smith (eds.), *The nature of play: Great apes and humans* (pp. 54–88). New York: Guilford.

Galda, L. (1984). Narrative competence: Play, storytelling and comprehension. In A. Pellegrini and T. Yawkey, *The development of oral and written language in social context* (pp. 105–119). Norwood, N.J.: Ablex.

Galda, L., and Pellegrini, A. D. (eds.) (1985). *Play, language, and stories: The development of children's literate behavior*. Norwood, N.J.: Ablex.

Gardner, H. (1980). Children's literacy development. In P. McGhee and A. Chapman (eds.), *Children's humor*. Chichester, U.K.: Wiley.

Gardner, R. A., and Gardner, B. T. (1969). Teaching sign language to a chimpanzee. *Science*, 165: 664–672.

Garvey, C. (1987: April). Creation and avoidance of conflict in preschool children's play. Paper presented at the biennial meeting of the Society for Research in *Child Development*, Toronto.

Garvey, C. (1989). The language of social pretend. *Merrill-Palmer Quarterly*, 9: 364–382.

Garvey, C. (1990). *Play*, 2nd ed. Cambridge, Mass.: Harvard University Press.

Geertz, C. (1972). Deep play: Notes on the Balinese cockfight. *Daedalus*, 101: 1–38.

Ginsberg, H. (2005). Mathematical play and playful mathematics: A guide for early educators. In D. Singer, R. M., Golinkoff, and K. Hirsh-Pasek (eds.), *Play = Learning* (pp. 145–168). New York: Oxford University Press.

Gomendio, M. (1988). The development of different types of play in gazelles: Implications for the nature and functions of play. *Animal Behaviour*, 36: 825–836.

Gómez, J-C., and Martín-Andrade, B. (2005). Fantasy play in apes. In A. D. Pellegrini and P. K. Smith (eds.), *The nature of play: Great apes and humans* (pp. 139–172). New York: Guilford.

Goodwin, M. (1990). *He-said she-said: Talk as social organization among black children*. Bloomington: Indiana University Press.

Gosso, Y., Otta, E., Morais, M., Ribeiro, F. Bussabb, V. (2005). Play in hunter-gatherer society. In A. D. Pellegrini and P. K. Smith (eds.), *Play in great apes and humans* (pp. 213–253). New York: Guilford.

Gottlieb, G. (1976). The roles of experience in the development of behavior and the nervous system. In G. Gottlieb (ed.), *Neural and behavioral plasticity* (pp. 24–54). New York: Academic Press.

Gottlieb, G. (1997). *Synthesizing nature-nurture: Prenatal roots of instinctive behavior*. Mahwah, N.J.: Erlbaum.

Gottlieb, G. (1998). Normally occurring environmental and behavioral influences on gene activity: From central dogma to probabilistic epigenesis. *Psychological Review*, 105: 792–802.

Gottlieb, G. (2003). On making behavioral genetics truly developmental. *Human Development*, 46: 337–355.

Gould, S. J. (1988). Irrelevance, submission, and partnership: The changing role of palaeontology in Darwin's three centennials, and a modest proposal for macroevolution. In D. Bennell (ed.), *Evolution: From molecules to man* (pp. 347–366). London: Cambridge University Press.

Grass, G. (1999). *My century*. New York: Harcourt.

Grass, G. (2006). *Peeling the onion: A memoir*. New York: Harcourt.

Gredlein, J., Bjorklund, D. F., and Hickling, A. (April, 2003). Play styles and problem-solving in preschool children. Paper presented at meeting of the Society for Research in *Child Development*, Tampa, Fla.

Greenfield. P. M., and Suzuki, L. K. (1998).Culture and human development: Implications for parenting, education, pediatrics, and mental health. In I. E. Sigel and K. A. Renninger (eds.), *Handbook of child psychology*, Vol. 4: *Child psychology in practice* (pp. 1059–1109). New York: Wiley.

Groos, K. (1898). *The play of animals*. New York: Appleton.

Groos, K. (1901). *The play of man*. London: Heinemann.

Gump, P. V., and Sutton-Smith, B. (1955). The "It" role in children's games. *The Group*, 17: 3–8.

Gunter, K. B., Baxter-Jones, A. D. G., Mirwald, R. L., Almstedt, H., Fuchs, R. K., Durski, S., and Snow, C. (2008). Impact exercise increases BMC during growth: An eight-year longitudinal study. *Journal of Bone and Mineral Research*, 10: 1359.

Guttman, M., and Frederiksen, C. (1985). Preschool children's narratives: Linking story comprehension, production, and play discourse. In L. Galda and A. Pellegrini (eds.), *Play, language, and stories* (pp. 99–128). Norwood, N.J.: Ablex.

Haight, W. L., and Miller, P. J. (1993). *Pretending at home*. Albany, N. Y.: State University of New York Press.

Hall, G. S. (1904). *Adolescence: Its psychology and its relation to physiology, anthropology, sociology, sex, crime, religion, and education*, Vols. 1–2. New York: Appleton.

Hall, G. S. (1916). *Adolescence*. New York: Appleton.

Halliday, M. A. K. (1969–1970). Relevant models of language. *Educational Review*, 22: 26–37.

Halliday, M. A. K. (1978). *Language as a social semiotic*. Baltimore: University Park Press.

Halliday, M. A. K, and Hasan, R. (1976). *Cohesion in English*. Longman: London.

Hallock, M. B., and Worobey, J. (1984). Cognitive development in chimpanzee infants (Pan troglodytes). *Journal of Human Evolution*, 13: 441–447.

Hamilton, W. D. (1964). The genetical theory of social behavior. *Journal of Theoretical Biology*, 7: 1–52.

Hare, B., Brown, M., Williamson, C., and Tomasello, M. (2002). The domestication of social cognition in dogs. *Science*, 298: 1634–1636.

Hare, B., Call, J., and Tomasello, M. (2001). Do chimpanzees know what conspecifics know? *Animal Behaviour*, 61: 139–151.

Hare, B., Call, J, and Tomasello, M. (2005). Human-like social skills in dogs? *Trends in Cognitive Science*, 9: 439–444.

Harkness, S. (2002). Culture and social development: Explanations and evidence. In P. K. Smith and C. H. Hart (eds.), *Blackwell handbook of social development* (pp. 60–77). Oxford: Blackwell.

Harlow, H. (1962). The heterosexual affection system in monkeys. *American Psychologist*, 17: 1–9.

Harlow, H., and Harlow, M. (1965). The affectional systems. *Behavior of Non-Human Primates*, 2: 287–334.

Harper, L. V. (2005). Epigenetic inheritance and the intergeneration transfer of experience. *Psychological Bulletin*, 131: 340–360.

Harper, L. V., and Huie, K. (1978). The development of sex differences in human behavior: Cultural impositions, or a convergence of evolved responses, tendencies, and cultural adaptations? In G. M. Burghardt and M. Bekoff (eds.), *The development of behavior: Comparative and evolutionary aspects* (pp. 297–318). New York: Garland STPM.

Harper, L. V., Sanders, K. (1975). Preschool children's use of space: Sex differences in outdoor play. *Developmental Psychology*, 11: 119.

Harris, P. L. (1990). The work of the imagination. In A. Whiten (ed.), *The emergence of mind-reading* (pp. 283–304). Oxford, U.K.: Blackwell.

Harris, P. L. (1991: March). Natural simulation of mental states. Paper presented in the symposium "Developmental Processes Underlying the Acquisition of Concepts of Mind," at the biennial meeting of the Society for Research in *Child Development*, Seattle.

Harris, P. L. (2007). Hard work for the imagination. In A. Gönçü and S. Haskins (eds.), *Play and development: Evolutionary, sociocultural and functional perspectives*. Mahwah, N.J.: Lawrence Erlbaum Associates.

Hart, C. (1993). Children on playgrounds: Applying current knowledge to future practice and inquiry. In C. Hart (ed.), *Children on playgrounds* (pp. 418–432). Albany, N.Y.: SUNY Press.

Hartup, W. W. (1983). Peer relations. In E. M. Hetherington (ed.), P. H. Mussen (Series ed.), *Handbook of child psychology*, Vol. 4: *Socialization, personality, and social development* (pp. 103–196). New York: Wiley.

Hartup, W. W. (1996). The company they keep: Friendships and their developmental significance. *Child Development*, 67: 1–13.

Hartup, W. W., Laursen, B., Stewart, M. I., and Eastenson, A. (1988). Conflict and friendship relations of young children. *Child Development*, 59: 1590–1600.

Havighurst, R. J. (1972). *Developmental tasks and education*. New York: Longmans.

Hayes, C. (1951). *The ape in our house*. New York: Harper.

Heath, S. (1983). *Ways with words*. New York: Cambridge University Press.

Heath, S. B. (with Hey-Kyeong Chin). (1985). Narrative play in second language learning. In L. Galda and A. Pellegrini (eds.), *Play language, and story: The development of children's literature* behavior. Norwood, N.J.: Ablex.

Henderson, B. B., and Moore, S., G. (1979). Measuring exploratory behavior in young children: A factor analytical study. *Developmental Psychology*, 15: 113–119.

Henig, R. M. (2008). Taking play seriously. New York Times Magazine, 17 February, http://www.nytimes.com/2008/02/17/magazine/17play.html. Accessed 24 March 2008.

Hetherington, E. M. (ed.) (1983), *Handbook of child psychology*, Vol. IV: *Socialization, personality and social development*. New York: Wiley.

Heyes, C. (2003). Four routes to cognitive evolution. *Psychological Review*, 110: 713–727.

Hill, C. (1971). *Antichrist in seventeenth-century England*. Oxford: Oxford University Press.

Hinde, R. A. (1974). *Biological basis of human social behavior*. New York: Academic.

Hinde, R. A. (1975). The concept of function. In C. Baerends, C. Beers, and A. Manning (eds.), *Function and evolution in behavior* (pp. 3–15). Oxford: Clarendon.

Hinde, R. A. (1978). Dominance and role. Two concepts with two meanings. *Journal of Social Biology Structure*, 1: 27–38.

Hinde, R. A. (1980). *Ethology*. London: Fontana.

Hinde, R. A. (1983). Ethology and child development. In J. J. Campos and M. H. Haith (eds.), *Handbook of child psychology: Infancy and developmental psychobiology*, Vol. 2 (pp. 27–94). New York: Wiley.

Hinde, R. A. (1999). Causes of social development from the perspective of an integrated developmental science. In G. Butterworth and P. Bryant, P. (eds.), *Causes of development* (pp. 161–185). London: Harvester Wheatsheaf.

Hines, M. (1982). Prenatal gonadal hormones and sex differences in human behavior. *Psychological Bulletin*, 92: 56–80.

Hines, M., Fane, B. A., Pasterski, V. L., Mathews, G. A., Conway, G. S., and Brooks, C. (2003). Spatial abilities following prenatal androgen abnormality: Targeting and mental rotations performance in individuals with congenital adrenal hyperplasia. *Psychoneuroendocrinology*, 23: 1010–1026.

Hines, M., and Kaufman, F. R. (1994). Androgens and the development of human sex-typical behavior: Rough-and-tumble play and sex of preferred playmates in children with Congenital Adrenal Hyperplasia (CAH). *Child Development*, 65: 1042–1053.

Hines, M., and Shipley, C. (1984). Prenatal exposure to Diethylstilbestrol (DES) and the development of sexually dimorphic cognitive abilities and cerebral lateralization. *Developmental Psychology*, 20: 81–94.

Hodges, E. V., and Perry, D. G. (1999). Personal and interpersonal antecedents of victimization by peers. *Journal of Personality and Social Psychology*, 76: 677–685.

Hovell, M. F., Bursick, J. H., Shockley, R., and McClure, J. (1976). An evaluation of elementary students' voluntary physical activity during recess. *Research Quarterly in Exercise Sports*, 49: 460–474.

Howes, C. (1993). *The collaborative construction of pretense*. Albany, N.Y.: State University of New York Press.

Hughes, T. (1895). *Tom Brown's school days*. Cambridge, U.K.: The Riverside Press.

Humphrey, N. (1976). The social function of intellect. In P. P. G. Bateson and R. A. Hinde (eds.), *Growing points in ethology* (pp. 303–317). Cambridge: Cambridge University Press.

Humphreys, A. P., and Smith, P. K. (1984). Rough-and-tumble play in preschool and playground. In P. K. Smith (ed.), *Play in animals and humans* (pp. 241–270). Oxford: Blackwell.

Humphreys, A. P., and Smith, P. K. (1987). Rough-and-tumble play, friendship, and dominance in school children: Evidence for continuity and change with age. *Child Development*, 58: 201–212.

Huston, A. (1983). Sex typing. In E. M. Hetherington (ed.), *Handbook of child psychology: Socialization, personality, and social development*, Vol. 4 (pp. 387–468). New York: Wiley.

Hutt, C. (1966). Exploration and play in children. Symposia of the Zoological Society of London, 18: 61–81.

Huxley, J. S. (1942). *Evolution: The modern synthesis*. London: Allen and Unwin.

Hymes, D. (1980a). Qualitative/quantitative research methodologies in education: A linguistic approach. In D. Hymes (ed.), *Language in education: Ethnolinguistic essays* (pp. 62–87). Washington, D.C: Center for Applied Linguistics.

Hymes, D. (1980b). What is ethnography? In D. Hymes (ed.), *Language in education: Ethnolinguistic essays* (pp. 88–103). Washington, D.C.: Center for Applied Linguistics.

Institute for Play: http://www.nifplay.org/about_us.html. Accessed 24 March 2008.

Jacklin, C. N., DiPietro, J. A., and Maccoby, E. E. (1984). Sex-typing behavior and sex-typing pressure in child/parent interaction. *Archives of Sexual Behavior*, 13: 413–425.

James, W. (1901). *Talks to teachers on psychology: And to students on some of life's ideals*. New York: Holt.

Jamison, D. T. and colleagues (eds.) (2006). *Disease and mortality in Sub-Saharan Africa*. New York: World Bank Publications.

Janikas, K. (1993). Hand clapping games: Rhythmic recordings of girlhood socialization. Newsletter of the Laboratory of Comparative Human Cognition, 15: 97–102.

Jarrold, C., Carruthers, P., Smith, P. K., and Boucher, J. (1994). Pretend play: Is it metarepresentational? *Mind and Language*, 9: 445–468.

Jenni, D. A. (1974). Evolution of polyandry in birds. *American Zoologist*, 14: 129–144.

Jensvold. M. L. A., and Fouts, R. S. (1993). Imaginary play in chimpanzees (Pan troglodytes). *Human Evolution*, 8: 217–227.

Johnson, J. E. (1976). Relations of divergent thinking and intelligence test scores with social and nonsocial make-believe play of preschool children. *Child Development*, 47: 1200–1203.

Johnson, J. E., Christie, J., and Yawkey, T. (1999). *Play and early childhood development*. New York: Longman.

Johnson, J. E., and Ershler, J. (1981). Developmental trends in preschool play as a function of classroom program and child gender. *Child Development*, 52: 995–1004.

Johnson, J. E., Ershler, J., and Bell, C. (1980). Play behavior in a discovery-based and a formal education preschool program. *Child Development*, 51: 271–274.

Johnson, W., McGue, M., and Iacano, W. G. (2005). Disruptive behavior and school grades: Genetic and environmental relations in 11-year-olds. *Journal of Educational Psychology*, 97: 391–405.

Jolly, A. (1966). Lemur social behavior and primate intelligence. *Science*, 153: 501–506.

Kagan, J. (1971). *Change and continuity in infancy*. New York: Wiley.

Kamii, C., and DeVries, R. (1978). *Physical knowledge in preschool education*. Englewood Cliffs, N.J.: Prentice-Hall.

Kamii, C., and Kato, Y. (2005). Fostering the development of logico-mathematical thinking in card game at age 5–6. *Early Education and Development*, 16: 376–383.

Kandel, D. (1978). Homophily, selection, and socialization in adolescent friendships. *American Journal of Sociology*, 84: 427–436.

Karmiloff-Smith, A. (1992). *Beyond modularity: A developmental perspective on cognitive science*. Cambridge, Mass.: MIT Press.

Karmiloff-Smith, A. (1998). Development itself is the key to understanding developmental disorders. *Trends in Cognitive Science*, 2: 389–398.

Kessen, W. (1965). *The child*. New York: Wiley.

Kessen, W. (ed.) (1975). *Childhood in China*. New Haven: Yale University Press.

Kohlberg, L., and Mayer, R. (1972). Development as an aim of education. *Harvard Educational Review*, 42: 449–496.

Köhler, W. (1925). *The mentality of apes*. New York: Harcourt Brace.

Konner, M. J. (1972). Aspects of the developmental ethology of a foraging people. In N. Blurton Jones (ed.), *Ethological studies of child behaviour* (pp. 285–304). London: Cambridge University Press.

Konner, M. J. (2005). Hunter-gatherer infancy and childhood: The ! Kung and others. In B. S. Hewlett and M. E. Lamb (eds.), *Hunter-gatherer childhoods: Evolutionary, developmental, and cultural perspectives* (19–64). New Brunswick, N.J.: Aldine Transaction.

Krasnor, L., and Pepler, D. (1980). The study of children's play. In K. Rubin (ed.), *Children's play* (pp. 85–95). San Francisco: Jossey-Bass.

Krebs, J. R. and Davies, N. B. (1993). *An introduction to behavioural ecology.* Oxford: Blackwell.

Krebs, J. R. and Davies, N. B. (eds.) (1997). *Behavioural ecology: An evolutionary approach.* 7th ed. Oxford, Blackwell Science.

Kuhn, D., and Siegler, R. S. (eds.) (2006), *Handbook of child psychology*, Vol. 2: *Cognition, perception, and language.* New York: Wiley.

Laboratory of Comparative Human Cognition. (1983). Culture and cognitive development. In J. Campos and M. Haith (eds.), *Handbook of child psychology*, Vol. 1 (pp. 295–352). New York: Wiley.

Ladd, G. (1983). Social networks of popular, average, and rejected children in school settings. *Merrill-Palmer Quarterly*, 29: 283–308.

Ladd, G. W., Kochenderfer, B. J., and Coleman, C. C. (1996). Friendship quality as a predictor of young children's early school adjustment. *Child Development*, 67: 1103–1118.

Ladd, G. W., and Price, J. M. (1987). Predicting children's social and school adjustment following the transition from preschool to kindergarten. *Child Development*, 58: 1168–1189.

Ladd, G. W., and Profilet, S. M. (1996). The Child Behavior Scale: A teacher-report measure of young children's aggressive, withdrawn, and prosocial behaviors. *Developmental Psychology*, 32: 1008–1024.

Lagault, F., and Strayer, F. F. (1990). The emergence of gender-segregation in pre-school peer groups. In F. F. Strayer (ed.), *Social interaction and behavioral development during early childhood* (pp. 73–76). Montreal: La Maison d'Ethologie de Montreal.

Laland, K. N., and Brown, G. R. (2002). *Sense and nonsense: Evolutionary perspectives on human behaviour.* Oxford: Oxford University Press.

Lamb, S., and Coakley, M. (1993). "Normal" childhood sexual play and games: Differentiating play from abuse. *Child Abuse and Neglect*, 17: 515–526.

Lancaster, J. B., and Lancaster, C. S. (1983). Parental investment: The hominid adaptation. In D. J. Ortner (ed.), *How humans adapt: A biocultural odyssey* (pp. 33–56). Washington, D.C.: Smithsonian Institution Press.

Lancy, D. F. (1996). *Playing on the mother-ground.* New York: Guilford.

Lancy, D. F. (2007). Accounting for variability in mother–child play. *American Anthropologist*, 109: 273–284.

Lancy, D. F. (In press). *The anthropology of childhood: Cherubs, chattel, changelings.* New York; Cambridge University Press.

Laursen, B., and Hartup, W. W. (1989). The dynamics of preschool children's conflicts. *Merrill-Palmer Quarterly*, 35: 281–297.

Lazarus, M. (1883). *Die reize des spiels.* Berlin: Ferd, Dummlers, Verlagbuchhandlung.

Lee, R. B. (1979). *The !Kung San.* Cambridge: Cambridge University Press.

Lerner, R. M. (ed.) (2006). *Handbook of child psychology*, Vol. 1: *Theoretical models of human development.* New York: Wiley.

Leslie, A. M. (1987). Pretense and representation: Origins of "theory of mind." *Psychological Review*, 94: 412–426.

Lessells, C. M. (1991). The evolution of life histories. In J. R. Krebs and N. B. Davies (eds.), *Behavioural ecology: An evolutionary approach*. 3rd ed. (pp. 32–68). Oxford, Blackwell Science.

Lever, J. (1976). Sex differences in the games children play. *Social Problems*, 23: 479–487.

LeVine, R. A., and LeVine, B. B. (1966). *Nyansongo: A Gusii community in Kenya*. New York: Wiley.

Lewis, K. P. (2000). A comparative study of primate play behaviour: Implications for the study of cognition. *Folia Primatologica*, 71: 417–421.

Lewis, K. P. (2005). Social play in great apes. In A. D. Pellegrini and P. K. Smith (eds.), *The nature of play: Great apes and humans* (pp. 27–53). New York: Guilford.

Lewis, K. P., and Barton, R. A. (2005). Playing for keeps: Evolutionary relationships between social play and the cerebellum in nonhuman primates. *Human Nature*, 15: 5–21.

Lewis, K. P., and Barton, R. A. (2006). Amygdala size and hypothalamus size predict social play frequency in nonhuman primates: A comparative analysis using independent contrasts. *Journal of Comparative Psychology*, 120: 31–37.

Lickliter, R., and Honeycutt, H. (2003). Developmental dynamics: Toward a biologically plausible evolutionary psychology. *Psychological Bulletin*, 129: 819–835.

Liddell, C., Kvalsvig, J., Strydom, N., Qotyana, P., and Shabalala, A. (1993). An observational study of 5-year-old South African children in the year before school. *International Journal of Behavioral Development*, 16: 537–561.

Lillard, A. S. (1993). Pretend play skills and the child's theory of mind. *Child Development*, 64: 348–371.

Lillard, A. S. (1993). Young children's conceptualization of pretense: Action or mental representational state. *Child Development*, 64: 372–386.

Lillard, A. S. (1994). Making sense of pretense. In C. Lewis and P. Mitchell (eds.), *Children's early understanding of mind* (pp. 211–234). Mahwah, N.J.: Erlbaum.

Lillard, A. S. (1997). Other folks' theories of mind. *Psychological Science*, 8: 271–274.

Lillard, A. S. (1998). Ethnopsychologies: Cultural variations in theories of mind. *Psychological Bulletin*, 123: 3–32.

Lillard, A. S. (2002). Pretend play as Twin Earth: A social-cognitive analysis. *Developmental Review*, 22: 1–37.

Lillard, A. S. (2006). Guided participation: How mothers structure and children understand pretend play. In A. Göncü and S. Gaskins (eds.), *Play and development* (pp. 131–154). Mahwah, N.J.: Erlbaum.

Lillard, A. S., Nishida, T., Massaro, D., Vaish, A., and Ma, L. (2007). Signs of pretense across age and scenario. *Infancy*, 11: 1–30.

Lillard, A. S., and Sorensen, L. (no date). Evidence for the persistence of pretend play into middle childhood. Unpublished distinguished major's thesis, University of Virginia.

Lloyd Morgan, C. (1896). On modification and variation. *Science*, 5: 139–155.

Loizos, C. (1967). Play behavior in higher primates: A review. In Morris, D. (ed.), *Primate ethology* (pp. 176–218). Chicago: Aldine.

Loizos, C. (1969). An ethological study of chimpanzee play. *Proceedings of the Second International Congress of Primatology*, Vol. I (pp. 87–93). New York: Karger.

Lorenz, K. (1965). *Evolution and modification of behavior*. Chicago: Chicago University Press.

Lorenz, K. (1969). Innate bases of learning. In K. Pribham (ed.), *On the biology of learning* (pp. 13–93). New York: Springer-Verlag.

Lorenz, K. (1981). *The foundation of ethology*. New York: Springer-Verlag.

Lovengiver, S. (1974). Socio-dramatic play and language development in preschool disadvantaged children. *Psychology in the Schools*, 11: 313–320.

Low, B. S. (1989). Cross-cultural patterns in the training of children: An evolutionary perspective. *Journal of Comparative Psychology*, 103: 311–319.

Low, B. S. (2000). *Why sex matters: A Darwinian look at human behavior*. Princeton: Princeton University Press.

Luria, A. R. (1961). *The role of language in self-regulation*. New York: Liveright.

Luria, A. (1976). *Cognitive development*. Cambridge: Harvard.

Lussier, L., and Buskirk, E. R. (1977). Effects of an endurance training regimen on assessment of work capacity in prepubertal children. *Annals of the New York Academy of Sciences*, 301: 734–747.

Lykken, D. (1968). Statistical significance in psychological research. *Psychological Bulletin*, 70: 151–159.

Maccoby, E. E. (1986). Social groupings in childhood: Their relationship to prosocial and antisocial behavior in boys and girls. In D. Olweus, J. Block, and M. Radke-Yarrow (eds.), *Development of antisocial and prosocial behavior: Research, theory, and issues* (pp. 263–280). New York: Academic Press.

Maccoby, E. E. (1998). *The two sexes: Growing up apart, coming together*. Cambridge, Mass.: Harvard University Press.

Maccoby, E., and Jacklin, C. (1987). Gender segregation in childhood. In H. Reese (ed.), *Advances in child development*, Vol. 20 (pp. 239–287).

MacDonald, K. (1987). Parent–child physical play with rejected, neglected, and popular boys. *Developmental Psychology*, 23: 705–711.

MacDonald, K. (1993). Parent–child play: An evolutionary perspective. In K. MacDonald (ed.), *Parent–child play* (pp. 113–143). Albany, N.Y.: State University of New York Press.

MacDonald, K., and Parke, R. D. (1984). Bridging the gap: Parent–child play interactions and peer interactive competence. *Child Development*, 55: 1265–1277.

MacDonald, K., and Parke, R. D. (1986). Parent–child physical play: The effects of sex and age of children. *Sex Roles*, 15: 367–378.

MacFarlane, A., and Coulson, G. (2002: September). Sexual segregation in Australian marsupials. Paper presented at the Workshop in Sexual Segregation, Department of Zoology, Cambridge University, Cambridge, U.K.

Mahoney, J. L., Larson, R. W., Eccles, J. S., and Lord, H. (2005). (eds.), Organized activities as developmental contexts. Mahwah, N.J.: Erlbaum.

Mahoney, J. L., Larson, R. W., Eccles, J. S., and Lord, H. (2005). Organized activities as developmental contexts for children and adolescents. In J. L. Mahoney, R. W. Larson, J. S. Eccles, and H. Lord (eds.), *Organized activities as developmental contexts* (pp. 3–22). Mahwah, N.J.: Erlbaum.

Maratsos, M. (1998). The acquisition of grammar. In D. Kuhn and R. S. Siegler (eds.), *Handbook of child psychology*, Vol. 2. *Cognition, perception, and language* (pp. 421–466). New York: Wiley.

Marsh, D. M., and Hanlon, T. J. (2004). Observer gender and observation bias in animal behaviour research: Experimental tests with red-backed salamanders. *Animal Behaviour*, 68: 1425–1433.

Martin, C. L., and Fabes, R. A. (2001). The stability and consequences of young children's same-sex peer interactions. *Developmental Psychology*, 37: 431–446.

Martin, P. (1982). The energy cost of play: Definition and estimation. *Animal Behaviour*, 30: 294–295.

Martin, P., and Bateson, P. P. G. (1993). *Measuring behaviour*. Cambridge: Cambridge University Press.

Martin, P., and Caro, T. (1985). On the function of play and its role in behavioral development. In J. Rosenblatt, C. Beer, M. Bushnel, and P. Slater (eds.), *Advances in the study of behavior*, Vol. 15 (pp. 59–103). New York: Academic Press.

Marx, K. (1906/1867). *Capital*, Vol. 1. Chicago: Charles Kerr and Co

Masten, A. S., and Coatsworth, J. D. (1998). The development of competence in favorable and unfavorable environments. *American Psychologist*, 53: 205–220.

Matas, L., Arende, X., and Sroufe, L. A. (1978). Continuity of development from the second year. *Child Development*, 49: 547–556.

Mathews, W., and Mathews, R. (1982). Eliminating operational definitions: A paradigm case approach to the study of fantasy play. In D. J. Pepler and K. H. Rubin (eds.), *The play of children: Current theory and research* (pp. 21–29). Basel: Karger.

Maynard Smith, J. (1979). Game theory and the evolution of behaviour. Proceedings of the Royal Society, 205: 475–488.

McCall, R. (1977). Challenges to a science of developmental psychology. *Child Development*, 48,333–344.

McCune, L. (1995). A normative study of representational play and the transition to language. *Developmental Psychology*, 31: 198–206.

McCune-Nicolich, L. (1981). Toward symbolic functioning: Structure of early pretend games and potential parallel with language. *Child Development*, 52: 785–797.

McCune-Nicolich, L., and Bruskin, C. (1982). Combinational competence in symbolic play and language. In D. Pepler and K. Rubin (eds.), *The play of children* (pp. 30–45). Basel, Switzerland: Karger.

McCune-Nicolich, L., and Fenson, L. (1984). Methodological issues in studying early pretend play. In T. D. Yawkey and A. D. Pellegrini (eds.), *Child's play* (pp. 81–104). Hillsdale, N. J: Erlbaum.

McGrew, W. C. (1972). *An ethological study of children's behaviour*. London: Metheun.

McGrew, W. C. (1981). The female chimpanzee as a female evolutionary prototype. In F. Dahlberg (ed.), *Woman the gatherer* (pp. 35–73). New Haven: Yale University Press.

McGrew, W. C. (1992). *Chimpanzee material culture*. Cambridge: Cambridge University Press.

McLoyd, V. (1980). Verbally expressed modes of transformation in the fantasy and play of black preschool children. *Child Development*, 51: 1133–1139.

McLoyd, V. (1981). Pretend play among low-income dyads as a function of age, sex, and structure of play materials. Paper presented at the biennial meeting of the Society for Research in Child Development. Boston.

McLoyd, V. (1982). Social class differences in sociodiamatic play. A critical review. *Developmental Review*, 2: 1–30.

Mead, G. H. (1934). *Mind, self, and society*. Chicago: University of Chicago Press.

Mead, M. (1928). *Coming of age in Samoa*. New York: Morrow.

Mead, M. (1930). *Growing up in New Guinea*. New York: Morrow.

Mead, M. (1946). Research on primitive children. In L. Carmichael (ed.), *Manual of child psychology* (pp. 667–706). New York: Wiley.

Mead, M. (1954). Research on primitive children. In L. Carmichael (ed.), *Manual of child psychology* (pp. 735–780). New York: Wiley.

Meaney, M. J., Stewart, J., and Beatty, W. W. (1985). Sex differences in social play. In J. Rosenblatt, C. Beer, M. C. Bushnel, and P. Slater (eds.), *Advances in the study of behavior*, Vol. 15 (pp. 2–58). New York: Academic Press.

Meltzoff, A. N. (1988). Infant imitation after a one-week delay: Long-term memory for novel acts and multiple stimuli. *Developmental Psychology*, 24: 470–476.

Meltzoff, A. N., and Borton, R. W. (1979). Intermodal matching by human neonates. *Nature*, 282: 403–404.

Meltzoff, A. N., and Moore, M. K. (1977). Imitation of facial and manual gestures by human neonates. *Science*, 198: 75–78.

Meltzoff, A. N., and Moore, M. K. (1992). Early imitation within a functional framework: The importance of person identity, movement, and development. *Infant Behavior and Development*, 15: 479–505.

Messick, S. (1983). Assessment of children. In W. Kesen (ed.), *Handbook of child psychology*, Vol. 1: *History, theory, and methods* (pp. 477–526). New York: Wiley.

Mill, J. S. (1843/1874). *A system of logic*. New York: Harper and Brothers.

Minuchin, P., and Shapiro, E. (1983). The school as a context for social development. In E. M. Hetherington (ed.), *Manual of child psychology*, Vol. 4 (pp. 197–274). New York: Wiley.

Mitani, J. C., Merriwether, A., and Zhang, C. (2000). Male affiliation, cooperation and kinship in wild chimpanzees. *Animal Behaviour*, 59: 885–893.

Mitchell, R. W. (2006). Pretense in animals: The continuing relevance of children's pretense. In A. Göncü and S. Gaskins (eds.), *Play and development* (pp. 51–76). Mahwah, N.J.: Erlbaum.

Moffitt, T. E. (1993). Adolescent-limited and life-course-persistent antisocial behavior: A developmental taxonomy. *Psychological Review*, 100: 674–701.

Moffitt, T. (2002: August). Behavioral genomics of antisocial behavior: How genetic research pushes environmental theory forward. Address to the International Society for the Study of Behavioral Development, Ottawa.

Mollar, L. C., and Serbin, L. A. (1996). Antecedents to toddler gender segregation: Cognitive consonance, sex-typed toy preference, and behavioral compatibility. *Sex Roles*, 35: 445–460.

Money, J., and Ehrhardt, A. A. (1972). *Man and woman: Boy and girl*. Baltimore, Md.: Johns Hopkins University Press.

Monson, D., and Sebesta, S. (1991). Reading preferences. In: J. Flood, J. Jensen, D. Lapp, and J. Squire (eds.), *Handbook of research on teaching the English language arts* (pp. 664–673). New York: Macmillan.

Montessori, M. (1964). *The Montessori method*. New York: Schocken Books.

Morelli, G. A., Rogoff, B., and Angelillo, C. (1993). Cultural variation in children's work and social activities. Paper presented at the biennial meetings of the Society for Research in Child Development, New Orleans.

Morrow, L. (1990). Preparing the classroom environment to promote literacy during play. *Early Childhood Research Quarterly*, 5: 537–554.

Müller-Schwarze, D. (1968). Play deprivation in deer. *Behaviour*, 31: 144–162.

Müller-Schwarze, D. (1984). Analysis of play behaviour. In P. K. Smith (ed.), *Play in animals and humans* (pp. 147–158). Oxford: Blackwell.

Müller-Schwarze, D., Stagge, B., and Müller-Schwarze, C. (1982). Play behavior in mammals: Persistence, decrease and energetic compensation during food shortage in deer fawns. *Science*, 215: 85–87.

Mussen, P. H. (1970). *Handbook of child psychology*, Vols. 1 and 2. Third edition. New York: Wiley

Mussen, P. H. (1983). *Handbook of child psychology*, Vols. 1–3. Fourth edition. New York: Wiley.

Nadler, R. D., and Braggio, J. T. (1974). Sex and species differences in captive-reared juvenile chimpanzees and orangutans. *Journal of Human Evolution*, 3: 541–550.

National Association for the Education of Young Children (1988). NAEYC position statement on standardized testing of young children 3 through 8 years of age. *Young Children*, 43(3), 42–47.

National Association for the Education of Young Children (1992). Developmentally appropriate practice in early childhood programs serving infants, toddlers, younger preschoolers. Washington, D.C.: Author.

National Vital Statistic Report—Mortality Rates (2006). http://www.data360.org/graph_group.aspx?Graph_Group_Id=347). Accessed March 4, 2009.

Neill, S. (1976). Aggressive and non-aggressive fighting in twelve-to-thirteen year old pre-adolescent boys. *Journal of Child Psychology and Psychiatry*, 17: 213–220.

Nelson, K. (1986). *Event knowledge: Structure and function in development*. New York: Cambridge University Press.

Nelson, K., and Gruendel, J. (1979). At morning it's lunchtime: A script view of children's dialogue. *Discourse Processes*, 2: 73–94.

Neuman, S., and Roskos, K. (1991). The influence of literacy-enriched play centers on preschoolers' conceptions of the functions of print. In J. Christie (ed.), *Play and early literacy development* (pp. 167–188). Albany, N.Y.: SUNY Press.

Neuman, S., and Roskos, K. (1991). Peers as literacy informants: A description of young children's literacy conversations in play. *Early Childhood Research Quarterly*, 6, 233–248.

Neuman, S., and Roskos, K. (1992). Literacy objects as cultural tools: Effects on children's literacy behaviors in play. *Reading Research Quarterly*, 27: 203–225.

Nicolich, L. (1977). Beyond sensori-motor intelligence: Assessment of symbolic maturity through analysis of pretend play. *Merrill-Palmer Quarterly*, 23: 89–99.

Nicolopoulou, A., McDowell, J., and Brockmeyer, C. (2006). Narrative play and emergent literacy: Storytelling, story-acting meet journal writing. In D. Singer, R. M. Golinkoff, and K. Hirsch-Pasek (2006) (eds.), *Play = learning* (pp. 124–144). New York: Oxford University Press.

Nurss, J., and McGauvran, M. (1976). *Metropolitan Readiness Tests: Levels I and II Test and Teacher's Manual*. New York: Harcourt, Brace, Jovanovich.

Obrist, P., Howard, J., Sutterer, J., Hennis, R., and Murrell, D. (1973). Cardiac-somatic changes during a simple reaction time study. *Journal of Experimental Child Psychology*, 16: 346–362.

Omark, D. R, and Edelman, M. S. (1976). The development of attention structures in young children. In M. R. A. Chance and R. R. Larsen (eds.), *The social structure of attention* (pp. 119–151). New York: Wiley.

Olson, D. R. (1977). From utterance to text: The bias of language in speech and writing. *Harvard Educational Review*, 47: 257–281.

Opie, L., and Opie, P. (1969). *Children's games in street and playground*. London: Oxford University Press.

Orme, N. (2001) *Medieval children*. New Haven, CT: Yale University Press.

Oswald, H., Krappmann, L., Chowduri, F., and Salisch, M. (1987). Gaps and bridges: Interactions between girls and boys in elementary schools. *Sociological Studies of Child Development*, 2: 205–223.

Paquette, D. (1994). Fighting and play fighting in captive adolescent chimpanzees. *Aggressive Behaviour*, 20: 49–65.

Parke, R. D., Cassidy, J., Burks, Carson, J., and Boyum, L. (1992). Familial contributions to peer competence among young children: The role of interactive and affective processes. In R. D. Parke and C. Ladd (eds.), *Family-peer relationships* (pp. 107–134). Hillsdale, N.J.: Erlbaum.

Parke, R. D., and Suomi, S. J. (1981). Adult male infant relationships: Human and nonhuman primate evidence. In K. Immelman, C. W. Barlow, L. Petronovitch, and M. Main (eds.), *Behavioral development* (pp. 700–725). New York: Cambridge University Press.

Parker, G. A. (1974). Assessment strategy and the evolution of fighting behavior. *Journal of Theoretical Biology*, 47: 223–243.

Parker, G. A. (2000). Scramble in behaviour and ecology. *Philosophical Transactions of the Royal Society of London*, 355: 1637–16.

Parker, S. T. (1977). Piaget's sensorimotor period series in an infant macaque: A model for comparing unstereotyped behavior and intelligence in human and nonhuman primates. In S. Chevalier-Skolnikoff and F. E. Poirer (eds.), *Primate bio-social development* (pp. 43–112). New York: Garland Press.

Parmar, P., Harkness, S., Super, C. M. (no date). Teacher or playmate? Asian immigrant and Euro-American parents' participation in their young children's daily activities. Unpublished manuscript, Penn State University, Commonwealth Campus.

Parrott, S. (1975). Games children play: Ethnography of a second recess. In J. Spradley and D. McCardy (eds.), *The cultural experience* (pp. 207–219). Palo Alto, Calif.: SRA.

Parten, M. (1932). Social participation among preschool children. *Journal of Abnormal and Social Psychology*, 27: 243–269.

Patrick, G. T. W. (1916). *The psychology of relaxation*. Boston: Houghton-Mifflin.

Patterson, G. (1980). Mothers: The unacknowledged victims. Monographs for the Society for Research in Child Development, 45 (5: Serial No. 186).

Pellegrini, A. D. (1980). The relationship between kindergarteners' play and achievement in prereading, language, and writing. *Psychology in the Schools*, 17: 530–535.

Pellegrini, A. D. (1982). Explorations in preschoolers' construction of cohesive test in two play contexts. *Discourse Processes*, 5: 101–108.

Pellegrini, A. (1983). The sociolinguistic context of the preschool. *Journal of Applied Developmental Psychology*, 4: 397–405.

Pellegrini A. (1984). The effect of dramatic play and children's generations of cohesive text. *Discourse Processes*, 7: 57–67.

Pellegrini, A. D. (1984). The Piaget-Vygotsky debate on the functions of private speech: A review of related research. In A. Pellegrini and T. Yawkey (eds.), *The development of oral and written language in social context* (pp. 57–70). Norwood, N.J.: Ablex.

Pellegrini, A. (1984). The effects of exploration and play on young children's association fluency: A review and extension of training studies. In T. Yawkey and A. Pellegrini (eds.), *Child's play: Applied and developmental* (pp. 237–253). Hillsdale, N.J.: Erlbaum.

Pellegrini, A. (1984). Identifying causal elements in the thematic-fantasy play paradigm. *American Educational Research Journal*, 21: 691–703.

Pellegrini, A. (1984). Social-cognitive aspects of children's play: The effects of age, gender, and play context. *Journal of Applied Developmental Psychology*, 6: 129–240.

Pellegrini, A. D. (1984). The social cognitive ecology of preschool classrooms. *International Journal of Behavioral Development*, 7: 321–332.

Pellegrini, A. D. (1985). The narrative organization of children's fantasy play: The effects of age and play context. *Educational Psychology*, 5: 17–25.

Pellegrini, A. D. (1985). Relations between children's symbolic play and literate behavior. In. L. Galda and A. Pellegrini (eds.), *Play, language, and stories* (pp. 79–98). Norwood, N.J.: Ablex.

Pellegrini, A. D. (1985). The relations between symbolic play and literate behavior: A review and critique of the empirical literature. *Review of Educational Research*, 55: 207–221.

Pellegrini, A. D. (1986). Play centers and the production of imaginative language. *Discourse Processes*, 9: 115–125.

Pellegrini, A. D. (1987). Children on playgrounds: A review of "What's out there." *Children's Environmental Quarterly*, 4(1): 1–7.

Pellegrini, A. D. (1987). The effects of play concepts on the development of children's verbalized fantasy. *Semiotica*, 65: 285–293.

Pellegrini, A. D. (1987). Rough-and-tumble play. Developmental and educational significance. *Educational Psychologist*, 22: 23–43.

Pellegrini, A. D. (1988). Elementary school children's rough-and-rumble play and social competence. *Developmental Psychology*, 24: 802–806.

Pellegrini, A. D. (1989). What is a category? The case of rough-and-tumble play. *Ethology and Sociobiology*, 10: 331–341.

Pellegrini, A. D. (1990). Elementary school children's playground behavior. Implications for children's social-cognitive development. *Children's Environment Quarterly*, 7 (2): 8–16.

Pellegrini, A. D. (1992). Preference for outdoor play during early adolescence. *Journal of Adolescence*, 15: 241–254.

Pellegrini, A. D. (1993). Boy's rough-and-tumble play, social competence, and group composition. *British Journal of Developmental Psychology*, 11: 237–248.

Pellegrini, A. D. (1994). The rough play of adolescent boys of differing sociometric status. *International Journal of Behavioral Development*. 17: 525–540.

Pellegrini, A. D. (1995). A longitudinal study of boys' rough-and-tumble play and dominance during early adolescence. *Journal of Applied Developmental Psychology*, 16: 77–93.

Pellegrini, A. D. (1995). *School recess and playground behavior*. Albany, N.Y.: State University of New York Press.

Pellegrini, A. D. (2002). The development and possible functions of rough-and-tumble play. In C. H. Hart and P. K. Smith (eds.), *Handbook of social development* (pp. 438–454). Oxford: Blackwell.

Pellegrini, A. D. (2002). Bullying and victimization in middle school: A dominance relations perspective. *Educational Psychologist*, 37: 151–163.

Pellegrini, A. D. (2003). Perceptions and functions of play and real fighting in early adolescence. *Child Development*, 74: 1552–1533.

Pellegrini, A. D. (2004). *Observing children in the natural worlds: A methodological primer*, 2nd ed. Mahwah, N.J.: Erlbaum.

Pellegrini, A. D. (2004). Sexual segregation in childhood: A review of evidence for two hypotheses. *Animal Behaviour*, 68: 435–443.

Pellegrini, A. D. (2005). *Recess: Its role in education and development*. Mahwah, N.J.: Erlbaum.

Pellegrini, A. D. (2006). The development and function of rough-and-tumble play in childhood and adolescence: A sexual selection theory perspective. In A. Goncu and S. Gaskins (eds.), *Play and development* (pp. 77–98). Mahwah, N.J.: Erlbaum.

Pellegrini, A. D. (In press). Play. In P. D. Zelazo (ed.), *Oxford handbook of developmental psychology*. New York: Oxford University Press.

Pellegrini, A. D., and Archer, J. (2005). Sex differences in competitive and aggressive behavior: A view from sexual selection theory. In B. J. Ellis and D. J. Bjorklund (eds.), *Origins of the social mind: Evolutionary psychology and child development* (pp. 219–244). New York: Guilford.

Pellegrini, A. D., and Bartini, M. (2000). An empirical comparison of methods of sampling aggression and victimization in school settings. *Journal of Educational Psychology*, 92: 360–366.

Pellegrini, A. D., and Bartini, M. (2001). Dominance in early adolescent boys: Affiliative and aggressive dimensions and possible functions. *Merrill-Palmer Quarterly*, 47: 142–163.

Pellegrini, A. D., and Bjorklund, D. F. (2004). The ontogeny and phylogeny of children's object and fantasy play. *Human Nature*, 15: 23–43.

Pellegrini, A. D., and Blatchford, P. (2000). *The child at school: Interactions with peers and teachers.* New York: Oxford University Press.

Pellegrini, A. D., Blatchford, P., Kato, K., and Baines, E. (2004). A short-time longitudinal study of children's playground games in primary school: Implications for adjustment to school and social adjustment in the U.S.A. and the U.K. *Social Development*, 13: 107–123.

Pellegrini, A. and Davis, P. (1993). Relations between children's playground and recess behaviour. *British Journal of Educational Psychology*, 63: 88–95.

Pellegrini, A. D., Dupuis, D., and Smith, P. K. (2007). Play in evolution and development. *Developmental Review*, 27: 261–276.

Pellegrini, A. D., and Galda, L. (1982). The effects of thematic fantasy play training on the development of children's story comprehension. *American Educational Research Journal*, 19: 443–452.

Pellegrini, A., and Galda, L. (1988). The effects of age and context on children's use of narrative language. *Research in the Teaching of English*, 22: 183–195.

Pellegrini, A. D., and Galda, L. (1991). Longitudinal relations among preschoolers' symbolic play, metalinguistic verbs, and emergent literacy. In. J. Christie (ed.), *Play and early literacy development* (pp. 47–68). Albany, N.Y.: SUNY Press.

Pellegrini, A., Galda, L. (1993). Ten years after: A reexamination of symbolic play and literacy research. *Reading Research Quarterly*. 28: 163–175.

Pellegrini, A., and Galda, L. (1998). *The development of school-based literacy: A social ecological approach.* London: Routledge.

Pellegrini, A. D., and Galda, L. (2001). I'm so glad, I'm glad, I'm glad: The role of emotions and close relationships in children's play and narrative language. In A. Göncü and E. Klein (eds.), *Young children in play, story, and school: Essays in honor of Greta Fein* (pp. 204–219). New York: Guilford.

Pellegrini, A. D., Galda, L., Bartini, M., and Charak, D. (1998). Oral language and literacy learning in context: The role of social relationships. *Merrill-Palmer Quarterly*, 44: 38–54.

Pellegrini, A. D., Galda, L., and Flor (1997). Relationships, individual differences, and children's use of literate language. *British Journal of Educational Psychology*, 67: 139–152.

Pellegrini, A. D., Galda, L., and Flor, D., Bartini, M., and Charak, D. (1997). Close relationships, individual differences, and early literacy learning. *Journal of Experimental Child Psychology*, 67: 409–422.

Pellegrini, A., Galda, L., and Rubin, D. (1984). Context in text: The development of oral and written language in two genres. *Child Development*, 55: 1549–1555.

Pellegrini, A. D., and Goldsmith, S. (2003) "Settling in": A short-term longitudinal study of ways in which new children come to play with classmates. *Emotional and Behavioural Difficulties*, 8: 140–151.

Pellegrini, A. and Greene, H. (1980). The use of a sequenced questioning paradigm as a facilitator of preschoolers' associative fluency. *Journal of Applied Developmental Psychology*, 1: 189–200.

Pellegrini, A. D., and Gustafson, K. (2005). Boys' and girls' uses of objects for exploration, play, and tools in early childhood. In A. D. Pellegrini and P. K. Smith (eds.), *The nature of play: Great apes and humans* (pp. 113–138). New York: Guilford.

Pellegrini, A. D., and Horvat, M. (1995). A developmental contextual critique of Attention Deficit Hyperactivity Disorder (ADHD). *Educational Researcher*, 24: 13–20.

Pellegrini, A. D., Horvat, M., and Huberty, P. D. (1998). The relative cost of children's physical activity play. *Animal Behaviour*, 55: 1053–1061.

Pellegrini, A. D., and Huberty, P. (1993). Relations between children's playground and classroom behavior. *British Journal of Educational Psychology*, 63: 88–95.

Pellegrini, A. D., Huberty, P. D., and Jones, I. (1995). The effects of recess timing on children's classroom and playground behavior. *American Educational Research Journal*, 32: 845–864.

Pellegrini, A. D., Kato, K., Blatchford, P., and Baines, E. (2002). A short-term longitudinal study of children's playground games across the first year of school: Implications for social competence and adjustment to school. *American Educational Research Journal*, 39: 991–1015.

Pellegrini, A. D., and Long, J. D. (2002). A longitudinal study of bullying, dominance, and victimization during the transition from primary to secondary school. British Journal of *Developmental Psychology*, 20: 259–280.

Pellegrini, A. D., and Long, J. D. (2003). A sexual selection theory longitudinal analysis of sexual segregation and integration in early adolescence. *Journal of Experimental Child Psychology*, 85: 257–278.

Pellegrini, A. D., Long, J. D., Roseth, C., Bohn, K., and Van Ryzin, M. (2007). A short-term longitudinal study of preschool children's sex segregation: The role of physical activity, sex, and time. *Journal of Comparative Psychology*, 121: 282–289.

Pellegrini, A. D., and Long, J. D. (2007). An observational study of early heterosexual interaction at middle school dances. *Journal of Research in Adolescence*, 17: 613–638.

Pellegrini, A. D., Melhuish, E., Jones, I., Trojanowska, L., and Gilden, R. (2002). Social contexts of learning literate language: The role of varied, familiar, and close peer relationships. *Learning and Individual Differences*, 12: 375–389.

Pellegrini, A. D., and Perlmutter, J. C. (1987). A re-examination of the Smilansky-Parten matrix of play behavior. *Journal of Research in Childhood Education*, 2: 89–96.

Pellegrini, A. D., and Perlmutter, J. (1989). Classroom contextual effects on children's play. *Developmental Psychology*, 25: 289–296.

Pellegrini, A. D., Roseth, C., Mliner, S., C. Bohn, Van Ryzin, M., Vance, N., Cheatham, C. L. and Tarullo, A. (2007). Social dominance in preschool classrooms. *Journal of Comparative Psychology*, 121: 54–64.

Pellegrini, A., and Smith, P. K. (1993). School recess. *Review of Educational Research,* 63: 51–67.

Pellegrini, A. D., and Smith, P. K. (1998). Physical activity play: The nature and function of a neglected aspect of play. *Child Development*, 69: 577–598.

Pellegrini, A. D., and Smith, P. K. (2005). The nature of play. In A. D. Pellegrini and P. K. Smith (eds.), *The nature of play: Great apes and humans* (pp. 3–12). New York: Guilford.

Peller, L. E. (1952). Models of children's play. *Mental Hygiene*, 36: 66–83.

Peller, L. E. (1954). Libidinal phases, ego development, and play. *Psychoanalytic Study of the Child*, 9: 178–198.

Pellis, S. (1988). Agonistic versus amicable rates of attack and defense: Consequences for the origins and function, and descriptive classification of play-fighting. *Aggressive Behavior*, 19: 85–104.

Pellis, S., and Pellis, V. (1987). Play-fighting differs from serious fighting in both target of attack and tactics of fighting in the laboratory rats *Rattus norvegicus*. *Aggressive Behavior*, 13: 227–242.

Pellis, S., and Pellis, V. (1988). Play-fighting in the Syrian Golden Hamster *Mesocricetus anratus Waterhouse*, and its relationship to serious fighting during post-weaning development. *Developmental Psychobiology*, 21: 323–332.

Pellis, S. M., Field, E. F., Smith, L. K., and Pellis, V. C. (1996). Multiple differences in the play fighting of male and female rats. *Neuroscience and Biobehavioral Reviews*, 21: 105–120.

Pellis, S. M., and Iwaniuk, A. N. (2000). Adult–adult play in primates: Comparative analyses of its origin, distribution, and evolution. *Ethology*, 106: 1083–1104.

Pellis, S. M., and Pellis, V. V. (1998). The structure-function interface in the analysis of play fighting. In M. Bekoff and J. A. Byers (eds.), Animal play: Evolutionary, comparative, and ecological perspectives (pp. 115–140). New York: Cambridge University Press.

Pellis, S. M., and Pellis, V. V. (2006). Play and the development of social engagement: A comparative perspective. In P. J. Marshall and N. A. Fox (eds.), *The development of social engagement: Psychobiological perspectives* (pp. 247–274). New York: Oxford University Press.

Pellis, S. M., Pellis, V. V., and Reinhart, C. J. (In press). The evolution of social play. In C. Worthman, P. Plotsky, and D. Schechter (eds.), *Formative experiences: The interaction of caregiving, culture, and developmental psychobiology*. New York: Cambridge University Press.

Pepler, D., and Ross, H. (1981). The effects of play on convergent and divergent problem solving. *Child Development*, 52: 1202–1210.

Petitt, G., Baksi, A., Dodge, K., and Cole, J. (1990). The emergence of social dominance in young boys' play groups: Developmental differences and behavioral correlates. *Developmental Psychology*, 26: 1017–1026.

Piaget, J. (1962). *Play, dreams, and imitation in childhood* (trans. C. Gattengno and F.M. Hodgson). New York: Norton (original work published 1951).

Piaget, J. (1965). *The moral judgment of the child*. New York: Free Press.

Piaget, J. (1966). Response to Brian Sutton-Smith. *Psychological Review*, 73: 111–112.

Piaget, J. (1970). Piaget's theory. In P. Mussen (ed.), *Carmichael's manual of child psychology*, Vol. I (pp. 703–732). New York: Wiley.

Piaget, J. (1967). *The psychology of intelligence*. London: Routledge and Kegan Paul.

Piaget, J. (1970). *Structuralism*. New York: Basic Books.

Piaget, J. (1974). *The language and thought of the child*. New York: Meridan.

Piaget, J. (1976). *Behaviour and evolution*. London: Routledge and Kegan Paul.

Piaget, J., and Inhelder, B. (1969). *The psychology of the child*. New York: Basic Books.

Pinker, S. (1994). *The language instinct: How the mind creates language*. New York: Morrow.

Pinker, S. (1997). *How the mind works*. New York: Norton.

Pinker, S. (1999). *Words and rules: The ingredients of language*. New York: Basic Books.

Pitcher, E. G., and Schultz, L. H. (1983). *Boys and girls at play: The development of sex roles*. South Hadley, Mass.: Bergin and Garvey.

Plomin, R., and Daniels, D. (1987). Why are children of the same family so different from each other? *Behavioural and Brain Sciences*, 10: 1–16.

Plomin, R., DeFries, J. C., Rutter, M., and McClearn, G. E. (1997). *Behavioral genetics: A primer*, 3rd ed. New York: W. H. Freeman.

Plomin, R., and Rutter, M. (1998). Child development, molecular genetics, and what to do with genes once they are found. *Child Development*, 69: 1223–1242.

Plotkin, H. (2004). *Evolutionary thought in psychology: A brief history*. Malden, Mass.: Blackwell.

Porges, S. W. (1992). Autonomic regulation and attention. In B. A. Campbell, H. Hayne, R. Richardson (eds.), *Attention and information processing in infants and adults* (pp. 201–213). Hillsdale, N.J.: Erlbaum.

Povinelli, D. J., and Cant, J. G. H. (1995). Arboreal clambering and the evolution of self-conception. *Quarterly Review of Biology*, 70: 393–421.

Power, T. G. (2000). *Play and exploration in children and animals*. Mahwah, N.J.: Erlbaum.

Pulaski, M. (1970). Play as a function of toy structure and fantasy predisposition. *Child Development*, 41: 531–537.

Pulaski, M. (1973). Toys and imaginative play. In J. Singer (ed.), *The child's world of make-believe* (pp. 75–103). New York: Academic.

Pusey, A. E., Williams, J., and Goodall, J. (1997). The influence of dominance rank on the reproductive success of female chimpanzees. *Science*, 277: 828–831.

Pusey, A. E., and Packer, C. (1997). The ecology of relationships. In J. Krebs and N. B. Davies (eds.), *Behavioural ecology*, 4th ed. Oxford: Blackwell.

Pusey, A. E. (1990). Behavioural changes at adolescence in chimpanzees. *Behaviour*, 115: 203–246.

Quadagno, D. M., Briscoe, R., and Quadagno, J. S. (1977). Effects of perinatal gonadal hormones on selected nonsexual behavior patterns: A critical assessment of the nonhuman and human literature. *Psychological Bulletin*, 84: 62–82.

Rahmani, L. (1973). *Soviet psychology. Philosophical, theoretical, and experimental issues*. New York: International Universities Press.

Ralls, K. (1976). Mammals in which females are larger than males. *The Quarterly Review of Biology*, 51: 245–276.

Ralls, K. (1977). Sexual dimorphism in mammals: Avian models and unanswered questions. *The American Naturalist*, 11: 917–938.

Ramsey, J. K., and McGrew, W. C. (2005). Object play in great apes: Studies in nature and captivity. In A. D. Pellegrini and P. K. Smith (eds.), *Play in great apes and humans* (pp. 89–112). New York: Guilford.

Renninger, K. A., and Sigel, I. E. (eds.) (2006). *Handbook of child psychology*, Vol. 4: *Applying research to practice*. New York: Wiley.

Repina, T. A. (1971). Development of imagination. In Zaporozhets, A. V., and Elknonin, D. B. (eds.), *The psychology of preschool children* (pp. 255–277). Cambridge: MIT Press.

Ritchie, S., and Howes, C. (2003). Program practice, caregiver stability, and child–caregiver relationships. *Journal of Applied Developmental Psychology*, 23: 497–516.

Rogoff, B. (1988). Commentary. *Human Development*, 32: 346–348.

Rogoff, B. (1991: Winter). U.S. children and their families: Current conditions and recent trends. Society for Research in Child Development Newsletter, pp. 1–3.

Rogoff, B., Göncü, A., Mistry, J., and Mosier, C. (1993). Guided participation in cultural activity by toddler and caregivers. Monographs for the Society for Research in Child Development 236 (58: Serial No. 8).

Rogoff, B., Mosier, C., Mistry, J., and Göncü, A. (1989). Toddlers' guided participation in cultural activity. *Cultural Dynamics*, 2: 209–237.

Roopnarine, J. L., and Field, T. (1984). Play interactions of friends and acquaintances in nursery school. In T. Field and J. L. Roopnarine (eds.), *Friendship in normal and handicapped children* (pp. 89–98). Norwood, N. J.: Ablex.

Roopnarine, J. L., Hooper, F., Ahmeduzzaman, A., and Pollack, B. (1993). Gentle play partners: Mother-child and father-child play in New Delhi, India. In K. MacDonald (ed.), *Parent-child play* (pp. 287–304). Albany, N.Y.: State University of New York Press.

Rosenberg, A. (1990). Is there an evolutionary biology of play? In M. Bekoff and D. Jamieson (eds.), *Interpretation and explanation in the study of animal behavior*, Vol. 1: *Interpretation, intentionality, and communication* (pp. 180–196). Boulder, Colo.: Westview Press.

Rosenthal, M. K. (1994). Social and non-social play of infants and toddlers in family day care. In E. V. Jacobs and H. Goelman (eds.), *Children's play in child care settings* (pp. 163–192). Albany, N.Y.: State University of New York Press.

Roseth, C. J. (2006). Effects of peacekeeping and peacemaking on preschoolers' conflict: A multi-method longitudinal study. Unpublished doctoral dissertation, University of Minnesota, Twin Cities.

Roseth, C. J., Pellegrini, A. D., Bohn, C. M., Van Ryzin, M., and Vance, N. (2007). Preschoolers' aggression, affiliation, and social dominance relationships: An observational, longitudinal study. *Journal of School Psychology*, 45: 479–497.

Roseth, C. J., Pellegrini, A. D., Dupuis, D., Bohn, Hickey, M., and Peshkam, A. Effects of peacekeeping and peacemaking on preschoolers' competitive conflict. Manuscript submitted for publication.

Roth, J. L., Brooks-Gunn, J., and Linver, M. R. (2003). What happens during the school day? Time diaries from a national sample of elementary school teachers. *Teachers College Record*, 105: 317–343.

Routh, D. K., Schroeder, C. S., and O'Tuama, L. A. (1974). Development of activity level in children. *Developmental Psychology*, 10: 163–168.

Rowland, T. W. (1985). Aerobic response to endurance training in prepubescent children: A critical analysis. *Medicine and Science in Sports and Exercise*, 17: 493–497.

Rubin, K. H. (1980) Fantasy play: Its role in the development of social skills and social cognition. In K. H. Rubin (ed.), *Children's play.* (pp. 69–84). San Francisco: Jossey-Bass.

Rubin, K. (1982). Nonsocial play in preschoolers: Necessary evil. *Child Development*, 53: 651–657.

Rubin, K. H., Bukowski, W., Parker, J. G. (1998). Peer interactions, relationships, and groups. In N. Eisenberg (ed.), *Manual of child psychology*, Vol. 3: *Social, emotional, and personality development* (pp. 619–700). New York: Wiley.

Rubin, K., and Clark, L. (1982). Preschool teachers' ratings of behavioral problems. Paper presented at the annual meeting of the American Research Association, New York.

Rubin, K. H., and Coplan, R. J. (1998). Social and nonsocial play in childhood: An individual difference perspective. In O. N. Saracho and B. Spodek (eds.), *Multiple perspectives on play in early childhood education* (pp. 144–170). Albany, N.Y.: State University of New York Press.

Rubin, K. H., Fein, G., and Vandenberg, B. (1983). Play. In E. M. Hetherington (ed.), *Handbook of child psychology*: Vol. 4: *Socialization, personality and social development* (pp. 693–774). New York: Wiley.

Rubin, K., and Maioni, T. (1975). Play reference and its relationship to egocentrism, popularity and classification skills in preschoolers. *Merrill-Palmer Quarterly*, 21: 171–179.

Rubin, K., Maioni, T., and Hornung, M. (1976). Free play in middle and lower class preschoolers: Parten and Piaget revisited. *Child Development*, 47: 414–419.

Rubin, K., Watson, R., and Jambor, T. (1978). Free-play behaviors in preschool and kindergarten children. *Child Development*, 49: 534–546.

Ruckstuhl, K. E. (1998). Foraging behaviour and sexual segregation in bighorn sheep. *Animal Behaviour*, 56: 99–106.

Ruckstuhl, K. E., and Neuhaus, P. (2002). Sexual segregation in ungulates: A comparative test of three hypotheses. *Biological Review*, 77: 77–96.

Ruckstuhl, K. E., and Neuhaus, P. (eds.) (2005). *Sexual segregation in vertebrates.* Cambridge: Cambridge University Press.

Ruff, H. A., and Saltarelli, L. M. (1993). Exploratory play with objects: Basic cognitive processes and individual differences. In M. Bornstein and A. W. O'Reilly (eds.), *The role of play in the development of thought* (pp. 5–15). San Francisco: Jossey-Bass.

Rushton, J., Brainerd, C., and Pressley, M. (1983). Behavioral development and construct validity: The principle of aggregation. *Psychological Bulletin*, 94: 18–38.

Russell, B. (1932/1972). *In praise of idleness and other essays.* New York: Simon and Schuster.

Sachs, J., Goldman, J., and Chaille, L. (1984). Planning in pretend play. In A. D. Pellegrini and T. Yawkey (eds.), *The development of oral and written language in social context* (pp. 119–128). Norwood, N. J.: Ablex.

Sachs, J., Goldman, J., and Chaille, C. (1985). Narratives in preschooler's sociodramatic play. In L. Galda and A. D. Pellegrini (eds.), *Play, language, and stories* (pp. 45–62). Norwood, N.J.: Ablex.

Saltz, E., Dixon, D., and Johnson, J. (1977). Training disadvantaged preschoolers on various fantasy activities: Effects on cognitive functioning and impulse control. *Child Development*, 48: 367–380.

Saltz, E., and Johnson, J. (1974). Training for thematic fantasy play in culturally disadvantaged children: Preliminary results. *Journal of Educational Psychology*, 66: 623–603.

Savage-Rumbaugh, E. S. and McDonald, K. (1988). Deception and social manipulation in symbol-using apes. In R. W. Byrne and A. Whiten (eds.), *Machiavellian intelligence* (pp. 224–237). London: Oxford University Press.

Savin-Williams, R. C. (1976). Dominance hierarchies in groups of early adolescence. *Child Development*, 47: 972–979.

Savin-Williams, R. C. (1987). *Adolescence: An ethological perspective.* New York: Springer-Verlag.

Scarlett, W. G., Naudeau, Salonius-Pasternak, and Ponte, I. (2005). *Children's play.* Thousand Oaks, Calif.: Sage.

Schank, R. C., and Abelson, R. P. (1977) *Scripts, plans, and understanding: An inquiry into human knowledge structures.* Hillsdale, N.J.: Erlbaum.

Schiller, F. (1795/1967). *On the aesthetic education of man.* London: Oxford University Press.

Schlosberg, H. (1947). The concept of play. Psychological Review, 54: 229–231.

Schofield, J. W. (1981). Complementary and conflicting identities: Images and interactions in an inter-racial school. In S. R. Asher and J. M. Gottman (eds.), *The development of children's friendships* (pp. 53–90). New York: Cambridge University Press.

Schrader, C. (1990). Symbolic play as a curricular tool for early literacy development. *Early Childhood Research Quarterly*, 5: 79–103.

Scollon, R., and Scollon, S. (1981). *Narrative, literacy, and face in interethnic communication.* Norwood, N.J.: Ablex.

Scribner, S., and Cole, M. (1978). Literacy without schooling. *Harvard Educational Review,* 48,448–461.

Serbin, L. A., Tonick, I. J., and Stemglanz, S. I-I. (1977). Shaping cooperative cross-sex play. *Child Development,* 48: 924–929.

Serbin, L., Connor, J., Burchardt, C., and Citron, C. (1979). Effects of peer presence on sex-typing of children's play behavior. *Journal of Experimental Child Psychology,* 27: 303–309.

Serbin, L. A., Moller, L. C., Gulko, J. Powlista, K. K., and Colburne, K. A. (1994). The emergence of gender segregation in toddler playgroups. In C. Leaper (ed.), *Childhood gender segregation: Causes and consequences* (pp. 7–17). San Francisco: Jossey-Bass.

Sharpe, L. L. (2005). Play does not increase social cohesion in a cooperative mammal. *Animal Behaviour,* 70: 551–558.

Sharpe, L. L., Clutton-Brock, T. H., Brotherton, P. N. M., Cameron, E. Z., and Cherry, M. I. (2002). Experimental provisioning increases play in free-ranging meerkats. *Animal Behaviour,* 64: 112–121.

Shephard, R. J. (1983). Physical activity and the healthy mind. *Canadian Medical Association Journal,* 128: 525–530.

Siegel, H. I. (1985). Aggressive behavior. In H. I. Siegel (ed.), *The hamster* (pp. 261–286). New York: Plenum.

Silverman, I., and Eals, M. (1992). Sex differences in spatial ability: Evolutionary theory and data. In J. Barkow, L. Cosmides, and J. Tooby (eds.), *The adapted mind* (pp. 533- 549). New York: Oxford University Press.

Silvern, S., Taylor, A., Williamson, P., Surbeck, E., and Kelly, P. (1986). Young children's story recall as a product of play. *Merrill-Palmer Quarterly,* 32, 73–86.

Simon, T., and Smith, P. K. (1983). The study of play and problem solving in preschool children. *British Journal of Developmental Psychology,* 1: 289–297.

Simon, T., and Smith, P. K. (1985). Play and problem solving: A paradigm questioned. *Merrill-Palmer Quarterly,* 31: 265–277.

Simons-Morton, B. C., O'Hara, N. M., Parcel, G. S., Huang, I. W., Baranowski, T., and Wilson, B. (1990). Children's frequency of participation in moderate to vigorous physical activities. *Research Quarterly for Exercise and Sport,* 61: 307–314.

Simons-Morton, B. C., O'Hara, N. M., Simons-Morton, D. C., and Parcel, C. 5. (1987). Children and fitness: A public health perspective. *Research Quarterly for Exercise and Sport,* 58: 293–302.

Singer, D., Golinkoff, R. M., and K. Hirsch-Pasek (2006) (eds.), *Play = learning.* New York: Oxford University Press.

Slade, A. (1987). A longitudinal study of material involvement and symbolic play during the toddler period. *Child Development,* 58: 367–375.

Slade, A. (1987). Quality of attachment and early symbolic play. *Developmental Psychology,* 23: 78–85.

Slobin, D. I. (1970). Universals of grammatical development in children. In G. B. Flores, J. Arcais, and W. J. M. Levelt (eds.), *Advances in psycholinguistics* (pp. 174–186). Amsterdam: North-Holland Publishing.

Sluckin, A. M. (1981). *Growing up in the playground: The social development of children.* London: Routledge and Kegan Paul.

Sluckin, A. M., and Smith, P. K. (1977). Two approaches to the concept of dominance in preschool children. *Child Development,* 48: 917–923.

Smilansky, S. (1968). *The effects of sociodramatic play on disadvantaged preschool children*. New York: Wiley.

Smilanksy, S. (1971). Can adults facilitate play in children? In N. Curry and S. Arnaud (eds.), *Play: The child strives toward self-realization*. National Association for the Education of Young Children: Washington, D.C.

Smith, P. K. (1973). Temporal clusters and individual differences in the behaviour of preschool children. In R. Michael and J. Crook (eds.), *Comparative ecology and behaviour of primates* (pp. 752–798). London: Academic Press.

Smith, P. K. (1974). Ethological methods. In B. Foss (ed.), *New perspectives in child development* (pp. 85–137). Harmondsworth: Penguin.

Smith, P. K. (1977). Social and fantasy play in young children. In B. Tizard and D. Harvey (eds.), *Biology of play* (pp. 123–145). London: Heinemann.

Smith, P. K. (1978). A longitudinal study of social participation in preschool children: Solitary and parallel play reexamined. *Developmental Psychology*, 14: 517–523.

Smith, P. K. (1982). Does play matter? Functional and evolutionary aspects of animal and human play. *The Behavioral and Brain Sciences*, 5: 139–184.

Smith, P. K. (1985). The reliability and validity of one/zero sampling: Misconceived criticisms and unacknowledged assumptions. *British Educational Research Journal*, 11: 215–220.

Smith, P. K. (1988). Children's play and its role in early development: A re-evaluation of the "play ethos." In A. D. Pellegrini (ed.), *Psychological bases for early education* (pp. 207–226). Chichester, U.K.: Wiley.

Smith, P. K. (1989) The role of rough-and-tumble play in the development of social competence. In B. Schneider, J. Nadel, and R. Weisbord (eds.), *Social competence in developmental perspective* (pp. 239–255). Hingham, Mass.: Kluwer Academic Publishers Group.

Smith, P. K. (1994). The war toy debate. In J. Goldstein (ed.), *Toys, play, and child development* (pp. 67–84). New York: Cambridge University Press.

Smith, P. K. (1997). Play fighting and real fighting: Perspectives on their relationship. In A. Schmitt, K. Atswanger, K. Grammer, and K. Schafer (eds.), *New aspects of human ethology* (pp. 47–64). New York: Plenum.

Smith, P. K. (2005). Social and pretend play in children. In A. D. Pellegrini and P. K. Smith (eds.), *The nature of play: Great apes and humans* (pp. 173–212). New York: Guilford.

Smith, P. K., and Boulton, M. (1990). Rough-and-tumble play, aggression, and dominance: Perception and behavior in children's encounters. *Human Development*, 33: 271–282.

Smith, P. K., and Connolly, K. (1972). Patterns of play and social interaction in pre-school children. In N. Blurton Jones (ed.), *Ethological studies in child behaviour* (pp. 65–96). London: Cambridge University Press.

Smith, P. K., and Connolly, K. (1980). *The ecology of preschool behaviour*. London: Cambridge University Press.

Smith, P. K., Hagan, T. (1980). Effects of deprivation on exercise play in nursery school children. *Animal Behaviour*, 28: 922–928.

Smith, P. K., Hunter, T., Carvalho, A. M. A., and Costabile, A (1992). Children's perceptions of playfighting, playchasing and real fighting: A cross-national interview. *Social Development*, 1.

Smith, P.K., and Lewis, K. (1985). Rough-and-tumble play, fighting, and chasing in nursery school children. *Ethology and Sociobiology*, 6: 175–181.

Smith, P. K., and Simon, T. (1984). The study of play and problem-solving in preschool children: Methodological problems and new directions. In P. K. Smith (ed.), *Play in animals and humans* (pp. 199–216). Oxford: Blackwell.

Smith, P. K., Smees, R., and Pellegrini, A. D. (2004). Play fighting and real fighting: Using video playback methodology with young children. *Aggressive Behavior*, 30: 164–173.

Smith, P. K., and Syddall, S. (1978). Play and group play tutoring in preschool children. Is it play or tutoring which matters? *British Journal of Educational Psychology*, 48: 315–325.

Smith, P. K., Takhvar, M., Gore, N., and Volstedt, R. (1986). Play in young children: Problems of definition, categorization, and measurement. In P. K. Smith (ed.), *Children's play* (pp. 39–55). London: Gordon and Breach.

Smith, P. K., and Vollstedt, R. (1985). On defining play: An empirical study of the relationship between play and various play criteria. *Child Development*, 56: 1042–1050.

Smith, P. K. and Whitney, S. (1987). Play and associative fluency: Experimenter effects may be responsible for previous positive findings. *Developmental Psychology*, 23: 49–53.

Smitsman, A. W., and Bongers, R. M. (2003). Tool use and tool making: A developmental action perspective. In J. Valsiner and K. J. Connolly (eds.), *Handbook of developmental psychology* (pp. 172–193). London: Sage.

Smoll, F. L., and Schutz, R. W. (1985). Physical fitness differences between athletes and nonathletes: Do changes occur as a function of age and sex? *Human Movement Science*, 4: 189–202.

Smuts, B. B. (1987). Sexual competition and mate choice. In B. B. Smuts, D. C. Cheyney, R. M. Seyforth, R. W. Wrangham, and T. Struhsaker (eds.), *Primate societies* (pp. 385–399). Chicago: University of Chicago Press.

Smuts, B. B. (1995). The evolutionary origins of patriarchy. *Human Nature*, 6: 1–32.

Snow, C. (1983). Literacy and language: Relationships during the preschool years. *Harvard Educational Review*, 53: 165–189.

Snow, C. E. (1989). Understanding social interaction and language acquisition: Sentences are not enough. In M. Bornstein and J. S. Bruner (eds.), *Interaction in human development* (pp. 83–103). Hillsdale, N.J.: Erlbaum.

Spencer, H. (1898). *The principles of psychology*, Vol. 2. New York: Appleton.

Špinka, M., Newbury, R. C., and Bekoff, M. (2001). Mammalian play: Can training for the unexpected be fun? *Quarterly Review of Biology*, 76: 141–168.

Sroufe, L. A., Egelund, B, Carlson, E. A. (1999). One social world: The integrated development of parent–child and peer relationships. In W. A. Collins, and B. Laursen (eds.), *Relationships as developmental contexts. The Minnesota symposia on child psychology*, Vol. 30 (pp. 241–261). Mahwah, N.J.: Erlbaum

Stamps, J. (1995). Motor learning and the value of familiar space. *American Naturalist*, 146: 41–58.

Stamps, J. (2003). Behavioural processes affecting development: Tinbergen's fourth question comes to age. *Animal Behaviour*, 66: 1–13.

Stearns, S. (1992). *The evolutions of life histories*. London: Oxford University Press.

Steinberg, L. (1986). Latchkey children and susceptibility to peer pressure. *Developmental Psychology*, 22: 433–439.

Stephens, D. W., and Krebs, J. R. (1986). *Foraging theory*. Princeton: Princeton University Press.

Stevenson, H. W., and Lee, S. Y. (1990). Contexts of achievement. Monographs for the Society for Research in Child Development, 55 (1–2: Serial No. 221).

Stipek, D., and Maclver, D. (1989). Developmental changes in children's assessment of intellectual competence. *Child Development*, 60: 521–538.

Strayer, F. F. (1980). Social ecology of the preschool peer group. In W. A. Collins (ed.), *The Minnesota symposia on child development.* Vol. 13: *Development of cognition, affect, and social relations* (pp. 165–196). Hillsdale, N.J.: Erlbaum.

Suomi, S. J. (1991). Early stress and adult emotional reactivity in rhesus monkeys. *Ciba Foundation Symposium,* 156: 171–189.

Suomi, S. J. (2002: August). Genetic and environmental contributions to deficits in rough-and-tumble play in juvenile rhesus monkey males. Paper presented the biennial meetings of the International Society for the Study of Behavioral Development, Ottawa.

Suomi, S. J. (2005). Genetic and environmental factors influencing the expression of impulsive aggression and serotonergic functioning in rhesus monkeys. In R. E. Tremblay, W. W. Hartup, and J. Archer (eds.), *Developmental origins of aggression* (pp. 63–82). New York: Guilford.

Suomi, S., and Harlow, H. (1972). Social rehabilitation of isolate-reared monkeys. *Developmental Psychology,* 6: 487–496.

Super, C., and Harkness, S. (1986). The developmental niche: A conceptualization at the interface of child and culture. *International Journal of Behavioral Development,* 9: 545–569.

Susser, M., and Stein, Z. (1994). Timing in prenatal nutrition: A reprise of the Dutch famine study. *Nutrition Reviews,* 52: 84–94.

Sutton-Smith, B. (1966). Piaget on play: A critique. *Psychological Review,* 73: 104–110.

Sutton-Smith, B. (1967). The role of play in cognitive development. *Young Children,* 22: 364–369.

Sutton-Smith, B. (1968). Novel responses to toys. *Merrill-Palmer Quarterly,* 14: 151–158.

Sutton-Smith, B. (1971). A syntax for play and games. In R. Herron and B. Sutton-Smith (eds.), *Child's play* (pp. 298–310). New York: Wiley.

Sutton-Smith, B. (1973). *The folk games of children.* Austin: University of Texas Press.

Sutton-Smith, B. (1975). *The study of games: An anthropological approach.* New York: Teachers College Developmental Studies.

Sutton-Smith, B. (1981). *A history of children's play.* Philadelphia: University of Pennsylvania Press.

Sutton-Smith, B. (1982). *Toys as culture.* New York: Garland.

Sutton-Smith, B. (1988). War toys and childhood aggression. *Play and Culture,* 1: 57–69.

Sutton-Smith, B. (1987). School play: A commentary. In J. Block and N. King (eds.), *School play* (pp. 277–290). New York: Garland.

Sutton-Smith, B. (1990). School playground as festival. *Children's Environment Quarterly,* 7: 3–7.

Sutton-Smith, B. (1997). *The ambiguity of play.* Cambridge, Mass.: Harvard University Press.

Sutton-Smith, B., Botvin, G., and Mahoney, D. (1976). Developmental structures in fantasy narrative, *Human Development,* 19: 1–3.

Sutton-Smith, B., and Rosenberg, B. G. (1970). *The sibling.* New York: Holt, Rinehart and Winston.

Sutton-Smith, B., Rosenberg, B. G., and Morgan, E. F., Jr. (1963). Development of sex differences in play choices during adolescence. *Child Development,* 34: 119–126.

Sylva, K., Bruner, J., and Genova, P. (1976). The role of play in the problem-solving of children 3–5 years old. In J. Bruner, A. Jolly, and K. Sylva (eds.), *Play—Its role in development and evolution* (pp. 244–261). New York: Basic Books.

Symons, D. (1974). Aggressive play and communication in Rhesus monkeys (*Macaca mulatta*). *American Zoologist*, 14: 317–322.

Symons, D. (1989). A critique of Darwinian anthropology. *Ethology and Sociobiology*, 10: 131–144.

Takhvar, M., and Smith, P.K. (1990). A review and critique of Smilansky's classification scheme and the "nested hierarchy" of play. *Journal of Research in Childhood Education*, 4: 112–122.

Tanner, J. M. (1970). Physical growth. In P. H. Mussen (ed.), *Manual of child psychology*, 3rd ed., Vol. 1 (pp. 77–156). New York: Wiley.

Tawney, R. H. (1969/1926). *Religion and the rise of capitalism*. Harmondsworth, U.K.: Penguin.

Taylor, M., Carlson, S. M., Maring, B. L., Gerow, L., and Charley, C. M. (2004). The characteristics and correlates of fantasy in school-age children: Imaginary companions, impersonation, and social understanding. *Developmental Psychology*, 40: 1173–1187.

Temerlin, M. K. (1975). *Lucy: Growing up human*. London: Souvenir Press.

Thelen, E. (1979). Rhythmical sterotypies in normal human infants. *Animal Behaviour*, 27: 699–715.

Thelen, E. (1980). Determinants of amounts of stereotyped behavior in normal human infants. Ethology and Sociobiology, 1: 141–150.

Thompson, G. G. (1944). The social and emotional development of preschool children under two types of education programs. *Psychological Monographs*, 56(5).

Thompson, R. A. (1998). Early sociopersonality development. In N. Eisenberg (ed.), *Manual of child psychology*, Vol. 3: *Social, emotional, and personality development* (pp. 25–104). New York: Wiley.

Thorne, B. (1986). Girls and boys together, but mostly apart: Gender arrangements in elementary school. In W. W. Hartup and Z. Rubin (eds.), *Relationships and development* (pp. 167–184). Hillsdale, N.J.: Erlbaum.

Thorne, B. (1993). *Gender play: Boys and girls in school*. Buckingham, U.K.: Open University Press.

Thorne, B., and Luria, Z. (1986). Sexuality and gender in children's daily worlds. *Social Problems*, 33: 176–190.

Thornhill, R., and Gangstead, S.W. (1993). Human facial beauty: Averageness, symmetry, and parasite resistance. *Human Nature*, 4: 237–270.

Tinbergen, N. (1963). On aims and methods of ethology. *Zeitschirift für Tierpsychologie*, 20: 410–413.

Tinbergen, N. (1969). *The study of instinct*. London: Oxford University Press

Tomasello, M. (1995). Joint attention as social cognition. In C. Moore and P. Dunham (eds.), *Joint attention: Its origins and its role in development* (pp. 103–150). Hillsdale, N.J.: Erlbaum.

Tomasello, M. (1999). *The cultural origins of human cognition*. Cambridge, Mass.: Harvard University Press.

Tomasello, M., and Call, J. (1997). *Primate cognition*. New York: Oxford University Press.

Tomasello, M., Kruger, A. C., and Ratner, H. H. (1993). Cultural learning. *Behavioral and Brain Sciences*, 16: 495–511.

Tomasello, M., Striano, T., and Rochat, P. (1999). Do young children use objects as symbols? *British Journal of Developmental Psychology*, 17: 563–584.

Tomporowski, P. D., and Ellis, N. R. (1986). Effects of exercise on cognitive processes: A review. *Psychological Bulletin*, 99: 338–346.

Tooby, J., and Cosmides, L. (1992). The psychological foundations of culture. In J. Barkow, L. Cosmides, and J. Tooby (eds.), *The adapted mind: Evolutionary psychology and the generation of culture* (pp. 19–136). Oxford: Oxford University Press.

Trivers, R. (1971). The evolution of reciprocal altruism. *Quarterly Review of Biology*, 46: 35–57.

Trivers, R. (1972). Parental investment and sexual selection. In B. Campbell (ed.), *Sexual selection and the descent of man* (pp. 136–179). Chicago: Aldine.

Trivers, R. L. (1974). Parent-offspring conflict. *American Zoologist*, 14: 249–264.

Troy, M., and Sroufe, L. A. (1987). Victimization among preschoolers: The role of attachment relationship history. *Journal of the American Academy of Child Psychiatry*, 26: 166–172.

Tudge, J., and Rogoff, B. (1989). Peer influences on cognitive development: Piagetian and Vygotskian perspectives. In M. Bornstein and J. Bruner (eds.), *Interaction in human development* (pp. 17–40). Hillsdale, N.J.: Erlbaum.

Tudge, J., and Winterhoff, P. (1991). Vygotsky, Piaget, and Bandura. Paper presented at the annual meeting of the American Educational Research Association, Boston.

Turner, P. J. (1991). Relations between attachment, gender, and behavior with peers in preschool. *Child Development*, 62: 1475–1488.

Ungerer, J. A., Zelazo, P. R., Kearsley, R. B., and O'Leary, K. (1981). Developmental changes in the representation of objects in symbolic play from 18 to 34 months of age. *Child Development*, 52: 186–195.

Vandenberg, B. (1980). Play, problem solving, and creativity. In K. Rubin (ed.), *Children's play* (pp. 49–68). San Francisco: Jossey-Bass.

van Leeuwen, L., Smitsman, A., and van Leeuwen, C. (1994). Affordances, perceptual complexity, and the development of tool use. *Journal of Experimental Psychology: Human Perception and Performance*, 20: 174–191.

Van Praag, H., Shubert, T., Zhao, C., and Gage, F. H. (2005). Exercise enhances learning and hippocampal neurogenesis in aged mice. *The Journal of Neuroscience*, 25 (38), 1–6.

van Schaik, C. P., Deaner, R. O., and Merrill, M. Y. (1999). The conditions of tool use in primates: Implications for the evolution of material culture. *Journal of Human Evolution*, 36: 719–741.

Vauclair, J. (1984). Phylogenetic approach to object manipulation in human and ape infants. *Human Development*, 27: 321–328.

Vaughn, B. E., and Santos, A. J. (2007). An evolutionary-ecological account of aggressive behavior and trait aggression in human children and adolescents. In P. H. Hawley, T. D. Little, and P. C. Rodkin (eds.), *Aggression and adaptation: The bright side of bad behavior* (pp. 31–64). Mahwah, N.J.: Erlbaum.

Vaughn, B. E., and Waters, E. (1981). Attention structure, sociometric status, and dominance: Interrelations, behavioral correlates, and relationships to social competence. *Developmental Psychology*, 17: 275–288.

Volle, M., Shephard, R. J., Lavalle, H., LaBarre, R., Jequier, J. C., and Rajic, M. (1982). Influence of a program of required physical activity upon academic performance. In H. Lavalle and R. J. Shephard (eds.), *Croissance et développement de l'enfant* (pp. 91–109). Trois Rivières: Universite de Quebec.

Vygotsky, L. S. (1962). *Thought and language*. Cambridge, Mass.: MIT Press.

Vygotsky, L. S. (1967). Play and its role in the mental development of the child. *Soviet Psychology*, 12: 62–76.

Vygotsky, L. S. (1971). *The psychology of art*. Cambridge, Mass.: MIT Press.

Vygotsky, L. S. (1978). *Mind in society*. Cambridge, Mass.: Harvard University Press.

Vygotsky, L. (1983). The prehistory of written language. In M. Martlew (ed.), *The Psychology of written language* (pp. 279–292). London: Witey.

De Waal, F. B. M. (1982). The integration of dominance and social bonding in primates. *Quarterly Review of Biology*, 61: 459–479.

De Waal, F., and Lanting, F. (1997). *Bonobo: The forgotten ape*. Berkeley: University of California Press.

Waddington, C. H. (1957). *The strategy of the genes*. London: Allen and Unwin.

Waddington, C. H. (1959). Evolutionary systems—animal and human. *Nature*, 183: 1634–1638.

Waddington, C. H. (1975). *The evolution of an evolutionist*. Ithaca, N.Y.: Cornell University Press.

Wallach, M. (1970). Creativity. In P. H. Mussen (ed.), *Carmichael's manual of child psychology*, 3rd ed., Vol. 1 (pp. 1211–1272). New York: Wiley.

Waters, E., and Sroufe, L. A. (1983). Social competence as a developmental construct. *Developmental Review*, 3: 79–97.

Watson, M. W., and Fischer, K. W. (1977). A developmental sequence of agent use in late infancy. *Child Development*, 48: 828–836.

Watson, M. W., and Fischer, K. W. (1980). Development of social roles in elicited and spontaneous behavior during the preschool years. *Developmental Psychology*, 16: 483–494.

Weber, E. U., Shafir, S., and Blais, A-R. (2004). Predicting risk sensitivity in humans and lower animals: Risk as variance or coefficient of variation. *Psychological Review*, 111: 43–445.

Weeks, B. K., Young, C. M., and Beck, B. R. (2008). Eight months of regular in-school jumping improves indices of bone strength in adolescent boys and girls: The POWER. PE. study. *Journal of Bone and Mineral Research*, 10: 1002–1011.

Welsh, M. C. and Labbé, E. F. (1994). Children and aerobic exercise: A review of cognitive and behavioral effects. *Journal of Experimental Child Psychology*, 58: 405–417.

Wertsch, J. (1978). From social interaction to higher psychological processes. *Human Development*, 22: 1–22.

Whiting, B., and Edwards, C. (1973). A cross-cultural analysis of sex-differences in the behavior of children age three through 11. *Journal of Social Psychology*, 91: 171–188.

Williamson, P., and Silvern, S. (1991). Thematic-fantasy play and story comprehension. In J. Christie (ed.), *Play and early literacy development* (pp. 69–90). Albany, N.Y.: SUNY Press.

Wilson, D. S. (1997). Incorporating group selection in to the adaptionist program: A case study involving human decision making. In J. A. Simpson and D. T. Kenrick (eds.), *Evolutionary social psychology* (pp. 345–386). Mahwah, N.J.: Erlbaum.

Wilson, D. S., and Wilson, E. O. (2007). Rethinking the theoretical foundation of socio-biology. *The Quarterly Review of Biology*, 82: 327–348.

Wilson, E. O. (1975). *Sociobiology: The new synthesis*. Cambridge, Mass.: Harvard University Press.

Winterhalder, B., and Smith, E. A. (2000). Analyzing adaptive strategies: Human behavioral ecology at twenty-five. *Evolutionary Anthropology*, 9: 51–72.

Wolf, D. P., Davidson, L., Davis, M., Walters, M., Hodges, M., and Scripps, L. (1988). Beyond the A, B, C: A broader and deeper view of literacy. In A. D. Pellegrini (ed.), *Psychological bases for early education* (pp. 123–152). Chichester, U.K.: Wiley.

Wolf, D. P., and Gardner, H. (1978). Style and sequence in early symbolic play. In M. Franklin and N. Smith (eds.), *Early symbolization* (pp. 117–138). Hillsdale, N.J.: Erlbaum.

Wolf, D. P., and Grollman, S. (1982). Ways of playing. In D. Pepler and K. Rubin (eds.), *The play of children* (pp. 46–63). Basel, Switzerland: Karger.

Wolf, D. P., and Pusch, J. (1985). The origins of autonomous text in play boundaries. In L. Galda and A. D. Pellegrini (eds.), *Play, language, and stories* (pp. 63–78). Norwood, N.J.: Ablex.

Wolfgang, C. (1974). An exploration of the relationship between the cognitive area of reading and selected developmental aspects of children's play. *Psychology in the Schools*, 11: 338–343.

Wood, D., Bruner, J.S., and Ross, G. (1976). The role of tutoring in problem-solving. *Journal of Child Psychology and Psychiatry*, 17: 89–100.

Wood-Gush, D. G., and Vestergaard, K. (1991). The seeking of novelty and its relation to play. *Animal Behaviour*, 42: 599–606.

Wood-Gush, D. G., Vestergaard, K., and Petersen, H. V. (1990). The significance of motivation and environment in the development of exploration in pigs. *Biology and Behaviour*, 15: 39–52.

Wrangham, R. (1987). The significance of African apes for reconstructing human social evolution. In W. G. Kinzey (eds.), *The evolution of human behavior: Primate models* (pp. 51–71). Albany, N.Y.: SUNY Press.

Wrangham, R. W. (1999). Evolution of coalitionary killing. *Yearbook of Physical Anthropology*, 42: 1–30.

Wrangham, R. W., Chapman, C. A., Clark-Arcadi, A. P., and Isabirye-Basuta, G. (1996). Social ecology of Kanyawara chimpanzees: Implications for understanding the costs of great ape groups. In W. C. McGrew, L. F. Marchant, and N. Toshisada (eds.), *Great ape societies* (pp. 45–57). Cambridge: Cambridge University Press.

Wrangham, R., and Peterson, D. (1996). *Demonic males*. Boston: Houghton Mifflin.

Wright, H. (1960). Observational child study. In P. H. Mussen (ed.), *Handbook of research methods in child development* (pp. 71–139). New York: Wiley.

Wright, M. (1980). Measuring the social competence of preschool children. *Canadian Journal of Behavioral Science*, 12: 17–32.

Wynne-Edwards, V. C. (1962). *Animal dispersion in relation to social behaviour*. Edinburgh: Oliver and Boyd.

Zahavi, A. (1977). The testing of a bond. *Animal Behaviour*, 25: 246–247.

Zaporozhets, A. V., and Elkonin, D. B. (eds.) (1971), *The psychology of preschool children*. Cambridge, Mass.: MIT Press.

Zigler, E., and Trickett, P. (1978). I.Q., social competence, and evaluation of early childhood intervention programs. *American Psychologist*, 33: 789–798.

Zigler, E. F., and Bishop-Josef, S. (2006). The cognitive child vs. the whole child: Lessons from 40 years of Head Start. In D. G. Singer, R. Michnick-Golinkoff, and K. Hirsh-Pasek. (eds.), *Play = learning: How children's play motivates and enhances children's cognitive, and social-emotional growth* (pp. 15–35). New York: Oxford University Press.

Index

Note: The locators with "*f*" and "t" denotes a figure or a table in that page.